SLOW TRAVEL

Dorset

Local, characterful guides to Britain' [illegible] places

Ale[illegible]

EDITION 2

Bradt Travel Guides Ltd, UK

The Globe Pequot Press Inc, USA

Bradt

TAKING IT SLOW IN

Dorset

A SNAPSHOT OF THE REGION

As one of the most rural counties in England, Dorset does Slow very well indeed. Become absorbed in its quintessentially English countryside and dramatic coastline, and relish its traditional country ways and rich history.

 CHRIS BUTTON/A

1 Durdle Door lies on the South West Coast Path. 2 Views of the Blackmore Vale from Hambledon Hill. 3 Horseriding on Studland Beach. 4 Swanage Heritage Railway passes beneath Corfe Castle. 5 The ancient tradition of falconry lives on in Dorset. 6 Local hunts demonstrate their skills at country fairs.

ALEXANDRA RICHARDS

1

RURAL LIFE

A proud farming tradition is central to Dorset's identity and is showcased at country fairs. Farming has shaped the landscape, from the tapestry of neat hedgerow-lined fields to the delightful villages where a sense of community remains strong and traditional country pursuits thrive.

2

ALEXANDRA RICHARDS

1 Straw bales on the Cranborne Chase. 2 Queen of the May celebrations and blessing of the cider orchard at Winterborne Houghton. 3 The ancient village of Stour Provost in the Blackmore Vale has strong farming roots. 4 A memorable encounter while badger-watching at Old Henley Farm. 5 Jersey cow at Modbury Farm, Burton Bradstock. 6 Sturminster Newton Mill on the River Stour. 7 Actor Martin Clunes and his Clydesdale 'Ronnie' winning at Buckham Down Fair.

1 SS

DORSET TOWNS & VILLAGES

Dorset has no large cities, but ancient market towns and quaint villages abound, crafted from local stone. You won't have to go far to find a photogenic, rose-covered thatched cottage. Evidence of thousands of years of habitation is visible in the county's varied architecture.

2 ALEXANDRA RICHARDS

ALEXANDRA RICHARDS

ALEXANDRA RICHARDS

ALEXANDRA RICHARDS

1 Milton Abbas, an early model village. 2 Abbotsbury is beautifully preserved. 3 The quay at Wareham. 4 The Pitchmarket houses at Cerne Abbas date from around 1500. 5 Wimborne Minster: DJ Dapper Dan is known as the 'rock 'n' roll town crier'. 6 Thatched lodge to Gaunts House in east Dorset.

LANGHAM WINE ESTATE

SAVOURING THE TASTE

Dorset boasts superb local produce. Some are well known, like its cheese and cider, others are relatively new and growing in popularity, like its wines.

1 Dorset's temperate climate produces some excellent wines. 2 Devonshire doesn't have the monopoly on cream teas. 3 Traditional Dorset Blue Vinny cheese. 4 The Hall & Woodhouse Brewery near Blandford Forum. 5 Dorset apple cake – a truly local treat.

ALEXANDRA RICHARDS

DORSET BLUE VINNY

MSHEV/S

ALEXANDRA RICHARDS

AUTHOR

Alexandra Richards (www.alexandrarichards.net) grew up in Dorset, where she developed a love of rural life, the natural world and outdoor pursuits. Following a degree in Modern European Languages at the University of Durham, which included a year teaching English on the Indian Ocean island of La Réunion, Alex evolved into a freelance travel writer and photographer. She has written four editions of the Bradt guidebook *Mauritius, Rodrigues and Réunion*. Alex now divides her time between Dorset and Australia.

AUTHOR'S STORY

I was fortunate enough to grow up in the tiny North Dorset village of Stour Provost and, as the first child born there for 25 years, I'm told my arrival was quite an event. It was a magical place for a childhood – I spent hours making camps, picking blackberries, riding ponies and fishing in our stretch of the River Stour, always accompanied by an assortment of pets, including a sheep named Perky. In those days the village was the domain of dairy farmers and farm workers, and the odd self-appointed squire; it was all rather *Vicar of Dibley*. The school run had to be timed with military precision to avoid being stuck behind the cows crossing the lane for milking; on a Saturday, the hunt would come charging over the hill, resplendent in their pink, hounds baying; village cricket and the church flower rota were serious business; and the pub was where all the big decisions were made. I have spent my life surrounded by colourful Dorset characters, some of the most genuine people you could wish to meet, and I was delighted to interview a few of them for this book.

Being based in Australia for the last few years, I've been returning to Dorset as a visitor with a new-found appreciation for its history, landscapes and culture; and writing this book gave me a reason to delve into corners of the county I didn't know particularly well. For instance, I'd never really appreciated the Jurassic Coast – my memories of it were of school art trips and being made to sketch Durdle Door from a windy cliff top. Returning there while researching this book I could see why our scatty art mistress thought the limestone arch a worthy artistic subject and I felt immense relief marvelling at it, photographing it and not having to draw it – art was never my strong suit. I must confess I was once one of the protective Dorset folk who referred to visitors as 'grockles', lamented the summer influx of 'townies' and bemoaned ramblers trampling over our land, but having returned home with fresh eyes and written this book, I can't wait to share it with anyone who wants to experience Slow Dorset.

Second edition published March 2015
First published 2012
Bradt Travel Guides Ltd
IDC House, The Vale, Chalfont St Peter, Bucks SL9 9RZ, England
www.bradtguides.com
Print edition published in the USA by The Globe Pequot Press Inc,
PO Box 480, Guilford, Connecticut 06437-0480

Project Managers: Anna Moores and Katie Wilding
Series design: Pepi Bluck, Perfect Picture
Cover design and research: Pepi Bluck, Perfect Picture

ISBN: 978 1 84162 867 7 (print)
e-ISBN: 978 1 78477 120 1 (e-pub)
e-ISBN: 978 1 78477 220 8 (mobi)

British Library Cataloguing in Publication Data
A catalogue record for this book is available from the British Library

Photographs
© individual photographers credited beside images & also those from picture libraries credited as follows: Alamy.com (A), Shutterstock.com (S), superstock.com (SS)

Front cover Corfe Castle (Lee Pengelly/A)
Back cover The cliffs at West Bay (Alexandra Richards)
Title page Gold Hill (SS)

Maps David McCutcheon FBCart.S and Liezel Bohdanowicz

Typeset by Pepi Bluck
Production managed by Jellyfish Print Solutions; printed in the UK
Digital conversion by www.dataworks.co.in

ACKNOWLEDGEMENTS

I would like to thank all those who took the time to show me around their businesses, among them farm shops, museums, bed and breakfasts, hotels, campsites, restaurants, nature reserves, cider orchards and breweries. I would also like to thank those who gave me memorable experiences to write about in this book, including but not limited to Allan and Alison Gates at Mere Down Falconry, Brandon Lennon (fossil hunter), the team at River Cottage, and the Dorset Wildlife Trust. My sincere thanks to John Wright, who showed me the delights of foraging and home-brewed alcohol and who took time out of his busy schedule to contribute to this book.

My thanks also to Fanny Charles and Gay Pirrie-Weir of the *Fine Times Recorder*, for their support of this project, their contributions to the book and their inspirational ideas.

I would like to thank all my Dorset friends for their anecdotes, advice and guidance, in particular Alf Wallis, Dominic and Marcia Paterson, Tim and Debbie Allard, Cleo and Chris Campbell, the White family and the villagers of Stour Provost past and present. My sincere thanks to Emma and Ed at Riversdale Farm for allowing me to continue returning to my beloved family home.

I am grateful to Neal Sullivan for assisting me with my research and for his help with the maps and photography for this book.

I would like to thank my parents for my Dorset childhood, my late father for all the research and writing he did on rural matters and Dorset life, and my mother for the hours she spent proofreading and reminding me of snippets about the county. My heartfelt thanks also to Baroness Sharples for her many years of help, encouragement and advice.

DEDICATION

I would like to dedicate this book to Zouk, my beloved Rhodesian ridgeback, who has kept me company writing this and many other books over the past ten years, patiently listening to my mutterings and providing entertaining breaks from work with his antics.

SUGGESTED PLACES TO BASE YOURSELF

These bases make ideal starting points for exploring localities the Slow way.

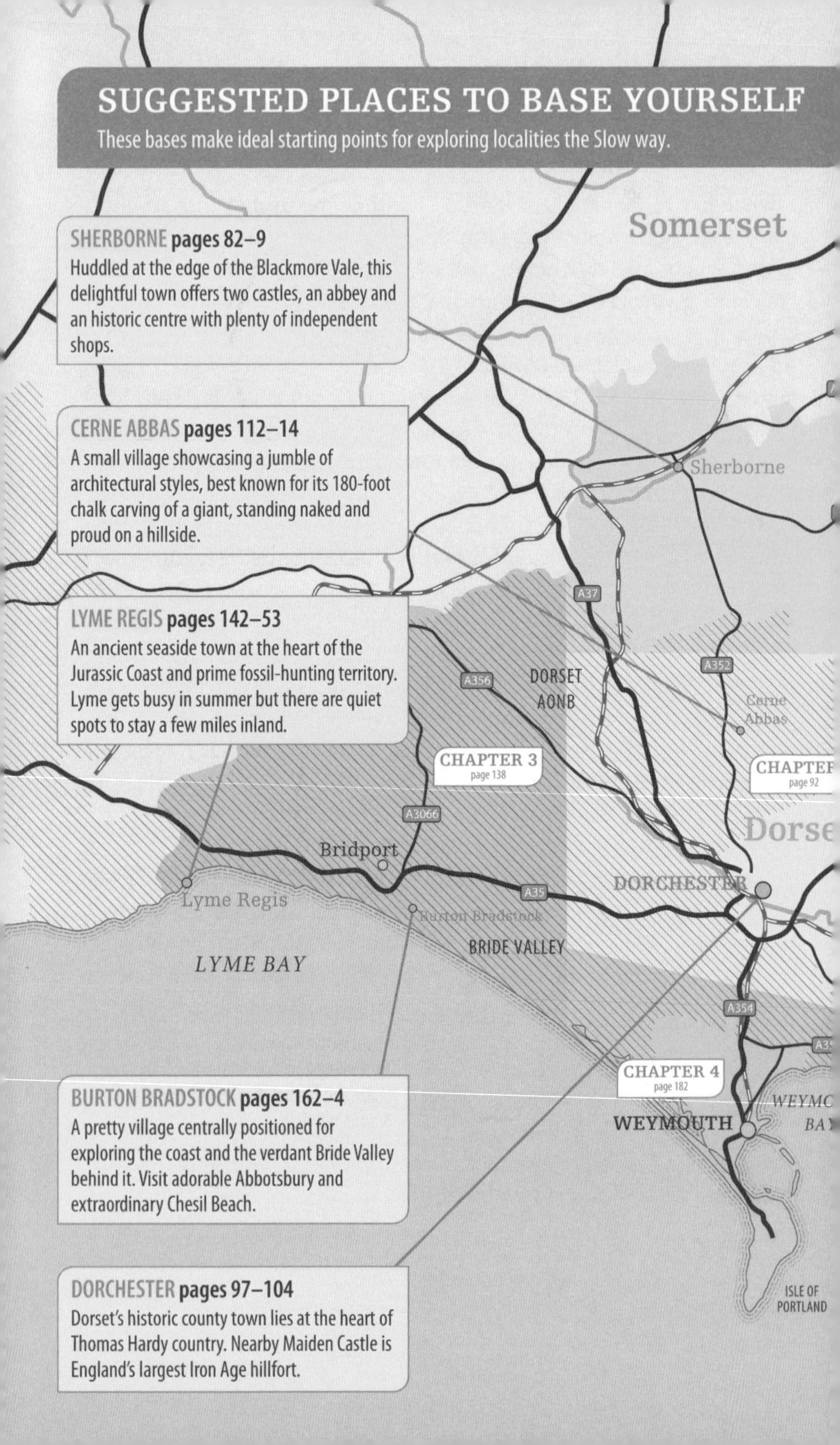

SHERBORNE pages 82–9
Huddled at the edge of the Blackmore Vale, this delightful town offers two castles, an abbey and an historic centre with plenty of independent shops.

CERNE ABBAS pages 112–14
A small village showcasing a jumble of architectural styles, best known for its 180-foot chalk carving of a giant, standing naked and proud on a hillside.

LYME REGIS pages 142–53
An ancient seaside town at the heart of the Jurassic Coast and prime fossil-hunting territory. Lyme gets busy in summer but there are quiet spots to stay a few miles inland.

BURTON BRADSTOCK pages 162–4
A pretty village centrally positioned for exploring the coast and the verdant Bride Valley behind it. Visit adorable Abbotsbury and extraordinary Chesil Beach.

DORCHESTER pages 97–104
Dorset's historic county town lies at the heart of Thomas Hardy country. Nearby Maiden Castle is England's largest Iron Age hillfort.

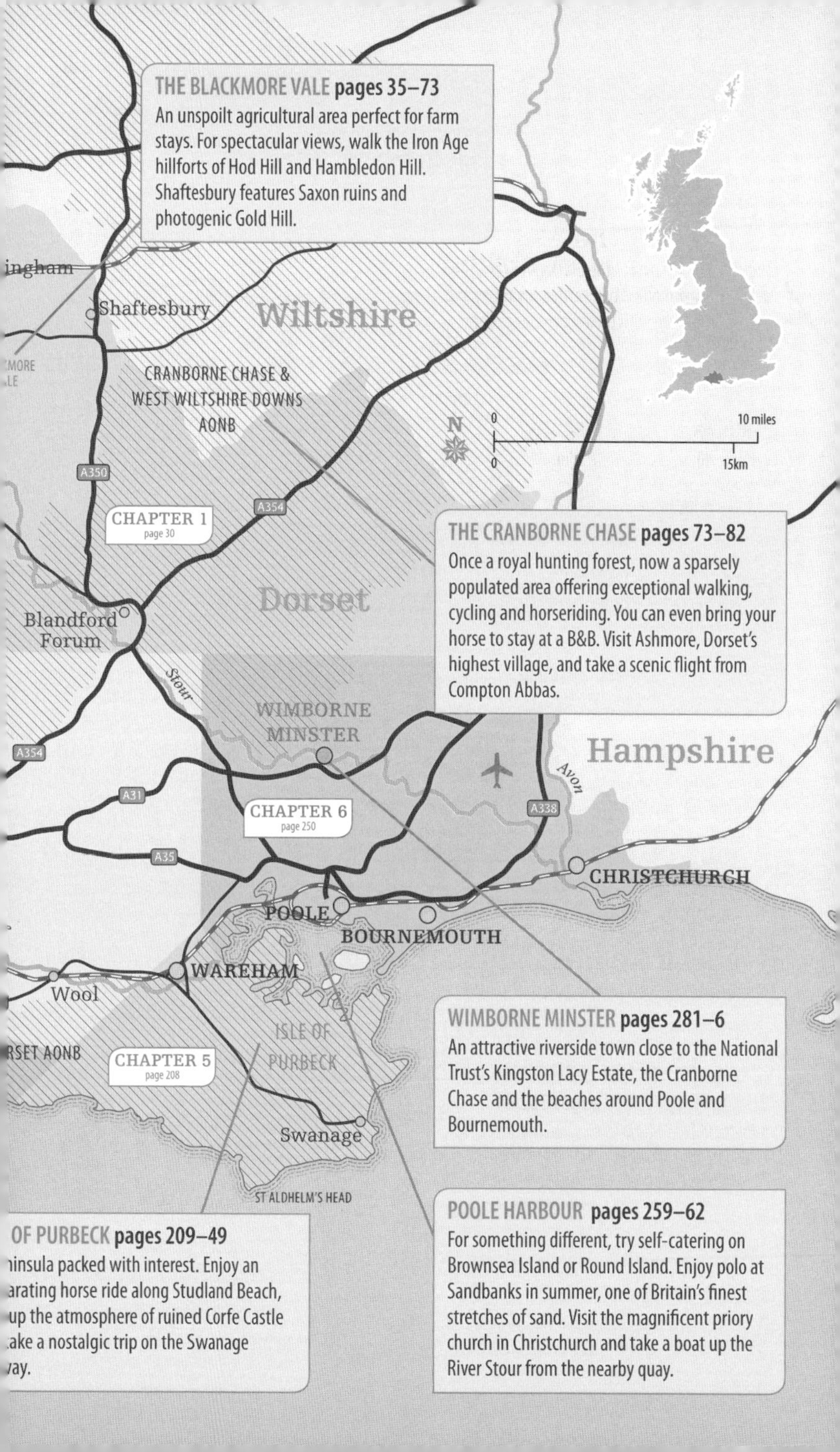
THE BLACKMORE VALE pages 35–73
An unspoilt agricultural area perfect for farm stays. For spectacular views, walk the Iron Age hillforts of Hod Hill and Hambledon Hill. Shaftesbury features Saxon ruins and photogenic Gold Hill.
Shaftesbury
Wiltshire
CRANBORNE CHASE & WEST WILTSHIRE DOWNS AONB
N
0
10 miles
0
15km
A350
A354
CHAPTER 1
page 30
THE CRANBORNE CHASE pages 73–82
Once a royal hunting forest, now a sparsely populated area offering exceptional walking, cycling and horseriding. You can even bring your horse to stay at a B&B. Visit Ashmore, Dorset's highest village, and take a scenic flight from Compton Abbas.
Dorset
Blandford Forum
Stour
WIMBORNE MINSTER
Hampshire
Avon
A354
A31
CHAPTER 6
page 250
A338
A35
CHRISTCHURCH
POOLE
BOURNEMOUTH
WAREHAM
Wool
ISLE OF PURBECK
CHAPTER 5
page 208
Swanage
ST ALDHELM'S HEAD
WIMBORNE MINSTER pages 281–6
An attractive riverside town close to the National Trust's Kingston Lacy Estate, the Cranborne Chase and the beaches around Poole and Bournemouth.
OF PURBECK pages 209–49
insula packed with interest. Enjoy an
arating horse ride along Studland Beach,
up the atmosphere of ruined Corfe Castle
ake a nostalgic trip on the Swanage
vay.
POOLE HARBOUR pages 259–62
For something different, try self-catering on Brownsea Island or Round Island. Enjoy polo at Sandbanks in summer, one of Britain's finest stretches of sand. Visit the magnificent priory church in Christchurch and take a boat up the River Stour from the nearby quay.

CONTENTS

GOING SLOW IN DORSET

I should mention from the outset that this is not your typical travel guidebook. It doesn't attempt to cover every aspect of the county and analyse all the accommodation and eateries. Instead, it is a personal look at what I love about Dorset, highlighting the elements that I believe encapsulate Dorset-ness and the Slow approach. There are, of course, many more places that fit the bill than I could squeeze into this book, so I must apologise to those that don't get a mention. I am always open to suggestions and you can send me your ideas via Bradt Travel Guides (see page 10).

In our fast-paced lives, where multi-tasking and time-saving devices are key to survival, the notion of travelling slowly and mindfully may seem unnatural but it is the perfect antidote to a hectic existence. This is one of a series of guides that builds on the Slow Tourism and Slow Food movements and encourages readers to take the time to explore an area thoroughly and at a relaxed pace, finding out what really makes it distinctive, rather than racing around and ticking off attractions from a glossy brochure. Slow Tourism involves seeking out special landscapes, engaging with local people, savouring the area's produce and discovering local culture and heritage; this book invites you to do just that.

Dorset does Slow very well indeed – its quintessentially English rural landscapes, bountiful local produce, even the lilting Dorset accent has an unhurried, lullaby quality. As I was wandering the county explaining that I was writing a book called *Slow Travel Dorset*, the response was frequently, 'Hmmm, I suppose we are pretty slow around here', accompanied by an enigmatic smile. It occurs to me that my parents and I, like many Dorset folk, lived in accordance with the Slow ethos but without giving it a label. We bought our meat fresh from a farm in the village, our milk from the local dairy, and our Christmas turkey from Mr Cox in Stour Row; collecting sloes, elderflowers, blackberries and mushrooms was an annual ritual, and homemade sloe gin in time for Christmas was one of the resulting treats. My parents didn't go out to work – our home was their livelihood – and most of our friends were

THE SLOW MINDSET

Hilary Bradt, Founder, Bradt Travel Guides

We shall not cease from exploration
And the end of all our exploring
Will be to arrive where we started
And know the place for the first time.

T S Eliot, 'Little Gidding', *Four Quartets*

This series evolved, slowly, from a Bradt editorial meeting when we started to explore ideas for guides to our favourite country – Great Britain. We wanted to get away from the usual 'top sights' formula and encourage our authors to bring out the nuances and local differences that make up a sense of place – such things as food, building styles, nature, geology, or local people and what makes them tick. Our aim was to create a series that celebrates the present, focusing on sustainable tourism, rather than taking a nostalgic wallow in the past.

So without our realising it at the time, we had defined 'Slow Travel', or at least our concept of it. For the beauty of the Slow movement is that there is no fixed definition: we adapt the philosophy to fit our individual needs and aspirations. Thus Carl Honoré, author of *In Praise of Slow*, writes: 'The Slow Movement is a cultural revolution against the notion that faster is always better. It's not about doing everything at a snail's pace, it's about seeking to do everything at the right speed. Savouring the hours and minutes rather than just counting them. Doing everything as well as possible, instead of as fast as possible. It's about quality over quantity in everything from work to food to parenting.' And travel.

So take time to explore. Don't rush it, get to know an area – and the people who live there – and you'll be as delighted as the authors by what you find.

in the same position. Villagers out for a walk or farmers passing in their tractors used to drop in for tea at any time – weekdays and weekends did not have the same meaning that they do for so many of us now, where we work flat out and it seems only two out of every seven days actually belong to us. That is one of the things I like about going back to Dorset; many of our friends have managed to keep that lifestyle going – they can still manage their own time, they know how to go slow. While they may have had to swap milking cows for running holiday cottages because of the decline in farming, they are still happy to stop for tea and a chat on a Wednesday afternoon.

A wise Dorset countryman, one of nature's gentlemen, once said to me in his broad West Country accent 'I like cities, I do.' I had known him for many years and had barely heard of him setting foot outside his native Blackmore Vale, so I was shocked by this pronouncement. He continued, 'I've never been to one but I like them because they keep all the idiots in one place.' Without wanting to insult the majority of the population, I concede he has a point – a lack of large cities is one of the intrinsic qualities that makes Dorset distinctive and ideal for Slow Travel.

As I chatted with Dorset friends about the places I had seen and things I had done in my quest for suitable material for this book, many of them said, 'I've never been there' or 'I never knew that.' I hope that locals as much as visitors will find this book helps them to become better acquainted with the county and encourages them to view it with the enquiring mind of an amateur sleuth, seeking out what makes Dorset Dorset. One local lady wrote to me while I was researching *Slow Travel Dorset*, 'I feel sure your book will be in great demand among the many of us who treasure our country ways and heritage'; if that is the case, I couldn't ask for more.

DORSET

> The county of Dorset is small, but is yet so varied in its configuration as to present an epitome of the scenery of Southern England. It is a land of moods and changes that knows no monotony, and is indeed so full of hills and dales that there is scarcely a level road within its confines, save by the banks of streams.
>
> Sir Frederick Treves, *Highways and Byways in Dorset*, 1906

Treves's words still hold true – Dorset's geological diversity crammed into a small area has produced varied and intimate landscapes, from fertile vales and chalk downland to pristine heathland and a rugged coastline. Visitors need not fear monotony around these parts.

Dorset lends itself to Slow Travel, and its status as one of only seven counties in England without a motorway seems to emphasise that fact. It has no large cities and its only heavily populated area (Poole and Bournemouth) is discreetly tucked into the southeastern corner. Slow Travel conjures up images of pottering about in unspoilt rural areas and Dorset is one of the most rural counties in England, with the highest proportion of conservation areas in the country, including an Area of Outstanding Natural Beauty covering 44% of it.

FEEDBACK REQUEST & UPDATES WEBSITE

At Bradt Travel Guides we're aware that guidebooks start to go out of date on the day they're published – and that you, our readers, are out there in the field doing research of your own. You'll find out before us when a fine new family-run hotel opens or a favourite restaurant changes hands and goes downhill. So why not write and tell us about your experiences? Contact us on 01753 893444 or info@bradtguides.com. We will forward emails to the author who may post updates on the Bradt website at www.bradtupdates.com/dorset. Alternatively you can add a review of the book to www.bradtguides.com or Amazon.

North Dorset is largely taken up by the **Blackmore Vale**, a landscape of lush fields defined by ancient hedgerows and dotted with tiny thatched villages. This is traditionally a dairy-farming area, although since the decline in that industry there are far fewer cows than there were when Treves wrote in 1906:

> Everywhere are there cows, for the smell of cows is the incense of North Dorset.

The Iron Age hillforts of **Hambledon Hill** and **Hod Hill** provide memorable walks, almost aerial views of the Blackmore Vale and archaeological interest. To the east of the vale is the **Cranborne Chase**, once a royal hunting forest and now a sparsely populated area offering exceptional walking, cycling and horseriding. Gentle, rolling chalk downland dominates the centre of the county, which is where the county town, **Dorchester**, is found. The west is more hilly, while the east features heathland and the county's major conurbation incorporating **Poole and Bournemouth**. The coastline in the east has fine sandy beaches but as you head west it becomes gradually more dramatic and culminates in the ancient cliffs of the Jurassic Coast.

The **Jurassic Coast** is England's first natural World Heritage Site, joining the likes of the Great Barrier Reef and the Grand Canyon as one of the wonders of the natural world. It was granted its status for its outstandingly diverse geology, capturing 190 million years of the earth's history in just 95 miles, making walking, cycling or sailing along this stretch of coast an exhilarating experience in time travel. It begins with the oldest red stone Triassic rock around Orcombe Point in east Devon, before it enters Dorset and the Jurassic period, then leads on to the younger Cretaceous period seen in the white chalk stacks at Old Harry Rocks, where the Jurassic Coast reaches its official eastern limit. The grey cliffs around Lyme Regis and Charmouth are rich in the fossils of creatures that swam in Jurassic seas some 190 million years ago. They are constantly eroded by the sea, releasing their fossils on to the beaches, where they are eagerly scooped up by delighted fossil hunters. You don't need to be a geologist to be blown away by the Jurassic Coast and get bitten by the fossil-hunting bug.

Another striking feature on the Jurassic Coast is **Chesil Beach**, a shingle bank stretching for 18 miles between West Bay and Portland and reaching around 40 feet at its highest point. Formed by rising seas at the end of the last Ice Age, it protects a large lagoon known as The Fleet, home to a diverse population of resident and migrating birds.

As you wander around Dorset, ancient manmade additions to the landscape stand as reminders that you are walking in the footsteps of much earlier inhabitants. It seems just about every hill you climb has a Neolithic site lying beneath your feet and the countryside is dotted with the telltale lumps and bumps of ancient burial grounds. **Maiden Castle** is the largest Iron Age hillfort in Britain and lies just outside Dorchester, which is laid out along the lines of its Roman antecedent and has the best-preserved Roman town house in the country. The Saxons left their mark all over the Kingdom of Wessex, visible in towns like **Shaftesbury**, where King Alfred built an abbey in AD888. **Sherborne** has some delightful medieval buildings and a fine abbey dating from the 15th century. The origin of one of Dorset's most famous landmarks, the **Cerne Abbas Giant** or 'Rude Man', is still much debated. The 180-foot-high figure of a naked man wielding a club, incised into the chalk of the hillside, has been variously identified as Roman, Celtic and Iron Age (or even post-medieval), and has been worshipped as a fertility symbol for centuries.

Perhaps one factor that has helped to preserve Dorset's character is that significant portions of it have remained in the hands of the same few families for centuries – it is one of the last bastions of feudalism. Several large estates still exist and their villages are carefully maintained – the areas around Lulworth Cove (Lulworth Estate) and Abbotsbury (Ilchester Estates) fall into this category. In 1981, Ralph Bankes bequeathed his family's 8,500-acre estate to the National Trust. At its heart is one of Dorset's finest houses, Kingston Lacy (pages 288–9), and it extends all the way to the coast at Studland, with its beautifully unspoilt beach and nature reserve.

One thing that strikes me about Dorset is how happy and proud people are to live here; they consider themselves lucky to dwell in this serene corner of England and are keen to preserve its landscapes and way of life. On your travels you are likely to see the Dorset flag – a white cross with a red border on a gold background – flying outside homes and businesses. Often referred to as St Wite's Cross, it recognises the female Anglo-Saxon saint buried at Whitchurch Canonicorum.

Any Dorset journey is inevitably enhanced by the implausibly delightful place names you encounter along the way; some of my favourites are Whitchurch Canonicorum, Toller Porcorum, Tincleton and Sixpenny Handley. The River Wriggle is found in the northwest of the county and the River Piddle winds through its centre, lined by a string of villages which take their amusing names from it: Piddlehinton, Piddletrenthide, Tolpuddle, Puddletown, Affpuddle and Briants Puddle. While we are on the subject of toilet humour, the town of Shitterton, near Bere Regis, is the butt of its fair share of jokes. I must also give a mention to the village of Fishpond Bottom in the Marshwood Vale, the uncomfortably named Scratchy Bottom near Durdle Door and its more contented counterpart Happy Bottom in Corfe Mullen near Wimborne Minster.

SOME PRACTICAL MATTERS

HOW THIS BOOK IS ARRANGED

Please note: no charge has been made for the inclusion in the main text of any business in this guide.

Maps

The map at the front of this book shows the area covered in each of the six chapters. In turn, each chapter begins with a sketch map of the area, highlighting the places mentioned in the text. The numbers on the map correspond to the descriptions in the text, helping you to find your way around. The symbol on these maps indicates that there is a walk in that area. There are also sketch maps for these featured walks.

Accommodation

At the back of this guide (pages 294–9), I've listed some accommodation ideas for each area, a mixture of camping, self-catering, bed and breakfast and hotel options. Each was chosen because it has a special quality, be that its location, character or service. For further reviews and additional listings, go to ⊘ www.bradtguides.com/dorsetsleeps.

The hotels, B&Bs and self-catering options are indicated by 🏠 under the heading for the area in which they are located. Campsites are indicated by ⛺.

Food & drink

I have included a cross section of food and drink options, including farm shops, food producers, cafés, pubs and restaurants. They were selected because they use local produce, serve homemade goodies, have a special character or follow sustainable principles – or a mixture of all four.

Attractions

For attractions, activities and eateries I have listed contact details and opening hours but it is worth checking websites for any changes. I have not listed admission fees as these change regularly, although I have mentioned if admission is free. If a description does not say admission is free, you should expect to be charged.

Getting to & around Dorset

I've given some suggestions for getting to and around each area, including car-free options wherever possible and ideas for cycling and walking. For some parts of Dorset car-free is not feasible as public transport is limited and the little-known, distinctive places I have tried to highlight are often, by their nature, out of the way and harder to reach than the usual tourist haunts.

General travel information is available at ⊘ www.visit-dorset.com, and ⊘ www.traveline.info is useful for journey planning; **bus timetables** are online at ⊘ www.dorsetforyou.com. **Bournemouth International Airport** links Dorset to other domestic and European airports, while **ferries** operate between Poole and Cherbourg. Coaches and trains connect Dorset to other English cities. **South West Trains** (⊘ www.southwesttrains.co.uk) is the main rail operator servicing the area, with regular trains from London Waterloo to Gillingham, Sherborne, Dorchester, Axminster (for Lyme Regis), Weymouth, Poole and Bournemouth.

Local buses can be helpful, although services are limited in rural areas and may only operate on certain days of the week; timetables and Dorset-wide maps are available at ⊘ www.dorsetforyou.com and the tourist information centres in each area. The **Jurassic CoastLinX53** bus is handy; it runs every two hours along the coastline between Exeter and Poole, and stops at all the key places *en route*. Getting the bus means you can safely look out of the window and admire the views of the coast, rather than trying to do so while driving.

Tourist information & additional resources

I have listed the tourist information centres for each area at the start of the relevant chapter, along with any websites on specific areas. For general information see www.visit-dorset.com and www.dorsetforyou.com.

For information on the region's arts and food scenes, including a calendar of events and reviews of theatre and film, the *Fine Times Recorder* (www.theftr.co.uk) is a handy resource and confidently grasps the essence of Slow.

MAKING THE MOST OF SLOW DORSET

Dorset's variety means it has a wide appeal – it has much to offer the lover of the natural world, the history buff, gastronome, archaeologist, hiker and adventure sports enthusiast, just to name a few. I had countless memorable experiences while pottering around Dorset researching *Slow Dorset*, and I hope you will be able to enjoy some of them too.

WALKING

Dorset's varied countryside and coastline provide excellent opportunities for walking and you will find some suggestions for short and medium-length walks in each chapter.

Information on walking is available at tourist information centres and online at www.dorsetforyou.com, from where you can download guides to some of the most popular trails, including the Wessex Ridgeway and the Stour Valley Way. Waymarked with a dragon symbol, the **Wessex Ridgeway** is a ridge-top trail from Marlborough in Wiltshire to Lyme Regis, part of the Great Ridgeway, an ancient trading route between the Devon and Norfolk coasts. The Dorset section begins at Ashmore in the Cranborne Chase and runs along a chalk ridge across the centre of the county, providing strikingly unhindered views of the surrounding countryside. Further information is available at www.dorsetaonb.org.uk. In contrast, the **Stour Valley Way** takes the low road, following the River Stour 64 miles from Stourhead to Christchurch, where the river flows into the sea. The Stour Valley Way is waymarked with a kingfisher symbol.

The South West Coast Path

The standout piece in Dorset's repertoire of walks is the hugely popular South West Coast Path, which combines heritage, flora, fauna, geology and spectacular coastal scenery. The UK's longest national trail, it runs for 630 miles from Minehead in Somerset to Poole in Dorset's east, tracing the coastlines of Cornwall, Devon and Dorset on the way.

The South West Coast Path website (🖰 www.southwestcoastpath.com) is extremely helpful for planning and its walk-finder tool can help you choose the right route for you. You can download a range of themed walks of varying lengths and levels of difficulty, including information about where to eat and drink *en route*. The path is easy to find from most coastal towns and villages or from the beach, and is waymarked by an acorn symbol.

The Dorset section offers some of the most spectacular seaside scenery and the path provides access to the entire length of the Jurassic Coast World Heritage Site, which runs from east Devon to Old Harry Rocks, off Studland. It passes through **Lyme Regis** and **Charmouth**, popular for fossil hunting. Between Charmouth and Seatown is **Golden Cap**, the highest point on England's south coast; it is a steep walk up from Seatown but the reward is expansive views along the coast, and on a clear day you can see as far as Dartmoor National Park (see page 157).

One of the most rewarding walks is the section of the path between **Lulworth Cove** and **Durdle Door**, two of the most spectacular features within the Jurassic Coast World Heritage Site. Durdle Door, a near perfect coastal arch of limestone rock, lies half a mile to the west of Lulworth Cove. The walk involves some moderately steep climbs along a remarkably well-preserved and photogenic section of coast.

A gentle four-mile walk leads from Studland along the cliffs to the dramatic chalk stacks of **Old Harry Rocks** (page 215), from where you can see across to another chalk formation: The Needles, off the Isle of Wight. Early mornings are the best time for this walk, when the sun casts its first gentle rays on the crisp, white rock.

The South West Coast Path provides plenty of opportunity for wildlife watching; on a clear day you may be lucky enough to spot basking sharks, seals or dolphins, particularly around **Durlston Country Park** near Swanage. **Portland** and **Poole Harbour** are good for watching resident and migrating seabirds, and you may catch a glimpse of rare butterflies on the Isle of Purbeck's chalk downland.

The South West Coast Path works well in combination with the **CoastLinX53 bus service** (see page 14). Luggage transfers (✆ 0800 043 7929 🖱 www.luggagestransfers.co.uk) is a very clever idea for walkers and cyclists – the company will transport your bags between your stop-off points along the South West Coast Path and around the South West.

HORSERIDING & CYCLING

Horseriders and cyclists can feel vulnerable on Dorset's narrow hedge-lined lanes but there are usually plenty of passing places to pull into out of anyone's way. A network of **bridleways** provides interesting off-road options and is complemented by the Wessex Ridgeway (see page 14), the North Dorset Trailway (page 33) and the Castleman Trailway (page 254) in the east of the county.

Suggestions for cycling routes and cycle hire are given in each chapter, and suggested horserides and stables are mentioned where applicable. The British Horse Society (BHS 🖱 www.bhs.org.uk) is the best resource for horseriders and provides a list of riding establishments offering trekking, instruction, etc. The BHS and 🖱 www.dorsetforyou.com provide lists of accommodation where both you and your horse can stay. On a second BHS website (🖱 www.emagin.org) you will find suggested rides and more lists of equestrian establishments.

"Some Dorset beaches are ideal for memorable horserides along the sand."

Some Dorset **beaches** are ideal for memorable horserides along the sand, in particular Studland (see pages 230–2), and also certain beaches around Christchurch (page 256). From the east of the county you can ride into the **New Forest**, while North Dorset offers excellent riding through woodland and open countryside, including in remarkable spots like the Iron Age hillfort on **Hod Hill**.

In recent years electric bikes have become all the rage in Dorset. **Jurassic Electric** (✆ 07796 135256 🖱 www.jurassic-electric.co.uk) offers guided electric bike tours of the south and west of the county, and you can also hire an electric bike from them.

SAVOURING THE TASTES OF DORSET

Dorset is ideally suited to the growing and savouring of seasonal, traditional and local food; its fertile soils, long farming history and food heritage combine to provide a rich variety of tasty treats, from fish caught off the Dorset coast, to artisan cheeses, breads and ciders. A visit to Dorset would not be complete without sampling Dorset Blue Vinny cheese (page 63), Dorset apple cake (see below) and Moores Dorset Knob biscuits (page 155). And remember, Devon does not have a monopoly on cream teas – the Dorset version is just as delicious. You will find many of the county's artisan food producers and suppliers plus the numerous local food festivals mentioned in this book.

Self-caterers are spoilt for choice when it comes to stocking up the pantry, and a picnic is a great way to enjoy the Dorset countryside. Rather than trudging around the supermarket, you can make gathering your ingredients into a treasure hunt by calling into local bakeries, farmers' markets and farm shops. As you are exploring the country lanes, look out for handwritten signs promising free-range eggs, homemade jams, honey, gooseberries and the like, which usually sit on a wonky table next to an honesty box. For dessert you can pick up one of the local farmhouse ice creams, such as those made by Barford Ice Cream (page 287) and Purbeck Ice Cream (page 249).

DORSET APPLE CAKE: A RECIPE

On every tea shop menu you will see Dorset apple cake, a truly local treat. Countless different recipes exist, each subtly different, but I really enjoy this slightly lemony one.

Ingredients

- 8 oz self-raising flour
- 4 oz butter
- 4 oz caster sugar
- 8 oz cooking apples – peeled, cored and diced
- Grated zest of 1 lemon
- 1 medium egg, beaten
- 2 oz sultanas (optional)

Method

Preheat the oven to 375°F/190°C. In a large mixing bowl rub the butter into the flour until the mixture resembles fine breadcrumbs. Stir in the sugar, apples, lemon zest and egg, and mix well. If you want to add the sultanas, you can do so now. Put the mixture into a well-greased 8-inch cake tin and bake for 30–40 minutes, or until golden in colour. Serve warm or cold, with or without custard or ice cream.

DORSET FOOD & DRINK – A TRUSTED BRAND FOR THE COUNTY

Fanny Charles,
Co-editor of the Fine Times Recorder *www.theftr.co.uk*

A producer group, Dorset Food & Drink, was set up as a not-for-profit organisation in 2013 by the Dorset Area of Outstanding Natural Beauty partnership to celebrate, promote and support Dorset's fantastic local food and drink culture.

The organisation had a successful first year, recruiting dozens of food and drink producers across the country.

In November 2013 a group of its producers took a taste of Dorset to the Houses of Parliament, showcasing Dorset food and drink in an event known as Dorset Day. The organisation is now building on that success, with a presence at most of the county's major food events, and is becoming a trusted brand and a key element in promoting Dorset to the wider world.

The attractive logo, which cleverly links the countryside, coast and local food, reflects the idea of 'eating the landscape', encouraging people to understand and value the connection between the beautiful landscape around them in Dorset and the food they eat in pubs and restaurants and buy in farm shops, at farmers' markets or in those supermarkets that offer local or regional selections.

Dorset Food & Drink represents both artisan producers and some of the county's biggest and oldest-established businesses, some of whom have shown their support by becoming Founder Members. They include Dorset Cereals, Eastbury Hotel, Purbeck Ice Cream, Blackmore Vale Dairy, Hive Beach Café, Ford Farm Cheddar, Moores Biscuits, Hall & Woodhouse Brewery and Olives Et Al.

There are a growing number of food festivals across the county each year – including Dorset Seafood Festival, Spring Tides at Hive Beach, the Frome Valley Food Fest and the Dorset Knob Festival at Cattistock, Church Knowle Food Festival in the Purbecks, Dorset Food and Arts Festival at Poundbury, Screen Bites Food Film Festival and the relaunched Dorset Food Week. The Dorset Food & Drink logo is prominent at all these events, with volunteers and producers on hand to offer tastings and some of the area's top chefs taking part in demonstrations and cook-offs to show the quality of the ingredients.

Information about Dorset Food & Drink can be found on the Area of Outstanding Natural Beauty (AONB) website, www.dorsetaonb.org.uk/food-and-drink, and there are plans to produce a printed directory which will be available from members, farm shops, bed and breakfasts and other locations. The website is also a handy resource for information on upcoming local food events.

The aim is to establish Dorset Food & Drink as a brand – an indication of quality and provenance, a celebration of the best Dorset has to offer, from the chalk downlands to the hidden valleys, from the waters off the Jurassic Coast to the lush pastures of the Blackmore Vale.

Drinking Dorset

To wash down your Dorset meal, you could try a locally made cider, like Cider by Rosie (pages 132–3). In early October, apple pressing days are held around the county, and many places invite you to bring your own apples for pressing.

My retired farming friend, Alf Wallis, remembers the days when badger leg was eaten in Dorset pubs; happily these days when you hear someone ordering a half a Badger in the pub they are after a beer from the Hall & Woodhouse Brewery (pages 66–7). Dorset is well stocked with breweries, such as the Piddle Brewery (page 118) and Palmers (page 159). Details of other local breweries and beers are available at www.dorsetbreweries.com.

Thanks to its temperate climate, the county even produces its own wine, available at farm shops, delicatessens and independent supermarkets. Furleigh Estate (Salway Ash DT6 5JF 01308 488991 www.furleighestate.co.uk) near Bridport is a dairy farm that has been transformed into a winery producing white, red, rosé and sparkling wines; cellar door sales and winery tours are available on Fridays and Saturdays. Wines from the Sherborne Castle Vineyard (www.sherbornecastle.com) are available at the castle shop (page 89) and other local outlets, while Melbury Vale Vineyard (Redmans Lane, Melbury SP7 0DB 01747 850773 www.melburyvaleco.co.uk) sells its wines in shops and restaurants in the Shaftesbury area. With 30 acres of land and 38,000 vines, Langham Wine Estate (Crawthorne, Dorchester DT2 7NG 01258 839095 www.langhamwine.co.uk) is the largest vineyard in the southwest of England. On Fridays between June and September, guided tours of the vineyard are available.

As we all know, dairy farmers have had to diversify. A creative diversification is Black Cow vodka (01308 868844 www.blackcow.co.uk), a smooth vodka made from milk and with a distinctly creamy quality. It is available in delicatessens and farmshops around Dorset.

DORSET FARMERS' MARKETS

See also www.dorsetfarmersmarkets.co.uk.

Blandford second Friday of the month (Market Place)

Bridport second Saturday of the month (Bridport Arts Centre, South Street)

Christchurch first Friday of the month (Saxon Square)

Dorchester fourth Saturday of the month (South Street)

LONG CRICHEL BAKERY

Long Crichel BH21 5JU 01258 830852 www.longcrichelbakery.co.uk Tue–Fri 09.30–17.00, Sat 09.00–13.30

This traditional bakery produces delicious handmade organic breads and cakes baked in a wood-fired oven. They use organic flour from the Stoate & Sons mill near Shaftesbury (page 46) and organic milk and cream from a local dairy farm. As well as six types of yeasted bread, they produce eight different kinds of sourdough and a variety of cakes and tarts. You can find their baked goods in farmers' markets and local shops or you can order direct from the bakery and have them delivered.

Poundbury first Saturday of the month (Queen Mother Square)
Shaftesbury first Saturday of the month (Town Hall)
Sherborne third Friday of the month (Cheap Street)
Sturminster Newton fourth Saturday of the month (Station Road)
Wareham second and fourth Thursday of the month (Town Hall)
Weymouth second Sunday of the month (Westham Bridge)
Wimborne Minster third Saturday of the month (Mill Lane)
As well as farmers' markets, watch out for the Anonymous Travelling Market (www.theatm.co.uk), which tours the West Country and combines food, drink, crafts and music.

FORAGING

Foraging is nothing new – until around 10,000 years ago all modern humans were hunter-gatherers – but in more recent times interest in foraging has waxed and waned and it is currently enjoying one of its periodic heydays. Foraging was encouraged during World War II, flourished during the hippy years and is now trendy again in our era of environmental awareness. Television shows are devoted to it, celebrity chefs espouse its virtues, and restaurant menus tempt diners with foraged delicacies, such as nettle soup, fish dishes topped with seaweed and just about anything accompanied by wild garlic.

Foraging is the ultimate rebellion against convenience food – there is nothing convenient about scrabbling through brambles, getting plastered in mud and being chased by an irate bull in the pursuit of a few morsels that have already been chewed and rejected by a grub of some description. Yet somehow it appeals to the hunter-gatherer in many of us, including me.

While researching this book I was lucky enough to spend a day foraging at the Kingcombe Centre with the charming and entertaining John Wright (see pages 179–80), who regularly appears on Hugh Fearnley-Whittingstall's *River Cottage* television series. He was kind enough to provide some words for this book on the subject of foraging.

Tips for happy foraging

John Wright ⊛ www.wild-food.net

I gave up growing my own fruit and vegetables years ago. Although it was fun and ultimately rewarding it was also unreliable and rather hard work. But my main objection to gardening is that it all takes too long. This book celebrates the concept of Slow Food but gardening, I think, is far too slow. For me instant gratification is everything. With gardening one needs to prepare the ground, sow the seed, weed, water and worry, and one day, all being well (and sometimes it isn't) you pick. Foraging however is quite a different matter – you just pick.

My foraging career began over 30 years ago when I moved to Dorset (in my village I am described as a 'relative newcomer'). An early passion for wild fungi found full expression in the fields and woods around the farmhouse I rented. 'Top field' would keep me for hours picking field mushrooms – 120 pounds one year – and 'eight-acre field' would supply a magnificently large form of the delicious shaggy parasol. St George's mushrooms in spring, puffballs in summer, field blewits and the riotously colourful wax caps in autumn, and jelly ears and velvet shanks in winter would fill my mushrooming year. Of course everyone thought I was mad and sure to poison myself.

But mad or not, I am also extremely careful and never, ever eat anything unless I am sure of its name. My best advice to anyone embarking on a mushroom hunt is to do the same. Get a couple of (you really need at least two) field guides and study them carefully. Collect just a few different species at first – no more than one or two specimens of each in case you have picked something rare – and carefully identify them by examining all their characteristics and using the advice in your books. Never jump to conclusions but always match all of the characteristics of your find to the description given. If the book says a species should have a ring on the stem or turns yellow when bruised it really means it – if any characteristic is missing then it must be something else and maybe a deadly something at that.

Identifying fungi is quite a tricky business but once you have a few species committed to memory you are set for life – you do not need to become an expert mycological taxonomist. My magnificent seven edible fungi are easy to identify, common and delicious: the parasol, giant puffball, horse mushroom, jelly ear, cep, charcoal burner and the hedgehog mushroom. If you only choose one then I suggest the last of these. It is the mushroom with everything – delicious, nutty texture, very common, never gets maggots and completely unmistakable. It grows in woodland, often in substantial rings, and has a 'chamois leather' cap with little spines hanging down underneath. Nothing else looks remotely like it making it the safest of all the wild mushrooms.

It would be remiss of me not to warn you of the species which causes 99% of all poisonings. The yellow stainer looks almost exactly like the field mushroom except the edge of the cap and the base of the stem turn a remarkable chromium yellow when bruised. This fades to brown after about 15 minutes. If you eat a yellow stainer you will have to cancel all engagements for a day or two before recovering completely, sadder but wiser.

"Caught by the foraging bug, I determined to explore other wild sources of food."

Of course there are times when mushrooms are not to be found and, caught by the foraging bug, I determined to explore other wild sources of food. My Dorset farm yielded the familiar blackberries and sloes but I wondered what else might be found and bought several guides to expand my repertoire. Most edible wild plants are easy to recognise. Everyone knows, usually to his or her cost, what a stinging nettle looks like and no-one hesitates when deciding whether the nut they are looking at is a hazelnut or some deadly impostor. Wild plants are, generally, much safer than wild mushrooms. However, some very common and excellent species can be a little more challenging: fat hen, red goosefoot, sea beet and even cherry plums may have the novice forager sensibly consulting a field guide. Incidentally, and I trust I am not putting you off the whole idea entirely, the most deadly of all plant and fungal toxins is found in a very common native plant. Its leaves look like that of flat-leaved parsley and it has substantial and tasty-looking roots. It is called hemlock waterdropwort, and a plateful will have you dead in three hours.

While most people will have picked wild plants at sometime or other, even if it is just blackberries, and mushroom hunting has become quite fashionable, few venture on to our rocky shores to collect that least likely addition to a dinner party – seaweed. When I started investigating seaweeds it was not with any expectation that I would actually enjoy eating any of them – their appearance, not to mention their smell, does not encourage the gourmet; and the evangelical zeal expressed in the few books I had on the subject I rejected as the misguided rantings of eccentrics. Well I seem to have taken up ranting myself and proclaim the virtues of seaweed at every opportunity.

Seaweeds are eaten the world over, with Japan being the most accepting of this unusual food. The main problem for the British, apart from a disinclination to eat anything that doesn't come in a packet, is that they just do not know how to cook it. With one exception there is no point collecting a basket of seaweed and trying to cook it like, say, cabbage – you end up with a smelly, slimy mess. Most of the half-dozen or so good, edible seaweeds found around these islands require special treatment. Laver – a membranous, brown seaweed found, mostly, attached to rocks – must be boiled for ten hours (no less!) to form the sticky paste that is laverbread. This is used, notably in south Wales, to make oatmeal cakes or as a (rather sticky) sauce for lamb. The slightly fishy flavour is of the 'umami' kind found in other delights such as Marmite and Parmesan cheese. Laver, put through a papermaking process, will be familiar to many as 'nori', the stuff that little bits of fish and rice are wrapped in to make sushi. With carragheen – a small, bushy seaweed found attached to rocks or in rock pools at low tide – you do not eat the seaweed at all; it is simply boiled for half an hour to extract the incredibly slippery/slimy substance called 'carragheenan' which is used to set such things as panna cotta. Gutweed – a bright green, hairlike seaweed of upper shores – can be deep fried to form genuine (the stuff you get in Chinese restaurants is actually cabbage) crispy seaweed. Sugar kelp is dried and fried to make seaweed crisps and the other kelps are used for their flavour-enhancing glutamates and removed from the dish prior to serving. The exception I mentioned earlier is dulse. The deep red, flat, fingered fronds can be cooked like any other vegetable and make an excellent 'seaweed bubble and squeak'. I do recommend you give seaweed a try. So much of it is 'wasted' for want of knowledge and courage.

Food collected from the wild is, of course, free and I hope I have been able to convince you that it is also delicious. But collecting wild food can feed the soul as well as the body. The forager comes to truly appreciate food.

Food from the supermarket is just a commodity, the origin of which we neither know nor care. When you eat food you have gathered yourself you understand it in a way not open to others. You know where it came from, how it lived, what problems it faced, how fresh it is and how jolly hard it may have been to come by in the first place. So, I entreat you, go foraging – it will be good for your karma.

DORSET WILDLIFE TRUST

Dorset is one of the richest counties in England in terms of biodiversity, with some precious habitats and wildlife. To assist in preserving this great asset, the Dorset Wildlife Trust (DWT; see advert in fourth colour section) works to champion wildlife and natural places, engage and inspire people and promote sustainable living. Its 42 reserves cover many of the most important wildlife havens, including ancient woodlands, wetlands, wildflower meadows and some of Britain's rare surviving lowland heaths. The DWT has scored many notable achievements, for example in restoring coppiced woodlands by careful management and by grazing neglected grasslands so that wildlife can flourish, and in campaigning for protection of marine habitats.

Most of the DWT's reserves are open daily and there are visitor centres providing a wealth of wildlife information at Brooklands Farm, Lorton Meadows, Kingcombe Meadows and Brownsea Island nature reserves, the voluntary Purbeck Marine Wildlife Reserve and the Urban Wildlife Centre at Upton Heath Nature Reserve. More information about DWT, its reserves and opportunities to volunteer is available at www.dorsetwildlifetrust.org.uk.

A SLOW LEARNING CURVE

If you find the Slow way of life in Dorset appealing, there are various short courses on offer with a Slow theme.

At Dorset Wildlife Trust's Kingcombe Centre (pages 179–80) you can improve your knowledge of **local flora and fauna** with courses on tracking wildlife, identifying butterflies and getting to know the area's wildflowers. They also teach rural skills and crafts, including beekeeping and willow-weaving, and for hobby farmers there are sessions on livestock management. Dorset Centre for Rural Skills (West Farm Barn, Farrington, Blandford Forum DT11 8RZ ✆ 01747 811099 ⌂ www.dorsetruralskills.co.uk) is a not-for-profit training centre teaching **traditional rural crafts** such as cob and lime building renovation, blacksmithing, hurdle-making and hedge-laying.

Wood working courses are available at Guy Mallinson's Woodland Workshop in West Dorset (page 173).

TALKING DORSET

Although the local dialect is less spoken than it once was, I hope that as you explore Dorset you will hear traces of it and the distinctive lilting regional accent. Although I grew up in Dorset I don't speak the dialect, nor do I have a West Country accent, but I know plenty of people around the Blackmore Vale who do, particularly among the older generation and the farming community. Friends will often chat to me about 'diddicoys' or 'diddies', meaning Gypsies, and when asking the whereabouts of something or someone, they will add 'to' to the end of their question, 'Where is Harry to?' The reply might be 'He's goen on', meaning he has left. 'Mind' is often added to statements, as in ''Tis a nice day, min', and 's' is often pronounced as 'z' and 'f' pronounced 'v'.

No-one has done more for the Dorset dialect than the poet William Barnes, whose *Poems of Rural Life in the Dorset Dialect* (1844) celebrated the lives, customs and language of the people among whom he was raised. It included a glossary of Dorset terms so that more genteel readers could understand it. Barnes was also a philologist, and in his *Glossary of the Dorset Dialect with Grammar* (1863) he recorded hundreds of words and expressions that he felt were in danger of dying out. Middle-class Victorians tended to look upon the dialect as a corruption of standard English; Barnes disagreed and maintained that the dialect of the South West was the closest form of speech to the Old English spoken in Wessex at the time of King Alfred, that it was purer and closer to the lives of those who spoke it than standard English. Subsequent publications on the dialect draw heavily on Barnes's pioneering work.

At the time of Barnes and Thomas Hardy, dialect had already begun to decline: Hardy noted that shortly after the railway arrived in Dorchester,

AN ARCHAEOLOGIST'S PERSPECTIVE ON DORSET

Dr Tim Clayden, Wolfson College, Oxford

Dorset's outstanding contribution to our understanding of ancient Britain is its Jurassic coastline, and the many prehistoric burial mounds (nearly 500) and hillforts (27 in all) that dot the landscape. After the AD43 conquest by the Romans of the local Celtic tribe, the Durotriges, Dorset never had a period of such riches again.

Websites and textbooks can tell you where the best sites or remains are, but Dorset is a county made for walking. Being in the landscape is a chance to touch the face of time, whether that be on one of the beaches which offers an endless treasure hunt for fossils, or on the Wessex Ridgeway about whose ancient track burial mounds cluster and hillforts shape the skyline. If you do nothing else in Dorset, fossicking for ammonites on **Charmouth Beach** (page 154) and walking Maiden Castle hillfort should not be missed (page 106).

The cliffs around Charmouth and Lyme Regis are being worn away by the sea. As they collapse, the sea washes and shifts the soil, causing bullet-like belemnites and ammonites made gold by the local soil to gather in rock pools or on the tideline, waiting to be found. Local experts offer fossil-hunting tours, or you can have a go yourself (page 149). It is difficult to comprehend the aeons that have passed since those fossilised creatures lived, and yet it is possible to take home in your pocket evidence of life millions of years ago.

Walking to the summit of **Maiden Castle**, you pass through a maze of banks and ditches, which formed part of the settlement's defences and were ultimately breached by the Romans in AD43. The Romans buried the dead in large pits, excavated by Mortimer Wheeler in the 1930s, and built a small temple inside the fort. A walk around the fort reveals social cohesion on a considerable scale. In the surrounding fields can be seen burial mounds of men and women, which were ancient even when Maiden Castle was built. Keep an ear open for the skylarks that rise out of the scrub and ascend on a song.

Abbotsbury Hillfort (page 168) is a bit battered and less visited than Maiden Castle, but the views along the coast, including of Chesil Beach, are wonderful. Being Dorset, there is more archaeology: in this little parish alone are 22 round barrows. Many are visible on the ridgeway that runs parallel to the sea.

The **Cerne Abbas Giant** (page 112) is hard to ignore. The huge figure of a naked man holding a club in his right hand, and his erect penis and ballooning testicles has understandably attracted archaeological investigation and much ribaldry. Theories as to its origin used to centre on it being prehistoric or Roman, depicting Hercules or a fertility deity, but more recent research suggests it may be a 17th-century creation intended to poke fun at the Puritan Oliver Cromwell. Either way it is a striking sight, better seen from a distance than close up.

Perhaps the best introduction to Dorset's archaeology and history is a visit to the **County Museum** in Dorchester (page 102).

London music-hall songs had started to replace the old folk tunes of the area. The teaching of standard English in schools, increased travel, migration of people from other areas and pervasive mass media have all contributed to the loss of England's dialects. However, some Dorset words have been reincarnated and found new modern usages; for instance, dumbledore, the Dorset word for bumblebee, is now the name of a character in J K Rowling's Harry Potter books.

Dorset dialect words are often far more fun and descriptive than their standard English cousins, for example:

betwattled – confused
biggity – conceited
chattermag – magpie or a woman who talks a lot
gallybagger – scarecrow
gurt lummock – big, clumsy person
tinklebobs – icicles
wops – wasp
zennit – seven nights (a week)
zull – plough
zummit – something

LITERARY DORSET

Dorset's scenery and its people have long inspired writers of prose and poetry, most notably the county's favourite literary son, **Thomas Hardy** (see box, page 29). However, Dorset has many other lesser-known literary connections, which you are likely to stumble upon as you explore the county.

A friend of Hardy's, and the son of a Blackmore Vale farmer, **William Barnes** (see box, page 35), wrote pastoral poetry in Dorset dialect, giving a voice to the county's humble farming folk and immortalising their lives and the county's landscapes in his emotive descriptions. He is buried at St Peter's Church in Winterborne Came near Dorchester, where he served as rector for 24 years.

Novelist **Henry Fielding** (1707–54) was also from the Blackmore Vale, more precisely the village of East Stour, near Shaftesbury, and some of his characters are based on people he knew while living in Dorset.

William Wordsworth (1770–1850) is commonly associated with the Lake District but he and his sister, Dorothy, spent two years in the 1790s in west Dorset near Pilsdon. It was here that he started to write seriously and Pilsdon Pen is said to have soothed his sister's longing for the hills of the Lake District. Poet **Samuel Taylor Coleridge** (1775–1834), who lived in neighbouring Somerset, visited them frequently.

Robert Louis Stevenson (1850–94) wrote *Kidnapped* while living in Bournemouth; he suffered from a weak chest and was one of many at the time who came to the seaside town for its healing air.

T E Lawrence (Lawrence of Arabia) lived at Clouds Hill, a cottage between Dorchester and Wareham, when he was stationed at Bovington Camp and he finished *Seven Pillars of Wisdom* and *The Mint* while living there. He died in 1935 as the result of a motorcycle accident near his home and is buried at Moreton. Clouds Hill is now run by the National Trust and is open to the public, and a walking trail links Bovington, Moreton and Clouds Hill, all being points associated with Lawrence (see pages 126–7).

Lyme Regis became a literary tourism destination as early as the 1820s, after **Jane Austen** described Louisa Musgrove falling from the steps on The Cobb in her novel *Persuasion* (1818). Austen loved Lyme Regis and the surrounding area and spent a good deal of time there. The Cobb later featured in **John Fowles's** well-known novel *The French Lieutenant's Woman* (1969); Fowles (1926–2005) had moved to Lyme Regis in 1968. He was a fan of Thomas Hardy's work and Tess is reputed to have been the inspiration for his own scandalised woman.

Children's writer **Enid Blyton** made regular visits to Dorset, in particular the Isle of Purbeck, where she bought a golf club; she later purchased a farm near Sturminster Newton in the Blackmore Vale. Dorset places and landscapes were the inspiration for many of the locations in her *Famous Five* and *Secret Seven* books. The golf club featured in *Five Have a Mystery to Solve*, her farm appeared in *Five on Finniston Farm* and Corfe Castle may have been the inspiration for Kirren Castle. Blyton's Whispering Island, also known as 'Keep-away island', was based on Brownsea Island in Poole Harbour, which during Blyton's day was owned by the reclusive Mrs Bonham-Christie who shunned visitors and let the island return to nature.

A handy resource for me in writing this book has been *Highways and Byways in Dorset* (1906) by **Sir Frederick Treves** (1853–1923), who managed to combine a successful career as a surgeon with travel writing, and in the former capacity famously rescued Joseph Merrick,

THOMAS HARDY

Thomas Hardy was born on 2 June 1840 in a small, thatched cottage at Higher Bockhampton, a hamlet east of Dorchester; his father was a master mason and his mother a servant and cook. The eldest of four children, Thomas was initially pronounced stillborn but an observant nurse realised the newborn was breathing.

Hardy's mother encouraged him to read and study, beyond the usual level for local children. He went to school in Bockhampton and then Dorchester and at the age of 16 was apprenticed to John Hicks architects in Dorchester. He practised as an architect at Hicks's London office for five years but returned to Dorset to write fiction, living first in Sturminster Newton and then at Max Gate, the house he had built in Dorchester. Hardy's first novel was rejected but in 1871 *Desperate Remedies*, set at Kingston Maurward, was published anonymously, followed by *Under the Greenwood Tree*. Over the next 25 years he wrote 12 novels, over 50 short stories and a significant amount of poetry, including *Wessex Poems*, an anthology written over 30 years and published in 1898.

When Hardy began writing about Dorset it was a little-known county beyond its seaside resorts. The Dorset countryside was immortalised in his writings as Hardy's Wessex, and although he slightly altered the place names it was easy to guess their true identities from the descriptions. Dorchester was the inspiration for the eponymous town in *The Mayor of Casterbridge* (1886), set in the county town in the 1850s, when Hardy was at school and starting his apprenticeship there. *Tess of the d'Urbervilles* (1891) was set in the Blackmore Vale, Hardy's 'vale of little dairies', and Tess was born in the village of Marlott, actually Marnhull. The publication of *Tess* and *Jude the Obscure* (1895) cemented Hardy's fame but not perhaps in the way he would have liked – many Victorians found the books' mildly racy content immoral and offensive.

Hardy married Emma Gifford in 1874 and although he later became estranged from his wife, her death in 1912 greatly affected him and was the subject of some of his finest poetry. In 1914, Hardy married his secretary, Florence Dugdale. He died in 1928 and his heart is buried alongside Emma in the churchyard at Stinsford, while his ashes are in Westminster Abbey.

Hardy aficionados can visit his birthplace at Higher Bockhampton (page 109), his home in Dorchester, Max Gate (page 103), and Stinsford (pages 108–9). A reconstruction of his study is on display at the Dorset County Museum in Dorchester (page 102).

the 'Elephant Man', who had been displayed as a circus freak. He was born in Dorchester and his forthright account of his tour of Dorset makes interesting and, in parts, amusing reading.

Today Bridport is the heart of the Dorset literary community: a literary festival is held there annually and incorporates the Bridport Prize for poetry and short stories (www.bridportprize.org.uk).

NORTH DORSET – THE BLACKMORE VALE, CRANBORNE CHASE & SHERBORNE

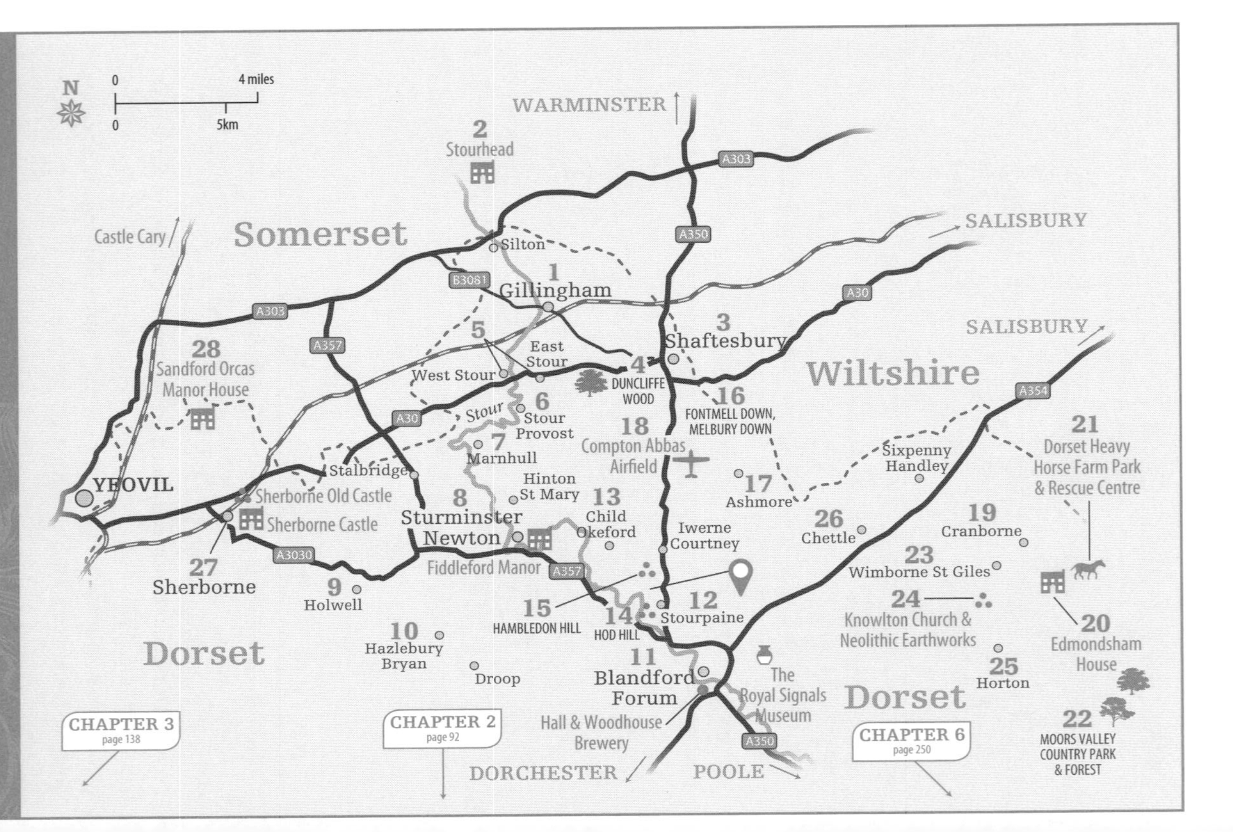

1
NORTH DORSET – THE BLACKMORE VALE, CRANBORNE CHASE & SHERBORNE

I admit to being biased when it comes to this part of Dorset, for this is where I grew up. I have travelled to many countries around the world but there is no landscape that makes my heart sing like the glorious **Blackmore Vale**, with its tapestry of verdant fields divided by neat hedges and sprinkled with beguiling villages.

The best way to appreciate the beauty of the vale is to look down on it from above, whether by taking a flight from Compton Abbas Airfield or by viewing it from the top of Hambledon Hill, Bulbarrow Hill or the Saxon town of Shaftesbury. Alternatively, you can see it up close, perhaps with a walk along the Stour Valley Way, which follows the River Stour through the vale.

The sparsely populated **Cranborne Chase**, which reaches into Hampshire and Wiltshire, offers equally exquisite landscapes and exceptional walking, cycling and horseriding. At Knowlton is a rare and intriguing sight, the ruins of a medieval church perched in the centre of a Neolithic henge.

Nestled in the wooded Yeo Valley in the northwest of the county, **Sherborne** is one of Dorset's, and perhaps England's, most appealing towns. It enchants the visitor with its blend of historic buildings, two impressive castles and imposing abbey.

North Dorset has historically been great farming country, in particular dairy farming. With the decline of the agricultural industry, many farmers have had to diversify but the area's farming heritage is obvious – in its landscapes and its first-rate local produce.

Tourists tend to bypass North Dorset and head straight for the coast, which means the area is largely unspoilt and you can expect genuine Dorset hospitality and real Dorset characters. The delightful sing-song of Dorset accents still hangs thick in the air around these parts.

GETTING THERE & AROUND

The areas within this chapter are easily reached from the A30 and the A303. Driving is a good option, especially if you are short of time, because public transport services are scant.

PUBLIC TRANSPORT

The towns of Gillingham (pronounced with a hard 'g' at the start), not to be confused with Gillingham in Kent (pronounced with a soft 'g'), and Sherborne are on the Exeter to London Waterloo **train** line (www.southwesttrains.co.uk). Trains are frequent (roughly every hour), catering for those prepared to suffer a daily commute of over two hours. Most trains divide at Salisbury, with only a few carriages continuing further south into Dorset and Devon, so choose your carriage carefully.

To reach the Dorset coast from Gillingham by train is not as straightforward as you may think. Getting to Bournemouth involves heading up to Salisbury, changing trains, then going across to Southampton, and changing again to hop on a train to Bournemouth. The journey time is something over two hours. Similarly, travel to Wareham involves changing at Salisbury and Southampton, with a journey time of almost three hours.

Public transport is limited in the Blackmore Vale and Cranborne Chase. However, there are hourly buses between Gillingham and Shaftesbury on weekdays (less often on Saturdays and none on Sundays or public holidays), plus less frequent services between Gillingham and Blandford Forum via Stour Provost, East Stour, Marnhull and Sturminster Newton (Line 309). Buses are regular between Blandford Forum and Poole and the journey takes about an hour.

CYCLING

The quiet **rural roads** and **bridleways** of the Blackmore Vale and Cranborne Chase have excellent scope for cycling.

You can download a leaflet on cycling in North Dorset (www.dorsetforyou.com) featuring seven suggested cycling routes which largely focus on the Blackmore Vale, although one ventures into the Cranborne Chase. The cycling section of the **Wessex Ridgeway** begins in Tollard Royal and cuts diagonally across Dorset through changing scenery: across the Blackmore Vale, through the chalk downland around Cerne Abbas to the Marshwood Vale in the southwest (www.dorsetaonb.org.uk).

The **North Dorset Cycleway** (regional route 41 www.gps-routes.co.uk) is a 73-mile circular on-road route linking Gillingham, Sturminster Newton, Blandford Forum and Shaftesbury. It wends its way along country lanes through classic Blackmore Vale landscapes with sections that run beside the River Stour, and skirts into the Cranborne Chase.

The **North Dorset Trailway** (www.northdorsettrailway.org) is a route for walkers, cyclists and horseriders along the old Somerset and Dorset railway line, which closed in 1966. Suggested routes can be downloaded from the website. The longest and most popular portion is between Stourpaine and Sturminster Newton, a six-mile route which links up with the Wessex Ridgeway.

CYCLE HIRE

Dorset Cycle Hire High St, Stalbridge DT10 2LL 01963 362476. A small cycle shop, which also does cycle hire.

WALKING

The Blackmore Vale and Cranborne Chase are criss-crossed by a dense web of footpaths and bridleways. A walk up one of the hills surrounding the Blackmore Vale, especially Hambledon or Bulbarrow, provides breathtaking views. Both are easily accessible with car parking nearby. The Iron Age hillforts of **Hambledon** and **Hod Hill** combine superb scenery with archaeological interest, while **Duncliffe Hill** offers the opportunity for an easy walk in one of the vale's few remaining wooded areas. The **Stour Valley Way** (www.stourvalleyway.co.uk) follows almost all of the 64-mile course of the river, passing through the Blackmore Vale from its source at Stourhead. It passes the remains of the many mills that once operated on this stretch of river, and it is worth taking a detour to visit some of them, such as the ones at Sturminster Newton and Stour Provost. The paths through the vale are far less used than those around Christchurch, making for some very pleasant, peaceful riverside walks.

"Duncliffe Hill offers the opportunity for an easy walk in one of the vale's few remaining wooded areas."

TOURIST INFORMATION

Blandford Riverside House, West St, DT11 7HW ✆ 01258 454770
Shaftesbury 8 Bell St, SP7 8AE ✆ 01747 853514
Sherborne Digby Rd, DT9 3NL ✆ 01935 815341 www.sherbornetown.com

The walking section of the **Wessex Ridgeway** (www.dorsetaonb.org.uk) begins in the village of Ashmore in the Cranborne Chase and drops down through the Blackmore Vale before continuing across the county to Lyme Regis on the coast. You don't have to stray far from Shaftesbury for some superb walks high on the **Cranborne Chase**, at Fontmell and Melbury Downs, and at Win Green, just over the Wiltshire border. The café at Compton Abbas Airfield is perfectly positioned for replenishing the energy stores.

HORSERIDING

North Dorset lends itself to being explored on horseback, as it has been for centuries. Bridleways are plentiful in the Blackmore Vale and Cranborne Chase, and the Wessex Ridgeway (www.dorsetaonb.org.uk) and the North Dorset Trailway (www.northdorsettrailway.org) are both open to riders. Some farm-based bed and breakfasts will allow you to bring your own horse, such as Glebe Farm in Ashmore (page 295). Unfortunately, there are now few places that offer hacking on their own horses.

RIDING STABLES

Hill View Stables Sunnyside Farm, Cathole Bridge Rd, Crewkerne, Somerset TA18 8PA ✆ 01460 72731 www.hillview-riding-stables.co.uk. Offers hacks in the Dorset and Somerset countryside, has an indoor arena and cross-country course.
Redlands Equestrian 4 George's Pl, Bathwick Hill, Bath BA2 4EN ✆ 01225 424413 www.redlandsequestrian.com. An equestrian travel company, which can arrange accommodation for both horse and rider in the Cranborne Chase, allowing you to take advantage of the area's excellent riding with your own horse.
The Stables at Bushes Farm Bushes Rd, Stourpaine DT11 8SU ✆ 01258 455846 www.thestables-bushesfarm.co.uk. Riding for all ages and abilities in the Blandford Forum area.
Three Gates Equestrian Leigh DT9 6JQ ✆ 01963 210284. A family-run riding school and livery yard near Sherborne, which can provide B&B accommodation and stabling for your horse.

THE BLACKMORE VALE

Most visitors to the West Country whizz down the A303, overlooking the Blackmore Vale just beneath it and, as a result, the area remains remarkably unspoilt. It lies in North Dorset and stretches just over the border into southwest Wiltshire, a wide, sheltered valley of fertile agricultural land dotted with charming, quintessentially English villages, many of which are built from warm, golden stone. The **Dorset Downs** and **Cranborne Chase** border it, with the towns of Shaftesbury (in the north) and Blandford Forum (in the south) being natural boundary markers. Hills such as Hambledon and Bulbarrow encircle the vale, and provide fine vantage points over its neat fields lined by hedges, its woodland and its villages. In spring and summer the landscape is sprinkled with yellow highlights – crops of oilseed rape. Those views would once have been quite different as the vale was densely wooded and the area around **Gillingham** a royal hunting forest. Few pockets of

WILLIAM BARNES

Mo Richards

William Barnes (1801–86) was born at Bagber, near Sturminster Newton in the Blackmore Vale, the son of a yeoman farmer. Although best known as a poet who wrote mostly in dialect, Barnes was also a philologist. He was fluent in Greek, Latin and several modern European languages and studied the close relationship between Dorset dialect and Old English. He called for the removal of foreign-derived words from the English language, so that it might be better understood by those lacking a classical education.

There is not a language Barnes loved more than that of the Dorset folk around him. His pastoral poetry written in Dorset dialect brought to life the voices of the county's ploughmen, milkmaids and farmers. His fondness for Dorset's landscapes, as well as its local people, shines through in his poetry.

From 1835 until 1862, Barnes ran a school in Dorchester and in 1844 he published *Poems of Rural Life in the Dorset Dialect*. From 1862 until his death, he was rector of St Peter's Church, Winterborne Came, and is buried in the churchyard.

Although younger than Barnes, Thomas Hardy was a fan of Barnes's work and the two became friends. Not everyone was impressed by Barnes's use of the Dorset dialect, but Hardy defended it: 'The veil of a dialect, through which except in a few cases readers have to discern whatever of real poetry there may be in William Barnes, is disconcerting to many, and to some distasteful, chiefly, one thinks, for a superficial reason which has more to do with spelling than with the dialect itself.'

woodland remain, the most notable being on **Duncliffe Hill**, which rises like a beacon from the flat base of the vale.

From its source at Stourhead, just over the Wiltshire border, the River Stour meanders through the vale on its way to the sea at Christchurch. A series of mills used to punctuate the water's journey through the vale, and several of them are named in the Domesday Book. Of some 50 mills that used to operate on the River Stour, many are now derelict but some have been lovingly restored. **Sturminster Newton Mill** is still in working order and is open to visitors in the summer months.

Dairy farming used to be the lifeblood of the Blackmore Vale, prompting Thomas Hardy to use it as the inspiration for his 'vale of little dairies'. Sadly, prolonged troubled times have meant many of the dairy farms have now shut up their milking parlours and had to diversify into other activities. The silver lining for the visitor is that those resilient, ingenious Dorset farming folk have built some fantastic rural businesses, including accommodation, farm shops, niche food production and even recreational fishing lakes.

The vale's towns, in particular **Shaftesbury** and **Sturminster Newton**, draw visitors for their history and beauty but perhaps the best way to appreciate the Blackmore Vale is to get out and walk its pristine countryside and hike the surrounding hills for a bird's-eye view. For generations the scenery has inspired artists, such as John Constable; writers, such as Thomas Hardy; and poets, such as William Barnes. Hardy's description of the view from the hills in *Tesss of the d'Ubervilles* still holds true today:

> Here, in the valley, the world seems to be constructed upon a smaller and more delicate scale; the fields are mere paddocks, so reduced that from this height their hedgerows appear a network of dark green threads overspreading the paler green of the grass.

1 GILLINGHAM & SURROUNDS

Stock Hill House (page 294) **Whistley Farm** Milton-on-Stour (page 295)

Being on the main train line to London, Gillingham is the gateway to the Blackmore Vale. Today the trains are used by suit-clad commuters making their daily journey to Salisbury, London or one of the cities in between but farmers June and Alf Wallis remember when the trains' cargo was quite a different one. June and Alf have been farming in Dorset all their lives and in nearby Stour Provost since 1963. They recall the days when cattle from nearby farms were loaded directly on to trains at Gillingham and the farmers' supplies of fertiliser arrived by train and they collected it from the station in their tractors. The station, and the town, must have had quite a different character in those days.

Gillingham gets a bit of a bad rap, largely because its neighbour, Shaftesbury, is considered far more attractive. Both towns have seen a great deal of new housing development in recent years, but Shaftesbury has done a better job of maintaining its charm. Gillingham wasn't always the ugly sister, however, as in the 19th century John Constable felt it a worthy artistic subject and painted the bridge, the mill and the entrance to the town. Of these, the most recognisable scene today is

CHESTER JEFFERIES – TRADITIONAL GLOVE MAKERS

Buckingham Rd, Gillingham SP8 4QE 01747 822629 www.chesterjefferies.co.uk

Tucked away down an alleyway on Station Road is a bustling workshop of which Gillingham can be proud. The Chester Jefferies company has been making high-quality leather and lambskin gloves in this building since 1963 using traditional methods, and enjoys a worldwide reputation for excellence.

Chester Jefferies, the company's namesake, came from a gloving family in Westbury, Wiltshire. He set up a glove-making partnership with a man named Gilbert Pearce in 1936, and his family forbade them from opening a factory within a hundred miles of their own for two years. For that reason, the first Chester Jefferies factory was in Slough. Gilbert bought Chester out in 1950; he kept the company name and moved the factory to Gillingham in 1963. Today the company is run by Gilbert's grandsons, Mark and Greg, and Mark's son Shaun.

The gloves are still handmade, some in the workshop, others by dedicated seamstresses in their own homes. The leather is carefully selected and cut the traditional way, by hand. The range of gloves is varied, and includes classic formal dress, casual, military, equestrian and shooting. In equestrian circles the gloves are highly sought after worldwide. The company has a long history of making gloves for theatre, film and television, including for productions such as *Titanic*, *Anna Karenina*, *Robin Hood*, the Harry Potter films and *Merlin*. Yes, Hagrid and Hercule Poirot have both worn Chester Jefferies gloves made in Gillingham. The company has also made gloves for members of the royal family and carefully crafted the Royal Horse Guards' white gauntlets for Queen Elizabeth II's Diamond Jubilee in 2012.

You will sometimes see a sign on Station Road saying 'glove sale', signalling your chance to pop into the workshop and pick up some superb gloves directly from the manufacturer (often at reduced prices), and at the same time you will be able to marvel at the busy folk within taking great pride in their work and the tradition behind it.

MERE DOWN FALCONRY

Manor Farm, Mere BA12 6HR ☎ 01747 824913 🖱 www.meredownfalconry.co.uk

Just over the border into Wiltshire, at the base of the Mere Downs, falconer Allan Gates carefully tends to his much-loved birds of prey: hawks, owls and falcons. He is a regular sight at local country shows, flying his birds over the heads of delighted spectators, while his wife Alison runs the ferret-racing part of the enterprise. For a truly memorable experience, you can have a go at flying Allan's birds under his expert supervision.

Of the various interactive experiences on offer, my pick is the full-day introduction to falconry. You spend the morning meeting and learning about the birds and flying them short distances near the aviaries, and after lunch you take a couple of them up on to the Mere Downs and fly them over the wide valley.

I accompanied Allan, his German short-haired pointer and two of his Harris hawks up on to the downs, where we flew the birds over the bowl created by the crescent-shaped hills. The views back towards Gillingham and the Blackmore Vale were breathtaking, providing a suitably impressive backdrop for these marvellous birds. The hawks and the dog hunted as a team, the dog flushing out prey and the birds watching keenly from above, and although we didn't catch anything that day that didn't seem to dull their enthusiasm. The majesty and power of these birds in flight is something to behold, but just as fascinating is Allan's relationship with them: they are clearly bonded to him but maintain that wild, instinctive spirit. Allan told me each bird very much has its own personality and he gives them the jobs to which they are best suited and, from what I saw, they enjoy their work.

A lot of time and effort goes into training these birds. Allan sometimes spends an evening in front of the television with a bird sitting on his arm, getting it used to the glove and food rewards. (Alison is a very tolerant wife.) He even delicately repairs any damaged feathers they may have. Allan learnt from one of the best falconers around, Merv Brown, who farmed in the Blackmore Vale village where I grew up, Stour Provost.

Falconry is an ancient countryside tradition practised in various countries around the world and is believed to date back to at least 3,500BC in the Middle East. The equipment used has barely changed since falconry began; you feel like you are stepping back in time as you stand on the hills and watch the birds soaring on the thermals over the valley and then swooping back to land on your glove with pinpoint accuracy. As Allan explained to me, many common expressions come from falconry, including 'under the thumb', referring to the bird's leash being tightly held.

Allan is doing a superb job of keeping this countryside pursuit alive. As well as half- and full-day flying experiences, he offers two-hour family handling sessions and occasionally runs special events such as owl night flights. He tells me the owls are particularly popular with children.

Gillingham Bridge, which lies three-quarters of the way down the High Street; Constable's depiction of it is in London's Tate Britain.

Before you rush off to Shaftesbury, the **Gillingham Museum** (✆ 01747 823234 🖱 www.gillinghammuseum.co.uk ⊙ Mon, Tue, Thu, Fri & Sat) is worth a look. It is located near the Gillingham library, opposite Waitrose supermarket on the Wyke Road and within walking distance of the train station. The museum tells the story of area's inhabitants, from Neolithic settlement to the present and reminds us that the Gillingham area was once a busy royal hunting forest, and that in 1210 King John is said to have rewarded two huntsmen for killing wolves here. The 1790 manual fire engine on display is the only surviving one of its kind. Also on show are reproductions of John Constable's paintings of the area.

There are some pleasing villages around Gillingham, notably Silton and **Milton-on-Stour**, where there are sturdy stone farmhouses and a bridge over the river, which rises in nearby Stourhead.

Silton

The village of Silton is worth visiting for its 15th-century **church of St Nicholas**, thought to stand on Saxon foundations. The interior walls carry a distinctive, dainty, stencilled decoration but the church's most striking feature is a highly theatrical 17th-century memorial to Sir Hugh Wyndham (1602–84), with him flanked by his two weeping wives. Wyndham was a judge of the court of common pleas and was one of 22 judges who sat in the Fire Court, set up in 1667 to hear cases relating to property damaged in the Great Fire of London. Wyndham bought the Manor of Silton in 1641, on the site of the present Manor Farm, just south of the churchyard.

In a field behind the church is the **Wyndham Oak**, one of Britain's oldest trees. It is said Sir Hugh Wyndham used to rest under the oak and admire the view, so it must have been a substantial size by the 17th century. It is thought that the tree may have been used for hangings following the Monmouth Rebellion, although this has not been confirmed. To visit the oak today is to be in the presence of plant majesty: its gnarly, split trunk and branches like witches' fingers attest to its momentous age. Personally, I wouldn't sit Wyndham-like beneath it as it doesn't look as robust as it must once have been. Should it finally give up the ghost, it will not be lost altogether because in the 1970s the residents of Manor Farm planted an acorn from the ancient oak in the same field as its ancestor so that it can one day take over the mantle.

FOOD & DRINK

Buffalo Inn Lydford Lane, Gillingham SP8 4NJ ✆ 01747 823759 ⏲ pub open daily, restaurant closed Mon. On the Wyke side of Gillingham, this traditional-looking pub contains a popular Italian restaurant. You won't leave hungry – the portions are huge. Reservation recommended.

Lagan Farm Shop Orchard Park Garden Centre, Shaftesbury Rd, Gillingham SP8 5JG ✆ 01747 835544 ⏲ daily. Stocks rare-breed lamb and beef, and the casual café is a popular meeting point for locals.

South Street Kitchen South St, Gillingham SP8 4AP ✆ 01747 824648 ⏲ Tue–Fri 18.00–21.30, Sat 10.00–15.00 & 18.00–21.30, Sun 10.00–15.00. Tucked away at the bottom of town, this innovative restaurant uses coal, wood and smoke to create tasty dishes using local produce. They also do a decent coffee and cake, and have a pleasant garden.

Stock Hill House Gillingham SP8 5NR ✆ 01747 823626 🖱 www.stockhillhouse.co.uk ⏲ lunch & dinner daily. An upmarket restaurant in this elegant country house hotel. Austrian chef Peter Hauser produces exceptional dishes, including Austrian specialities. Many of the vegetables and herbs are grown in the impressive gardens. Reservation recommended.

2 STOURHEAD HOUSE & GARDENS

Stourton BA12 6QD ✆ 01747 841152 ⏲ garden: 09.00–18.00 all year; house: opening times vary; National Trust

Just over the Wiltshire border, the 2,650-acre Stourhead Estate is one of the area's key attractions. As the name indicates, it is here that the River Stour rises. The house is a Palladian mansion brimming with antique furniture and artwork, and evokes the lives of its former residents, the Hoare family, who made their fortune in banking. The 18th-century gardens are magical, inspired by the great landscape painters of the 17th century and grand tours of Europe. A magnificent lake constitutes the centrepiece, fed by the infant River Stour, which shimmers with the reflections of autumn colours as the leaves change hue. Classical temples, a romantic bridge and a mysterious grotto create a dreamy atmosphere; the European influence is clear with a mini Pantheon and a Temple of Apollo among the features.

"Classical temples, a romantic bridge and a mysterious grotto create a dreamy atmosphere."

Nearby is King Alfred's Tower, a 160-foot folly built in 1772 in honour of the Saxon king by Stourhead's then owner, Henry Hoare II. The woods around the tower offer memorable walks and when the tower is open in summer you can walk to the top for superlative views of the surrounding countryside.

THE GILLINGHAM & SHAFTESBURY SHOW

Turnpike Showground, Motcombe SP7 9LP www.gillshaftshow.co.uk

One of the highlights of the Blackmore Vale calendar is the annual agricultural show, held on the third Wednesday in August at Motcombe, between Gillingham and Shaftesbury. It has all the best features of an agricultural show: livestock classes, dog classes, equestrian classes, heavy horses, the local hunts, agricultural trade stands, local food producers and handicrafts. Locals spend many months preparing their entries for the fiercely contested jam, cake, vegetable, embroidery and art classes.

3 SHAFTESBURY

Grosvenor Arms (page 294)

'Welcome to Shaftesbury, a Saxon Hilltop Town': the sign seems to sum it up, but there is more to this place because it shows immense skill in combining functionality, history and beauty. It stands on a greensand promontory at 700 feet, overlooking the Blackmore Vale; its centre is compact, packed with enticing, independent shops and easy to explore on foot. It was founded by King Alfred the Great around AD880 and is one of four Dorset towns named in the Burghal Hidage, which recorded Alfred's plan to provide fortified safe havens for local people at times of invasion (see page 43 for more details). Although many of the town's buildings are Georgian and Victorian, constructed from distinctive local greensand stone, traces of its Saxon origins can be seen around the site of the abbey. Key to the town's beauty is the picture-perfect Gold Hill, a cobbled street lined with tiny cottages.

Thomas Hardy had plenty to say about Shaftesbury: he referred to it as 'Shaston' in his writings and it appeared in both *Jude the Obscure* and *Tess of the d'Urbervilles*. He described it as 'one of the queerest and quaintest spots in England', 'breezy and whimsical' and said 'beer was more plentiful than water'. It is certainly quaint and, thanks to its hilltop position, has a tendency to be breezy. Mercifully, the water supply is now far more reliable than it once was and although there is a healthy population of pubs serving local ales, I doubt beer is more plentiful than water. On a dull day, the town is often shrouded in cloud and this, combined with its cold greensand stone, has given it a reputation as a rather dreary, melancholy place. Catch it on a fine day and you will be amply rewarded by this queer, quaint, whimsical town that so fascinated Hardy.

The appealing town centre is an easy walk from the car parks at the top and bottom of the High Street, and buses stop outside the Town Hall, in the very centre of town. The **Town Hall** is a Georgian building whose battlements seem designed to project a serious, castle-like image; the weekly **street market** takes place here on Thursdays. Next to the Town Hall is the diminutive **St Peter's Church**; built in the late 15th century, it is the oldest church in Shaftesbury.

Just behind the Town Hall is the much-photographed, much-painted **Gold Hill**. This impossibly steep, cobbled street with its row of attractive cottages and pastoral Blackmore Vale backdrop is a local celebrity. The highlight of its career was appearing in the 1973 Hovis bread commercial directed by Ridley Scott, which featured a boy pushing a bicycle up the hill. A mildly comical statue of a Hovis loaf sits next to the Town Hall, a reminder of that pinnacle of Gold Hill's fame. Along one side of Gold Hill a formidable stone wall is all that remains of the walls that once encircled Shaftesbury Abbey. At the top of Gold Hill is a café, where you can sit and pity the poor folk walking up the steep incline. Nearby is **Gold Hill Museum** (pages 45–6). Don't be surprised if you hear the odd bleating sheep (although I never have) as apparently a tenant's right to keep six sheep was bestowed on all households on Gold Hill and that permission remains in place today.

A narrow alleyway (Park Lane) leads from the top of Gold Hill to **Park Walk**, which has peaceful public gardens, breathtaking views across the Blackmore Vale and the **Abbey Museum and Garden** (pages 44–5). With the abbey ruins behind and the mesmerising countryside in front, the gardens are an ideal place to sit and ponder the history of the place and how it might have been when King Alfred ruled the roost around these parts.

"The gardens are an ideal place to sit and ponder the history of the place."

Shaftesbury Abbey was built by King Alfred around AD888 on the site of a pagan temple; it was the first religious house solely for women and Alfred's daughter, Aethelgifu, was the inaugural abbess. The remains of Saxon king Edward the Martyr were brought to the abbey after his murder at Corfe Castle in AD978 (see box, page 225); his shrine and the promise of associated miracles attracted streams of pilgrims. The abbey thrived and became one of the largest in the country, with around 350 inhabitants and large tracts of land in

Dorset, Wiltshire and beyond. It attracted royal visitors, including King Canute who died here in 1035. In 1491 Henry VII stayed at the abbey, as did Catherine of Aragon in 1501 on her way to marry Prince Arthur, elder brother of Henry VIII. After 650 years of continuous worship, the abbey closed in 1539 as part of Henry VIII's Dissolution of the Monasteries and soon fell into disrepair. The ruins are visible within the Abbey Museum and Garden, while the ramparts on Gold Hill are all that remain of the outer walls.

The views from Park Walk are rivalled by those from **Castle Hill**, which is within walking distance of the abbey ruins. Head along Abbey

KING ALFRED THE GREAT

Alfred is the only English king to be known as 'The Great', an epithet bestowed for his valiant defence of his kingdom against a formidable enemy, for securing peace with the Vikings and for his educational and legal reforms.

He was born in AD849 in what is now Wantage, Oxfordshire, fifth son of Aethelwulf, king of the West Saxons. In AD871, at the age of 21, he succeeded his brother Aethelred as King of Wessex.

Viking armies had been raiding England since around AD790 and had taken much of the North; in AD870 they attacked the last remaining independent Anglo-Saxon kingdom, Wessex. After turning to guerrilla tactics to defeat the Danes in several protracted battles, Alfred negotiated a partition treaty with them in AD886, whereby the areas between the rivers Thames and Tees became Danish territory and Alfred took charge of an extended Wessex, which now included West Mercia and Kent.

To protect his kingdom, Alfred established a navy and built a series of well-defended settlements across southern England, fortified marketplaces or 'burhs', where residents could seek shelter. Settlers received plots in return for manning the defences in times of war. The programme was recorded in the Burghal Hidage, a document detailing the building and operation of Wessex and Mercian burhs according to their size, the length of their ramparts and the number of men needed to garrison them. This network of burhs, with strong points on the main river routes, ensured that no part of Wessex was more than 20 miles from the refuge of one of the settlements.

Alfred believed strongly in education, learnt Latin in his late thirties and was patron of the Anglo-Saxon Chronicle, a patriotic history of the Anglo-Saxons. He lamented that much of the population could not understand Latin and so arranged the translation into Anglo-Saxon of a series of important books he thought 'most needful for men to know'. He also advocated justice and order and significantly reformed Anglo-Saxon law. Alfred reigned until his death in AD899 and was buried in Winchester, capital of Wessex.

Walk then turn left when you reach Bimport; after a short distance, a lane on your right leads to Castle Hill, once the site of a Saxon fort. The views across the Blackmore Vale to the Somerset and Wiltshire border are topped off by King Alfred's Tower in the distance. Thomas Hardy described the scene as:

> As sudden a surprise to the unexpected traveller's eyes as the medicinal air is to his lungs.

Aside from Gold Hill, some of the best-preserved greensand cottages, with tiny doors and thatched roofs, are found at the top of town in Bell Street and at the bottom of town in **St James**, an area at the base of Gold Hill. In St James look out for a u-shaped collection of workers' cottages set back from the road, known as Pump Court and still with the pump at its centre.

You will see plenty of references to the Grosvenor family in and around Shaftesbury, for they owned much of the town until less than a hundred years ago. In 1820, Earl Grosvenor (later Marquis of Westminster) bought the 'Property of Shaftesbury' (the 400 premises large enough to have voting rights) in order to control elections in the borough. The Grosvenors grew very wealthy and were responsible for much of the development in the town, and it is for that reason that it has an estate village character; the keen-eyed will spot many cast-iron windows of similar design and uniform rows of workers' cottages. The family also alleviated one of the town's greatest problems, a lack of water, when in the mid-1800s the marquis provided a well and a steam engine to pump free water to the residents. In 1918, Robert Grosvenor's great-grandson sold his Dorset estates, and Shaftesbury was again put up for sale. It was bought by a Londoner and then re-sold to a consortium of three men of the town: the doctor, the innkeeper at the Grosvenor Arms and the manager of a grocer's shop. They subsequently held the 'sale of Shaftesbury' in which, over three days, most tenants bought their own houses and shops.

Shaftesbury Abbey Museum & Garden

Park Walk, SP7 8JR ☎ 01747 852910 ⊕ www.shaftesburyheritage.org.uk ⊙ Apr–Oct daily

This small museum sits on the site of the abbey and gives a feel for what life would have been like for the women who lived there. It is best visited in decent weather, as you can explore the excavated foundations of the abbey in the walled garden. The foundations are all that remain of the abbey,

DORSET BUTTONS

Dorset buttons, with their characteristic wheel appearance, used to be handmade in households around the county. Their manufacture was at a peak between 1622 and 1850. Originally, they were made on a disc cut from the horn of a Dorset Horn sheep, which was covered with needle-worked thread; in around 1720, the horn was replaced with a metal ring.

It was in 1622 that Abraham Case set up a commercial button-making enterprise in Shaftesbury. He had a workshop there but as the business grew Case paid people to make buttons in their own homes and buttony became an important cottage industry. For many, especially those who could not work in the fields, it was their main source of income.

Abraham's descendants carried on the family business and by 1720 the company had additional premises in Bere Regis, Milborne St Andrew, Sherborne, Poole, Langton Matravers and Tarrant Keynston. By the end of the 18th century, the business employed over 4,000 people.

However, a button-making machine displayed at the 1851 Great Exhibition in Crystal Palace spelt the beginning of the end of buttony as a viable cottage industry. Handmade buttons were gradually replaced by those made by these machines in factories in England's growing cities. The decline hit Dorset hard, as many households had relied on the industry to survive. Some people were forced into the workhouse, others emigrated to Australia, Canada or the USA, including 350 people from Shaftesbury.

The Blandford Fashion Museum (page 65) tells the story of Dorset buttons and sells modern versions in its shop.

as much of the stone was taken for building elsewhere, and a small herb garden commemorates the nuns' extensive use of herbs; the commanding statue of King Alfred was made as recently as 1989. Indoor exhibits include a model of the abbey church as it would have been in the 11th century. The free audioguide provides an excellent commentary.

Gold Hill Museum

Gold Hill, SP7 8JW ✆ 01747 852157 🖱 www.goldhillmuseum.org.uk ⏲ Apr–Oct 10.30–16.30; free admission

This well-run museum in a cottage at the top of Gold Hill was once a dosshouse (cheap lodging) for the drovers, jugglers and traders who came to Shaftesbury's markets and fairs. Exhibitions cover archaeology and local history. The industries on which the town was built are given due attention: agriculture, lace-making and the production of Dorset buttons. Murals by local artist, Janet Swiss, help to bring the history to life.

STOATE & SONS STONEGROUND FLOUR

Cann Mills, Shaftesbury SP7 0BL ✆ 01747 852475 🖱 www.stoatesflour.co.uk ⏲ closed Tue, Sat & Sun, & between 13.00 & 14.00 Mon, Wed & Fri

The Stoate family began milling in the West Country in 1832, and in 1947 took over this mill about a mile south of Shaftesbury on the A350 to Blandford. Their mill is powered largely by the River Sturkel, a tributary of the Stour, and the flour is ground using French burr stones. They produce a range of organic and non-organic flours, including spelt, rye and wholemeal.

You can buy Stoates flour direct from the mill or from farm shops, healthfood shops and bakeries across the South West. Several good local bakeries use Stoates flour, such as Long Crichel Bakery and Leakers in Bridport.

Paul Merry runs artisan bread- and pastry-making courses at the mill itself, which include a mill tour (✆ 01747 823711 🖱 www.panary.co.uk).

The most extraordinary object on display is the Byzant, an exotic gilded totem embellished with peacock feathers. While it may look like the product of a school project, the Byzant was central to securing the town's water supply. Shaftesbury had no water supply of its own, so the Byzant was processed annually to nearby Enmore Green, along with gifts of ale, bread, a calf's head and gloves, to secure the town's right to water from that area. The Byzant is recorded as early as 1364 and the ceremony continued until 1830, when Shaftesbury acquired its own water.

FOOD & DRINK

Beggars' Banquet Music Café Mustons Lane, SP7 8AD ✆ 01747 850332 ⏲ Mon–Sat 09.00–17.00 & Fri evening. Deservedly popular vegetarian café, which also caters for vegan and gluten-free diets. The former stables and courtyard on a quiet lane halfway down the High Street make a pleasant setting. On Friday evenings it becomes a bar and hosts regular live music nights.

Grosvenor Arms The Commons, SP7 8JA ✆ 01747 850580 🖱 www.thegrosvenorarms.co.uk. ⏲ daily. The Grosvenor Arms was bought by 2 local farmers in 2013 and local produce is now central to the sophisticated and creative menu. The food is carefully prepared and presented, and the choice of wines is excellent. The comfy bar and courtyard are open all day for coffee and snacks, while the restaurant serves breakfast, lunch and dinner daily.

King Alfred's Kitchen 17 High St, SP7 8JS ✆ 01747 858452 ⏲ daily. Traditional tea rooms in a delightfully wonky 13th-century building, complete with low ceilings and original beams. It is thought it may have been the original kitchen for the abbey. Breakfasts, lunches, cream teas and cakes are homemade, including a textbook Dorset apple cake. Tall people will find there is more headroom upstairs.

La Fleur de Lys Bleke St, SP7 8AW ✆ 01747 853717 🖱 www.lafleurdelys.co.uk ⏲ Mon–Sat for dinner & for pre-booked lunches Wed–Sun. An upmarket restaurant at the entrance to the town. Reservation recommended.

Salt Cellar Gold Hill Parade, SP7 8JW ✆ 01747 851838 ⏲ daily. This café's greatest asset is its location, right at the top of Gold Hill. If you have climbed the hill, you will have earned tea and cake here. Light lunches are available.

Turnbulls 9 High St, SP7 8HZ ✆ 01747 858575 🖱 www.turnbulls.co.uk. A popular deli and café at the top of the High Street. The owner, Charlie Turnbull, is an international cheese judge and there is a huge choice of cheese on sale alongside a range of local produce.

Ye Olde Two Brewers 24 St James St, SP7 8HE ✆ 01747 855477 ⏲ closed Sun evening & Mon. A traditional pub at the bottom of Gold Hill serving reasonably priced food. The dining room and large garden have stunning views of the Blackmore Vale.

4 DUNCLIFFE WOOD

A visit to Duncliffe is perhaps the best way to gain an impression of what Blackmore and Gillingham would have been like when they were royal hunting forests. As the many farms grew up in the area, the land was cleared but on Duncliffe Hill a pocket of well-preserved woodland remains, cared for by the Woodland Trust. The Domesday Book records a wood here, which was traditionally coppiced, and is said to have been the inspiration for Thomas Hardy's *The Woodlanders*. Much of the ancient oak, ash and hazel was felled in the 1950s and replanted with Norway spruce, oak, larch and beech. Today, the Woodland Trust manages it in such a way as to encourage a greater mix of native broadleaf species.

Footpaths and a bridleway lead through the 228-acre wood to the top of the hill (690 feet), which provides far-reaching views of the surrounding farmland. Whenever I walk through the wood, I always half expect to encounter the wildlife characters from a children's book – it has that magical feel – and if you walk there on a summer's evening you are likely to catch a glimpse of many of them – the local roe deer, badgers, pheasants and foxes. Butterflies are also abundant, including silver-washed fritillary, white admiral and purple hairstreak.

Duncliffe Wood lies off the A30 between Shaftesbury and East Stour; from the A30 take the turning signed Stour Row. There is a car park and sign showing the various paths you can follow through the wood.

5 EAST STOUR & WEST STOUR

The importance of the River Stour is evident in this area, with a string of villages named after it. This is an area of small farms, watched over by Duncliffe Hill. East Stour and West Stour lie on the A30 between Shaftesbury and Sherborne; both villages were mentioned in the Domesday Book but now have a noticeable amount of modern development, East Stour in particular. Thankfully it also has handsome original farms and the short, squat **church**, which was rebuilt in 1842 on the site of an earlier one. Henry Fielding, author of *Tom Jones*, lived in the old rectory which has now been demolished; Church Farm stands on the site. As you enter East Stour from Shaftesbury you pass the marvellous **Udder Farm Shop**, which has breathed new life into the area (see box, opposite).

From East Stour the A30 continues through West Stour, providing views back across the fields towards Stour Provost, where the River Stour flows. The **Ship Inn**, a handsome coaching inn built in 1750, is a good starting point for walks across the fields to Stour Provost.

FOOD & DRINK

Kings Arms Inn East Stour Common, SP8 5NB 01747 838325 www.kingsarmseaststour.com daily for lunch & dinner. On the A30 between Shaftesbury and East Stour, this is a popular pub with locals, especially for its Sunday lunch carvery. It offers a choice of traditional pub food or more upmarket meals.

Ship Inn West Stour SP8 5RP 01747 838640 daily. A traditional coaching inn; the menu is diverse and uses local ingredients wherever possible. The bulk of the parking is across the road, so do take care when crossing as visibility is poor.

6 STOUR PROVOST

I grew up in this tiny community, which is little more than a single street lined with conspicuously picturesque golden limestone houses, some of them thatched, and a smattering of farms. When I came into the world in 1977, I was the first child born in the village for 25 years and something of a novelty. The pace of life has remained pretty slow ever since, although the character of the village has altered. When I was growing up at Riversdale Farm, Stour Provost still had a village shop and a pub but they are long gone. There were several working dairy farms and it was not uncommon to see herds of cows, including our own small family of beef cattle, being walked through the village to pastures new.

THE UDDER FARM SHOP

Manor Farm, East Stour SP8 5LQ ✆ 01747 838899 www.theudderfarmshop.co.uk ⊙ daily

This fabulously named large farm shop (see advert in fourth colour section) sells a wonderful array of local produce and is a great place for self-caterers to stock up. There is an on-site butcher, a delicatessen and a large selection of gifts with a local flavour. The café has become the definitive place in the area to meet up with friends. It serves excellent light lunches and delicious cakes, has views of Duncliffe Hill, an outdoor children's play area and wheelchair access.

The shop is the brainchild of local farming personalities Brian and Jane Down. I have known Brian and his family since I was born – they used to farm the land adjoining ours in Stour Provost, although their farm is in East Stour on the A30.

For years I only ever saw him on a tractor and I suspect he only ever saw me on a pony. His grandfather came to Manor Farm in 1938 and it has remained in the family. In the 1990s, when my father was the European correspondent for a Canadian newspaper, he interviewed Brian and his father, Jim, for an article about the approaches of the different generations to farming. Brian had spent some time on a very progressive farm in New Zealand in the 1980s and returned full of ideas to modernise Manor Farm, some of which met with a lukewarm reception from his father. Like so many father-and-son farming teams they figured out their own *modus vivendi*, supported by a shared love of their piece of the Blackmore Vale. I thought it only right that all these years later I interview Brian about his latest venture and ask what Jim makes of it.

It was 2005 when Brian, like so many dairy farmers, came to the realisation that diversification was the only way forward. If nothing else, it would make the bad years easier to bear and with any luck provide an asset he and Jane could leave to their children. The East Stour village shop had closed, leaving a significant gap in the local community, and they came up with the idea of a farm shop. They were determined the project should benefit the community as much as possible, employing local labour as well as providing a service. It seems apt that the company they used to build the frame of the Udder Farm Shop barn was the same rural firm that built Brian and Jim's milking parlour in 1994.

They have created a hugely successful enterprise selling a tempting array of locally made products. Brian finally gave up milking 18 months after the Udder Farm Shop opened but you can't stop a farmer doing what comes naturally so he continues to run beef cattle. Much of the beef you see in the Udder Farm Shop butcher's corner is Brian's, and the pork is supplied by his uncle.

I asked who had come up with the name, and Brian took the credit and said they settled on it when Jane refused to wear the T-shirt bearing his first-choice, 'The Crazy Cow'. As for Jim's reaction, he initially had some reservations about the farm shop but he got behind the project and helps out where he can. No-one can deny the Udder Farm Shop has really put East Stour on the map.

These days most of the farms are farms in name only, bought by Londoners who use them as weekend pads. A few diehard locals remain and the village still has that small community feel but it is a smarter, more sophisticated version of its former self, without a single cowpat on the street. For the visitor it offers unabashed architectural beauty, an ancient church and tranquil walks along the River Stour.

Stour Provost's history has helped to preserve its character because until less than a hundred years ago the village as a whole was owned by one entity. From the 11th century until 1467 it was owned by the nuns of the Saint Léger de Préaux Abbey in Normandy, and was known as Stour Préaux. During the wars with France, Henry V rescinded the title of various French-held lands in England, including the village, and Henry VI gave it to Eton College. Edward IV subsequently gave it to King's College, Cambridge, which owned much of the village until 1925, when it began to sell the houses to individuals.

St Michael and All Angels Church was largely built in 1302, probably on the site of an earlier Saxon church, but has undergone alterations over the centuries. An avenue of pollarded lime trees leads to the small church; sadly it is not usually left open but you can get the key from one of the church wardens. The interior is modest but with some elaborate stained glass, while the font is Purbeck stone and dates from the 15th century. Adjacent is **Church House**, a fine 16th-century building. The thatched cottage known as **Mundy's**, which lies towards the bottom of the main street, was a house for 'poor orphan children and other poor of the parish' in the 18th century.

The River Stour runs at the base of the gardens of the houses on the west side of the street. At Riversdale Farm (my childhood home) is an oxbow which was used as the local swimming pool until the 1960s, and known as Lucky Dip. At the opposite end of the village, at the end of Mill Lane, is the **Mill House**. A footpath runs through here so the mill, its waterwheel and the millpond can be seen close up. The Domesday Book of 1086 records a mill here; the present waterwheel was made in 1886, fell into disuse and was restored in 1988 by the then owners of the house, the Llewellyn family, and run to provide electricity to the house.

A **circular walk** takes you from the mill across fields to the village of **Fifehead Magdalen** and from there across fields to **West Stour**, where you can stop off for refreshments at the Ship Inn (page 48). From the Ship Inn a footpath leads directly back to the other end of Stour Provost, taking you through fields and over a footbridge (ideal for Pooh sticks) and arriving in Stour Provost near Riversdale Farm. From there you can simply walk up The Street back to the centre of the village.

7 MARNHULL

Crown Inn (page 294) **Todber Manor** Todber (page 295)

Thomas Hardy enthusiasts seek out Marnhull, which Hardy referred to as Marlott, for it was here that the eponymous heroine of *Tess of the d'Urbervilles* was born and raised. The historic, partly thatched Crown Inn on the edge of the village was the Pure Drop Inn in the novel. I fear that visitors expecting a village barely changed since Hardy's day will be disappointed; it is a large scattered community with much new development. Marnhull certainly isn't the prettiest village around but is perhaps not quite as bad as Sir Frederick Treves makes out in *Highways and Byways in Dorset* (1906):

> It is a disappointing village, prim and stiff, with houses mostly of slate and stone, together with many villas of the Brixton and Camberwell type. It is as little rustic as a place on the edge of the Blackmore Vale could be. Its long listless street crowns a modest height above the River Stour.

There are, however, plenty of attractive, old buildings in the local, creamy white limestone, quarried at nearby Todber. Particularly handsome are the village's stone farmhouses, such as **Senior's Farm**, adjacent to the church, which dates from 1500, and **Chantry Farmhouse** (formerly Pope's Farm) on the road to Stalbridge. The **church of St Gregory** is largely 15th century and its tall tower can be seen from miles around. Within the church is the alabaster figure of a recumbent knight flanked by his two wives, which dates from the 1470s. Treves (and many other writers) recorded a memorial to parish clerk John Warren, who died in 1752, which is sadly no longer visible:

> Here under this stone lie Ruth and old John,
> Who smoked all his life and so did his wife,
> And now there's no doubt,
> But their pipes are both out
> Be it said without joke
> That life is but smoke
> Though you live to fourscore,
> 'Tis a wiff and no more.

His case would do the anti-smoking lobby no good at all, as he lived to 94 years of age.

Marnhull was reportedly famous for bull-baiting until 1763, when it was banned because of the hooligan behaviour of supporters. The annual contest, held on 3 May, saw bulls brought from the surrounding area but rivalry was so intense it often led to violence, which spread from Marnhull to outlying villages.

FOOD & DRINK

The village is well equipped with village shops and two pubs.

Blackmore Vale Inn Burton St, DT10 1JJ 01258 820701 daily for lunch & dinner. Fresh home-cooked pub food, including traditional dishes like hommity pie.

Crown Inn Crown Rd, DT10 1LN 01258 820224 daily for lunch & dinner. This thatched, 16th-century pub appeared in Thomas Hardy's writings as the 'Pure Drop Inn' and it oozes history with its chunky beams, wonky walls and original flagstone floor. Popular with locals, the pub gets busy at weekends.

8 STURMINSTER NEWTON

Plumber Manor (page 294) **Stock Gaylard Yurt Holidays** (page 295)

Sturminster Newton, known to locals as Stur, has been the nucleus of life in the Blackmore Vale for centuries. The town's livestock market, dairy farming, button- and candle-making brought great prosperity to Sturminster Newton and the surrounding area, particularly from 1863 when the Somerset and Dorset Railway opened and the area's milk, cheese and other produce could be sold further afield. The railway closed in 1966 but parts of it now form the **North Dorset Trailway**, a cycle and footpath which links Sturminster Newton to surrounding villages (see page 33).

Sturminster Newton is justifiably proud of its literary connections. Dorset poet and author William Barnes (see box, page 35) was born on its outskirts, christened in the church of St Mary and went to school in the town. Thomas Hardy lived in the town with his wife Emma while writing *The Return of the Native* (1876–78).

Although there is much new development on the outskirts of Stur, the town centre, and the marketplace in particular, is overflowing with a variety of historic buildings and architectural styles, including 17th- and 18th-century thatched cottages, Georgian stone houses and 19th-century brick buildings. **Church Street** and **Tanyard Lane** have some particularly pretty houses. Prominent in the marketplace are the well-worn stone remains of a 15th-century **market cross**, which was reportedly shaped like a mushroom until 1540 when it was smashed by thieves. A Monday market is held here and features local foods, crafts and clothing.

In a quaint 16th-century thatched building in the town centre is **Sturminster Museum** (Old Market Cross House ✆ 01258 817116 ⌂ www.sturminsternewton-museum.co.uk ⏲ Easter–Dec Mon, Thu, Fri 10.00–15.00, Sat 10.00–12.30, Jan–Mar Mon, Fri, Sat 10.00–12.30; free admission), where the history of the livestock market and local dairy farming features strongly.

The Station Road livestock market, once the largest in Britain, was central to the vale's important agricultural industry until it closed in 1997. As I grew up in nearby Stour Provost, the Stur Monday market was very much part of my childhood and I recall the sadness that swept the area when it was announced it would close. The historic market had originated from a royal charter of 1219 and there was a fear that Stur would lose its identity when the market was demolished and a seven-acre gaping hole left in the town. However, ten years after the market closed, and thanks to a committed band of locals, **The Exchange** (✆ 01258 475137 ⌂ www.stur-exchange.co.uk) opened on the site and its art exhibitions, theatre, cinema and community activities now draw crowds from around the vale just as the market once did. It is an impressive facility for a small country town and the complex in which it stands also houses a much-needed medical centre and some shops. Just as the concept of the new community centre was a local one, so was the building of it. The committee engaged an architect from Shaftesbury and a local builder, while Stur's blacksmith, Ian Ring, created the delightful wrought-iron balustrade on the staircase.

At the bottom of Station Road is **Harts of Stur** (Station Rd, DT10 1BD ✆ 01258 472240 ⌂ www.hartsofstur.com), affectionately described by locals as Stur's answer to Harrods. This family-run shop has been operating since 1918 and stocks a huge range of kitchenware, hardware and clothing.

At the southern end of town a handsome six-arched 16th-century stone **bridge** spans the River Stour; a 19th-century plaque warns would-be graffiti artists, 'Any person wilfully injuring any part of this county bridge will be guilty of felony and upon conviction liable to be transported for life'. You have been warned.

From the bridge you catch your first glimpses of **Sturminster Mill** (☎ 01747 854355 ⏲ Apr–Sep Mon, Thu, Sat & Sun 11.00–17.00), 250 yards upstream. When the mill is open, volunteers are on hand to show you around, explain its workings and recount its history. The Domesday Book records a mill on this site and until recently it was thought the present one dated from the 17th and 19th centuries. However, in 2013 lime plaster began to peel off one of the mill's interior walls and revealed new evidence that cast doubt on earlier assessments of its age: a stone bearing the date 1566 and other fascinating carvings. Millers had carved their initials into the stone over the centuries, creating a sort of

JOHN CONSTABLE & THE LAWYER'S WIFE

The late K J Richards (this is adapted from an article written by my father for a Canadian newspaper, *Farm and Country*, in which he wrote a regular column on European rural affairs; he was an author, farmer, film director and entrepreneur)

When we first moved to Riversdale Farm in Stour Provost some of the more ancient locals referred to the place as 'Tinney's', yet none of them knew quite why. They were right: a man called John Pern Tinney did once own the farm and John Constable's painting of *Stratford Mill* used to hang above the fireplace. The story I stumbled across played out in a Dorset village tucked away in the Blackmore Vale, and combined the agony and the ecstasy of an artist, the stubborn possessiveness of a house-proud wife and the intermediacy of a wise friend.

Stour Provost consists of a village street, almost unchanged since Constable's time, and a lane leading down to the farm. Tinney, a small town lawyer, had become the proud owner of *Stratford Mill*, now more commonly known as *The Young Waltonians*, in part payment for a law suit that he had successfully undertaken on behalf of John Fisher, Dean of Salisbury Cathedral. Fisher was Constable's closest friend and perhaps the first to realise the genius of the temperamental painter. Many in the Establishment had little time for Constable's landscapes and his canvasses regularly returned unsold from exhibitions. With a family to support he was approaching middle age increasingly riven and in despair.

The picture must have reached the farm in early summer 1821, for on 19 July Dean Fisher wrote: 'King George IV crowned this day! My dear Constable, your picture is hanging up in a temporary way at Tinney's till his new room is finished. It excites great interest and attention.' For Mrs Tinney, probably no great connoisseuse of the arts, it quickly became the most treasured possession in her home.

Slowly but surely, and in no small measure due to Fisher's patronage, Constable's work began to find recognition and in its exhibition of 1825 the Royal Academy agreed to find a space for one of his larger canvasses. The picture Constable chose to show was *Stratford Mill*, milling wall of fame. Volunteer Pete Loosmore, a retired teacher whose grandfather worked at the mill, explained to me the meaning behind a more magical-looking carving on the same stone: the date 1610 inside a rectangle with a shark's-teeth pattern around the edge. Experts believe the shark's teeth depict VM (Virgin Mary) and ask for her help to protect the mill against witchcraft. Pete described the curious carving as a forerunner of the many horseshoes that have been hanging from the building's beams for centuries to bring the mill good luck.

"Millers had carved their initials into the stone over the centuries."

and he wrote to Tinney requesting its loan for the period of the exhibition. Tinney, who had begun to fancy himself as a patron of the arts and had already made offers for further works by the painter, readily agreed, although it can be assumed that Mrs T was more than a little vexed to see her best room denuded of its much-admired decoration. Nevertheless, *Stratford Mill* took the stage to London.

Later that year Constable was approached to give his support to the first exhibition of the newly formed Scottish Academy and again wrote to Tinney asking him to lend the painting for the purpose. This was too much for Mrs T. Quite a few angry words must have been exchanged between the lawyer and his wife in front of the fireplace and this time she prevailed. Sharpening his quill and with his wife's shadow cast from spluttering candles above his shoulders, Tinney penned a letter to Constable, 'With respect to the beautiful picture which is the principal ornament of our house, Mrs Tinney says she will not consent to its being again removed as it was last year for so a long a time ... I hope you will not think her unreasonable.'

Constable did think the lady unreasonable and exploded into an artistic fury that must have shaken his studio to its foundations. His reply to Tinney marked the end of a friendship and the end of the lawyer's brief sway as a collector of contemporary art; Constable cancelled the arrangements under which he had agreed to sell further canvasses to Tinney.

Dean Fisher acted as intermediary and with a series of wise letters calmed the fiery Constable, who eventually accepted, 'My name (though looked for) will not appear at the opening of the noble institution in Edinburgh – I should have liked to have struck a blow in that quarter – but I must submit to circumstances'. Without the calming influence of the dean, Constable would surely have severed an ear, as well as disposed of his reason.

Stratford Mill remained with Tinney for his lifetime and was doubtless the object of minute adjustments and daily dustings by the obstinate Mrs T.

STURMINSTER NEWTON – A BLEND OF OLD & NEW

Jane Williams

Stur is a charming little town which honours its history and embraces the future. Newcomers and visitors often remark on the welcoming atmosphere of the town and it is impossible for locals to 'pop into town quickly' because there are always friends to greet and snippets of news to share.

The old and the new mix well here. The pretty little museum right in the middle of town is fascinating but only a short walk away is a modern hall and arts centre called The Exchange. I love many things about The Exchange. I will always meet somebody I know and perhaps join them in a cuppa while we pick out what we will book from the variety of cinema, theatre and music on the programme. I love the fact that the whole centre is an exchange – it's like a bring-and-buy sale of goodwill. Everybody comes with something to offer, whether it's their time, their advice, ideas or energy, and in return they get entertainment, stimulation, a feeling of belonging. To explain how all this came about, I need to go back a few years to the closure of the livestock market.

When a market town loses its market the silence is deafening. Instead of clatter, gossip and laughter there's a gaping hole. In many small country towns, the livestock market is the reason for being. Stur's market bell rang for the last time in 1997. Big blank fences went up and sadness hovered over the site and the town like bereavement. Would Stur go the way of so many small market towns with their empty shops and loss of purpose? Absolutely not! In stepped a group of residents who formed SturQuest, a community group with enormous vision, patience and tenacity. The town was determined to meet the challenge of life after livestock and to be a part of planning its own future.

Ten years to the day after the market closed, and after extraordinary community efforts in lobbying, negotiation and fund-raising,

Until 1991 this was a working mill, but today it grinds into action on the second weekend of each month between April and September. The flour it produces is sold on site and at the Sturminster Museum.

The River Stour is wide here and it is easy to see why generations of artists, including John Constable, have been inspired to paint the mill. On a summer's day the water seems to drift unhurriedly towards its destination, lilies provide colourful decoration and cows graze nonchalantly in the adjacent fields. The scene is best appreciated from the fields opposite the mill, which you can reach across the bridge over the weir, and where a footpath leads along the river towards Hinton St

The Exchange opened its doors: within were a hall for concerts, cinema, theatre and banquets, plus half a dozen other rooms and spaces for almost any activity you could wish for, from pannier markets to exercise classes and a gallery and bar.

Within weeks the place was buzzing. I am a therapist, and one wet week night in November I remember hosting my regular meditation group in a small room there and every other room was booked – there was a family history group, foreign language class, bowls, belly-dancing, a Chamber of Trade meeting and a gallery full of people enjoying an exhibition of sculpture and art. All this, midweek in a country town of 3,500 inhabitants! The venue has not just acted as a replacement for a tired old hall; it has rejuvenated the town, given it another reason for being and encouraged visitors from all over Dorset and beyond.

There is one thing I love above all and that for me captures the spirit of this resilient little town. When the market closed its doors a local farmer managed to retrieve the big market bell complete with signals for cattle, sheep, pigs and so on. He didn't know what he was going to do with it, but among the destruction and chaos he needed to salvage an icon of a treasured way of life. The bell now sits proudly at The Exchange to call theatre-goers in for the start of a performance but was first rung there at its opening ceremony, ten years after it had last rung at the market, by a ten-year-old boy, born on the day the market closed.

It is a joy to be part of this kind of community and that is the key – there is so much to be a part of, to engage with. People have been consulted and plans have taken into account how we live here, so things flow.

Newcomers are attracted to the town because of its beautiful setting, snuggled into the Blackmore Vale on the Stour; they travel many a mile to the annual cheese festival, celebrating the area's great reputation for quality produce, and they stay because it immediately feels like home.

Mary in one direction and Fiddleford in the other. The picnic benches around the mill make a pleasant lunch spot.

Locals are used to watching out for **deer** along the A3030 about four miles southwest of Sturminster Newton because the road runs through the **Stock Gaylard Estate** (DT10 2BG ✆ www.stockgaylard.com) and alongside its 80-acre **deer park**. Although the common deer and menil fallow have been there for generations, they always seem surprised and a little indignant to see cars pass by. The estate's small Georgian house is visible from the road and is occasionally open to the public (see website). In front of the house is a tiny 12th-century church, where services are held monthly. In August the estate hosts an **Oak Fair**, which celebrates all things woody and is a great opportunity to meet and buy from local hedgelayers, coppicers and woodturners. Yurt camping is available on the estate (page 295).

Fiddleford Manor

DT10 1HD ✆ 0117 9750700 ⊙ Apr–Sep daily 10.00–18.00, Oct–Mar 10.00–16.00; free admission; English Heritage

This hugely atmospheric medieval manor a mile east of Sturminster Newton on the A357 is one of the oldest buildings in Dorset and is certainly worth a visit. In 1355, the land passed through marriage to William Latimer, later sheriff of Somerset and Dorset. The main parts of the house, which was grand for its time, are thought to have been built for Latimer around 1370. The arched timber braces of the Great Hall and Solar are spectacular and, combined with the low ceilings, wood panelling and hefty fireplaces, give an impression of what a medieval Dorset house may have been like. Upstairs, in what was the family's quarters, is a 14th-century wall painting of the Angel Gabriel announcing that Mary would give birth to the son of God. It was discovered in 1990 under layers of whitewash and is remarkably well preserved. It is a privilege to admire the 14th-century craftsmanship in this building, and the 16th- and 17th-century additions. As you look out of the upstairs window at the river and the fields beyond, it is humbling and exciting to think of the characters that have stood in the same spot over the centuries, enjoying a view that has barely changed.

FOOD & DRINK

Three years after the closure of the livestock market, Stur suffered another body blow in 2000: the closure of the Sturminster Creamery, a major employer in the town. It had come into existence in 1913 as the initiative of a co-operative of local farmers, who sought to supply fresh milk and Cheddar cheese to the area. Today, Stur's cheese-making history is celebrated via the town's annual **Cheese Festival**, one of the largest in England (www.cheesefestival.co.uk).

Comins Tea House Bridge St, DT10 1BZ ✆ 01258 475389 www.cominsteahouse.co.uk. After a visit to India, Michelle and Rob Comins were inspired to bring high-quality single estate tea to the UK. As well as selling their teas online, they have opened this delightful tea house where you can enjoy a memorable cuppa, accompanied by homemade sweet or savoury treats, including Japanese gyoza dumplings. They value the ritual of tea drinking and take pains to explain how best to enjoy each variety. Their bespoke British teaware is also for sale here.

Fiddleford Inn Fiddleford DT10 2BX ✆ 01258 475612 www.thefiddlefordinn.com ⊙ daily from 12.00. A traditional pub on the outskirts of Sturminster Newton serving pub fare at reasonable prices.

Holebrooks 6 Market Pl, DT10 1AR ✆ 01258 472077 www.holebrooks.co.uk. In the centre of town, Al and Nikki Wingate-Saul sell an excellent range of local meat, including from their own farm, plus baked goods and deli items.

Plumber Manor DT10 2AF ✆ 01258 472507 www.plumbermanor.com ⊙ daily for dinner, lunch on Sun. Fine dining in elegant surroundings at this well-respected small hotel (page 294).

Sturminster House Tea Rooms Bath Rd, DT10 1AT ✆ 01258 471808 www.sturminsterhousetearooms.co.uk ⊙ Mon–Sat 10.00–17.00, Sun 10.00–14.00, Fri & Sat dinner by appointment, check the website for theme nights. Mother and daughter team, Wendy and Louise, put their heart and soul into this venture. In a characterful building, Sturminster House Tea Rooms has a traditional feel that is enhanced by the vintage china on sale. As well as cakes and cream teas, light lunches are on the menu, and there are plenty of gluten-free options. On a sunny day, you may like to take your tea in the courtyard.

9 HOLWELL

Golden Hill Cottage Stourton Caundle (page 295) **The Ark** Naish Farm (page 295)

Holwell isn't a particularly pretty village and it's very spread out; divided into two halves, one part medieval and the other, known as Barnes Cross, mostly 19th century. Its layout is not conducive to a sense of community, and one resident told me 'if you want a social life, don't live in Holwell'. Having said all this, some may wonder why I've included Holwell at all – there are three reasons: a church, a postbox and a bakery.

"Some may wonder why I've included Holwell at all – there are three reasons: a church, a postbox and a bakery."

The **church of St Lawrence** is in the older part of the village, down a dead-end lane lined with Holwell's most appealing houses. It is largely 15th century and outside it are an unwelcoming set of stocks. The church is usually only open on service days but I was lucky enough to visit when the warden was mowing the graveyard. He let me into the church and we got chatting; it turned out he was my old school bursar – Dorset is a small place. He explained that the churchyard is a nature reserve; he only mows a narrow path through the graveyard because churchyard seed beds can be up to 600 years old and leaving the grass wild supports the local ecology. Many other Dorset churches are now treating their churchyards similarly. Inside the church I found a delightful, authoritative, historic wall-hanging entitled 'A table of kindred and affinity'. A handy document, it provides clear guidelines as to which relatives one should not marry. There are two lists, one for men and one for women, and I was relieved to see that 'grandmother' topped the list for men but surprised that mother came in at number ten, below wife's mother's sister!

Tucked away on a quiet lane, bashfully shunning the fame its title could bestow, is the oldest Royal Mail **pillar box** in use in Britain. Made between 1853 and 1856, it is cast with Queen Victoria's cipher and the tiny letter slot is vertical. The box is at the Barnes Cross end of the village, not far from the turning to the church, outside Barnes Cross Cottage.

FOOD & DRINK

Bee Shack Naish Farm, DT9 5LJ ☎ 01963 23597 ⌂ www.honeybuns.co.uk ⏲ 11.00–16.00 on the first Sat of each month between Apr & Dec. The rustic café of the Honeybuns Bakery (where Emma Goss-Custard bakes superb cakes using locally sourced ingredients) serves tasty gluten-free and vegetarian treats, and light lunches in informal surroundings in the farm's former chicken shed. All proceeds from the café are used in their BeeGreen project – building nest boxes and bat boxes, tree planting, in the team veggie plot & polytunnel, hedge laying and improving the nature reserve which surrounds the bakery. Children can explore the nature reserve or meet Cino, the friendly donkey. Check the website for special events. Glamping weekends are available in The Ark, a vintage 1940s cedar-clad caravan (page 295).

10 HAZLEBURY BRYAN

This scattered and confusing village consists of seven tiny hamlets, each with its own name. Hazlebury Bryan is one of those deliciously descriptive Dorset village names, so it is rather deflating to learn that the older part of the village, including the church, lies in the area known as Droop. The **church of St Mary and St James** is charming, a simple golden stone building by a large pond. It is of mainly 15th-century construction; the wooden door and wagon roof date from that period, and are well preserved.

The **Red Barn Village Stores and Post Office** (☎ 01258 818303 ⏲ daily) is a handy resource for the community, stocking an eclectic mixture of grocery, deli, bakery and household goods.

OLIVES ET AL

1 North Dorset Business Park, Sturminster Newton DT10 2GA ✆ 01258 474300 www.olivesetal.co.uk

Small businesses often have intriguing stories behind them and Olives Et Al is right up there with the quirkiest that I've heard. When someone told me an ex-army officer and a former ballerina had set up a company making marinated olives, I had to find out more.

Giles Henschel left the army in 1991 and was living on a houseboat in London with his new wife, Annie, a former ballerina and flight attendant. They weren't exactly sure how they were going to earn a living but decided that a long-overdue 'gap year' was in order. They embarked on a year-long adventure that would be the inspiration for Olives Et Al, motorbiking through the Mediterranean, Middle East and North Africa. Giles told me that there was a common thread – wherever they were offered great local hospitality, they were offered great local olives. No matter the religion, the political instability or the standard of living, the olive was ubiquitous, prepared with its own local twist. They collected recipes from countries such as Spain, Greece, Turkey, Syria and Libya, and worked on olive plantations as they went.

From what Giles tells me, their return to England brought them back down to earth with a jolt. They had sold everything before they went abroad, and so ended up sharing a bedsit in Southampton with one of Giles's old army chums. One day Giles suggested to Annie that rather than spend another evening worrying about the future, they set up their tents, drink wine, eat olives and pretend they were travelling again. Giles's plan was only foiled by the jar of olives he had picked up at the supermarket, which tasted nothing like those they had had on their adventure. It seemed that the only way to get decent olives was to buy them and ferment them themselves. Giles bought olives in bulk and, using the recipes they had collected, fermented them in the only vessel they could find that was large enough – the bath. Friends raved about them and persuaded Giles and Annie they should sell them. They took a batch to a rural living show in Bath in 1993 and sold out. Within a year, Giles and Annie were selling olives via mail order and producing them for a large London retailer.

Today, they marinate over 40 million olives per year and the Olives Et Al range has grown to include oils, dressings, kiln-roasted nuts and other snacks. The products remain true to the lessons Giles and Annie learnt on their travels: use the finest ingredients, tried and tested methods and no artificial colours, flavourings or preservatives. The olives are naturally ripened, come from trusted olive farmers, and are brought back to Dorset to be fermented. As Giles pointed out, 'it takes time, care and attention to produce a good quality product' and while the recipes may be exotic, Dorset know-how is at the heart of this business.

You will see Olives Et Al products in farm shops and delis throughout the West Country. They also have a shop at their headquarters on the edge of Sturminster Newton and a café/deli at Poundbury called the Potting Shed (page 106).

Some 150 yards from the Thyme after Time farm shop and café is the 35-acre **Alners Gorse Butterfly Reserve**, one of Dorset's few remaining areas of common land and open to visitors on foot. The area of wet grassland, scrub and woodland is being restored after years of neglect, and is grazed by Fell ponies. It supports an important population of butterflies and moths; the Blackmore Vale is the only area of Dorset where the brown hairstreak is found; other species you may see include grizzled skipper, silver-washed fritillary and white admiral.

FOOD & DRINK

Thyme after Time Woodrow Dairy, DT10 2AH ✆ 01258 818004 www.thymeaftertime.co.uk ⏲ Tue–Fri 09.00–15.00, Sat 08.30–12.30. Bubbly Dorset lady, Margot Annelle Finlay has put her heart and soul into her super little shop and café, where she also operates a catering business. The café has a genuinely homely feel and a woodburner in winter. Margot buys local ingredients and turns them into tasty cakes, pies, jams, chutneys and cordials, and offers a good choice of light lunches, all served in generous (farmer) portions. Her motto is 'Dorset born, Dorset fed', a twist on the saying 'Dorset born, Dorset bred, strong in the arm, thick in the head'. Local artwork and books on Dorset are on sale. Watch out for the event evenings, such as curry night and lamb night with a local farmer who brings and spit roasts his own organic lamb.

11 BLANDFORD FORUM

Ellwood Cottages (page 295) **Inside Park** (page 295)

Blandford is hailed as one of the finest Georgian rural market towns in England, and occupies an enviable position in a wooded valley on the banks of the River Stour. Much of the original town was destroyed by a devastating fire in 1731, which began in a tallow chandler's (candle maker's) shop on the site now occupied by the Kings Arms. Over 450 people lost their homes and at least 14 townsfolk died; the town museum (page 65) has a model showing the extent of the damage. Memorably named local architects and builders John and William Bastard were engaged to design and rebuild the town: the elegant, coherent Georgian town centre is the result. Its uniformity gives it a very different feel to other Dorset towns.

The **church of St Peter and St Paul** (⏲ Mon–Fri 09.30–12.00) dominates the town centre, a simple, classical building built on the site of its medieval predecessor. Its most recognisable feature, the wooden cupola on its tower, was not part of the original design. The Bastard

DORSET BLUE VINNY CHEESE

Woodbridge Farm, Stock Gaylard DT10 2BD ✆ 01963 23133 ⊛ www.dorsetblue.com

Dorset has many fine food traditions and one of the best known is Dorset Blue Vinny cheese. The Davies family makes this unpasteurised farmhouse cheese at their farm just outside Sturminster Newton, along with a range of fresh soups.

There was a time when the manufacture of Dorset Blue Vinny cheese was virtually ubiquitous throughout the county's farmhouses. It was a by-product of butter-making, using the milk after the cream had been skimmed off.

However, the production of Dorset Blue Vinny ceased following the establishment of the government's Milk Marketing Board in 1933. The board purchased all of the milk produced by a farm, which meant the farmer's wife was no longer able to set aside milk for making cheese. Michael Davies revived the Dorset Blue Vinny tradition in the 1980s. During the time of milk lakes and butter mountains, Michael began to question his commitment to early mornings and milking; he had originally trained as a cheese maker and thought it might be time to put those skills to use. According to his daughter Emily, 'he was truly one of the first to diversify and value-add – the buzzwords of today'. The family produced its first Dorset Blue Vinny in 1982, matured in the farmhouse pantry; it turned the walls, cornflakes and marmalade blue.

The 24-hour process of making this cheese begins with the milk from their herd of Friesian cows, which graze the lush pastures of the Blackmore Vale. Once the milk has been brought up to temperature they hand-skim the cream from the milk, then add skimmed milk powder to raise the fat content back up to give it a creamy, subtle character. A penicillin promotes the blueing of the cheese. Once the milk has hardened, it is cut into small pieces and left overnight. The resulting whey is drained off and the curd cut into blocks, ground, salted and packed into moulds. After a few days, the moulds are transferred to the ripening room where they stay for between three and five months, and are turned and spiked according to whether the blue needs to develop.

brothers intended a steeple to be built but apparently the money ran out and they had to make do with the cupola, which was added in 1758. (By all accounts, the Bastard brothers were not impressed with this deviation from their plan.) The interior is unashamedly grand, with Portland stone columns supporting a vaulted ceiling. The ornately carved wooden Mayor's Chair was made in 1748.

In front of the church is the **Fire Monument** designed by John Bastard and dated 1760, known as the Bastard's Pump. It was intended to provide water for firefighting in the event of a further fire.

The inscription acknowledges, with just a touch of hyperbole, 'the divine mercy that has since raised this town, like the Phaenix from its ashes to its present beautiful and flourishing state'. John Bastard signs himself off as 'a considerable sharer in the great calamity'.

Opposite the church, marked with a plaque, is the house that was built for John and William Bastard following the fire. Along with the Town Hall and the former Greyhound Inn (with a hare and a hound painted above the entrance), it is one of the town's finest buildings. A few buildings survived the fire, including the Ryves Almshouses of 1682 in Salisbury Street and the Old House of 1660 in The Close. Most of East Street escaped unscathed as it had been rebuilt in brick after an earlier fire in 1713.

Today's Blandfordians can see the lighter side of the 'calamity': a paving stone in front of the Town Hall bears the inscription, 'Recipe for regeneration: take one careless tallow chandler and two ingenious Bastards', words drafted by the Blandford poetry group for the Millennium project.

The Georgian marketplace comes into its own on Thursdays and Saturdays, when it hosts a bustling food and bric-a-brac **market**. Blandford is justifiably proud of its Georgian heritage and a **Georgian Fayre** (✆ 01258 480333 🖱 www.blandfordgeorgianfayre.co.uk) is held on the May Day Bank Holiday every other year in the town centre, when people dress in period costume and enjoy cultural presentations, stalls and a funfair.

Blandford has strong military links, with Blandford Camp lying just outside the town. Guided tours of Blandford Forum are organised in the summer months by the Blandford and District Civic Society, and can be booked through the Blandford Tourist Information Centre.

THE GREAT DORSET STEAM FAIR

Tarrant Hinton ✆ 01258 860361 🖱 www.gdsf.co.uk

From modest beginnings in 1968, the Great Dorset Steam Fair has grown into the largest steam and vintage fair in the world, attracting over 200,000 visitors over five days. It is held on a 600-acre site just outside the village of Tarrant Hinton, near Blandford Forum. The focus is heritage machinery: 200 working steam engines are on display, some of them hard at work sawing wood, hauling loads or driving ploughs and threshing machines. You can also expect classic cars, military vehicles, tractors, heavy horses, and country crafts and pursuits in addition to the steam-driven funfair and a huge modern one.

Blandford Town Museum

Beres Yard, Market Pl, DT11 7HQ ✆ 01258 450388 🖰 www.blandfordtownmuseum.org
◷ Apr–Oct Mon–Sat 10.30–16.30; free admission

An assistant curator of this outstanding local museum, Jack Greaves, told me 'we have just about everything, from palaeontology to music'. A series of detailed exhibits gives a glimpse of life in the town as it used to be, and includes a reproduction of the 19th-century forge used to service the local Portman Hunt horses, of a Victorian kitchen and of the Blandford market as it was in the 18th century. Particularly interesting is the model of the town following the fire of 1731, showing the devastation caused and the few areas which survived. Behind the museum is a small Victorian garden; the shop sells plants grown there, along with honey products from bees kept by one of the museum staff. A dedicated team of volunteers keeps the museum running and as Jack put it, 'they restore your faith in human beings after all the bad things that are happening in the world'.

Jack also pointed out to me the metal doors on the outside of the building. In 1788 a band of smugglers was apprehended near Sixpenny Handley and their loot taken to Blandford and put into an excise store. The following night some unsavoury characters broke into the store, grabbed the tea and liquor and rode through the town handing it out to the townspeople.

The Blandford Fashion Museum

Lime Tree House, The Plocks, DT11 7AA ✆ 01258 453006 🖰 www.theblandfordfashionmuseum.co.uk ◷ Mon, Thu–Sat 11.00–16.00, closed Dec–mid-Feb

Within an attractive red-brick house built by the Bastard brothers just after the fire that destroyed Blandford, the costume collection dates from the 1730s to the 1970s and was begun by the late Betty Penny MBE after World War II. For 35 years Mrs Penny toured the country with her historical fashion show, *Cavalcade of Costume*, raising money for charity. A benefactor bought Lime Tree House for Mrs Penny in 1996 to house her collection and it provides the perfect setting. Enthusiastic volunteers are on hand to show you around and will even help you try on a corset, and in one of the rooms mannequins are dressed in clothing from the era in which the house was built. For me, the highlights were the Victorian wedding collection and crinolines, and the display of Dorset buttons (see box, page 45). There is a resources room for students and a very good tea room (page 68).

SHEPHERDS' HUTS

Shepherds' huts are making a comeback. These wheeled huts are thought to have been used to shelter shepherds tending their flocks in fields around England since the 16th century, and some were even used as Home Guard outposts during World War II. The huts typically contained a small stove, a straw bed over a cage where lambs could be kept and a basic medicine cupboard with a range of potions to treat both shepherd and sheep.

Today, people are buying them to use as garden decorations, artist studios, children's cubby houses or guest accommodation. **Alf Wallis** of Stour Provost (✆ 01747 838783) carefully crafts shepherds' huts in the same way they would have been made many years ago, but adds a touch of luxury. The huts' exteriors are covered in tin and the interiors are lined with wood, they have dainty windows and the layout can be tailored to the buyer's requirements.

Hall & Woodhouse Brewery

The Brewery, Blandford St Mary DT11 9LS ✆ 01258 486004 www.hall-woodhouse.co.uk
tours Jan–Nov Mon, Tue, Thu–Sat 11.00

The badger logo of the Hall & Woodhouse Brewery is a familiar sight around Dorset, as are its quirkily named beers, among them Fursty Ferret, Pickled Partridge and Poacher's Choice (all sold under the name Badger rather than Hall & Woodhouse).

Hall & Woodhouse is run by the fifth generation of the Woodhouse family and has a formidable history. A Dorset farmer, Charles Hall, founded a brewery at Ansty in 1777, providing beer to the troops during the Napoleonic Wars. In 1847 Robert Hall, the founder's son, went into partnership with George Woodhouse. The badger was adopted as the brewery's trademark in 1875 and in 1899 the brewery moved to its present site, where it has been brewing ever since. It has developed into a successful independent brewery with a network of 240 pubs across the south of England. In 2011, in order to keep pace with its own growth, the company built a new brewery adjacent to the one it has been using for over a hundred years.

The visitor centre tells the story of the brewery and guided tours are available, ending with a tasting. I enjoyed a tour of the brewery with head brewer, Toby Heasman. It was an assignment for which I felt particularly under-qualified as I have never been a beer drinker; in fact I can barely tolerate the smell of it. The tour turned out to be an experience full of surprises and lessons learnt.

Firstly, Toby didn't fit my image of a head brewer at all; I had envisioned a short, round, balding chap in overalls but I was greeted by a tall, slim, dapper gentleman in his early thirties, wearing chinos and a tweed jacket, who told me he had a degree in brewing and had studied for a further five years to become a master brewer. I was fascinated by the highly complex process and the antique machinery that is still in use in some sections of the brewery. Many of the techniques used here have barely changed over the past 250 years, and the water has been supplied by the same wells since 1899.

The family-company culture is delightfully evident throughout the brewery, and a roll of long service shows an amazing number of local people who have been with the company for over 30, and even 40, years. This is just as well for Toby because one of the earlier Woodhouses coined the company motto 'never trust a thin brewer' and Toby has a fair way to go before he acquires a trustworthy shape.

Needless to say, I was a little apprehensive when tasting time came but even I, with a totally uneducated beer palette, could discern the subtle differences between the beers (with a few hints from the experts).

A well-stocked shop on site sells Hall & Woodhouse beer, plus wine and soft drinks. You can sample the brewery's Badger beers in the numerous Hall & Woodhouse pubs dotted around Dorset.

The Royal Signals Museum

Blandford DT11 8RH ✆ 01258 482248 🖱 www.royalsignalsmuseum.com ⊙ Mon–Fri all year & Sat–Sun Feb–Oct

This museum tells the story of military communications through the ages. It lies within Blandford Camp Military Base, two miles northeast of Blandford Forum. As it is on base, visitors need to sign in; you will need photo identification and you will have your photograph taken. Fascinating displays on codes and code-breaking include the story of the Special Operations Executive (SOE) in World War II and the ENIGMA cipher machine. Motorcycle enthusiasts may enjoy the collection of military motorcycles from 1914 to the present.

FOOD & DRINK

To stock up on local meat, game and deli items, head to **Dorset Larder** (11 Market Pl, DT11 7AF ✆ 01258 452846 🖱 www.thedorsetgamelarder.co.uk ⊙ Tue–Fri 08.00–17.00, Sat 07.30–16.00) in the market square near the Town Hall.

Cafés and restaurants seem to come and go regularly in Blandford, but there are always plenty of them. Currently the best place for a cuppa and a piece of cake around the market square is **Café SoBa** (8 West St, DT11 7AJ ✆ 01258 269314 ⏲ daily), a boutique coffee house with a trendy feel, lovingly run by Michael and William. They use their own blend of coffee and their edible treats are homemade; they have licensed events from time to time. There are also some decent cafés up the hill from the square, on Salisbury Street, including the delightful tea rooms at the Fashion Museum (see below).

Crown Hotel West St, DT11 7AJ ✆ 01258 456626 ⏲ daily. A Hall & Woodhouse pub within a large Georgian red-brick building at the far western end of the marketplace. The restaurant and beer garden are nicely laid out and the food is of a good standard.

Fashion Museum Tea Rooms Lime Tree House, The Plocks, DT11 7AA ✆ 01258 453006 ⏲ Mon, Thu–Sat 11.00–16.00; closed Dec to mid-Feb. Very reasonably priced Dorset cream teas and homemade cakes are served by cheerful volunteers. The tea room has a vintage Dorset feel and the tea is served in pretty blue and white Poole Pottery teaware. You don't need to pay the museum entry fee to enjoy the tea room and there is a courtyard for sunny days, where dogs are welcome.

Georgian Tea Room 7 Georgian Passage, East St, DT11 7DX ✆ 01258 450307 ⏲ Mon–Sat 09.00–16.30. A small, unassuming café down an alleyway, away from the busy main street, serving reasonably priced cakes and light lunches. Gluten-free options are also available.

Yellow Bicycle Café 30a Salisbury St, DT11 7AR ✆ 07718 315852 ⏲ Mon–Sat 08.30–17.00. Run by husband and wife, Steve and Ali, the café prides itself on its homemade food. Even the dough for the flatbreads is made on site each morning. Traditional children's toys are also on sale.

12 STOURPAINE

The busy A350 runs through the village but there are some attractive, quiet spots away from the road, in particular near the Holy Trinity Church. Here you will find dainty cottages, some thatched, with flower-filled gardens; the smell of roses and other flowers hangs in the air on a summer's day. Just north of the church is a crossroads; the turning to the left leads to the **Trailway**, a foot, cycle and bridle path which runs to Shillingstone (2½ miles) and Sturminster Newton (5½ miles). To the right of the Trailway is a track leading to a footpath running through woodland beside the River Stour and up on to Hod Hill.

In 2010, Stourpaine suffered a loss that has been felt by many villages around the country – its post office and village shop closed. A year later, thanks to village spirit and 'The Pub is the Hub', they re-opened at the White Horse pub on the main road. The Pub is the Hub

(www.pubisthehub.org.uk) is a scheme initiated in 2001 by Prince Charles, champion of preserving rural ways of life; his venture encourages local people, breweries and pub owners to provide essential services, like a village shop, within rural pubs.

Stourpaine did just that and villagers now have access to a well-stocked little shop and a postal counter open two days a week, rather than having to travel into Blandford. The shopkeeper told me locals are very supportive of the shop and it has breathed new life into the community. A letter from the Prince of Wales's office in support of the move has pride of place on the wall of the shop, and in May 2011 Prince Charles and the Duchess of Cornwall visited the White Horse to see the changes for themselves.

FOOD & DRINK

White Horse Shaston Rd, TQ1 4TS 01258 453535 daily for lunch & dinner. A popular pub with village shop on the main A350, which serves traditional food and local beers. Each summer, London theatre company Shooting Stars puts on a Shakespeare play in the car park.

3 CHILD OKEFORD

Child Okeford is a large village with some appealing 18th- and 19th-century houses and farm buildings, and several modern housing developments on the outskirts. Its principal attraction is that it lies in the shadow of Hambledon Hill and is a good starting point for walks up it to view the Iron Age hillfort on the summit.

In the 1560s the village vicar, William Kethe, composed the well-known hymn, The Old Hundredth ('All People That on Earth do Dwell'). A Bible from his era (1568) is on display in the church, although the church would have looked rather different in his day; while the tower is 15th century, the rest dates from the mid-1800s.

Gold Hill Organic Farm

DT11 8HB 01258 861916 www.goldhillorganicfarm.com Thu–Sat 10.00–16.00, Sun 10.00–14.00

Gold Hill was one of the first organic farms in Dorset, started over 25 years ago. The farm shop sells an inviting variety of organic meat, dairy products and vegetables, which are picked the same morning. Some of the farm buildings have been converted to house local businesses and it has developed into a small complex with arty shops and a café.

DIKE & SONS SUPERSTORE

Ring St, Stalbridge DT10 2RG ✆ 01963 362204 🖰 www.dikes-direct.co.uk

Tucked away in the village of Stalbridge is something you don't see very often a family-run, independent supermarket. This isn't a corner shop with supermarket aspirations; Dikes is large, well stocked and offers plenty of variety. Despite the presence of the big supermarkets in surrounding towns, Dikes is still a firm favourite with locals and it is a mutually beneficial relationship because the store supports local farmers and small businesses. It has over a hundred local suppliers, meaning food miles are kept to a minimum, and makes its own sandwiches, pizzas and salads.

The Dike family have had a shop in Stalbridge since 1851 and current manager, Andrew Dike, represents the fifth generation.

It regularly hosts events (see website for details), including travelling markets. Gold Hill also delivers boxes of freshly picked vegetables all around Dorset (✆ 01747 811077 🖰 www.goldhillorganics.com).

14 HOD HILL

National Trust; free access

Hod Hill stands unassumingly beside its more celebrated neighbour, Hambledon Hill, yet Hod's hillfort is larger: 54 acres versus Hambledon's 30. Its multiple ramparts protected an Iron Age village of over 250 roundhouses, the footprints of many of which are still visible as depressions in the ground. The Romans, led by Vespasian, captured the Celtic settlement of the Durotriges tribe around AD44 and built their own camp in the northwest corner. By that stage, they had already taken Maiden Castle, near Dorchester.

There is a small car parking area at the base of Hod Hill; to reach it take the Child Okeford and Hanford turning from the A350. Several paths begin here; one leads through woodland and along the River Stour to Stourpaine, while a bridleway leads to the top of Hod Hill. A steep walk up rewards you with glorious views of the surrounding countryside and a fabulous archaeological juxtaposition: the rigid lines of the Roman fort and the softer, more organic ones of the earlier settlement. This is a fine place to contemplate life for the original inhabitants and what must have gone through their minds when they saw the mighty Roman army

"A steep walk up rewards you with glorious views of the surrounding countryside."

advancing across the countryside. These days it is remarkably peaceful on top of the hill: the only sound is the breeze and the occasional shriek of a buzzard circling over the vale, while livestock graze nonchalantly, oblivious of the many layers of history beneath them.

Hod Hill is a rich chalk grassland site with a colourful carpet of wildflowers. Cowslips are prolific in spring, followed by milkwort, horseshoe vetch, rock rose and common spotted orchids. It is a popular butterfly-watching spot thanks to its populations of Adonis blue, chalkhill blue, marsh fritillary and grizzled skipper.

5 HAMBLEDON HILL

National Trust; free access

The view from Hambledon Hill is one to soothe the soul and replenish the energy stores, which is just as well as the walk to the summit is one to tire the legs. The hill juts out into the Blackmore Vale, providing a natural viewing platform over the tapestry of small fields and villages.

"Hambledon Hill is where the Dorset Clubmen were routed by Cromwell in 1645 during the Civil War."

Archaeologists flock to Hambledon Hill and although its earliest occupation was Neolithic, it is best known as an Iron Age hillfort. The site seems to have been abandoned around 300BC, possibly in favour of nearby Hod Hill. When I was walking on Hambledon Hill in 2011, photographing the view towards Shaftesbury, a group of archaeologists on a guided tour came up behind me and I heard several shrieks of excitement. It was the end of a particularly hot and dry spell and the weather had exposed the outline of a Neolithic enclosure, which even the tour leader had never seen before.

Hambledon Hill is where the Dorset Clubmen were routed by Cromwell in 1645 during the Civil War. Armed only with clubs, about 2,000 to 4,000 farmers and yeomen banded together to protest at the plundering by the armies traversing Dorset. They were not in favour of either the king or the parliament, they had simply lost patience with troops from both sides trampling their crops, stealing their livestock and ransacking their barns. Their motto made their grievance clear:

> If ye offer to plunder or take our cattle, be assured we'll give you battle.

A walk around Hambledon Hill & Hod Hill

OS Explorer map 118; start: Cricketers Pub, Iwerne Courtney, SY859127; approximately 5.5 miles; medium (some steep hills). Refreshments at The Cricketers pub (see opposite). To walk Hod Hill only start at the car park at the base of Hod Hill, SY853112.

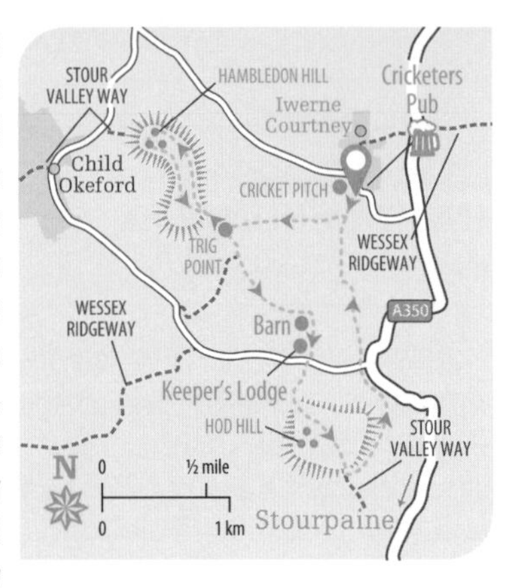

This walk is mostly well signed, and uses parts of the Stour Valley Way and the Wessex Ridgeway. The hillforts are natural vantage points for fabulous views over North Dorset's enchanting farmland. The footpath is signed from behind The Cricketers pub. Keep the cricket pitch on your right and head for the chalk path up the hill, then bear right through the fields, which are often lined with poppies. At the top of the hill is a trig point, from where you get your first sight of the hillfort on your right. You are free to wander the hilltop and the impressive ramparts, which are owned by the National Trust, but be aware that Hambledon Hill is typically grazed by livestock.

Return to the trig point and take the path signed Steepleton Iwerne. When you reach the large barn you will need to head through the gate and turn right down the hill, following the hedgerow. Hod Hill is visible in front of you. At the bottom you will cross the road near Keeper's Lodge and start the climb up Hod Hill. The path takes you diagonally across the hillfort, where signs of its ancient settlements are visible. A gate at the other side leads to Stourpaine, where there is a pub if you fancy a detour, but for this route turn left before the gate and follow the path below the ramparts. Go through the next gate on your right and turn left then follow the path to the bottom of the hill. You will need to cross the road again then head up the bridleway, which takes you back to The Cricketers pub. Doing this walk in autumn offers the chance to fuel yourself on blackberries on the way.

Cromwell attacked with a thousand men; a dozen farmers were killed and some 300 taken prisoner in Iwerne Courtney Church, where Cromwell rebuked them before releasing them.

Of various starting points for walks up Hambledon Hill, a particularly good one is from just behind The Cricketers pub in **Iwerne Courtney** (also known as Shroton) because of the promise of a hearty meal on your return.

FOOD & DRINK

The Cricketers Main St, Iwerne Courtney (Shroton), Blandford Forum DT11 8QD ☎ 01258 860421 www.thecricketersshroton.co.uk ⊙ daily. A popular family-run pub, opposite the village green and backing on to Hambledon Hill – the perfect spot from which to explore this huge prehistoric hillfort, the pub even supplies a leaflet with a suggested walking route. A good selection of high-quality pub food, with daily deliveries of fresh fish, meat and local produce.

CRANBORNE CHASE

The B3081 from Shaftesbury takes you up on to the hills of the Cranborne Chase for sweeping panoramas of the Dorset and Wiltshire countryside. **Win Green** (National Trust) lies just over the Wiltshire border; it is the highest point in the Cranborne Chase and draws an assortment of walkers, model aircraft enthusiasts and kite-flyers. The hill is crowned by a clump of trees growing on a Bronze Age bowl barrow.

Cranborne Chase was once a royal hunting ground, hence the 'Chase' part of the name, and originally covered the area between Shaftesbury, Salisbury, Ringwood, Wimborne and Blandford Forum. An impressive line-up of monarchs hunted here, including King John, Henry VIII and James I. In those days much of the area would have been wooded but today it is characterised by open downland with pockets of woodland. The land remained in royal ownership until James I handed the estate to Robert Cecil, First Earl of Salisbury and the royal hunting lodge became Cranborne Manor, which remains at the heart of the estate. In the 18th century, the chase's remoteness attracted smugglers, who hid contraband here.

The unblemished Cranborne Chase draws walkers, cyclists and horseriders, as well as archaeologists, who come in search of the **Dorset Cursus**, a Neolithic cursus monument spanning 6¼ miles of chalk downland. A cursus consists of large, parallel linear banks with external ditches, perhaps used as a processional route or as part of ceremonial competitions. The Dorset Cursus, the longest known example of its kind, crosses a river and three valleys, and runs close to Knowlton and its Neolithic henge topped with the ruins of a medieval church (page 80).

En route to the village of Cranborne from Shaftesbury the road sneaks briefly into Wiltshire again around Tollard Royal and the Rushmore Estate. This well-managed estate incorporates a popular golf course, preparatory school and the **Larmer Tree Gardens** (Tollard Royal,

Wiltshire SP5 5PT ☎ 01725 516971 🖱 www.larmertreegardens.co.uk). Opening times for the garden vary; a popular music festival is held here every July (🖱 www.larmertree.co.uk).

16 FONTMELL & MELBURY DOWNS

The unclassified upper Blandford road from Shaftesbury takes you through the village of **Melbury Abbas** and up on to Fontmell and Melbury Downs, which open up before you in a burst of bucolic beauty. The quintessentially English rolling hills with patches of woodland provide inspiring views and walks on the western edge of the Cranborne Chase. Many locals escape here to walk the dog, or just admire the scenery.

At 720 acres, Fontmell and Melbury Downs is the National Trust's largest chalk downland site, and in summer the area is awash with wildflowers, birdlife and butterflies, including the Adonis blue and chalkhill blue. Access to the walks above Melbury Abbas is from small car parks on Spread Eagle Hill; take care along this road as visibility is poor and traffic moves at high speeds. It is an easy, mostly level walk of three miles along the hilltop to **Melbury Beacon**, erected in 1588 to warn of the invading Spanish Armada. The walk skirts around the edge of the Blackmore Vale, providing far-reaching views across the fields and villages. Buzzards can often be seen drifting on the currents that swirl around the bowl formed by the hills, and skylarks provide a tuneful accompaniment to a walk. On the opposite side of the road, another walk leads along the base of Melbury Down, with Compton Abbas Airfield on the hilltop above.

"Buzzards can often be seen drifting on the currents that swirl around the bowl formed by the hills, and skylarks provide a tuneful accompaniment to a walk."

The Dorset Wildlife Trust manages 148 acres on **Fontmell Down**, above the village of Fontmell Magna. A variety of wildflower species grow here, including nine different orchids and the rare early gentian, while 35 species of butterfly have been recorded on the reserve. Glow worms are plentiful in summer and winged residents include sparrowhawks, green woodpeckers and yellowhammers. Evidence of Bronze Age habitation is visible in the form of two cross dykes, which were probably used as territorial boundary markers. On the flatter land on top of Fontmell Down are traces of a Bronze Age field system, most easily seen when the sun is low in the evening.

17 ASHMORE

Glebe Farm (page 295)

As you enter Ashmore, the highest village in Dorset, you might feel transported back to an earlier era. It is a tiny village, with 17th- and 18th-century stone houses huddled around a village pond, which some believe is of Roman origin.

One of the major problems for hilltop settlements like Ashmore was that of water supply. The chalk drained the water away, so to preserve water the hilltop settlers dug 'dew ponds' and lined them with clay to retain water. Ashmore's **dew pond** is one of the few remaining in the area.

The pond is the venue for the village's annual **Filly Loo** festival, held to celebrate the summer solstice. This is rural tradition at its best: a Green Man kicks off the dancing to folk music, which continues throughout the evening. At dusk the celebrations reach their climax with the 700-year-old Abbots Bromley Horn Dance. This is a torchlit procession with six men wearing antlers and four other colourful costumed characters: Maid Marion, a bowman, a hobbyhorse and a fool. It is accompanied by a haunting solo flute melody. The celebration finishes with everyone joining hands around the pond for a final torchlit dance.

Ashmore is worth a visit at any time of year, and being so high the area around the village offers uninterrupted views towards the Dorset coast. On a clear day you can even see the Isle of Wight.

On the way from Ashmore to Cranborne, travelling along the B3081, you pass through the curiously named village of **Sixpenny Handley**, whose name is derived from two medieval 'hundreds', 'Sexpena' and 'Hanlega'. Over the years, local folk and the highways authority have reduced it to the memorable 6d Handley, and it sometimes appears on signposts as that.

18 COMPTON ABBAS AIRFIELD

Ashmore SP5 5AP 01747 811767 www.abbasair.com daily

This family-run grass airfield is near Ashmore, high on Spread Eagle Hill, overlooking Shaftesbury. It has a tremendous sense of community and a very welcoming atmosphere, and houses almost 50 aircraft, many of which are owned by syndicates made up of local people. It was first utilised as an airfield in 1960 by the farmer who owned the land; he used it to fly his Tiger Moth and then opened the runway up to others. The current owners bought the site in 1988 and the airfield is now managed by their two young, accomplished daughters, Laura and Emma Hughes.

The light-aircraft flights and trial flying lessons offered here are unforgettable ways to see the South West's countryside, and you will usually get a chance to take the controls. For a bit of nostalgia, you can take a flight in the resident Tiger Moth and, if you get a taste for flying, you can study for your pilot's licence here. Film-maker Guy Ritchie, who owns an estate nearby, is one of the airfield's alumni. If you don't fancy taking to the skies, watching the light aircraft from the airfield restaurant is a very enjoyable way to spend a couple of lazy hours.

FOOD & DRINK

Compton Abbas Airfield SP5 5AP ✆ 01747 811767 ◷ daily 09.30–17.00. An informal café and restaurant with indoor and outdoor seating overlooking the runway and with superb countryside views.

19 CRANBORNE ESTATE & CRANBORNE VILLAGE

The seemingly endless acres of fertile farmland and woodland that you see in this area have been the property of just one family since 1604, when King James I granted Cranborne Manor and the lordship of the Chase to Sir Robert Cecil, the First Earl of Salisbury. King John built the original house at Cranborne as a hunting lodge and the first earl enlarged it and modernised it. Cranborne Manor is the home of the current Viscount Cranborne, the eldest son of the Seventh Marquess of Salisbury.

"Cottages with doors painted in the ubiquitous Cranborne blue belong to the estate."

Adjacent to the manor is the village of Cranborne, where (unusually for Dorset) most of the buildings are brick. The village is centred around an attractive square; in 1748, a fire destroyed many of the older buildings – the north side is 18th century and the south side Edwardian. Cottages with doors painted in the ubiquitous Cranborne blue belong to the estate. At the superb **Cranborne Stores** (1 The Square, BH21 5PR ✆ 01725 517210) you can buy game and other meat from the surrounding area, while locals catch up on gossip.

The predominance of red brick belies Cranborne's true age. The village, which lies on a winterborne (a stream which flows only in winter) called the Crane, dates from Saxon times. There was a Benedictine Abbey here from circa AD980 until the Dissolution of the Monasteries in 1539. Until the 18th century Cranborne was a thriving market town on the main route from Salisbury to Poole but in the 1750s the Great Western Turnpike from Salisbury to Blandford was built, bypassing Cranborne, and its trade declined. Thomas Hardy described it as 'a decayed market town' but it has a pleasant feel today and is unmistakably an estate village.

The **church of St Mary and St Bartholomew** dates from the 12th century; the faded wall-paintings are 14th century and the tower 15th century. On the wall a memorial commissioned by Lady Norton for her grandson, John Elliot, features a statue of a boy with a skull on his knee. According to the inscription he was a very promising boy who had made 'an almost supernatural progress' in his studies, and who died suddenly at school on 2 February 1641, reputedly from choking on a fish bone.

Cranborne Manor Garden

BH21 5PP ✆ 01725 517248 www.cranborne.co.uk ⏲ Mar–Sep Wed 09.00–17.00

Although the manor house is not open to the public, visitors are able to wander through its quintessentially English garden during opening hours. One of Dorset's finest, the garden was partly laid out by 17th-century gardener John Tradescant, and more recently owes its splendour to the Dowager Marchioness of Salisbury, a noted garden designer. The walled gardens, herbaceous borders, espaliered apple trees and yew hedges are particularly fine. In the rather fun Sundial Garden a sundial stands sentinel on a mound surrounded by raised parterres. Various statues and sculptures catch the eye as you wander, and the garden runs down to the River Crane, a winterborne, where a mass of spring bulbs flower in April and May. Although it has a formal layout, parts of the garden are left wild and it is regularly used by the family, making it feel very much like you have wandered into a much-loved private garden. On site are a well-stocked garden centre (www.cranbornegardencentre.co.uk), which sells specialist plants, a shop and a good café (see below and advert in the fourth colour section).

FOOD & DRINK

La Fosse London House, The Square, BH21 5PR ✆ 01725 517604 ⏲ Mon, Fri, Sat for dinner & Sun for lunch. A small restaurant that punches above its weight, serving excellent, creative British dishes made using locally sourced ingredients.

Café at Cranborne Garden Centre BH21 5PP ✆ 01725 517248 ⏲ Daily. A pleasant, informal café within the attractive walled garden that houses the garden centre. Freshly prepared food, locally sourced wherever possible.

20 EDMONDSHAM HOUSE

Edmondsham BH21 5RE 01725 517207 house: Apr–Oct Wed afternoon, Easter Sun & bank holidays; garden: Sun afternoons during the same period

The owner, Julia Smith, gives guided tours of her home, an Elizabethan building with Georgian extensions. The six acres of attractive grounds are typical of a country house of this size, with colourful herbaceous borders and a fine walled garden. A circular grass hollow is believed to have been the site of a **medieval cock-fighting pit**. The grand Victorian stable block will be the envy of most horse owners and the octagonal Victorian dairy is built over an underground stream, with louvered windows in order to keep it cool.

21 DORSET HEAVY HORSE FARM PARK & RESCUE CENTRE

Edmondsham, near Verwood BH21 5RJ 01202 824040 www.dorset-heavy-horse-centre.co.uk Apr–Oct daily

This centre provides a home for heavy horses in need and has over 20 rescued gentle giants of various breeds. At the other end of the scale, there are miniature ponies, kunie kunie pigs, sheep and goats. Before you visit, check the daily schedule on the website; there is plenty to entertain the children, including wagon rides, pony rides, pony grooming, feeding the farm animals, play areas, fairground rides and a café. There are presentations daily, including on the Romany people and on the resident heavy horses.

22 MOORS VALLEY COUNTRY PARK & FOREST

Horton Rd, Ashley Heath BH24 2ET 01425 470721 www.moors-valley.co.uk 08.00–dusk; free admission but car parking is charged

The 1,000 acres of forest, woodland, grassland, heath and lakes here are run as a countryside recreation facility, as a joint venture between East Dorset District Council and the Forestry Commission. The emphasis is on family fun: you can walk, cycle (bike hire is on site) or catch a narrow-gauge steam train around the park; there are high-ropes courses, adventure play areas, orienteering, segways and an 18-hole golf course. Coarse fishing is available from June to March; you can buy a day ticket or season ticket from the visitor centre, but note that anyone over 12 years of age will need to show a valid Environment Agency rod licence. Wheelchair access is good, and dogs are allowed. You can bring a picnic or take advantage of the restaurant.

23 WIMBORNE ST GILES

This small, peaceful community is the estate village at the centre of the Earl of Shaftesbury's 5,500-acre landholding. The ancestors of the Ashley-Cooper family arrived here in the 15th century and reminders of them can be seen all around. Facing the village green is a row of **almshouses** and **St Giles Church**. The almshouses were built in 1624 by Sir Anthony Ashley and were intended to house 11 poor people; an inscription above the door reads, 'he hath delivered me out of all trouble'.

"This small, peaceful community is the estate village at the centre of the Earl of Shaftesbury's 5,500-acre landholding."

The church has been through several incarnations. In 1732, the Dorset architects responsible for rebuilding Blandford Forum after the 1731 fire, John and William Bastard, were commissioned to build a church on the site of an earlier, disused one. In 1908 it burnt down in a fire accidentally started by workmen repairing the lead roof and the Shaftesburys called in renowned architect Ninian Comper to conduct the restoration. The result is a magnificent and colourful interior, far more elaborate than that of most village churches. An ornate rood screen carved in dark wood separates the altar from the nave. Prevalent are impressive tombs of various members of the Ashley-Cooper family, including Sir Anthony Ashley who has the unglamorous claim to fame of being the first person to grow cabbages in England. The seventh earl (1801–85) was a philanthropist and social reformer, who improved the lot of working children through a series of reforms; he was offered burial in Westminster Abbey but declined and is buried here.

I sat down with the young and energetic Twelfth Earl of Shaftesbury to discuss his plans for the estate, which currently operates arable and dairy enterprises, a commercial shoot, a trout farm, forestry, a livery yard and fishing on the River Allen.

Nick Ashley-Cooper was not expecting to inherit the peerage, but did so in 2005 in his mid-twenties, after the tragic deaths of his father and later his elder brother. Nick had been travelling down a different path, following a passion for music and working as a DJ in New York, when his life suddenly changed direction. After taking stock of the situation, he returned to Wimborne St Giles to better manage his responsibilities. In 2011, he and his wife embarked on a massive restoration of the family home, **St Giles House**, which had been empty since 1961, when his antecedents, who were struggling to maintain the big house, moved into the dower house. Nick told me he realised that it was important not only for his family, but also for the community, that he would do everything in his power to preserve the history of the Shaftesburys. He was spurred on in his challenge by the loyalty and support of the estate workers and the wider community. When I visited in mid-2014, years of building work were finally coming to an end and the house was looking marvellous. The handsome building sits in 400 acres of classic 18th-century parkland and regular events are held there, including the Grand Shaftesbury Run (a half marathon and 10km run), the Great Dorset Chilli Festival and Paws in the Park (a dog show raising money for Worldwide Veterinary Science). Details of the various activities and events at the estate, including information on hiring it as a wedding venue, are available on the website (www.shaftesburyestates.com).

24 KNOWLTON CHURCH & NEOLITHIC EARTHWORKS

BH21 5AE; free admission, and free parking 150 yards away; English Heritage

At **Knowlton**, on the B3078 south of Cranborne, you can visit two monuments in one: a ruined medieval church stands in the middle of a Neolithic henge. It is a magical, almost eerie, sight, and is said to be haunted by a ghostly horse and rider galloping through the rings, a nun who kneels within the church and the ringing of a non-existent bell. In the snow, the site resembles a decoration on top of a tiered Christmas cake. On a deeper level, it represents the transition from pagan to Christian worship – it is thought the church was built to symbolically destroy the power of the Neolithic rings.

The henge is circular with a substantial ditch around it and is just one part of a complex of **Neolithic earthworks** in the area. The clump of trees 200 feet to the east of the henge stands on the Great Barrow, the largest individual barrow in Dorset. The church is 12th century with a 15th-century tower; it was abandoned after the roof collapsed in the 18th century. Not many people visit Knowlton, so you may well have the site to yourself, making it all the more atmospheric.

25 HORTON

On a hill on the edge of the scattered, low-lying village of Horton is **Horton Tower**, a triangular, turreted brick structure 140 feet high. Local landowner Humphrey Sturt built this folly in 1750, possibly as a vantage point from which to watch the hunt when he became too old to ride to hounds. Although it can be seen from miles around and a bridleway runs nearby, the tower stands on private land and is not open to the public. It was the location for the cockfight in the 1966 film *Far from the Madding Crowd*; in recent years it has found a new purpose, as a discreet mobile phone tower.

The Duke of Monmouth was reportedly captured in Horton in 1685 after his failed rebellion. Following his defeat at the Battle of Sedgemoor, Monmouth disguised himself as a shepherd and headed towards Poole, where he planned to catch a boat to Holland. Monmouth was crossing the Cranborne Chase when he was recognised by an old woman, who reported him to the authorities. A search ensued and he was discovered hiding in a ditch under an ash tree, now known as Monmouth's ash (although it's unlikely to be the same tree).

26 CHETTLE

Museum Inn Farnham (page 294)

Chettle is a remarkable place, the very essence of an English rural idyll, with lovingly maintained thatched cottages and the obligatory manor house and church. It is something of a rarity, being one of only a handful of villages still owned by the manor house, and that is what has helped to preserve it. **Chettle House** is an elegant Queen Anne manor (not open to the public), which you may glimpse across the fields as you enter the village.

Chettle has a population of just about 90, but has avoided the sad fate of many small villages, where outsiders buy up the houses as weekend homes, thereby driving up property prices and leaving the village empty except on weekends, and where the village shop and post office close and the young local people can't afford to buy in their own area. Chettle doesn't have that problem because outsiders can't buy houses here. The 42 farms and cottages are owned by the Chettle Estate and are rented out to people who actually live and work in the village, at below market value. Priority is given to families of those who work on the estate, and residents are required to abide by a series of rules designed to preserve the village's character, such as not erecting satellite dishes or street lamps. As a result the village has a distinctly old world flavour. Residents support their village shop and there is a tremendous sense of community. The village's story is the subject of a book entitled *Enduring Village*, which was published in 2008.

FOOD & DRINK

Castleman DT11 8DB ☎ 01258 830096 🖱 www.castlemanhotel.co.uk ⏲ daily for dinner & Sun for lunch. Like the rest of the village, the Castleman is managed by a member of the Bourke family. The building was the dower house to Chettle House and contains some impressive art and furniture belonging to the Bourke family. Enjoy an aperitif in one of the elegant sitting rooms or the garden to soak up the atmosphere before moving to the dining room. Local ingredients are used to produce tasty but unfussy dishes.

Museum Inn Farnham DT11 8DE ☎ 01725 516261 🖱 www.museuminn.co.uk ⏲ daily for lunch & dinner. This gastropub offers an extensive menu of creative dishes. Meat is sourced locally and much of the game is shot by the chef. The bar prides itself on its range of beers.

SHERBORNE & AROUND

This ancient town marking the boundary of the Blackmore Vale has much to offer the visitor, including two castles, a splendid abbey and a charming town centre. Allow at least one full day to explore.

27 SHERBORNE

Eastbury Hotel (page 294)

Sherborne is attractive, and knows it. If Sherborne were a woman, she would be an incredibly pretty, popular socialite who relishes the envy she generates in everyone else. It has an impressive aristocratic pedigree spanning hundreds of years and exudes a refined sense of style. In most towns and villages in the Blackmore Vale you will see a farmer fresh from his tractor (which may be parked around the corner) or a woman in well-worn jodhpurs and wellies popping into the bank or the grocer, but this doesn't seem to happen here. I get the impression that Sherborne would frown upon such activity because it is the sort of place where you get dressed up and slap on some make-up to go shopping.

Sherborne's aristocratic pedigree is embodied in its finest buildings, Sherborne Abbey, Sherborne Old Castle and Sherborne Castle (built by Sir Walter Raleigh), which are all open to the public. A stroll around the town centre with its medieval buildings is enough to gain an appreciation for the town's history; it dates back to the Saxons, who named the town 'scir burne', meaning the place of the clear stream, and made it the capital of Wessex. Today it is a vibrant market town and a centre of learning, thanks to its three private schools, Sherborne Boys, Sherborne Girls and Leweston.

With its compact centre and abundance of buildings of architectural interest, the town is best explored on foot. The tourist information centre stocks helpful booklets on the town and surrounding area, including the excellent *Official Guide to Sherborne*. Guided walks leave from the tourist office at 11.00 on Fridays between July and September, and take around 90 minutes.

Cheap Street

The name of Sherborne's main shopping street is misleading, for it is crammed with upmarket shops, art galleries, antique shops and eateries. Refreshingly, many of them are small independents. Be sure to look above the tempting shop windows to appreciate the blend of architectural styles, with many buildings dating from the 16th century. Some 19th-century shopfronts survive, as do some of the grand houses that were built for merchants made wealthy by the silk-throwing and cloth-, glove-, button- and lace-making industries that existed in Sherborne until the 19th century.

Just above the junction with Long Street is **The Conduit**, a hexagonal stone structure that was originally the monk's *lavatorium* or washhouse; it was moved here in 1539 following the closure of the monastery for use by the local community. It is mentioned in Thomas Hardy's *The Woodlanders* as the place where Giles Winterborne, who was seeking work, stood in the marketplace 'as he always did at this season of the year, with his specimen apple tree'. The Conduit has been used variously as a police station, a bank and a reading room. At Christmas it houses a nativity scene, one of many festive features which draw visitors from miles around at that time of year.

Near The Conduit, an alleyway leads to the abbey, with the 15th-century **Bow Arch** spanning the gap above, from where it is believed 12 local Monmouth followers were hanged in 1685 following their unsuccessful rebellion. It is along here that you will find the **Sherborne Museum** (pages 86–7).

Henry Willis Antique Silver (38 Cheap St, DT9 3PX ✆ 01935 816828) is within a wooden, jettied building dating from around 1490, the Shoemaker's House. It is worth popping in to browse the lovely, shiny items inside and to see the preserved square of wattle and daub in the wall, which is now visible behind glass. The large stone fireplace was re-discovered in 1992, and according to Henry it would have been built before the wooden frame of the building, giving it stability. Today the fireplace provides a characterful backdrop for an every-changing display of antique silver.

The small, **independent shops** along Cheap Street contribute to the town's bygone-era flavour. Among them are the **Toy Box** (7 Cheap St, DT9 3PT ✆ 01935 817913), an old-fashioned toy and sweet shop, and the **Chocolate Musketeer** (16 Cheap St, DT9 3PX ✆ 01935 815139), a family-owned handmade chocolate shop. The **Swan Gallery** (51 Cheap St, DT9 3AX ✆ 01935 814465) is a family-run business selling fine watercolours, oil paintings, antique maps and prints, and it has a section devoted to antique prints and maps of Dorset. It stands at the entrance to **Swan Yard**, a small pedestrianised shopping area converted from stables.

At the top of the hill Cheap Street leads into **The Green**. On the corner stands **Julian House**, a 16th-century stone-built hospice with mullioned windows, which now contains shops. Beside it is the 16th-century **George Inn**, Sherborne's oldest surviving inn.

Markets are held in Cheap Street on Thursday and Saturday, and there's a farmers' market on the third Friday of each month (⏲ 09.00–13.00).

Sherborne Abbey (Abbey Church of St Mary the Virgin) & around

www.sherborneabbey.com ⏲ daily; free guided tours Tue 10.30 & Fri 14.30

The centrepiece of Sherborne is undoubtedly its abbey, a glorious spectacle of architecture and history. Resplendent in its golden hamstone, it stands proudly on a perfectly groomed lawn platform, surveying the goings-on of the town. In front a memorial commemorates George Winfield Digby of Sherborne Castle, one of the principal financiers of the abbey's Victorian restoration.

The land on which the abbey stands has been consecrated for over 1,300 years. In AD705 King Ine divided the Diocese of Winchester in two, created a new seat at Sherborne and appointed Aldhelm, Abbot of Malmesbury, as the first bishop of the West Saxons. The Cathedral of Sherborne served Aldhelm and 26 succeeding Saxon bishops until the bishop's seat was moved to Old Sarum (near Salisbury) shortly after the Norman Conquest. The abbey became the church of a Benedictine monastery until 1539, when it was dissolved as part of King Henry VIII's Reformation. The building as it stands today was largely the work of Abbot Ramsam (1475–1504).

Perhaps the abbey's most striking architectural feature is its superb **fan-vaulted stone roof**, the earliest in England. In his book, *England's Thousand Best Churches*, Simon Jenkins proclaims, 'I would pit Sherborne's roof against any contemporary work of the Italian Renaissance.' Another highlight is the **engraved glass reredos** (1968) by Lawrence Whistler in the Lady Chapel. St Katherine's Chapel contains most of the abbey's surviving medieval glass and is where Sir Walter Raleigh attended services, while the rear choir stalls feature ornate 15th-century misericords.

"Perhaps the abbey's most striking architectural feature is its superb fan-vaulted stone roof, the earliest in England."

Fascinating tombs and monuments are dotted about the abbey, vestiges of various periods in its history. The north choir aisle contains Saxon tombs believed to be those of two kings of Wessex, Ethelbald and Ethelbert, elder brothers of Alfred the Great. In the south transept is an impressive marble monument to John Digby, Third and Last Earl of Bristol, dated 1698 and featuring a rather troubling skull and crossbones. In the north transept, within the Wykeham Chapel, a monument of 1564 honours Sir John Horsey, who bought the abbey estates from the Crown during the Reformation and then sold the abbey back to the people of Sherborne as their parish church. Life-sized effigies of Horsey and his son lie next to each other, both of them wearing armour dating from around 1470, presumably to emphasise the fact they were from an old family. Horses' heads, looking like chess pieces with enigmatic expressions, adorn the top of the monument.

Today, the abbey holds regular classical music concerts and performances, in particular during the annual Sherborne Abbey Festival held over five days in May. It is also a memorable and extremely popular venue for a Christmas service.

Behind the abbey, occupying some of the former monastic buildings, is **Sherborne Boys' School**, which was founded in 1550 as King Edward's School. The handsome stone buildings may look familiar, as the school has been used as a location for various films, including *The Guinea Pig*, *The Browning Version* and *Goodbye Mr Chips*.

Not far from the abbey, past the almshouse, is the shop of **Edward Oliver** (The Old Stables, Trendle St, DT9 3NT ✆ 07947 468674 www.edward-oliver.co.uk), who restores furniture. Housed in 18th-century stables, it makes for fun browsing.

The Almshouse of St John the Baptist & St John the Evangelist

Half Moon St, DT9 3LJ 01935 813245 www.stjohnshouse.org May–Sep Tue, Thu, Fri & Sat 14.00–16.00

In front of the abbey is this monastic-looking almshouse, built between 1440 and 1445 and extended in 1864, when additions included the cloister and the Victorian railings. Now a residential home for the elderly, it has been providing assistance to local people for over 500 years. In 1437, Henry VI granted a licence for a home for 'twelve pore feeble and ympotent old men and four old women' to be cared for by a housewife whose duty was to 'feeche in and dyght to the victaill wash wrying make beddys and al other things do'. When new residents first arrived they had to bring their few possessions with them and surrender them to the house on their death. They also swore to obey the rules of the house and could be evicted for serious misdemeanours; daily religious services were compulsory. Residents were required to wear uniform; for women in Victorian times this was a red cape and black bonnet, while the men were dressed in black.

"The almshouse has been providing assistance to local people for over 500 years."

Inside, a chapel features fine medieval stained-glass windows and a vivid triptych (c1480), a three-panelled altarpiece of oil on wood depicting five of the miracles of Christ. For a small fee, you can take a guided tour of the main areas, chapel and gardens. Aside from the chapel, other highlights include the uniforms worn by earlier residents, copies of the royal licence and foundation deed, a solid wooden chest requiring five separate keys, a letter from Sir Walter Raleigh to the Almshouse Master and a collection of 18th-century pewter plates.

Sherborne Museum

Church Lane, DT9 3BP 01935 812252 www.sherbornemuseum.co.uk Mar–Dec Tue–Fri 10.30–16.30, Jan–Mar Tue & Thu 10.30–12.30

Between Cheap Street and the abbey, this museum is dedicated to the history of the town and the surrounding area. It covers prominent buildings, such as Sherborne Castle and the abbey, as well as giving an insight into the life of local agricultural workers and tradesmen. A scale model of the old castle before it was seized puts the ruins visible today into perspective.

In the early 1400s the monks of Sherborne Abbey wrote and illuminated the **Sherborne Missal**, the largest and most ornately decorated English medieval service book to survive from the Middle Ages. The original is held in the British Library but a digital copy can be viewed here.

Sherborne Old Castle

Castleton DT9 3SA ✆ 01935 812730 ◷ Apr–Oct daily 10.00–16.00; English Heritage

This atmospheric ruin lies to the east of the town, in the grounds of the new Sherborne Castle, and is all that remains of the original, which was destroyed by Cromwell's troops during the Civil War. It reportedly took 16 days for Cromwell's men to bring the castle down in 1645; only the imposing gatehouse, parts of the keep and the outer walls survive, surrounded by a moat. The entrance passes over a modern bridge with the piers of the medieval one beneath it. It is a serene spot with fine beech trees, views of the surrounding countryside and the town. It oozes history and mystery, conjuring up images of medieval banquets and battles.

"It oozes history and mystery, conjuring up images of medieval banquets and battles."

The castle was built in the 12th century by Roger de Caen, Bishop of Salisbury and Chancellor of England. In 1592, Queen Elizabeth I gave the castle, which was already deteriorating, to explorer Sir Walter Raleigh. Raleigh initially tried to modernise it but gave up and built a home (Sherborne Castle) in the deer park opposite; he kept the old castle for ceremonial use.

Sherborne Castle

New Rd, DT9 5NR ✆ 01935 812072 🖱 www.sherbornecastle.com ◷ Apr–Oct Tue–Thu, Sat–Sun 11.00–16.30

Having decided that Sherborne Old Castle was not fit for habitation, Sir Walter Raleigh built this Elizabethan mansion on the other side of the River Yeo in 1594. Raleigh and his wife enjoyed their new home for less than nine years before his execution during the reign of James I. In 1617 the estate, with its two castles, was purchased by Sir John Digby and has remained in the family ever since. At its core is the house built by Raleigh with polygonal turrets in each corner. It was extended in a similar style (more turrets) by various Digbys through the generations, giving it its rather unusual shape. During World War I the house was used by the Red Cross as a hospital, and in World War II as the headquarters for the commandos involved in the D-Day landings.

The interior presents a parade of styles from different eras: Tudor, Jacobean, Georgian and Victorian. The furniture, art and family memorabilia give it a very human touch. There is a lot to take in, so it is just as well that there are guides on hand to explain each room. The slightly comical ostrich with a horseshoe in its beak, which you can see depicted all around the building, has been the heraldic symbol of the Digby family since 1350. The symbol is said to originate from around 100BC when the king of Numidia (now Tunisia) put warriors on ostriches to fight the Roman cavalry; the speedy ostriches outflanked the Romans and they fled. The ostrich and horseshoe crest was later used in Hungary but it is not clear why it was adopted by the Digbys. The 18th-century library is striking, with formidable-looking busts tucked into recesses between the highly decorative bookcases. The green drawing room has Raleigh's arms on the ceiling and three beautiful 17th-century fireplaces.

The spectacular gardens were created in 1753 by Capability Brown with a 50-acre lake fed by the River Yeo as their centrepiece. Around the lake are sweeping lawns, majestic old trees and colourful flower borders, while the remains of Old Sherborne Castle in the distance provide a romantic backdrop. Exploring the grounds is like being lost in a Jane Austen adaptation. I, for one, was certainly hoping that Mr Darcy would ride up on his powerful, grey gelding to invite me to a sumptuous picnic

SHERBORNE CASTLE COUNTRY FAIR

www.sherbornecountryfair.com

Sherborne Castle plays host to an annual country fair, usually held in early June. It was started by a small group of volunteers in 1996, with the aim of collecting money for local charities, especially those working with children, and to date it has raised over three-quarters of a million pounds. The fair makes for a thoroughly entertaining day out, and it showcases country pursuits and crafts, including Morris dancing, rare breed shows, heavy horses, gun dog trials, falconry and local hunts and their hounds. A more unusual inclusion on the schedule is the dragon-boat racing on Sherborne Castle lake. The food hall, crammed with delicious local produce, is another highlight.

by the lake, and perhaps a lifetime as Mrs Darcy. As you walk around the lake in the direction of Sherborne Old Castle you come to **Raleigh's seat**, a large stone seat where the adventurer reportedly used to sit to survey the estate and keep an eye on the road below, the main route to Dorchester. Raleigh's role in popularising tobacco in England is well documented and legend has it that a servant happened upon Sir Walter smoking his pipe at the stone seat and, thinking his master was on fire, threw a pitcher of beer over him to extinguish the flames. Raleigh's ghost reportedly walks the castle grounds and sits on the stone seat gazing longingly across the estate.

Both the castle and its gardens are open to visitors; you can visit both or just the gardens. The gardens provide a beautiful, peaceful spot to enjoy a picnic or to walk the dogs around the lake. There is a good tea room in the former nursery building and the estate produces wine, on sale in the gift shop.

FOOD & DRINK

Oxford's 34 Cheap St, DT9 3PX 01935 812642 Mon–Sat 09.00–17.00. A wonderful, traditional bakery, established in 1911 and now run by the fourth generation of the family, Steve Oxford. The preservative-free bread is baked daily in the nearby village of Alweston and delivered to their shops in Sherborne, Blandford, Canford Cliffs and Westbourne. They use local flour wherever possible, such as that from Cann Mills near Shaftesbury (page 46).

The Arch Swan Yard, Cheap St, DT9 3AX 01935 817022 Wed–Sat 11.00–17.00. A pub tucked away in a pedestrian alleyway off the main street. A light and fresh interior, a real fire in winter and a walled garden create a pleasant atmosphere. A simple menu, including some tasty cakes for afternoon tea.

Bakery Café 1 The Green, DT9 3HZ 01935 813264 Mon–Sat 08.00–17.00, pizza evenings Thu & Fri from 17.00. Seating is upstairs at school-like long tables, making for an informal, friendly atmosphere. On offer are freshly baked breads, cakes, pizzas and the like.

Eastbury Hotel Long St, DT9 3BY 01935 813131 daily. Home-grown and local is the culinary theme at this boutique hotel; the menu tells you exactly which producers supplied the ingredients. Creative dishes, beautifully presented.

Olivers 19 Cheap St, DT9 3PU 01935 815005 daily. Casual, counter-service café with long tables and a back room with unusual 2-person booths. Serves homemade cakes and uses as much local produce as possible, including coffee roasted by Reads of Sherborne.

Three Wishes 78 Cheap St, DT9 3BJ 01935 817777 daily. A popular café/bistro that prides itself on using local ingredients in its carefully presented dishes. On the menu is the 'Sherborne Stodger', a bun containing dried fruit and spices.

MY ORCHA'D IN LINDEN LEA

The following poem by Dorset dialect poet William Barnes is considered to be an unofficial Dorset anthem. It was set to music by Ralph Vaughan Williams.

'Ithin the woodlands, flow'ry gleaded,
By the woak tree's mossy moot,
The sheenen grass bleades, timber-sheaded,
Now do quiver under voot;
An' birds do whissle auver head,
An' water's bubblen in its bed,
An' ther vor me the apple tree
Do lean down low in Linden Lea.

When leaves that leately wer a-springen
Now do feade 'ithin the copse,
An' painted birds do hush ther zingen
Up upon the timber's tops;
An' brown-leav'd fruit's a-turnen red,
In cloudless zunsheen, auver head,
Wi' fruit vor me the apple tree
Do lean down low in Linden Lea.

Let other vo'k meake money vaster
In the air o' dark-room'd towns,
I don't dread a peevish measter;
Though noo man do heed my frowns,
I be free to goo abrode,
Or teake agean my hwomeward road
To where vor me the apple tree
Do lean down low in Linden Lea.

28 SANDFORD ORCAS MANOR HOUSE

The Manor House, Sandford Orcas DT9 4SB ✆ 01963 220206 ⏲ Easter Mon 10.00–17.00, May & Jul–Sep Sun & Mon 14.00–17.00

Sandford Orcas is an appealing stone village three miles north of Sherborne, just inside the border with Somerset. The manor house was constructed in the mid 16th century from local hamstone, on the site of an earlier house; it is little altered and a rare example of the small Tudor manor houses that were once dotted throughout the countryside. The house was built for Edward Knoyle and only two families, the Knoyles and the Medlycotts, have owned it since. When the house is open, you are likely to be shown around by a member of the Medlycott family.

The entrance is impressive, passing through a gatehouse to reveal the atmospheric courtyard, bordered by the former coachhouse and stables. It's very easy to imagine making an entrance in a horse-drawn carriage, gravel crunching beneath the wheels. Above the door of the house the coat of arms of the Knoyle family is still visible, and three stone lions crouch on the gables. One of them is original, the others are Victorian copies. Visitors are shown around about eight rooms of the house; the centrepiece is the hall, which has fine wood panelling, an impressive carved stone fireplace and some original stained glass.

The house is reputed to be haunted by a litany of ghostly characters; somewhat suspiciously most of the ghost stories originate from the 1960s when the then tenant, Colonel Claridge, opened it to the public to raise funds, leaving one to wonder whether the ghost stories may have been an attempt to boost ticket sales. It is a theory Sir Mervyn Medlycott confirmed when I spoke to him and he is adamant there are no ghostly occupants.

The herbaceous borders of the typically English garden provide a colourful contrast to the farmland that surrounds the house. The giant clam shells are a surprising feature and were brought to the house from Tahiti in 1881.

Adjacent to the house, is the adorable little medieval **church of St Nicholas**. Inside, above the door is a memorial to William Knoyle, son of Edward, dated 1607. He is depicted as a knight with his two wives and 11 children. The four children from his first marriage are shown to be deceased, wrapped in red swaddling clothes. On a wall at the back of the church is half of a stone coffin lid dating from around 1280 to 1315. When I last visited there was a litter tray in the centre of the church bearing the polite instruction 'bats are respectfully requested to use the facilities provided'. An absence of bat droppings on the church floor indicated the bats had been doing as they were told.

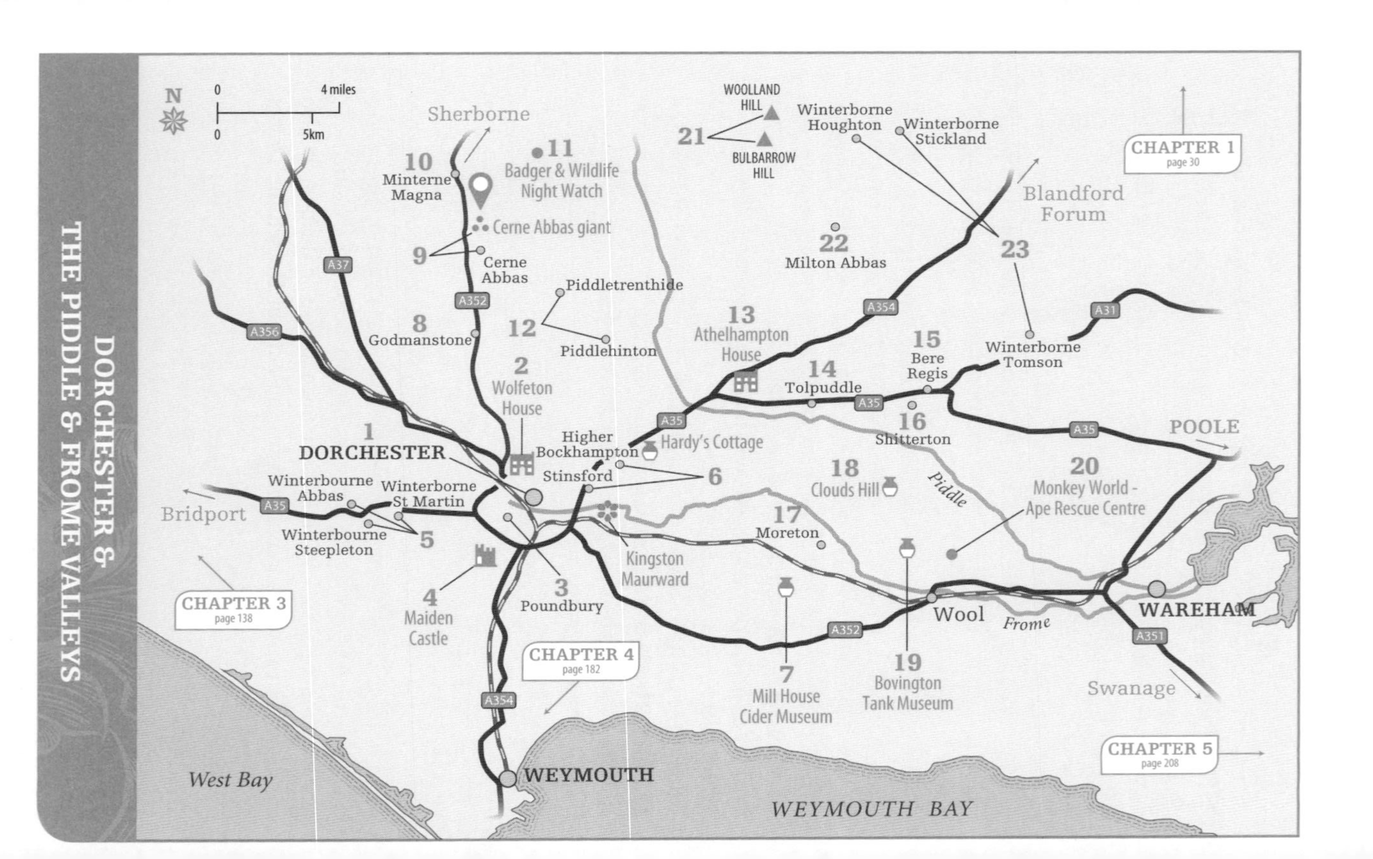
DORCHESTER &
THE PIDDLE & FROME VALLEYS
N
0
4 miles
0
5km
Sherborne
10
Minterne Magna
11
Badger & Wildlife Night Watch
Cerne Abbas giant
9
Cerne Abbas
8
Godmanstone
A37
A356
A352
12
Piddletrenthide
Piddlehinton
2
Wolfeton House
1
DORCHESTER
Winterbourne Abbas
Winterbourne St Martin
Winterbourne Steepleton
5
Bridport
A35
4
Maiden Castle
3
Poundbury
Higher Bockhampton
Stinsford
6
Hardy's Cottage
Kingston Maurward
WOOLLAND HILL
BULBARROW HILL
21
Winterborne Houghton
Winterborne Stickland
22
Milton Abbas
13
Athelhampton House
14
Tolpuddle
15
Bere Regis
16
Shitterton
17
Moreton
18
Clouds Hill
Piddle
23
Blandford Forum
Winterborne Tomson
A354
A31
20
Monkey World - Ape Rescue Centre
POOLE
Wool
Frome
WAREHAM
A351
Swanage
7
Mill House Cider Museum
19
Bovington Tank Museum
A352
A354
WEYMOUTH
WEYMOUTH BAY
West Bay
CHAPTER 1
page 30
CHAPTER 3
page 138
CHAPTER 4
page 182
CHAPTER 5
page 208

2
DORCHESTER & THE PIDDLE & FROME VALLEYS

At the heart of Dorset is a captivating landscape of rolling chalk downland, wooded hills and river valleys. The area is sparsely populated, its chalk hills with their short springy grass being relatively inhospitable farmland compared with the fertile, neighbouring Blackmore Vale. Visitors tend to bypass the area in favour of the Dorset coast, yet it has much to offer those who want to slow down and really get to know what lies at the centre of the county.

Strings of villages huddle in clusters along the river valleys, like those along the **River Frome** and the evocatively named **River Piddle**. In the east the Frome and Piddle valleys lead into water meadows and from there to an area of heathland, which spreads towards the Isle of Purbeck and Poole Harbour. The chalk hills hold a large water table, which means there are many seasonal rivers that flow depending on the level of the water. The area has 15 villages with names prefixed by 'Winterborne', indicating they lie on a stream which only runs in winter.

Dorchester, the county town, and the surrounding area have a strong sense of history, having been settled since around 4,000BC. Dorchester still bears the imprint of Roman occupation, including the only fully exposed and best-preserved Roman town house in Britain. It also has arguably the most comprehensive museum in Dorset, the Dorset County Museum.

Just outside Dorchester is **Maiden Castle**, the largest Iron Age hillfort in Britain. It is one of several prehistoric sites in this area, along with Maumbury Rings and Badbury Rings. Dorset's past inhabitants have left their mark all over this part of the county. It seems chalk hills do have their uses – you can make enormous carvings in them which last for centuries and glisten white for all to see. That is precisely what someone (no-one knows quite who or when) has done at **Cerne Abbas**, where the chalk carving of a naked, club-wielding, 180-foot giant dominates the landscape.

Dorchester and the surrounding countryside inspired one of Dorset's most famous sons, author Thomas Hardy, who was born in a tiny hamlet near Dorchester in 1840 and later moved into the town. In this part of the county are innumerable reminders of Hardy's work and thankfully much of the landscape has changed little since his day. The various sites for aficionados to visit include the cottage where he was born.

GETTING THERE & AROUND

Unless you have all the time in the world, a car really is the best way to reach the delightful hidden places in this area. The main roads are good (the A35 running east to west and the A352 running north to south) but getting away from them and exploring is where the real fun is. Dorchester is straightforward to negotiate by car, there is plenty of parking and the town doesn't usually feel crowded.

The Dorchester tourist information centre stocks a leaflet entitled 'Discover the heart of Hardy's Wessex', which includes a Hardy trail linking together sites where he lived, places he wrote about and the church at Stinsford where his heart is buried. Parts of the trail are designed to be walked, such as Dorchester to Hardy's birthplace at Higher Bockhampton, but most of it follows the road and can be covered by car.

PUBLIC TRANSPORT

Travelling to Dorchester via public transport is relatively easy. London Waterloo to Weymouth **train** services (South West Trains) call at Dorchester South station, while Bristol to Weymouth services (Wessex Trains) call at Dorchester West. A **National Express bus** service runs from London Victoria to Dorchester via Bournemouth.

Getting beyond Dorchester and out into the villages and more remote points of interest is less straightforward. However, regular **bus services** are available between Dorchester and some of the main attractions, including Maiden Castle, Cerne Abbas, Milton Abbas and Bovington Tank Museum. A useful service is the 387 operated by Damory Coaches, which runs from Dorchester to Poole via Athelhampton House, Tolpuddle and Bere Regis (Mon–Sat only).

Hardy's Cottage at Higher Bockhampton is not well served by public transport: the closest bus stop is on the A35, but you need to walk across the busy road and then on to the cottage. A simpler solution is a **taxi** from Dorchester, which is inexpensive.

CYCLING

The charming countryside and relatively quiet roads make for some very pleasant cycling country. National Cycle Network (NCN) **Route 2** covers 30 miles between Lyme Regis and Dorchester, taking you through the West Dorset countryside. The route passes through the Marshwood Vale, around Bridport and through the beautiful Bride Valley. It runs close to the Hardy Monument and Maiden Castle on the approach to Dorchester. The 'Cycling in West Dorset' leaflet is available from tourist information centres and can be used in conjunction with ❋ OS Explorer maps 116 and OL15. Various branches allow you to detour to see local sites of interest, such as Abbotsbury. NCN **Route 26** begins in Dorchester and runs 28 miles north to Sherborne, passing Cerne Abbas *en route*.

CYCLE HIRE

Cycle Life Electric Wessex 181 Bridport Rd, Poundbury DT1 3BN ☏ 07734 054277 ⊛ www.cyclelifeelectricwessex.co.uk. Sale and hire of electric bikes.
Dorchester Cycles 31 Great Western Rd, Dorchester DT1 1UF ☏ 01305 268787 ⊛ www.dorchestercycles.co.uk

WALKING

The town of **Dorchester** lends itself to being explored on foot and The Walks, following the Roman town walls, are a good place to start. The tourist information centre can provide information on guided walks. The town crier, Alistair Chisholm, offers guided walks of the town, including a Thomas Hardy tour (page 100).

The prehistoric site of **Maiden Castle** offers a memorable short stroll, as well as the chance to soak up thousands of years of history and some breathtaking views of the countryside.

The **Cerne Valley** is criss-crossed by footpaths and bridleways that can tie in with a memorable walk up Giant Hill to get a closer look at the chalk carving.

For those with an interest in **Lawrence of Arabia**, a themed trail starts at the Bovington Tank Museum and takes in Clouds Hill

TOURIST INFORMATION CENTRE

General information www.westdorset.com, www.dorchesterdorset.com
Dorchester Antelope Walk, DT1 1BE 01305 267992

and Moreton. A leaflet on the trail is available from local tourist information centres (such as Wareham) and free to download online (www.dorsetforyou.com).

If you want to walk in quintessential **Hardy country**, the obvious starting point is Hardy's Cottage, and the walk into Thorncombe Wood and Duddle Heath ('Egdon Heath' in Hardy's writings), or perhaps along the river from Lower Bockhampton to the church at Stinsford. The 212-mile trail known as the **Hardy Way** links together many of the key sites.

Bulbarrow Hill lies on a section of the Wessex Ridgeway and has superb views of the Blackmore Vale. You can easily reach it from car parks on the hilltop and along the Ridgeway or you can combine it with a longer walk, such as starting from Ibberton beneath the escarpment, climbing steeply to the top, then from Bulbarrow dropping down through Woolland.

Just to the south, there's a beautiful stroll from Milton Abbas to Milton Abbey; the best longer walks around the village lie to the north, including Hilton and Winterborne Houghton.

The **Dorset Jubilee Trail** runs 90 miles from Forde Abbey on the Somerset border across Dorset to Bokerley Dyke on the Hampshire border and takes in several places mentioned in this chapter, including Moreton, Bere Regis and Milton Abbas.

HORSERIDING

The area is rich in bridleways, including around the Cerne Abbas Giant where you can enjoy superb views of the Cerne Valley. The **Wessex Ridgeway** crosses the centre of the county and you can download a trail guide from www.dorsetforyou.com.

RIDING STABLES

Golden Equestrian Blagdon Hill, Winterborne St Martin (Martinstown) DT2 9HY 07950 749993. A family-run stables offering hacking for all levels of experience, including through the heathland surrounding Hardy's monument (see page 187).

DORCHESTER & AROUND

You may be tempted to assume that **Dorchester**, being Dorset's county town, is large, crowded and surrounded by new, soulless housing developments. That is not the case. Dorchester is full of old-world charm and with around 20,000 inhabitants is a very manageable size. The countryside and villages around it are alluring and it only takes a brief look at a road atlas to see that many of Dorset's archaeological and historical attractions are in this area, including the hillfort at Maiden Castle. As for new housing developments, they don't come any more remarkable than Poundbury, the community designed in the 1990s by HRH Prince of Wales.

Dorchester is the heart of **Hardy country**: devotees come here to pay homage to the author. High on the list of Hardy haunts to visit are his birthplace at **Higher Bockhampton** and his former home at **Max Gate** in Dorchester.

1 DORCHESTER

> The town is populous, tho' not large, the streets broad, but the buildings old, and low; however, there is good company and a good deal of it; and a man that coveted a retreat in this world might as agreeably spend his time, and as well in Dorchester, as in any town I know in England.

I am inclined to agree with Daniel Defoe's description in his *A tour thro' the whole island of Great Britain* (1724–26).

Dorchester as you see it today has been forged over a long and fascinating history. One of the great pleasures of wandering around the town is the chance to trace portions of that history by visiting sites of Neolithic, Roman, medieval and more recent importance. The Dorchester area has been inhabited since Neolithic times, c4000BC, with settlements based around what later became the Iron Age hillfort of Maiden Castle to the southwest of the town (page 106). When the Romans arrived in AD70 they laid out what is now the town of Dorchester, which they called Durnovaria, in their usual cruciform manner surrounded by a wall. The basic structure of the town remains unchanged. Today, pleasant avenues lined with lime, chestnut and sycamore trees, trace the town walls. Known as **The Walks**, the avenues were laid down in the 18th century and to wander along them is an enjoyable way to get a feel for the town. As you explore, it may strike you that Dorchester does not look as old as you may expect. That is because much of medieval Dorchester was lost in five devastating fires between 1613 and 1775 but the rebuilding left streets of handsome 18th-century houses.

A good place to start any visit to Dorchester is the **tourist information centre** on Antelope Walk. It is well stocked with books and brochures; the staff are helpful and can provide leaflets on walks around the town and in the area.

Dorchester has a surprisingly long and varied list of museums, some devoted to themes that have little to do with the area, such as the Tutankhamun Exhibition and the Terracotta Warriors Museum. Of the town's museums, two really stand out as worth visiting: the **Dorset County Museum** (page 102) and the **Keep Military Museum of Devon and Dorset** (pages 102–3).

The clues pointing to Dorchester's Roman origins were certainly not lost on Thomas Hardy. In his novel *The Mayor of Casterbridge*, Hardy based the fictional town on Dorchester, which he knew well, being born and raised in the area. His description of Casterbridge may as easily have been a description of Dorchester: 'Casterbridge announced old Rome in every street, alley and precinct. It looked Roman, bespoke the art of Rome, concealed the dead men of Rome.' Dorchester's Roman origins are even more evident today than they were in Hardy's time, for Hardy would not have seen the most striking proof of Roman occupation, the **Roman Town House** (☎ 01305 221000 🖱 www.romantownhouse.org). The house, which dates from the 4th century, was found in 1937 during the building of a new County Hall and is the only fully exposed Roman town house in the country. It is perhaps surprising (and certainly refreshing) that you are able to walk freely around the ruins and that no entry fee is charged. Parts of the ruins are protected by roofs and glass walls but the basic structure, mosaic floors and underfloor heating are clearly visible. An audioguide is available through your mobile phone, or there are display panels for the less technically minded. The items found during the excavation of the town house are on display in the Dorset County Museum (page 102). The only disappointing aspect of the ruins is their location, backing on to the county council's rather unlovely offices.

Not far from the Roman town house, on the banks of the River Frome, is **Hangman's Cottage**. This very pretty thatched building in the traditional Dorset style is believed to have been home to the town's executioner.

JUDGE JEFFREYS & THE BLOODY ASSIZES

In May 1685, the Duke of Monmouth set sail from Holland, where he had been in exile, bound for Lyme Regis. Monmouth, the Protestant son of Charles II, intended to overthrow the Roman Catholic King James II. Lyme Regis was strongly Protestant; Monmouth gathered over 3,000 supporters and marched towards Somerset. Monmouth was defeated on 6 July at the Battle of Sedgemoor, around 1,200 men were taken prisoner and Monmouth was executed. Judge Jeffreys held his infamous 'Bloody Assizes', a series of trials which began in Winchester and then moved through Salisbury, Dorchester, Taunton and Wells. While presiding over the trials in Dorchester, Judge Jeffreys lodged at 6 High West Street (now a restaurant) and on 5 September, 312 trials were held in the Oak Room of the Antelope Hotel (now a tea room). The 'hanging judge' sentenced 292 Monmouth supporters to death and around 800 to be transported to the West Indies. After the hangings, the heads of some of the executed were impaled on church railings, and left there for several years as a warning of the penalty for treason.

In 1688, when King James II was overthrown by William of Orange, Judge Jeffreys was imprisoned in the Tower of London. He died a year later, aged 44, of kidney disease.

In 1856, at the age of 16, Hardy was present at the execution of Martha Brown, and the memory of this public hanging, on top of the north-facing main entrance to the prison only 150 yards downstream from Hangman's Cottage, stayed with him. Town crier Alistair Chisholm told me some Hardy scholars link the event to the ultimate fate of Tess of the d'Urbervilles. Thomas Hardy's short story 'The Withered Arm' features the hangman's cottage on this site and, Alistair told me, the association has remained to this day, reinforced by stories of hangman's ropes being found in the roof in the late 19th century.

Near Hangman's Cottage is **John's Pond**, part of the intricate drainage system of the water meadows which enabled low-lying areas to be flooded in winter to stop the ground freezing and allow fertile silt to settle. The name is reportedly in memory of a hapless prisoner, who, having managed to escape the nearby jail on a dark night, fell into the pond and was drowned.

Dorchester's **High Street** is inviting, brimming with character, points of interest and some decent shops. On the south side of High West Street are the only timber-framed buildings surviving in anything like their original state. The black-and-white building now housing a restaurant (6 High West St – see page 104) is where **Judge Jeffreys** ('The Hanging Judge')

GUIDED TOURS & WALKS AROUND DORCHESTER

07773 286197 www.thomas-hardy-explorer.co.uk

Dorchester's town crier, Alistair Chisholm, offers entertaining guided tours and walks around Dorchester and the surrounding area. Some of the most popular are evening ghost walks (focusing on Judge Jeffreys and the Bloody Assizes), Thomas Hardy tours and visits to Tolpuddle to trace the martyrs' story.

Alistair has been Dorchester's town crier since 1997 and has been national champion town crier seven times. His enthusiasm for Dorchester, which he describes as 'the small town with the big story', is wonderfully evident. Details of his tour programme are available online.

lodged during the trials of those who took part in the Monmouth Rebellion of 1685 (see box, page 99). The trials, known as the **Bloody Assizes**, were held in the Oak Room (now a tea room – see page 104) of the **Antelope Hotel**. Judge Jeffreys, whose deadly zero-tolerance policy made him highly unpopular, is said to have had a secret passage leading there from his lodgings.

The **Shire Hall**, built in 1797 of Portland stone, contains the **Old Crown Court** (Stratton House, 58–60 High West St, DT1 1UZ 01305 267992 Mon–Fri 10.00–12.00 & 14.00–16.00), where the Tolpuddle Martyrs were tried in 1834 (see box, page 121). Inscribed on the outside of the building, at a level for stagecoach passengers to read, are the distances to the nearest towns. The court is owned by the Trades Union Congress (TUC) and was restored as a memorial to the martyrs in 1956. At selected times in summer you can take a guided tour of the cells as well as the court – call for tour times.

St Peter's, at the junction of South Street and High Street, is the town's only surviving medieval church. The church was restored by the Dorchester architect John Hicks in 1856, along with his 16-year-old assistant, the future author Thomas Hardy, who trained as an architect. The plans Hardy drew for the church are on display in the south chapel. Outside the church is a statue erected in 1888 to the Dorset dialect poet **William Barnes** (see box, page 35), who lived in Dorchester from 1837 until 1886. Barnes was a rector of nearby Winterborne Came and a great friend of Thomas Hardy. Dorchester couldn't possibly have a statue of Barnes without one of Hardy too; the Hardy one is at the western end of High West Street, near the top-of-town roundabout.

Opposite St Peter's Church is the **Corn Exchange** of 1848. The rather playful clock tower was added in 1864.

A quiet retreat within the town is the flower-filled **Borough Gardens** on Cornwall Road, where the colourful bandstand and clock provide a Victorian feel. On the southern side of town, opposite where the market is held, is the new **Brewery Square** development. The site of the former Eldridge Pope brewery is now home to modern shops, a cinema and pleasant public spaces. The centrepiece is the stunning and gigantic bronze sculpture of a dray horse by Shirley Pace, who came out of retirement in 2013 at the age of 81 to complete the work. The horse is Drummer, the last dray horse to work at the brewery. The sculpture was paraded through the town on a horse-drawn dray cart before being placed in its present position in 2014.

"The site of the former Eldridge Pope brewery is now home to modern shops, a cinema and pleasant public spaces."

Nearby **Maumbury Rings** (www.maumburyrings.co.uk; free access) acts almost as a physical representation of a timeline charting the area's history. The rings began life as a Neolithic henge around 2,500BC. Just over 2,500 years later the Romans turned the site into an amphitheatre and held gladiatorial conquests here. During the Middle Ages it was a venue for bear-baiting and when the Civil War came, it became an artillery fort. In the 17th and 18th centuries Maumbury Rings was again used as an amphitheatre, drawing excited crowds to its public executions or 'Hanging Fairs'. The site continues to host public entertainment today, although the violent displays of the past have been replaced by more genteel activities, such as choral recitals, plays and Dorchester's Arts Festivals. You can visit and walk along the banks, although busy roads run around it and the views are very urban. Finds from excavations of Maumbury Rings can be seen at the Dorset County Museum (page 102).

Grey's Bridge on London Road leads over the River Frome and towards Poole and Bournemouth. The bridge is one of several in Dorset bearing a sign that warns any person damaging it is liable to be transported for life. During World War II fear of invasion resulted in Royal Engineers drilling holes in the stonework, ready for explosives. No invasion took place but in 1942 several bombs fell on the water meadows and riverbank, killing ten cows and a horse, injuring several people, and damaging nearby houses.

Dorset County Museum

High West St, DT1 1XA ✆ 01305 262735 www.dorsetcountymuseum.org
Jan–Oct Mon–Sat, Nov–Mar Tue–Sat

The fetching mock-medieval-style building (1884), with high ceilings and fine cast-iron work inspired by the Great Exhibition of 1851, provides a fitting backdrop for the exhibits. Its collections comprehensively cover Dorset's social history, literature, archaeology, geology and natural history. The Jurassic Coast exhibition, complete with fossilised dinosaur remains, is bound to be a hit with children, while Dorchester's early history is well represented with finds from digs of Iron Age, Roman, Anglo-Saxon and medieval sites. The floor of the Victorian Hall, the museum's magnificent main gallery, is one of the few places in England where you can actually walk on a Roman mosaic floor. The mosaics inlaid into the floor came from Roman town houses excavated in and around Dorchester. There are fascinating finds from Maiden Castle (page 106), including the skeleton of a member of the Durotriges tribe of Iron Age Britons with a Roman ballista bolt lodged in his spine.

The Keep Military Museum of Devon & Dorset

Barrack Rd, DT1 1RN ✆ 01305 264066 www.keepmilitarymuseum.org Apr–Sep Mon–Sat 09.30–17.00, Oct–Mar Tue–Fri 10.00–16.30

The museum occupies the imposing former gatehouse of the Dorsetshire Regiment barracks, built in 1879 from Portland stone. The regiments of Devon and Dorset have a history spanning over 300 years. Here you can follow their story right up to 2007, when the Devon and Dorset Light Infantry was disbanded and absorbed into The Rifles.

I found this a highly emotive museum, dedicated to the many West Country folk who have left their beloved towns, villages and farms to serve their country in a faraway land. During World War I they were joined by many of the area's finest horses. The **Queen's Own Dorset Yeomanry Horses** are best known for their 26 February 1916 charge of the Senussi forces at Agagia in Egypt. Despite being outnumbered almost three to one, the Yeomanry charged across the desert in the face of rifle and machine-gun fire. They lost half their horses and a third of their men but won the ensuing battle and captured General Jaafa Pasha. On the ground floor of the museum is a life-size model of Second Lieutenant Blaksley on horseback, carrying the original sword he used in the battle. On 3 March 1916 he wrote to his mother: 'I was within 30 yards of the enemy when my horse came down, shot through the heart. He was, I think, the nicest horse I have ever ridden, a well known hunter in the Blackmore Vale.' For me, this was perhaps the starkest illustration of what a shock it must have been for both soldier and horse to be plucked from the tranquillity of Dorset and sent to a battlefield in northern Africa.

The museum is brilliantly laid out and has some gems that you may not expect to see tucked away in Dorset, such as Hitler's desk. The Dorsetshire Regiment recovered the desk from the ruins of the Chancellery in Berlin in 1945. From the roof there are breathtaking 360° views of Dorchester and the surrounding countryside.

Max Gate

Alington Av, DT1 2AB ✆ 01305 262538 www.maxgate.co.uk ⏲ 1 Apr–30 Oct Wed–Sun & Bank Holiday Mon 11.00–17.00; National Trust

Max Gate, on the eastern peripheries of town near the A35, was the home of Thomas Hardy from 1885, when he was aged 45, until he died in 1928. Construction of the house was a family affair – it was designed by Hardy and built by his brother. It was here that the author wrote *Tess of the d'Urbervilles*, *Jude the Obscure*, *The Woodlanders* and much of his poetry, and entertained other literary figures of the day, including Robert Louis Stevenson, Rudyard Kipling and T E Lawrence. Hardy had no children with either of his wives (Emma and Florence) but had a number of pets, including a dog called Wessex, who are buried in the garden. The house provides a rare glimpse into Hardy's personal life, as many of his letters were destroyed upon his death, in accordance with his will.

FOOD & DRINK

A large weekly market is held opposite the Brewery Square development (Weymouth Avenue) every Wednesday and includes a **farmers' market**.

Brewhouse and Kitchen 17 Weymouth Av, DT1 1QY ✆ 01305 265551 www.brewhouseandkitchen.com ⏲ daily. Appropriately located in the Brewery Square development is this micro-brewery serving its own and other beers, as well as pub food. If you fancy a go at brewing, information about their brewing days is available online.

The Fridge 17 Tudor Arcade, DT1 1BN ✆ 01305 269088 www.thefridge.biz ⏲ Mon–Sat. This shop has been supplying desirable deli items and local produce to the area since 1995.

The Horse with the Red Umbrella 10 High West St, DT1 1UJ ✆ 01305 262019 ⏲ Mon–Sat 07.00–16.30. A popular, casual café in the former Loyalty Theatre building. Serves sandwiches, jacket potatoes and a good range of cakes.

No 6 6 North Sq, DT1 1HY ✆ 01305 267679 ⊙ Tue–Fri for lunch & dinner, Sat for dinner. French restaurant which uses Dorset ingredients. Uncharacteristically for a French restaurant there is a good selection of vegetarian dishes. Reservation recommended.
Oak Room 5b Antelope Walk, DT1 1BE ✆ 01305 250760 ⊙ Mon–Sat 09.00–17.00, Sun 11.00–15.00. The atmosphere here makes this a top choice for a tea break or lunch. The oak-panelled room above the alleyway served as Judge Jeffreys' court during the Bloody Assizes – a portrait of the grumpy judge hangs near one of the two fireplaces and a card telling the room's grim history is available. The room now has a gentler purpose, as a traditional tea rooms in the style of a Lyons Corner House. The lunches and homemade cakes are reasonably priced.
Potter's Café 19 Durngate St, DT1 1JP ✆ 01305 260312 ⊙ Mon–Sat 09.30–16.00, Sun 10.00–14.30. Centrally located and with a courtyard garden for sunny days. On offer is a variety of lunch dishes, delicious cakes (including gluten free) and homemade smoothies. Generous portions, reasonably priced.
Prezzo 6 High West St, DT1 1UJ ✆ 01305 259678. This Italian restaurant's big draw card is the incredible Judge Jeffreys' building which houses it. The notorious 'hanging judge' lodged here when he presided over the Bloody Assizes in 1685.
Re-loved 2 Cornhill (South St), DT1 1BA ✆ 01305 257070 ⊙ Mon–Thu 09.00–17.30, Fri–Sat 09.00–21.00, Sun 10.00–16.00. A family-run, vintage-style tea rooms above a secondhand shop. Quirky and full of character, it serves old-fashioned favourites like bubble and squeak and corned beef hash. The cakes are homemade and many are gluten free. Tranforms into a bistro on Friday and Saturday evenings.
Sienna 36 High West St, DT1 1UP ✆ 01305 250022 ⊙ Tue–Sat for lunch & dinner A tiny, upmarket but friendly restaurant, this comes with impressive credentials: a Michelin star and 3AA rosettes. Uses seasonal, local produce to great effect.

2 WOLFETON HOUSE

Wolfeton Gatehouse (page 296)
Wolfeton, near Dorchester DT2 9QN ✆ 01305 263500 www.hha.org.uk ⊙ Jun–Sep Mon, Wed, Thu 14.00–17.00

This fine medieval and Elizabethan manor to the north of Dorchester is the home of the Thimbleby family, and was the home of the Lady Penelope in Thomas Hardy's *A Group of Noble Dames*. The house has magnificent carved oak panelling, ornate ceilings, grand fireplaces and stone stairs. There is also an impressive collection of art and furniture. The house can be visited at certain times (best to check the website as these can vary) and the gatehouse is available for letting through the Landmark Trust (see page 296).

3 POUNDBURY

Poundbury is the well-known western extension of Dorchester, constructed on Duchy of Cornwall land as an initiative of Prince Charles. The development was designed in accordance with the prince's town-planning theories, outlined in his 1989 book, *A Vision of Britain*. Building began in 1993 and is due to be completed in 2025, the target being a total of 2,500 dwellings and a population of about 6,000.

"Unsurprisingly, given its high profile, Poundbury has attracted its fair share of critics."

Unsurprisingly, given its high profile, Poundbury has attracted its fair share of critics. However, the theories behind it seem sound. Aiming to create an integrated community of shops, businesses and housing, it comprises many thoughtfully designed buildings – the architecture is largely traditional and incorporates period features. The streets are planned with people rather than cars in mind, with narrow roads and wide pavements. The most alluring parts of Poundbury are the oldest ones, at the Dorchester end.

Just to the north of the development lies a much older Poundbury: **Poundbury Hillfort**, a middle Bronze Age enclosure dating from around 1500BC. As well as the relatively simple ramparts of the roughly rectangular fort, the channel of the Roman aqueduct which supplied water to Durnovaria is clearly visible as a terrace in the hillside. The aqueduct cut across the northern and eastern sides of the hillfort's outer defences. On the northern side of the fort, the ramparts slope steeply down to the River Frome and there are good views of Dorchester and the surrounding countryside. It may be much smaller than Maiden Castle, but it is relatively easy to access.

FOOD & DRINK

A **farmers' market** is held in Pummery Square under the Brownsword Hall on the morning of the first Saturday of each month. Nearby is a village shop.

Café on the Green 7 Dinham Walk, DT1 3WU ☎ 01305 259359 ⏲ Mon–Sat 09.30–17.00. In 2010, Gill Symes and her daughter Kelly were made redundant from a local college where they worked with young people with learning difficulties. They turned their misfortune into something incredibly positive and opened this training café, which gives young adults with learning difficulties valuable work experience. It is in a great location overlooking the fountain and has plenty of free parking. Light meals, homemade cakes and cream teas are all served.

House of Dorchester 10 Victor Jackson Av, DT1 3GY ✆ 01305 264257 ⌚ Mon–Fri 09.00–15.00. Once you have found this litte secret, you will want to keep coming back! This chocolate maker has a seconds shop just near the green. Behind the blue door lies a small room crammed with not-quite-perfect chocolates; whether they be misshapen or close to their best-before date, they still taste delicious and cost far less than usual.
Octagon Café 4 Pummery Sq, DT1 3GW ✆ 01305 261555 ⌚ Mon–Sat 08.30–17.00. Simple, friendly café in an octagonal building on the edge of the square. Serves breakfast, lunch and snacks.
Olives Et Al @ The Potting Shed Poundbury Farm Way, DT1 3RT ✆ 01305 216788 🖱 www.olivesetal.co.uk ⌚ Mon–Sat 09.00–17.30, Sun 10.30–16.30. Deli and licensed café run by Dorset company Olives Et Al (see box, page 61). As you would expect, there is a great range of local produce and freshly made lunches.

4 MAIDEN CASTLE

Free to access, this magnificent earthen fortification around two miles southwest of Dorchester is the largest Iron Age hillfort in Britain. The terraced ramparts, which rise to almost 90 feet, enclose an area the size of 50 football pitches. Although it is best known as an Iron Age settlement, the hilltop was first inhabited much earlier, some 6,000 years ago, in the Neolithic period.

Maiden Castle was a bustling settlement populated by the Durotriges tribe. In AD43, the Romans, led by Vespasian, attacked and the Durotriges, armed with only slings and stones, were massacred. A war cemetery excavated near the east gate revealed 34 defenders buried there.

The Romans built a temple on the hilltop, the foundations of which are still visible in the northeast sector. However, they had no real use for an oversized hillfort, so they abandoned the site and established Durnovaria, now Dorchester.

It is a short walk from the car park at the base of the fort to the hilltop. Dorchester and the busy roads around it are clearly visible but are far enough away not to detract too much from the atmosphere of the place. It is only by walking around the site that you can appreciate the scale and complexity of the ramparts and the area they protected. It is easy to imagine how petrified the Durotriges must have been as they saw the advancing Roman armies, and how formidable those ramparts must have looked to the opposition.

Some of the finds from excavation of the site are in the Dorset County Museum (page 102).

5 THE SOUTH WINTERBORNES

The area has two clusters of villages with the 'winterbourne' (or winterborne) prefix to their name, indicating they lie on a stream which flows only in winter. The South Winterbornes are those just west of Dorchester and the North Winterbornes are those near Blandford.

The winterbourne near Dorchester rises above Winterbourne Abbas and joins the River Frome at West Stafford, passing through Winterbourne Steepleton, Winterborne St Martin, Winterborne Monkton and Winterborne Came. The spelling of 'Winterborne' has never been consistent, but traditionally Winterbourne Abbas and Winterbourne Steepleton retain the 'u'.

Attractive **Winterbourne Abbas** is rather spoilt by the A35 running through it. Just west of the village a small Bronze Age stone circle on the edge of a beech wood is known as **Nine Stones**. The canopies of the beech trees cast dappled light over the stones but their proximity to the busy main road is unfortunate.

Winterbourne Steepleton has stone or stone and flint cottages with thatched roofs, mostly dating from the 17th and 18th centuries. The delightful little St Michael and All Angels Church is Saxon and Norman; a rare Saxon sculpture of a flying angel hangs on the north wall of the chancel. The rather fine Steepleton Manor is now a retirement home.

Winterborne St Martin, also known as **Martinstown**, is an adorable village, with the stream running down the main street alongside the houses, which are reached by small footbridges over the water. Not surprisingly, it won the title of Dorset's Best Kept Large Village in 2007 and again in 2010. The village still has a post office, pub, village shop and **Stevens Farm Shop**, which has good views of the valley. In the centre is the **church of St Martin**, which dates from the 12th century and has a 15th-century tower. Inside is a square Purbeck marble font dating from around 1125. Nearby a seasonal stream, or winterbourne, crosses under the road, just in front of the Brewers Arms, which was built as a girls' private school in 1848. If you follow the path upstream past the Brewers Arms you will see the stone **sheep washing pool**, which was used to wash the sheep before sale, as a higher price could be obtained for clean fleeces. It may look simple but it was certainly effective as it was in use as recently as the 1960s. Today, the stream outside the pub is the venue for the village's annual yellow-plastic **duck race**, held in May.

From the centre of the village it is an easy walk to **Maiden Castle**. The round distance is 3½ miles, although this can be extended by walking around the ramparts of the hillfort. As you walk, look out for the many prehistoric mounds known as tumuli or barrows (set up as tombs and landmarks in the Bronze Age) around the Winterbornes and particularly concentrated around Winterborne St Martin.

FOOD & DRINK

Brewers Arms DT2 9LB 01305 889361 Tue–Sun for lunch, Tue–Sat for dinner. A popular, traditional, dog-friendly pub in the centre of the village, built in 1848 as a school. If you stop at the pub be sure to head up the lane along the stream for a look at the sheep washing pool (page 107).

Stevens Farm Shop DT2 9JR 01305 889216 www.stevensfarmshop.co.uk daily, the café serves roast lunches on Sun. The Barnes family have farmed here for over 35 years and opened the farm shop in 2005. It stocks local produce and gifts, and also has a café. It is a good farm shop for children because of the notable array of animals near the entrance – when I visited the varied beasts included cows, goats, pigs and chickens.

6 HIGHER BOCKHAMPTON, STINSFORD & SURROUNDS

Woodsford Castle (page 296)

The hamlets of Higher Bockhampton and Stinsford just east of Dorchester are best known for their links to Thomas Hardy, who was born in a small, highly picturesque cottage in Higher Bockhampton (see opposite). He was christened in the **church of St Michael** in Stinsford and attended services there as a child.

Although he was famously agnostic, Hardy loved this peaceful, little church and it is easy to see why. The building is largely 13th century, with a 14th-century tower. Above the church door is a relief of St Michael installed in 2011 by local stone mason, Rebecca Freiesleben. It replaced the Saxon version, which is now in the south aisle of the church.

Hardy's family had a long association with the church. Hardy's grandfather, father and uncle all belonged to the parish's string choir, which played from the gallery. Thomas is said to have played the violin with them on occasion. A tablet within the church commemorates the family's participation. Hardy remembered Stinsford and the band with great affection naming the village 'Mellstock' in his novel *Under the Greenwood Tree*.

Hardy is commemorated in a beautiful stained-glass window of 1930 in the south aisle; it is based on his favourite Old Testament reading, Elijah and the still small voice (1 Kings 19). Many members of Hardy's family, including his parents, sister, his first wife, Emma, and second wife, Florence, are buried in the churchyard. The Hardy family graves are on the left as you enter from the car park. Hardy's heart is buried alongside Emma but his ashes are in Poet's Corner within Westminster Abbey. Just along from the Hardy graves is the grave of Cecil Day Lewis (1904–72), Poet Laureate and detective novelist.

Hardy's Cottage

Higher Bockhampton DT2 8QJ ✆ 01305 262366 ◷ Mar–Oct Wed–Sun 11.00–17.00; National Trust

It is fortunate that Thomas Hardy was born in a picture-perfect thatched cob cottage with flower-filled garden, for this must be one of the most photographed addresses in Dorset. The cottage, now held by the National Trust, is nestled at the base of Thorncombe Wood, a five- to ten-minute walk from the car park. The most direct route is along a fairly level but rough track or there is a pretty, slightly longer and steeper path through the woods.

The cottage was built by his great-grandfather and was Hardy's home, on and off, from his birth in 1840 until he married Emma Gifford in 1874. Visiting it gives you an appreciation for how quiet, secluded and reflective Hardy's young life must have been. You have the chance to wander the tiny rooms, negotiate the perilously steep staircase and see where he wrote *Under the Greenwood Tree* and *Far from the Madding Crowd*. The cottage has changed little since he lived here and described it in his earliest surviving poem, 'Domicilium':

Red roses, lilacs, variegated box
Are there in plenty, and such hardy flowers
As flourish best untrained. Adjoining these
Are herbs and esculents; and farther still
A field; then cottages with trees, and last
The distant hills and sky.

Behind, the scene is wilder. Heath and furze
Are everything that seems to grow and thrive
Upon the uneven ground. A stunted thorn
Stands here and there, indeed; and from a pit
An oak uprises, springing from a seed
Dropped by some bird a hundred years ago.

Kingston Maurward Gardens & Animal Park

DT2 8PX 01305 215003 www.kmc.ac.uk daily 10.00–17.30

Kingston Maurward House lies between Stinsford and Lower Bockhampton. The house was built in 1720 in the classic Palladian style for George Pitt, cousin of William Pitt the Elder, who became prime minister in 1766. During World War II it was occupied by American servicemen and the estate used as a fuel depot for the D-Day landings. Today, Kingston Maurward is a well-regarded agricultural college. The impressive gardens are open to the public and showcase a number of different horticultural styles, including Arts and Crafts. Although the house is not open to the public, it is visible from the gardens, elegant but overwhelmingly grey and rather austere. The animal park is well laid out with a host of pet and farm animals, including rare breeds, to delight visiting children. Spring brings the chance to see lambing. Your entry fee provides access to the animal park and the gardens.

"The house was built in 1720 in the classic Palladian style for George Pitt."

FOOD & DRINK

Yalbury Cottage Lower Bockhampton DT2 8PZ 01305 262382. A highly regarded restaurant in this small, thatched hotel. The menu changes daily according to the produce available. Reservation recommended.

7 MILL HOUSE CIDER MUSEUM & A DORSET COLLECTION OF CLOCKS

33 Moreton Rd, Owermoigne DT2 8HZ 01305 852220 www.millhousecider.com Tue–Sun & public holidays

This museum (north of the A352) provides an insight into traditional cider-making and includes displays of antique cider-making equipment. In October you can see apples being transformed into cider using 19th-century machinery. You can even bring your own apples and put them through the museum's crusher and press to make apple juice or cider. Some villages pool their apples and take them to the museum by the trailer load to produce a communal supply. Also on site are a shop selling West Country produce and a garden nursery specialising in seed potatoes.

Adjacent, a separate clock museum houses an extensive collection including over 30 grandfather clocks. They are beautifully displayed and will delight anyone with even a passing interest in timepieces.

NORTH FROM DORCHESTER TOWARDS THE BLACKMORE VALE

The A352 runs north from Dorchester to Sherborne and North Dorset. Between Dorchester and Minterne Magna the road runs parallel to the River Cerne and takes you through the pretty villages of the Cerne Valley. It is along this road that you will see one of Dorset's most distinctive sights, the **Cerne Abbas Giant**.

8 GODMANSTONE

Green Valley Yurts (page 296)

Five miles north of Dorchester, the small village of Godmanstone lies along the River Cerne at the base of the valley.

With a bar measuring just 20 feet by 10 feet, the **Smith's Arms** at Godmanstone once claimed (among many others) to be the smallest pub in England. It is visible from the A352 as you pass through Godmanstone: a thatched 15th-century building of mud and flint.

Tradition has it that King Charles II stopped at a blacksmith's forge in Godmanstone and requested a glass of porter. The blacksmith responded, 'I cannot oblige you Sire, as I have no licence.' The king reportedly granted one on the spot and the Smith's Arms came into being.

In 1982 the licensee of The Nutshell at Bury St Edmunds challenged the Smith's Arms's claim to be the smallest pub. The rival landlords decided to settle the matter with a football match, which The Nutshell won. The Nutshell has subsequently lost the title to even tinier competitors.

The Smith's Arms operated as a pub for many years but a sign on it now announces that it has closed indefinitely.

Nearby, a footpath across the River Cerne behind the former mill takes you up on to the hillside for impressive views across the valley. On the other side of the road from the pub a lane leads to a charming, little 11th-century **church**.

FOOD & DRINK

Green Valley Farm Shop Longmeadow, DT2 7AE 01300 342164 Tue–Sat 09.30–16.00. A well-run farm shop stocking organic vegetables from the family farm, organic meat and goodies from other local suppliers. Their own Longmeadow organic apple juice is excellent. They also have a small tea room serving organic cream teas. Accommodation is available here in yurts and bell tents (page 296).

9 CERNE ABBAS & ITS GIANT

New Inn (page 295) **Abbots B&B** (page 295)

Travellers along the A352 are treated to a very unusual and surprising sight – the 180-foot-tall chalk carving of a naked man known as the **Cerne Abbas Giant**. He is also known as 'The Rude Man', for reasons (actually one very obvious reason) which become apparent when you look at him from the roadside viewpoint. I strongly suspect that the postcards of the Rude Man in his birthday suit are the county's best-sellers.

The giant is a Scheduled Ancient Monument in the care of the National Trust although his origins are uncertain. Some believe that he represents the Roman god, Hercules, and is over 1,500 years old. This theory is supported by the fact that he is brandishing a club and by studies indicating he once wore a cloak. However, there is no known record of the carving prior to 1694 and it is often argued that the giant is of 17th-century origin, perhaps a caricature of any one of a number of historical figures – Oliver Cromwell is the primary candidate. Whatever the truth, he has been worshipped as a fertility symbol for centuries and appears to be highly effective in this regard, at least as far as the local population is concerned: in 2010 it was revealed that North Dorset has the highest birth rates in the country, with women having an average of three children.

There is far more to Cerne Abbas than the giant – it is a captivating village with a mixture of architectural styles evoking different eras, from medieval to Georgian. It grew up around a Benedictine abbey founded in AD987 but largely destroyed after the Dissolution of the Monasteries in the 16th century. What little remains of the abbey is now part of a private house at the top of Abbey Street but can be visited for a small fee: the **Abbot's Porch**, built as the entrance to the abbey in the early 1500s, and the **abbey guesthouse**, a rare surviving example of a monastic guesthouse. As you walk up Abbey Street towards the abbey ruins, you will pass an attractive duck pond and just beyond it a gate leads into a **burial ground** believed to date from the time of the abbey. Looking a little out of place among the gravestones is the medieval **Preaching Cross**, a stone shaft set into a squat hexagonal base, which travelling priests would have used to give communion to local residents.

"It is a captivating village with a mixture of architectural styles evoking different eras, from medieval to Georgian."

A walk around the giant

❋ OS Explorer map 117; start: Abbey St, Cerne Abbas, SY665014; 2½ miles; medium (one steep hill). Refreshment at the Abbots Tea Rooms in Cerne Abbas (page 114).

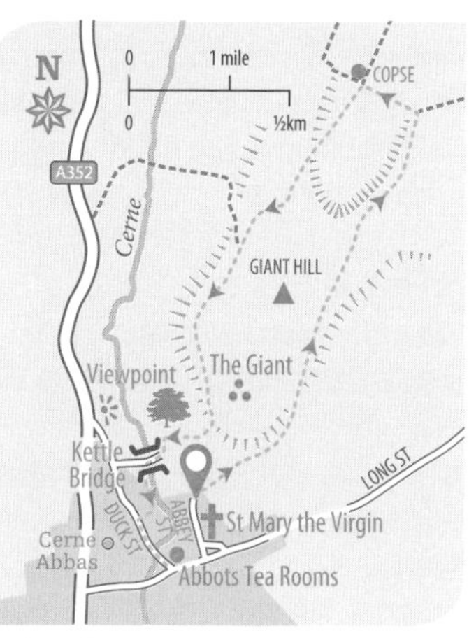

The best views of the giant are from the viewpoint on the A352. The giant is fenced off but this walk takes you around him. The walk starts at the burial ground at the end of Abbey Street, where a gate in the wall leads into fields. Once through the gate, turn right and head around the base of the woodland, then left up the hill. The climb provides glorious views of the Cerne Valley, where buzzards are frequently seen making good use of the thermals. At the top of the hill you will cross a field, heading towards a copse, then head back to the bottom left corner of the same field. Follow the path downhill and left along the hillside from there, and you will soon be walking under the giant's feet. Drop down into some woodland on the edge of the village and follow the signs for Kettle Bridge, an adorable stone and flint bridge across the River Cerne. Cross the bridge and it is a pleasant, short walk along the river back to the village, where the Abbots Tea Rooms does a superb cream tea.

If you follow the wall on your right as you go into the burial ground you will come to **St Augustine's Well**. Also known as the Silver Well, this is another of the few relics remaining from the days of the abbey. According to legend, **St Augustine of Canterbury** (died AD604) visited Dorset and met some shepherds in the then uninhabited Cerne Valley. He asked if they would prefer beer or water to quench their thirst. When they replied 'water', the saint struck the ground with his staff and the spring started to flow. Some cynical folk have suggested that the Benedictine monks of Cerne Abbey fabricated the story to attract pilgrims.

Also on Abbey Street, the **church of St Mary the Virgin** was built by the abbey and dates from the 15th century, although the chancel is earlier, being circa 1300, and there were various additions in the 17th and 18th centuries. Opposite the church is a row of wonderfully wonky wooden houses dating from around 1500, known as the **Pitchmarket** because the farmers' would pitch their corn sacks here on market days for buyers to inspect.

Heading back towards the A352, along the road known as The Folly, it is worth taking a detour to walk along the footpath marked Barton Farm Meadows, because from the path you get a reasonable view of the **Tithe Barn**. This magnificent barn dates from the 14th century and was probably much longer than the building you see today. It is now a private house and not open to the public.

FOOD & DRINK

Abbots Tea Rooms 7 Long St, DT2 7JF ✆ 01300 341349 www.abbotsbedandbreakfast.co.uk ⏲ Easter–Oct daily 10.00–16.30. Quaint, licensed tea rooms in the centre of the village with a tea garden. Breakfast, lunch and afternoon tea are carefully homemade by owner Nicola, including the excellent scones. The best-value lunch option in the village, and plenty of choice on the menu. Keep an eye out for their evening events.

New Inn 14 Long St, DT2 7JF ✆ 01300 341274 www.newinncerneabbas.com ⏲ daily for lunch & dinner, but with a bar menu only on Sun evenings. The restaurant within this 16th-century coaching inn is full of beams and character, and specialises in local fish and game prepared to a high standard. Easily the most expensive option in town.

Royal Oak 23 Long St, DT2 7JG ✆ 01300 341797 ⏲ daily. This ivy-covered freehouse dates from 1540 and serves traditional pub food.

10 MINTERNE MAGNA

As you travel north from Cerne Abbas towards Sherborne on the A352, you pass through the pretty village of Minterne Magna. The church here, **St Andrew's**, is based on an original Saxon church now incorporated into the chancel. The nave and chancel were built in the early 15th century, while the north chapel was added between 1610 and 1620. Next door to the church is the entrance to **Minterne Gardens** (see below).

Minterne Gardens

DT2 7AU ✆ 01300 341370 www.minterne.co.uk ⏲ garden: Mar–Nov 10.00–18.00

Although the house is only open by appointment, visitors can walk around the impressive garden of this private home. You will need to leave your car in the car park opposite St Andrew's Church and walk across the road to enter the grounds, which were landscaped in the 18th century in the manner of Capability Brown. The owner at that time, Robert

Digby, reportedly used to visit the family home at Sherborne Castle whenever Brown was working there and pick his brain for ideas. Keen gardeners will enjoy walking the 1½ miles of paths, which wind through the garden and criss-cross the stream. Himalayan rhododendrons and azaleas feature heavily in the design, so it is particularly colourful from March to June. In April and May, bluebells and wild garlic add soft colour and a woodland perfume. The garden's appeal is greatly enhanced by its location, in a wide valley where sheep graze nonchalantly below a band of woodland.

THE PIDDLE VALLEY & BERE REGIS

The River Piddle (also known far less amusingly as the River Trent) rises near the church in the village of Alton Pancras and flows towards Wareham, entering the sea at Poole Harbour along with the River Frome. The name Piddle is thought to derive from the Saxon, meaning clear water. Many of the villages it passes through are named after the river, creating some of the best village names in existence: Puddletown, Tolpuddle, Piddlehinton, Piddletrenthide, Affpuddle, Briantspuddle and Turnerspuddle. All but two of those names now contain 'puddle' rather than 'piddle'. The reason for that is up for debate. A popular story tells that the villages were renamed prior to a visit by Queen Victoria to avoid offending her sensibilities but there is no firm evidence of this. A more prosaic theory is that the names were altered in response to a request from the post office.

"The River Piddle rises near the church in the village of Alton Pancras and flows towards Wareham, entering the sea at Poole Harbour along with the River Frome."

11 BADGER & WILDLIFE NIGHT WATCH & HENLEY HILLBILLIES

Old Henley Farm, DT2 7BL ☎ 01300 345293, 07860 759996 🖱 www.badgerwatchdorset.co.uk, 🖱 www.henleyhillbillies.co.uk; booking essential

This farm in Henley, a tiny hamlet between Buckland Newton and Alton Pancras on the B3143, is a hugely rewarding place for anyone interested in wildlife to spend an evening. The viewing of the badgers is from two hides (each can take up to 12 people) positioned in front of the farm's badger setts. You arrive at 18.15 for an 18.30 start, which means you

THE ART OF THATCHING

With Edward Taylor, Master Thatcher

01297 489528, 07966 209561 www.thatching.biz

A thatched cottage with a rose wandering around the door is one of the quintessential images of English rural living, and with chocolate-box cottages around every Dorset corner thatch is very much part of the landscape and culture.

Thatching is one of the oldest ways of protecting houses from the elements, and in Britain is believed to date back to the Bronze Age. Not all of the thatched properties you see in Dorset are old, however: many new building projects include houses that are thatched in order to blend in with the surroundings and clear the planning authorities.

Dorset master thatcher, Edward Taylor, more commonly known as 'Spike', has been working in the thatching trade ever since he left school. Before he could call himself qualified, he had to complete a seven-year apprenticeship. According to Spike, the ancient craft takes this long to learn because numerous styles, techniques and materials are used – styles which also vary from county to county.

Spike works mainly with combed wheat reed and water reed. Today, much of the water reed used in England is imported from countries where it is cheaper to produce, but local alternatives can be found. Spike grows several varieties of thatching straw, which can be seen on the roofs he creates. Reed is still cut at Abbotsbury and used on the Ilchester Estate buildings, including the 14th-century Tithe Barn, which is by far the largest thatched building in the area. It is fascinating to think that the barn must have been re-thatched by many hands over the centuries yet always with reeds from the same stretch of land.

Spike explained to me that thatching wheat is cut with a reaper/binder and the sheaves (bundles) are 'stooked' up in the fields. It is at this point that I began to realise thatching has its own language of ancient technical terms, so Spike had to translate – eight sheaves make

have a good chance of seeing the shy creatures in daylight. The evening I went was warm and sunny – lovely weather for badgers and even better for badger watchers. We only had to wait about 20 minutes before the first badger appeared from the hedgerow. She poked her head out and cautiously sniffed the air, then waddled down towards the hide, where she snuffled around in the grass, just a few yards from us, hoovering up tasty morsels. At one point she appeared to be having a battle with a particularly stubborn worm as she dug in her heels and tugged tenaciously on what looked like a piece of elastic; it finally gave way

"We saw four or five different badgers merrily going about their business."

a stook, 16 make a stock. The sheaves are left in the stook for two weeks to dry slowly and evenly, and are then put into the rick before going on the threshing machine or reed comber. Here, the short straws, leaf and flag are combed out and the grain and chaff removed. The long stems are kept perfectly straight. Finally, the straw is trussed up and bundled, ready to use.

Laying the thatch is tough physical work and often a battle with the elements. The primary tool is a legget, which is used to coerce the material into position, a process known as 'dressing'. A 'spar', a branch of split hazel wood tapered to a point at each end and twisted into a V shape, is used to staple the thatch into place. Each course overlaps the one below it, providing a continuous depth of straw over the entire roof. The ridge is where the thatcher can really leave his mark; Spike favours the traditional pointed end, which has been used for centuries.

Most of Spike's tools have been made by local blacksmiths and his legget heads cast at Bridport Foundry. He scours the antique farm machinery section at country fairs, looking for the original tools of his trade, now prized above some of the newer versions. He even coppices his own hazel, to make traditional fixings for the thatch – spars, ledgers, liggers and sways.

Spike points out that qualifying and working as a master thatcher is not for the faint-hearted: the few men who carry on this ancient craft do so for the love of it and are fiercely proud.

While we all love the look of a thatched roof, people are divided as to whether they would want to live under one. Beauty doesn't come cheap: the roof needs to be re-thatched about every 25 years and the ridge needs to be replaced around every ten years. Depending on the roof and the materials used re-thatching can cost around £25,000; on top of that there is usually an insurance premium because of a perceived fire risk. Thankfully, the undeniable charm of a thatched roof means that they will remain part of the rural landscape, just as they have for the past 4,500 years.

and she staggered backwards with her reward. Throughout the evening we saw four or five different badgers merrily going about their business, oblivious that they were taking part in a thrilling reality show for the viewers within the hide. As darkness fell, soft lights came on under the hides allowing us to continue watching the wildlife. We saw rabbits (of course) and bats, and the sightings book in the hide showed that previous visitors had also seen foxes, deer and barn owls.

As well as badger watching, Old Henley Farm offers daytime activities which are more 'Extreme Dorset' than 'Slow Dorset'. Thrill seekers can career around a track on quad bikes, mini maveriks and hovercrafts. Clay shooting, air-rifle shooting and crossbows are also on offer.

12 PIDDLETRENTHIDE & PIDDLEHINTON

Piddletrenthide and its neighbour Piddlehinton are largely made up of stone and flint-banded cottages. Stretched along the river valley and the B3143, **Piddletrenthide** gets its memorable name from the fact that it is on the River Piddle and was assessed for 30 hides in the Domesday Book. A hide was a unit used to measure land value in order to calculate tax, and was originally the amount of land that could be ploughed in a year using one plough and an eight-ox team. The area thus varied with soil quality and a 'hide' could range from 60 to 180 acres. Piddletrenthide has a good village shop and, at the northern end of the village, a fine **church** with a splendid tower dated 1487.

"Piddletrenthide is on the River Piddle and was assessed for 30 hides in the Domesday Book."

The name of the river was a marketing gem waiting to be exploited. In 2002, a micro-brewery was set up in Piddlehinton, the **Piddle Brewery** (www. piddlebrewery.co.uk), which now markets a series of beers with names like Piddle in a Bottle, Jimmy Riddle and Silent Slasher. You will see their beers in pubs and shops throughout the county.

FOOD & DRINK

The Blue Vinny Puddletown DT2 8TE 01305 848228 www.thebluevinny.co.uk. Mon–Sat for lunch & dinner, Sun for lunch. The clean, fresh interior bodes well and the food doesn't disappoint. Head chef Anthony Riley loves to experiment so you will see some daring creations on the menu, which is extensive and includes vegetarian and gluten-free options. The kitchen takes pride in the way the food is presented, so it looks expensive but is in fact reasonably priced. Reservation recommended.

Poachers Inn Piddletrenthide DT2 7QX 01300 348358 daily for breakfast, lunch & dinner. A large 17th-century pub on the B3143, which serves unpretentious meals. It is right on the road but has a riverside garden behind.

13 ATHELHAMPTON HOUSE & GARDENS

River Cottage at Athelhampton (page 296)

Athelhampton DT2 7LG 01305 848363 www.athelhampton.co.uk Mar–Oct Sun–Thu 10.30–17.00, Nov–Feb Sun 11.00–dusk

Thomas Hardy was a frequent visitor to this beautiful manor house dating from the 15th century, and he referred to it in his writings as 'Athelhall'. Today, the owners live in the Edwardian extension and open the oldest parts of the house to the public.

A carved stone monkey wearing a chain sits above the front door, and he makes appearances throughout the house, including in its stained-glass windows. He is also said to make ghostly appearances. The story goes that he lived as a pet in the hall in the 15th century but was accidentally imprisoned in a secret passage, starved to death and has haunted the house ever since.

> *"A carved stone monkey wearing a chain sits above the front door."*

The oak-panelled Great Hall was built in 1485. Hidden in the panels next to the large fireplace is a Tudor doggy door, and if you ask nicely the guides will show it to you. After the household had finished eating, the dogs would be let in from the wine cellar to clean up the leftovers in the dining hall. On the second floor is a gallery displaying the work of the artist Marevna, who lived at the house from 1948 to 1957.

Visitors are free to wander the delightful Grade I-listed gardens surrounding the house. Largely laid down in the late 19th century, they feature perfect topiary pyramids and colourful herbaceous borders. Highlights include a supremely photogenic 15th-century dovecote and a 19th-century toll house.

There is a good restaurant open for lunch, morning and afternoon tea (see below), and a self-catering cottage sleeping six (page 296).

FOOD & DRINK

The Restaurant at Athelhampton House Athelhampton DT2 7LG ✆ 01305 848363 www.athelhampton.co.uk ⊙ Sun–Thu 10.00–17.00. You don't need to pay the entry fee for the house to eat at the restaurant here, which is in a converted thatched stable block. The menu offers plenty of choice; the food is of a good standard, is freshly made and uses locally sourced ingredients wherever possible.

14 TOLPUDDLE

The small village of Tolpuddle has secured its place in history thanks to the actions of six farm labourers in 1834, now known as the Tolpuddle Martyrs (see box, page 121). The labourers spoke up about their intolerable poverty and took an oath of mutual support, essentially forming an early trade union. This did not go down at all well with the local landowners; the farm labourers were charged with swearing an illegal oath and were transported to Australia. Public outcry eventually led to their pardon and they returned to England.

The village has become a place of pilgrimage for its links to the trade union movement. The Trades Union Congress (TUC) holds an annual festival at Tolpuddle in honour of the martyrs on the third Sunday in July. The festival, which attracts as many as 10,000 people, culminates in a procession through the village by representatives of various trade unions, accompanied by marching bands. The festival also involves live music, speeches by prominent socialists and stalls selling local produce.

On the west side of the village are six memorial cottages built by the TUC in 1934 to commemorate the 100th anniversary of the martyrs' transportation and to provide accommodation for retired agricultural trade unionists. In the centre of these is the small **Tolpuddle Martyrs Museum** (DT2 7EH 01305 848237 www.tolpuddlemartyrs.org.uk Apr–Oct Tue–Sun & bank holidays, Nov–Mar Thu–Sun; free admission), devoted to the martyrs and the history of the trade union movement. This interesting and well laid-out little museum evolved from a library intended for residents of the cottages but which soon became a depository for artefacts, documents and memorabilia relating to the martyrs. Over the years, it developed into the Tolpuddle Martyrs Museum.

"The village has become a place of pilgrimage for its links to the trade union movement."

When I visited the museum, there was an elderly gentleman wearing a TUC cap sitting on a bench in the sunshine just outside the cottages. His name, it transpired, was Ernest (Ernie) Chaffey. Ernie and I got chatting and it turned out he lived in one of the six TUC cottages. Ernie told me proudly that in 51 years of working as a farm labourer he had only had one day unemployed, and that was a bank holiday which happened to fall between the end of one job and the start of another. Ernie explained that he had worked for over 30 years on a 3,000-acre dairy farm near Dorchester, during which time he lived in a farm worker's cottage on the estate. When he retired he had to move out of the cottage and, even after all those years of hard work, Ernie had no home of his own. He was lucky enough to be allocated one of the TUC cottages. Ernie mused, 'I suppose I could have gone into a retirement flat, but I have the wife and the dog to consider and I don't think we would have liked it. It was obvious to me that this man was not meant to be confined to a flat. Even as we spoke, I could see his eyes scanning the rolling fields and I suspect he was longing to be back in the tractor seat. We talked about farming and the changes it

THE TOLPUDDLE MARTYRS

In the 1830s life was tough for farm labourers in Dorset. Increased mechanisation of farming practices in the early part of the 19th century meant landowners became less dependent on labourers and lowered the average agricultural wage. Labourers in Dorset had traditionally been poorly paid in comparison with their counterparts in the rest of England and eventually wages in the county fell to just seven shillings a week. It became impossible for a labourer to support his family.

In 1833, a group of farm labourers from Tolpuddle made representation to their local landowners and employers for an increase in wages. This request was met by a decree that wages would be reduced further to six shillings a week.

Under the leadership of George Loveless (a respected Methodist lay preacher), some of the aggrieved labourers organised themselves into a 'Friendly Society of Agricultural Labourers', effectively an early trade union. The group would meet either under what has now become known as the 'Martyrs Tree' on the village green or in the cottage of group member John Standfield.

Local landowners, led by James Frampton of Moreton House, were determined to quash any uprising, particularly given what had happened to their French counterparts during the French Revolution.

On a cold February morning in 1834, police arrested six members of the group: George Loveless and his brother James, Thomas Standfield and his son John, James Hammett and James Brine. These men were tried at Dorchester Assizes, and found guilty of unlawful assembly and administering an illegal oath. Forming a union had been made legal in 1824, but they had made the mistake of swearing an oath which meant that they could be tried under the Mutiny Act of 1797. Sentencing them to transportation to Australia for a period of seven years, the judge noted he wanted to make an example of them. At the trial, George Loveless reportedly said: 'If we have violated any law, it was not intentionally. We have injured no person or property. We were uniting to preserve ourselves, our wives and our children from utter degradation and starvation.'

The public outcry at the martyrs' harsh treatment, driven by a fledging trade union movement, was so great that it led to pardons being granted in March 1836. It was three years before the martyrs were brought back to Dorset. During their absence, their families were sustained by the trade union movement. The martyrs returned first to Essex, where land had been set aside for them, but several later migrated to London in Ontario, Canada. The only martyr to remain in Tolpuddle was James Hammett, who returned to England a year later than the others and worked as a builder. He died in Tolpuddle in 1891 and is buried in the churchyard.

has seen in Ernie's lifetime. These days all of Ernie's agricultural attention and energy is focused on the garden at the back of the cottage, where vibrantly healthy vegetables stand to attention in neat rows.

The village of Tolpuddle has a pleasing blend of brick and cob cottages, many of them thatched. Some newer houses have been added but thankfully in a similar architectural style to the old ones, and the whole village seems well looked after. At the centre of the village is a small green, on which stands the largest sycamore in Dorset. This is the tree under which the martyrs used to meet but it seems it was there long before the martyrs came along – the National Trust has dated the tree as having started its life in the 1680s. Next to it is a thatched shelter dedicated to the martyrs, erected as part of the 100th anniversary celebrations in 1934. A new sycamore was planted in 1984 to replace the old one when the time comes.

"This is the tree under which the martyrs used to meet but it seems it was there long before the martyrs came along."

St John's Church is a striking stone and flint building. Although the original church dates from the 12th century it has been altered and restored over the years, most significantly in 1855. In the graveyard is the grave of the only one of the Tolpuddle Martyrs who returned to live in the village, James Hammett, who died in 1891.

FOOD & DRINK

The Martyrs Inn DT2 7LG 01305 848249 daily for morning tea, lunch & dinner. A Hall & Woodhouse pub serving traditional pub food. The beef comes from a farm just 5 miles away.

15 BERE REGIS

The Old Mill (page 295) **Dorset Resort** (page 296)

Bere Regis is one of those villages that used to have a main road running through it, but has now been bypassed, leaving it feeling a little lost. It is not a particularly attractive village; historically it has always been relatively poor and it doesn't feel very prosperous now, although it has managed to keep its local shop and two pubs. Much of Bere Regis was destroyed in a series of fires, the worst of which occurred in 1788, and as a result it is largely a mixture of 18th-century and more modern buildings. The one exception is the marvellous **church of St John the Baptist**, which dates from 1050.

The uninspiring approach to the church from the car park in town takes you through an estate of modern houses and does not do the church justice, but do persevere. The church bell ringers were in full swing when I visited on a sunny evening in May. A 16th-century tower in flint and stone sets an impressive note, and inside it is even better. Look up as you enter the church and you will see two large iron hooks above the door. Chair of the parish council, Ian Ventham, explained to me that they were an early fire-fighting tool. They date from around 1600 and were placed there for the men of the village to use to pull thatch from the roofs of buildings ahead of an advancing fire. The nave has a magnificent 15th-century carved oak ceiling with figures of the Apostles looking down from above. Much of the wood is painted and gilded: coin-operated lights highlight the ceiling to bring out its colours and detail. The central bosses depict Cardinal Morton, his shield of arms, a Tudor rose and a golden cord, symbolising the marriage he arranged between Henry VII and Elizabeth of York in 1486, so ending the Wars of the Roses. A small amount of the 1050 church survives at the northeast end of the nave. Just inside the door at the edge of the nave are 12th-century capitals with some curious carvings: the head of a monkey, a king and two people apparently with toothache.

There is a slab in the floor over the entrance to the Turberville vault, which reads '1710 Door of the sepulchre of the ancient family of the Turbervilles'. The manor house at Bere Regis was the home of the Turberville family from the 13th century to the 18th century, when that branch of the family became extinct. It was the fall of the powerful Turbervilles which inspired Thomas Hardy's *Tess of the d'Urbervilles* and Bere Regis featured in the novel as 'Kingsbere'.

While you are in the church look out for the Bere Regis funeral bier – the September 1898 model. A sign tells that it could be hired as a burial board by Bere for 2/6d, Kingston for 5/- and other parishes for 10/-; that's respectively 12½p, 25p and 50p in today's money.

In the churchyard, some of the older graves of interest are marked with numbers and boards clarifying their worn lettering. Particularly moving, and apt for the Bere Regis/Shitterton area, is the grave marked number five. According to the inscription on the small headstone Thomas Fry was 'killed by the over-thro of a dung cart June ye 12th 1722 in ye 11th year of his age'.

FOOD & DRINK

Drax Arms West St, BH20 7HH ✆ 01929 471386 ⏲ daily for breakfast, lunch & dinner. Traditional pub in the centre of Bere Regis, popular with locals. Reservation recommended.
Pampered Pigs Rye Hill Farm Rye Hill BH20 7LP ✆ 01929 472327 ⏲ Tue–Sat 09.00–17.00,

Sun 09.30–15.00. Animal welfare is a priority for this free-range farm, which raises traditional breeds of cattle, pigs and sheep. The meat is available in the small farm shop, which has a café corner. Several members of the family cannot eat gluten, so gluten-free items are in good supply.

Royal Oak West St, BH20 7HQ ✆ 01929 471203 ⏲ Mon–Sat for lunch & dinner, Sun for lunch. A 16th-century coaching inn serving decent pub food in the pleasant bar area, beer garden or courtyard. Good vegetarian options.

16 SHITTERTON

You won't be surprised to hear that the hamlet of Shitterton, which adjoins Bere Regis, is best known for its name, which appeals greatly to those with a fondness for lavatory humour and ranks at number nine in *Rude Britain: The 100 Rudest Place Names in Britain.* While some prudish folk leave out the 'h', many of the residents are proud to tell you precisely where they live and even emphasise the 'sh'. In a broad Dorset accent, the name has even more of a ring to it.

The most irritating thing about living in Shitterton was, until fairly recently, the lack of a road sign, which played havoc with home deliveries. Due to frequent theft of Shitterton's sign by souvenir hunters, the council gave up replacing it. In July 2010, after nearly three years without a sign, residents, led by chair of the parish council, Ian Ventham, banded together to purchase a slab of Purbeck stone and have it engraved. Of some 50 Shitterton households, well over half contributed and the local council chipped in too. It would take a highly committed souvenir hunter to make off with the 1½-ton stone slab, which now announces, rather grandly, the hamlet's name. In 2012, to commemorate the diamond jubilee of Queen Elizabeth II, Ian arranged for similar stones to be carved and placed at the three entrances to Bere Regis, also funded by local donations.

Shitterton is far more comely than its name may indicate. It was protected by the Bere River from the fires that destroyed Bere Regis, so still retains some older, mostly thatched buildings. A pretty stream runs through Shitterton, although it loses some of its charm when you learn the origin of the hamlet's name, which apparently means stream used as a midden, in other words a dung heap.

Just one narrow no-through lane runs through Shitterton, but if you venture down it you may see a blackboard towards the end of the lane, advertising Di's homemade jams for sale. They are delicious, and home-produced honey and eggs are also available here.

THE FROME VALLEY

17 MORETON

The small village of Moreton is firmly on the Lawrence of Arabia trail, for it was in **St Nicholas's Church** that Lawrence's funeral took place on the afternoon of 21 May 1935. It was well attended, including by Sir Winston Churchill, Robert Graves and Siegfried Sassoon. Lawrence is buried in the cemetery to the south of the village; his grave is at the far end on the right. The headstone records Lawrence's real name, although he had changed his name by deed poll to T E Shaw in 1923 to escape his celebrity status (see box, pages 126–7).

Regardless of its connections to Lawrence of Arabia, St Nicholas's Church is fascinating. The original church was demolished in 1776 and replaced by a Georgian, Gothic building, thanks to the Frampton family (cousins of T E Lawrence), who lived in Moreton House behind the church.

"The small village of Moreton is firmly on the Lawrence of Arabia trail, for it was in St Nicholas's Church that Lawrence's funeral took place."

The church's best-known feature is its unusual engraved windows by Laurence Whistler. The windows were installed in 1955 and 1974–84. A German bomb destroyed the original stained-glass windows on 8 October 1940, along with the north wall of the church. The theme of the replacement windows is light: one depicts candles, another lightning, one the sun, and the effect of the clear glass is striking. You are so accustomed to not being able to see the view from a church, yet this one allows you to enjoy the sky and trees outside and allows light to flood in. Near the church in a charming former schoolhouse with latticed windows is Moreton Tea Rooms, a convenient lunch or tea stop.

FOOD & DRINK

Moreton Tea Rooms 01929 463647 www.moretontearooms.co.uk Tue–Sun 10.00–17.00. The carefully co-ordinated rustic chic interior of this former schoolhouse hints at the fact this is far more than your average tea rooms, and displays on the life of T E Lawrence are reminders of the area's claim to fame. The menu is extensive and creative, with local produce at its heart. You can expect tasty lunch dishes, such as local game stew, and a tempting array of cakes, all prepared on site. There is a warming fire in winter and a large outdoor walled patio area for warmer days.

18 CLOUDS HILL

Near Wareham BH20 7NQ ✆ 01929 405616 ⏲ Mar–Oct Wed–Sun; National Trust

This unassuming former forester's cottage is where T E Lawrence (Lawrence of Arabia; see box, below) lived between 1923 and 1935 as T E Shaw.

Lawrence first rented the cottage in 1923 while stationed at Bovington Camp with the Tank Corps, and bought it in 1925 from his cousins, the Framptons, the landlords of the Moreton Estate. It was here that Lawrence completed *Seven Pillars of Wisdom* and *The Mint*.

The interior has been recreated to appear as it was when Lawrence lived there. The house is deliberately spartan – Lawrence wrote: 'Nothing in Clouds Hill is to be a care upon the world. While I have it there shall be nothing exquisite or unique in it. Nothing to anchor me.' The cottage served as Lawrence's retreat, where he read, wrote and listened to music, so it is fitting that his collection of music and books remains. An exhibition provides further insight into Lawrence's extraordinary life.

In 1935, Lawrence left the RAF and retired to Clouds Hill. A few months later, at the age of 46, he was involved in a fatal accident on his Brough Superior motorcycle close to the house.

LAWRENCE OF ARABIA

Thomas Edward Lawrence, also known as Lawrence of Arabia, was born in Wales on 16 August 1888. From the age of eight he lived in Oxford, where he later read modern history at Jesus College.

In 1911, Lawrence worked as an archaeologist in Syria, where he gained knowledge of the Arab culture and language. He made several further trips to the Middle East until the outbreak of World War I.

In 1914, he joined the British Army and was posted to Military Intelligence in Cairo. In June 1916, he was sent to investigate the Arab revolt in the Hejaz, where he formed a bond with the local Arab leader, Amir Feisal. Feisal's troops were committed but ill-disciplined and Lawrence planned to harness their passion by focusing on guerrilla tactics to disrupt the Turkish Army's activities. He led Bedouin tribesmen in guerrilla raids against the Turkish Army, which eventually contributed to British and Arab forces taking Damascus. Lawrence lived the life of a Bedouin, eating what they ate, wearing Arab dress and riding a camel, which earned him an almost mythical status among the Arabs who fought with him.

He returned to Britain in 1918 as Colonel Lawrence and lobbied unsuccessfully for Arab independence. Lawrence attempted to escape from the public eye by changing his identity and in 1922 enlisted in the RAF as Aircraftman Ross. His alias was

9 BOVINGTON TANK MUSEUM

Bovington BH20 6JG ✆ 01929 462359 www.tankmuseum.org ⏲ daily 10.00–17.00

The tank museum adjoins Bovington Camp, home of the British Army's Armour Centre. As the name indicates, the museum tells the story of the tank from its invention in 1915 to the present day. The first thing to strike you about this museum is its size – it is vast. You will need to allow at least three hours to get around. A useful large café overlooks the arena.

The collection of tanks is one of the biggest and most varied in the world. It was Rudyard Kipling who pressed for the creation of a museum after a visit to Bovington in 1923, when it held a small selection of tanks that had survived World War I. The museum was opened to the public in 1947.

Almost 300 vehicles from 26 countries are on display, each with a story to tell. They include 'Little Willie', the first tracked vehicle, which was developed in 1915 by the Landships Committee, which had been established by First Lord of the Admiralty, Winston Churchill, to tackle the problems of trench warfare.

The World War I trench experience is particularly moving, taking you from the recruiting office to the front line in the boots of a young soldier.

---

soon discovered and he was forced out of the RAF.

In 1923, as T E Shaw, he joined the Tank Corps and was stationed at Bovington Camp. He didn't much care for army life and purchased nearby Clouds Hill as a retreat. In 1925, Lawrence rejoined the RAF, and after a spell in Karachi, was posted to Plymouth, where he lobbied successfully for faster rescue boats. He spent the rest of his career developing and testing high-speed rescue boats, which formed the basis of the air-sea rescue service.

Lawrence retired to Clouds Hill in 1935, where, only a few months later, he was involved in a serious collision on his Brough Superior motorcycle. He died six days later in the military hospital at Bovington Camp. Lawrence's mother arranged for his body to be buried at Moreton Church, in the family plot belonging to his cousins, the Framptons of Moreton House.

You can walk the 6¾-mile 'Lawrence of Arabia Trail' tracing his life in the area. It starts at the Bovington Tank Museum and takes in Clouds Hill and Moreton. A leaflet on the trail is available from local tourist information centres (such as Wareham) and online (www.dorsetforyou.com, look under 'walking in Purbeck'). If you want to know more but don't fancy the walk, Wareham Town Museum (page 219) has a display devoted to Lawrence, as does the Moreton Tea Rooms (page 125).

When I visited I was lucky enough to see the Battlegroup Afghanistan exhibition revealing the work of the Royal Armoured Corps in that area. The reconstruction of a forward operating base provides an insight into what life is like for troops on the front line. Installed for the centenary of World War I is the new Warhorse to Horsepower exhibition, which looks at the rise of the tank and the role of the cavalry.

On weekdays during the school summer holidays (and at some other specific times) live tank displays take place on the Kuwait Arena and are a big hit with children. Tank experience days are available and involve riding in a tank and driving an armoured personnel carrier.

20 MONKEY WORLD – APE RESCUE CENTRE

Near Wool BH20 6HH 01929 462537 www.monkeyworld.org daily except Christmas Day; see advert in fourth colour section

In a 65-acre park between Bere Regis and Wool live some unlikely Dorset residents: over 250 rescued and endangered apes and monkeys call Monkey World home. As well as making a perfect day out for children and adults, this is first and foremost a rescue centre and every one of the animals at Monkey World is there because it needs to be. The centre has about 60 chimpanzees living in four social groups, plus orang-utans, woolly monkeys, squirrel monkeys, capuchins and more. One of the highlights for visitors is a walk-through **lemur enclosure**, which allows you to get up close to these curious creatures.

"In a 65-acre park between Bere Regis and Wool live some unlikely Dorset residents: over 250 rescued and endangered apes and monkeys call Monkey World home."

New Yorker Jim Cronin started the rescue centre in 1987, on the site of a derelict pig farm near Wool. There was a good degree of scepticism in the local community and beyond, but Jim had a vision and the energy and enthusiasm to bring it to life. He met his wife Alison when she visited in 1992. She had a background in biological anthropology and animal behaviour, and had been working on the rescue of bears. Jim and Alison married in 1996 and, together with Jim's right-hand man, Jeremy Keeling, continued to rescue primates. Their work and the centre drew international acclaim and touched a wide audience through the television programmes *Monkey Business* and *Monkey Life*. Sadly, Jim died suddenly of cancer in 2007 at the age of 55, a year after he and Alison were awarded

NEOLITHIC DORSET

All around are reminders that Dorset has been inhabited for thousands of years. Its ancient hillforts, such as at Hambledon (pictured here), Hod Hill, Maiden Castle and Badbury Rings make for splendid walks.

DAVID CROSBIE/S

ALEXANDRA RICHARDS

DORSET BY THE WATER

The Jurassic Coast, England's first natural World Heritage site, captures 190 million years of history in 95 miles and offers fine fossil-hunting. The South West Coast Path features spectacular scenery and the county's peaceful rivers are perfect for messing about in boats.

STOCKER1970/S

ALEXANDRA RICHARDS

NEAL SULLIVAN

IAN WOOLCOCK/S

HELEN HOTSON/S

DAVID CROSBIE/S

ALEXANDRA RICHARDS

WILLOW DEMPSEY/S

ALEXANDRA RICHARDS

1 Golden Cap is the highest point on England's south coast. **2** Boat hire at West Bay. **3** Colourful beach huts at Hengistbury Head. **4** Fossil-hunting on the Jurassic Coast. **5** The beach at Lyme Regis. **6** The chalk stacks known as Old Harry Rocks. **7** Weymouth has been a seaside resort for hundreds of years. **8** The lighthouse at Portland Bill guides vessels through the strong currents. **9** Walking the South West Coast Path. **10** Worbarrow Bay near Tyneham is only accessible on foot.

NEAL SULLIVAN

RURAL SKILLS & CRAFTS

Traditional rural skills have played an important part in moulding the Dorset you see today. They are still valued in the county and many are taught – try your hand at foraging, woodworking, coppicing, hedge-laying, blacksmithing, stone carving and more.

1 Roofs are re-thatched around every 25 years. 2 Chester Jefferies gloves are handmade in Gillingham. 3 Dorset folk have been managing woodland through coppicing for hundreds of years. 4 Tout Quarry is one of several on the Isle of Portland.

IN2THELIGHT PHOTOGRAPHY/CHESTER JEFFERIES

ALEXANDRA RICHARDS

ALEXANDRA RICHARDS

the MBE for services to animal welfare. Alison, Jeremy and their team continue the centre's valuable work and the realisation of Jim's vision.

Monkey World was one of the world's first primate rescue centres. Initially its mission was to provide homes for chimpanzees rescued from a miserable life as props for beach photographers in Spain. By necessity, that mission expanded to rescuing primates from circuses, laboratories and the entertainment industry worldwide. Monkey World now works to assist governments around the world to stop the smuggling and mistreatment of primates. The centre also runs important captive-breeding programmes for endangered species, including orang-utans, golden-cheeked gibbons and woolly monkeys.

In January 2008, Monkey World completed the largest primate rescue in history, when 88 capuchin monkeys were rescued from a medical research laboratory in Santiago, Chile. They had been living in solitary confinement in small cages, some for as long as 20 years.

Like the capuchins, many of the rescued primates who arrive at Monkey World have been kept in unnatural conditions, neglected or suffered cruel treatment. They arrive in poor condition, with physical and psychological problems. As you wander around Monkey World, it is a joy to see the rehabilitated animals living in large enclosures with plenty of stimulation and good company. Watching the antics of Monkey World's primates is bound to bring a smile to any visitor's face. The keepers are a devoted bunch, and hold regular, informative talks. Guided tours are available by appointment and you can even get married here.

"It is a joy to see the rehabilitated animals living in large enclosures with plenty of stimulation."

Monkey World does not receive government funding: it depends on donations and funds raised by opening the rescue centre to the public. By visiting you are helping to support the valuable work conducted here. If you are as moved by the centre's animals as I was, you may wish to consider primate adoption. In exchange for a small fee, you can 'adopt' a particular primate. Monkey World will send you a photograph of your chosen primate, an adoption certificate, three editions of the centre's newsletter and you will receive free entry for a year. Adoption also makes a great gift – I gave my mother adoption of a young orang-utan and she was delighted. (I suppose that makes the orang-utan my stepbrother!) Further details are available on Monkey World's website.

BULBARROW HILL, MILTON ABBAS & SURROUNDS

At 902 feet, **Bulbarrow Hill** is the third-highest point in Dorset and affords far-reaching views over the Blackmore Vale and towards Somerset. It can be reached on foot from the much-photographed village of **Milton Abbas**, passing Milton Abbey School *en route*.

21 BULBARROW HILL & WOOLLAND HILL

At any time of year the views from Bulbarrow and Woolland Hill are breathtaking. Up here you can see five counties, namely Dorset, Somerset, Wiltshire, Hampshire and Devon. Standing out on the horizon are King Alfred's Tower near Stourhead in Wiltshire and Duncliffe Hill (page 47). In summer the patchwork fields of the Blackmore Vale are every shade of green and yellow, while in winter the bare trees stand like skeletons silhouetted against a frosty backdrop. They are views which have been delighting visitors for hundreds of years, at least. Renowned Dorset historian, Reverend John Hutchins, described the view from Bulbarrow as 'surpassing imagination'. In his *Highways and Byways in Dorset*,

OXFORD SANDY & BLACK PIGS AT ANSTY

Broadclose, Ansty DT2 7PN ✆ 01258 880143

When David Norman and his wife Jenny started breeding Oxford Sandy and Black pigs in the late 1990s there were only around a hundred of these animals in existence. Like many native breeds they were dangerously close to extinction. The Oxford Sandy and Black is one of the oldest British breeds and, David told me, it was saved by the perseverance and sheer bloody-mindedness of a few individuals who formed a breed society in 1985. David is the breed's British Pig Association representative.

David explained that the exact origin of the breed is unknown but it is believed to have developed some two centuries ago in Oxfordshire. Oxford Sandy and Blacks are an excellent multi-purpose pig producing succulent pork, bacon and ham. Some of David and Jenny's prize-winning herd are bred to end up as hog roasts and sausages. A firm favourite for those who are lucky enough to have tasted the sausages is the pork and marmalade variety.

David and Jenny sell most of their sausages by word of mouth from their home next to the Fox Inn at Ansty: if you would like to try some, contact them at the above address.

Sir Frederick Treves (1853–1923) poetically portrayed it as a waving valley of green fields stretching for miles, 'with trees in lines, in knolls, in avenues, in dots; a red roof, the glitter of a trout stream, the trail of a white road, and at the end blue-grey hills so far away that they seem to be made of sea mist'.

Ever popular with paragliders and model aircraft enthusiasts, **Bulbarrow Hill** has on its promontory Rawlsbury Camp, an Iron Age hillfort with discernable traces of its twin embankments. Also on the summit are two tall masts which served as radio location posts during World War II. As one of Dorset's grandest viewpoints, this makes a highly rewarding objective for walks; the well-signposted Wessex Ridgeway runs along the road between Bulbarrow Hill and Ibberton Hill.

There is a car park and local nature reserve at nearby **Woolland Hill**, one of the largest remaining fragments of chalk heath in Dorset at over ten acres. This rare habitat enables acid-loving plants, such as heather, to grow in an alkaline area. Profuse bird and butterfly life includes stonechats and meadow brown butterflies.

22 MILTON ABBAS & MILTON ABBEY

Fox Inn Ansty (page 295)

Milton Abbas is typically described with a combination of overused phrases, including 'chocolate-box' and 'picture-postcard'. With its two neat rows of pleasingly uniform white cob thatched cottages on either side of a wide road, it is hard to imagine a village more deserving of those descriptions. It did not evolve but was deliberately planned in the 18th century as an estate village for the nearby Abbey House. The cottages were designed to house two families and there was a good deal of overcrowding and poverty. Most of them have since been converted to single dwellings. Some house names point to the identity of their original inhabitants: baker, blacksmith and brewer. On the main street there is also a pub, almshouses, a post office and a church. The almshouses, dated 1674, were moved from the original estate village of Middleton.

The Benedictine Abbey at Milton Abbas was founded circa AD934 by King Athelstan, grandson of Alfred the Great, and became one of the richest in the West Country with estates of over 14,000 acres. Following the Dissolution of the Monasteries in 1539 the abbey was sold. In 1752, it was bought by Joseph Damer (Lord Milton and later Earl of Dorchester). Damer demolished many of the monastic buildings and built a grand Gothic mansion, **Abbey House**, adjacent to the abbey church.

Damer drafted in famed landscape designer Capability Brown to design gardens worthy of his new home. Damer and Brown felt that the town of Middleton was spoiling the view from the big house, so Damer set about demolishing it in order to replace it with an ornamental lake. The only obstacle was what to do with the townspeople, but Damer found a straightforward solution. He commissioned the building of one of the first model villages in order to house the displaced Middletonians.

CIDER BY ROSIE

www.ciderbyrosie.co.uk

If you see bottles of Cider by Rosie in the shops you may be tempted to assume, like I did, that the name (playing on the title of the Laurie Lee book) and the label with its cartoon drawing of a cheery, rosy-cheeked woman in an orchard next to a thatched cottage are just clever marketing. For once, that is not the case. This craft cider is lovingly made by Rose Grant ('Rosie') from apples grown in her own orchard in the small village of Winterborne Houghton. And, yes, she does live in a beautiful thatched cottage (with a fabulously colourful garden), just like the one on the label.

Now in her seventies, Rose has been making cider and selling it commercially since 2003. Essentially it was a retirement project that snowballed – 'it enlivens my retirement', Rose told me. Cider by Rosie is sold in pubs, farm shops and markets around Dorset. It is a true craft cider, with nothing added, not even sugar or water: the drink is simply the result of the natural fermentation process.

To make her cider, Rose uses over 20 varieties of apples gathered over a whole season from her orchard and others around Dorset. According to Rose, the blend of the correct apple varieties is vital to producing a good-quality cider. The apples are harvested between September and December and pressing takes place from November to January in the former farm buildings at her cottage. There is around a ten-week window of intense work during some of the coldest months of the year. I asked Rose if she hires any help: 'I have had young men come and help but they usually only last a few days because it is such hard work.' Even more amazing is that not only does Rose produce the cider almost single-handedly, she delivers it to the pubs herself. 'If I was completely retired I would just potter about at home reading and gardening. Making, selling and delivering cider gives me a chance to get out and visit the pubs and see the beautiful Dorset countryside at the same time.'

Rose is passionate about orchards and traditional cider-making and she has made it her mission to bring real cider back to Dorset. The demise of cider-making began when cider ceased to be used as payment for farm workers: many orchards were ripped up and replaced with more profitable beef and cereal crops. Somerset however, where Rose spent her teenage years, never lost its cider-making

After all, they would still be needed to run the house and the estate. Capability Brown assisted with the design of the new village and Milton Abbas was built in 1780, just one mile from the original town of Middleton. When the last residents of Middleton refused to leave the town, Damer opened the sluice gates of the new dam and flooded the area. Unfortunately for Damer, one of those residents was a lawyer, who sued and won.

tradition and it was there that she was first introduced to the drink. Rose believes that a cider revival is well under way, 'all the young are drinking it – cider is the new lager', she told me. It seems Rose is right – the Bath and West Show now receives around 500 entries in its champion cider competition, a prize Rose's cider has won several times. Rose recommends cider to accompany fish and chips – it counteracts the greasiness, she says.

Rose is a retired electronic engineer, who worked both in the RAF and private industry. Her engineering background undoubtedly shapes her approach to cider-making. She uses traditional and antique machinery, which she has carefully restored, including a beautiful French apple press built in the 1920s. To assist with the physically challenging tasks and increase efficiency, Rose has erected systems of pulleys and lifts, which even she describes as Heath Robinson. The process is very precise and scientific, and I can see how it would appeal to a former engineer. According to Rose, however, it isn't just about the science; you also have to have a feel for it.

Making her own alcohol has long been a hobby for Rose. For a while she dabbled with making country wines and the odd beer and cider to compete with the chaps at work. Her cider came into its own though in 2002, the year of the Queen's Golden Jubilee. The village needed to raise money to put on a party to celebrate the milestone and various fund-raising events were organised. Rose had around 30 jars of homemade cider lurking in her utility room so put on a cheese and cider tasting to raise some funds for the party. She was delighted with how well received her cider was. It was the villagers' enthusiasm that spurred her on to increase production to a level that would allow her to sell it commercially.

The whole village has become involved in Rose's revival of the cider tradition. In May, the villagers crown the Queen of the May and bless Rose's orchard for the coming season. They carry the young queen, a teenage girl from the village, around the orchard on a throne made from a rocking chair and hazel twigs bedecked with flowers.

It is hard to imagine a better example of Slow and local produce than Rose's cider, made in the traditional way in her own home. More information, including where to buy Cider by Rosie, is available on the website.

Abbey House is now part of **Milton Abbey School**, one of Dorset's many fine private schools. It is easy to see why Damer thought it the perfect spot for a house, nestled in a natural amphitheatre of wooded hills. The lawns in front of the house make an idyllic spot for playing cricket, which is precisely what you will see the schoolboys doing on a summer's day.

Every two years the villagers hold a **fair** with an 18th-century flavour to celebrate the rebuilding of the village. The main street is closed to traffic, and residents and stallholders dress in 18th-century costume. The day includes traditional music and dancing, local craft stalls and a farmers' market.

Milton Abbey Church

You can take the estate road in to see the church. Additionally, a public footpath crosses the estate – from the bottom of Milton Abbas, walk down to the junction, turn right and the signposted path soon goes off on the left. To give it its full and rather convoluted title, the Abbey Church of St Mary, St Sampson and St Branwalader is now the chapel of Milton Abbas School and occupies a spectacular location next to the mansion with expansive views of the valley. It comprises a chancel, tower and transepts; the nave was never built and the chapels have been demolished. As it stands today it is large but were it complete it would be enormous. What remains dates largely from the 14th and 15th centuries; the original buildings were destroyed by fire in 1309 after lightning struck the spire.

"Every two years the villagers hold a fair with an 18th-century flavour to celebrate the rebuilding of the village."

Joseph Damer (page 131) married Caroline Sackville, daughter of the First Duke of Dorset. After her death in 1775 the Italian sculptor, Carlini, was commissioned to make a monument to her. In the north transept of the abbey, the white marble carving depicts Caroline Damer lying on a sofa with her grieving husband beside her.

A story that is often repeated in connection with the Abbey Church is that of John Tregonwell, son of the owner of the house, who in 1588 and aged five is reputed to have fallen 60 feet from the top of the church tower. As was customary at the time, he was wearing several petticoats, which acted as a parachute and he landed on the ground unharmed. He went on to become the High Sheriff of Dorset. Whatever the accuracy of the story, it does conjure up an intriguing image.

The **chapel of St Catherine** overlooks the Abbey Church. It was once reached by a set of grass steps leading from the garden of the house but the steps are no longer used. The chapel was part of King Athelstan's original construction, although what remains today dates largely from the 12th century and later restoration work.

FOOD & DRINK

Fox Inn Ansty DT2 7PN ✆ 01258 880328 ⊛ www.anstyfoxinn.co.uk ⊙ daily for lunch and dinner. This is a popular, well-known and dog-friendly pub near Milton Abbas. The menu here features a good selection of traditional dishes with a creative twist and there is also a carvery on Sunday.

Hambro Arms DT11 0BP ✆ 01258 880233 ⊙ daily for lunch and dinner. A traditional pub in the centre of Milton Abbas, almost camouflaged among the white thatched cottages. The restaurant and bar have plenty of character, with wooden beams and an open fire. Local and seasonal produce are used where possible.

23 THE NORTH WINTERBORNES

Referred to as the North Winterbornes to differentiate them from those southeast of Dorchester, these villages sit at the base of a valley just south of the Blackmore Vale. As their names indicate, they lie near a stream which only runs in winter: Winterborne Houghton, Winterborne Stickland, Winterborne Clenston, Winterborne Whitechurch, Winterborne Kingston, Winterborne Tomson (also known as Anderson) and Winterborne Zelston. The River Winterborne joins the River Stour near Sturminster Marshall to continue its journey to the sea at Christchurch.

All of the villages are rewarding to potter around, with a mixture of thatched cottages and more modern houses. Winterborne Whitechurch is the only one to suffer from having a main road passing through it and is larger than its relatives; the others are relatively unblemished.

Winterborne Houghton and **Winterborne Stickland** are within striking distance of Bulbarrow Hill and Woolland Hill (pages 130–1), both of which command spectacular views over the Blackmore Vale. Winterborne Houghton feels remote and almost disappears into the hill at whose base it sits. It is within a thatched cottage in this village that local character Rose Grant produces her much-loved cider (see box, pages 132–3). Winterborne Stickland is slightly larger and has managed to hold on to its post office, village shop and school.

THE DORSET RED POST

On the A31, between Bere Regis and Wimborne Minster, at Winterborne Zelston, is a distinctive, bright red signpost. It is one of three in Dorset painted that colour, the others being near Evershot and Sherborne.

The sign is believed to have been erected for the benefit of illiterate guards escorting prisoners as they were marched from Dorchester Gaol to Portsmouth for transportation to Australia.

It marked the turning to the substantial barn at Botany Bay Farm, where they would spend the night secured. The barn burnt down in the 1930s and only the base of the walls remains.

Winterborne Tomson has a strangely shaped (Norman apsidal) church, St Andrew's (DT11 9HA), which looks rather like an upturned boat. The small weatherboard belfry, resembling a dovecote, dates largely from the 12th century but has undergone various renovations along the way. The church is now in the care of the Churches Conservation Trust and is usually open to visit. Inside you will find total simplicity: whitewashed walls and 18th-century oak pews, screen and pulpit, installed by Archbishop of Canterbury, William Wake, who had grown up in the village of Shapwick. The church was saved from dereliction in the 1920s when it was carefully restored: prior to that it was being used as an outbuilding by the neighbouring farm.

FOOD & DRINK

East Farm Shop and Tea Rooms Winterborne Whitechurch DT11 9AW ✆ 01258 881398 ◷ Mar–Sep Mon, Thu–Sun 10.30–17.00. A small shop on a working farm, selling produce from the farm and surrounding area, and it also has a tea room.

THE MARSHWOOD VALE & WEST DORSET

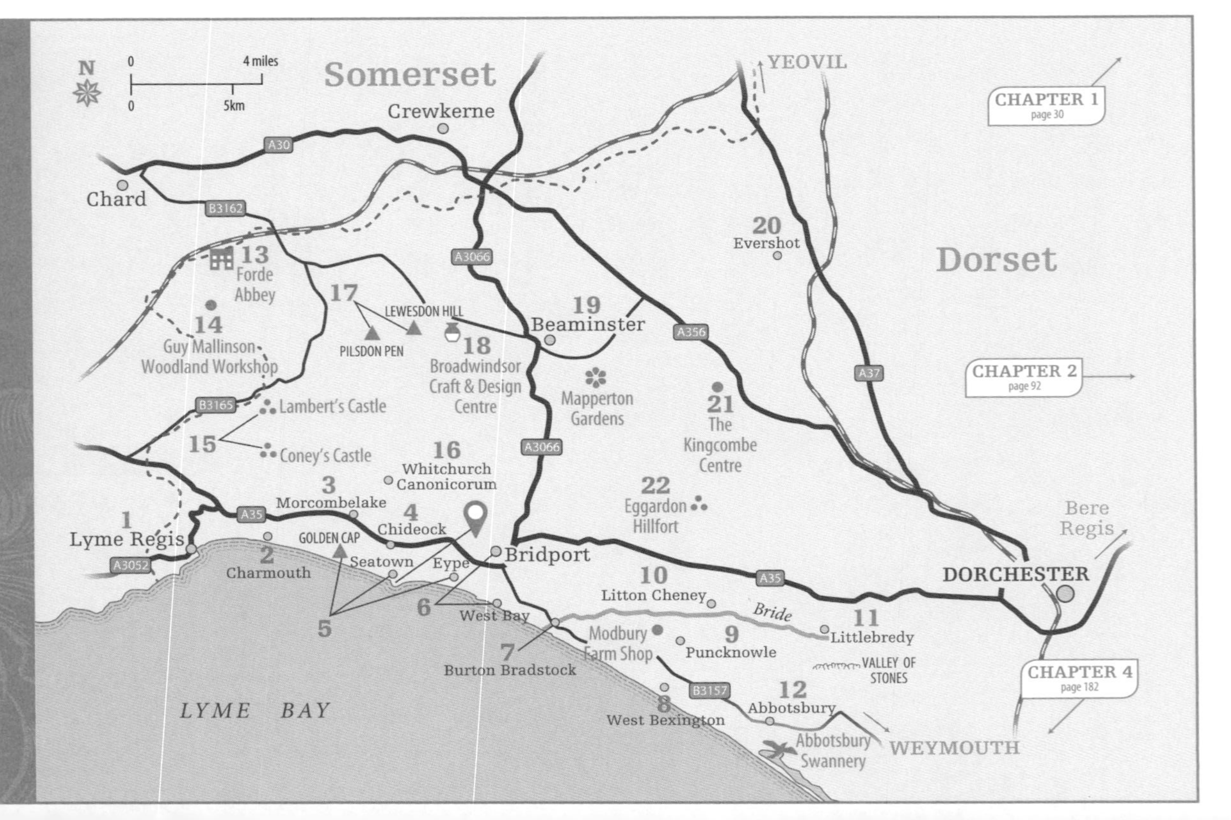

3
THE MARSHWOOD VALE & WEST DORSET

West Dorset is endowed with one of the most enticing sections of the **Jurassic Coast World Heritage Site**. The Jurassic Coast stretches 95 miles from east Devon along the Dorset coastline to Old Harry Rocks in the Isle of Purbeck and records 185 million years of the earth's history. At its heart, just inside the Dorset border, lies the supremely characterful resort of **Lyme Regis**. Lyme, as it is often known, is a popular holiday destination for its quaint buildings, sheltered beach and fossil hunting. From here you'll find a choice of excellent walks, notably a particularly beautiful stretch of the South West Coast Path which incorporates Golden Cap, the highest point on the south coast.

The market town of **Bridport** has a rich food culture and its myriad food and drink producers, farm shops and restaurants are showcased each June during the annual Bridport Food Festival. Bridport's harbour, **West Bay**, marks the start of **Chesil Beach**, a shingle bank which stretches 18 miles east to Portland and protects a natural lagoon known as **The Fleet**. The coastline between West Bexington and Abbotsbury has a rugged, untouched appeal. A journey inland through the beguiling **Bride Valley** is equally rewarding.

As you travel inland between Lyme Regis and Bridport the roads turn quickly to narrow lanes winding through farmland dotted with hamlets and villages – this is the picturesque **Marshwood Vale**. For exhilarating views over the vale and towards the coast, you can't beat a walk up **Pilsdon Pen** or **Lewesdon Hill**, the two highest points in Dorset.

The Dorset Wildlife Trust's **Kingcombe Centre** has the best-preserved lowland meadow in southern England. The centre offers courses and activities, such as beekeeping and foraging, or you can simply enjoy seeing the countryside as it would have looked years ago.

GETTING THERE & AROUND

Drivers will find the West Dorset coast easy to access, with most of the places described in this chapter easily reached from the A35, which in turn links up with the A303.

PUBLIC TRANSPORT

Local tourist information centres stock a useful leaflet entitled 'Jurassic Coast: Explore without Your Car', which suggests car-free routes.

There is no mainline train station in this part of Dorset but London Waterloo to Exeter services (South West Trains) call at Axminster in Devon, from where you can pick up a bus to Lyme Regis. Alternatively, you can get a **train** from London to Dorchester and then hop on a bus.

The **Jurassic Coast bus** (CoastLinX53) runs every two hours along the coastline between Exeter and Poole, and stops at all the key places in West Dorset, including Lyme Regis, Bridport, Burton Bradstock and Abbotsbury.

Inland, services to places described within this chapter are very limited, although there are regular buses between Bridport and Beaminster.

BY BOAT

Travelling by boat along the Jurassic Coast can give you a real appreciation of the area's geology and the multi-layered cliffs that run along the coastline. West Dorset's two harbours, Lyme Regis and West Bay, both have a slipway for public use; visiting craft are welcome but there is a long waiting list for the moorings that are let on an annual basis. Lyme Regis Sailing Club (www.lymeregissailingclub.co.uk) offers temporary membership for visitors. Further information about using the harbours is available at www.dorsetforyou.com, while general information about exploring the Jurassic Coast by boat is available at www.jurassiccoast.com.

You can take **fishing, sightseeing and diving trips** from both Lyme Regis and West Bay. Lyme Bay RIB charter (07971 258515 www.lymbayribcharter.co.uk) operates a **water taxi** between Lyme Regis and West Bay, and Jurassic Coast cruises departing from Lyme Regis. For a bit of variation you can take the CoastLinX53 bus from Lyme Regis to West Bay and then the water taxi on your return trip. The Lyme Regis Pleasure Boat Company (07765 501539) offers **self-drive hire boats** from the harbour in Lyme Regis, if you prefer to explore the coast at your own pace.

CYCLING

West Dorset offers some very special cycling country, if you don't mind a few hills. The roads along the coast can get pretty crowded in summer but at least there are no big towns or cities to negotiate.

National Cycle Network (NCN) **Route 2** covers 30 miles between Lyme Regis and Dorchester, taking you through the Marshwood Vale, around Bridport and across the Bride Valley, then close to the Hardy Monument and Maiden Castle on the approach to Dorchester. The 'Cycling in West Dorset' leaflet is available from tourist information centres and can be used in conjunction with ❊ OS Explorer maps 116 and OL15.

The **West Dorset Pedal** is a series of five shorter routes uncovering West Dorset's finest food and arts. Available from tourist information centres is a leaflet pack detailing the routes and describing eateries, farm shops, art galleries and attractions found along the way.

CYCLE HIRE

Jurassic Electric ✆ 07796 135256 🖱 www.jurassic-electric.co.uk. Offers electric bike hire, as well as guided electric bike tours.

Lyme Regis Cycles 56 Henry's Way, Lyme Regis DT7 3BW ✆ 07522 799242 🖱 www.lymeregiscycles.wix.com/lymeregiscycles

Mud, Sweat and Gears Grove Works, West Rd, Bridport DT6 5JT ✆ 01308 420586 🖱 www.mudsweatngears.co.uk

WALKING

Some long-distance trails pass through West Dorset, including the South West Coast Path and the Wessex Ridgeway. Rather lesser known is the **Dorset Jubilee Trail**, which runs 90 miles from Forde Abbey on the Somerset border across Dorset to Bokerley Dyke on the Hampshire border. The route incorporates the Iron Age hillfort of **Pilsdon Pen** for views of the Marshwood Vale, and the Dorset Wildlife Trust's reserve at the **Kingcombe Centre** (pages 179–80). A walk to the top of **Golden Cap** near Seatown will take you to the highest point on England's south coast for breathtaking views, which on a clear day can even include Dartmoor (page 157); immediately inland it's interestingly hilly enough for some hugely satisfying round walks linking up with Golden Cap itself.

One of the most rewarding areas for walking is around **Abbotsbury**, where within a few miles you can walk up on to the hillsides immediately

TOURIST INFORMATION CENTRES

General information www.westdorset.com
Guide to events in Lyme Regis www.whatsoninlyme.co.uk
Bridport South St, DT6 3NY 01308 424901
Lyme Regis Church St, DT7 3BS 01297 442138

north of the village for glorious views, and climb up the hill to St Catherine's Chapel, explore the swannery and head out to the end of Chesil Beach (which itself is painfully slow progress for walking but worth contemplating from this point).

HORSERIDING

The back of a horse is the ideal vantage point from which to appreciate the fabulous West Dorset scenery, it also allows someone else's legs to do the hard work up the hills. The Wessex Ridgeway is open to horseriders and there are memorable sections around Beaminster and the Marshwood Vale. You can download a trail guide from www.dorsetforyou.com.

RIDING STABLES

Bidlake Stables Broadoak DT6 5PY 07796 517888 www.bidlakeridingstables.co.uk. Offers lessons and hacking for all levels of experience near Bridport.
Woodhouse Farm Stables Hawkchurch, Axminster, Devon EX13 5UF 01297 639202. This stables just over the Devon border, around three miles from Lyme Regis, offers hacks for all levels of experience from one hour to a full day.

LYME REGIS TO BRIDPORT & WEST BAY

1 LYME REGIS & SURROUNDS

Dorset House (page 296)

Somehow Lyme Regis doesn't look real: with its rows of houses of every shape and size huddled together along the seafront beneath open fields and woodland, it looks more like a painting in a children's book, or perhaps a model town. You might half expect to see an oversized adult bending down peering through the windows of the cottages.

Lyme Regis snuggles up against the Dorset/Devon border, on the River Lim. The Jurassic blue-grey cliffs on either side of the town are

THE MARINE THEATRE, LYME REGIS

Hilary Bradt

Lyme's little Marine Theatre sits practically *in* the sea, and is one of the joys of this lovely town. It started life in 1806 as a seawater bath and the pumphouse, which brought water up from the sea below, is still there, incorporated into one of the dressing rooms. After a turn as a drill hall, it became the Marine Cinema, and finally in 1962 it reopened as the Marine Theatre and is now run by the Lyme Arts Community Trust.

So, a great history, but it is the people behind the scenes who make it what it is, most notably, for us Theatre Friends, the manager Nigel Day. Nigel's ability to persuade us to donate our junk to his various projects is legendary. In 2013 the bar needed to be completely redesigned; Nigel has since described it as a 'shabby-cheek [sic] make-under', and to reveal the end result would be to spoil the surprise. The first long list contained such items as 'old trunks, suitcases, tea chests etc, the older and tattier the better. Dead musical instruments, totally beyond repair. One (the left one) very very tarty high stiletto shoe (you may donate this anonymously).' And so it went on. It was almost disappointing to hear that 'The bar is fully functional again, looking great, and we've spent next to nowt, thanks to all your kind donations.' Not that the emails stopped; there were some further messages such as 'Who gave my lampshade tassels Viagra? Come on, own up. You know who you are. If you haven't a clue what I'm talking about take a look in the bar'. So take a look in the bar, you visitors to Lyme, even if you don't go to the show. It is truely amazing.

In the mix of famous names who grace the stage, the theatre staff sometimes manage to put in an unscheduled appearance. During a recent performance by Wendy Cope, the poet must have been mystified by the laughter when she read her version of *The Pied Piper of Hamelin*. At the mention of rats, a black-and-white cat walked purposefully across the stage behind her. 'Oh no!' said Nigel when I mentioned it. 'I thought I'd shut TC away'. TC stands for Theatre Cat. He's not the only TC. A recent email told us: 'As most of you will know, Mark Hix and company came in this week with the 'Crab Fest', raising over a thousand pounds towards the new roof. Fantastic and thank you Mark, but it would seem that you didn't take ALL your stuff away – we found a lone crab making its way across the stage the following night just before the 'Steve Jobs' show!'

filled with layers of fossils, making the beaches of Lyme Regis excellent for fossil hunting. The narrow, twisting (and in parts steep) streets lead down through the town to the attractive seafront and the manmade harbour protected by the ancient breakwater known as **The Cobb**.

The town centre

The town is best explored on foot as the centre is compact, packed with small shops, eateries and art galleries, and there is little room for cars. At the northern end of the seafront you will find the **tourist information centre**, which, as well as the usual brochures on accommodation, eateries and activities can provide tide times – essential if you plan to go fossil hunting. Nearby is the **Marine Theatre** (Church St, DT7 3QA ✆ 01297 442394 🖱 www.marinetheatre.com), an active, traditional seaside theatre with regular performances and events (see box, page 143).

A little further up the hill is **St Michael's Church**, a charming building with two Norman pillars in the entrance. Inside the church, on the left, is a stained-glass window commemorating fossil hunter **Mary Anning** (pages 150–1). Mary and her brother Joseph are buried in the churchyard almost opposite the window. Their grave is a site of pilgrimage for palaeontologists and geologists, and you will frequently see small fossils found on the beach left on the grave as a tribute.

As you head back down the hill towards the seafront, the eccentric tower of the **guildhall** almost encroaches on to the narrow road; tucked away behind it is the **Lyme Regis Museum** (Bridge St, DT7 3QA ✆ 01297 443370 🖱 www.lymeregismuseum.co.uk 🕒 Easter–Oct daily, Oct–Easter Wed–Sun). The museum is within a quirky turreted brick building built in 1901 and, like the town, is a warren full of hidden corners to be explored. As you would expect, it has good exhibits on local geology and fossils, and Lyme's literary connections. The museum runs a regular programme of activities, such as guided walks, rock pooling and fossil hunting, which can be booked in advance. Down the hill from the museum the road crosses the river; the bridge is largely medieval underneath but you will need to be looking back from the seafront to see evidence of its age.

The eastern end of the seafront

A promenade leads northeastwards along the seafront from the town centre, past the Marine Theatre in the direction of Charmouth. The cliffs here have long been particularly unstable and in 2014 a new sea defence wall was built along this stretch as part of a broader project to stabilise the coastline, prevent erosion and save the houses in the East Cliff area from being washed into the sea. The sea wall provides a wide, elevated and flat platform along which to walk and enjoy the views around the bay to Charmouth and beyond. A large ammonite found during the construction by local consultant geologist Paddy Howe is set into the end of the wall. The new structure should also prevent the re-occurrence of an earlier problem: skeletons poking out of the cliff from the graveyard at St Michael's Church. The walk along the wall leads to Back Beach, known for its rock pooling and fossil hunting.

Around The Cobb

Lyme Regis is perhaps at its most enchanting viewed from **The Cobb** at sunset, when the sun illuminates the hills above the harbour and you can see the geological layers within the cliffs, stacked like a deck of cards. Sheltering behind the breakwater is a colourful array of fishing and pleasure boats. The Cobb has been protecting the harbour and the town from erosion since the 13th century. It was originally made from huge boulders inside oak walls and detached from the land at high tide. It was joined to the land in 1756 and rebuilt in Portland stone in the 1820s, as the gently tilting serpentine wall that you see today.

It may look like a tiddler of a harbour but in its heyday Lyme Regis was a major port – the second largest in Dorset in the 14th century. Ships from Lyme Regis traded all over the world until the 20th century. Attached to the front of The Cobb's buildings, near the aquarium (page 146), is a venerable toll board dated 1879 and entitled 'Rates of Merchandise'. It lists the amount of tax levied on imports and exports to and from the harbour with incredible detail, such as 'for every barrel of salted beef, cod, herring ... 4d', 'for every Hogshead of Ale, Beer or Porter ... 6d', 'for each horse, mule, cow or ox ... 6d'.

"In its heyday Lyme Regis was a major port – the second largest in Dorset in the 14th century."

The Cobb has seen its fair share of drama, real and fictional. It was at The Cobb that James Scott, Duke of Monmouth, landed with his followers in 1685, intent on taking the throne from his uncle, James II. Monmouth, the son of King Charles II, chose Lyme Regis because the West Country was strongly Protestant. A month after they landed, Monmouth and his followers were defeated at the Battle of Sedgemoor in Somerset. Following the trial known as the 'Bloody Assizes', which was presided over by the notorious Judge Jeffreys (page 99), 292 Monmouth supporters were executed. A dozen of them were hanged, drawn and quartered on the spot where they had disembarked in Lyme Regis.

You won't be in Lyme Regis for long before finding mention of its connection with John Fowles's *The French Lieutenant's Woman*, the story of a romance between Sarah Woodruff and Charles Smithson, a fossil hunter. Fowles was living in a farmhouse in Lyme Regis when he wrote the book. The Cobb is the setting of the dramatic opening scene of the film, when Sarah, played by Meryl Streep, is standing alone looking out to sea. Lyme Regis's other literary claim to fame involves Jane Austen, who stayed in the town in 1803–04. The Cobb features in her novel, *Persuasion*, which describes Louisa Musgrove falling from the steps.

On The Cobb, within a building dating from 1723, is the small, unpretentious **Lyme Regis Aquarium** (01297 444230 www.lymeregismarineaquarium.co.uk mid-Feb–Nov daily 10.00–17.00), run by the Gallop family since 1958. It contains a modest collection of species found in the local waters and children will enjoy helping to hand feed the mullet. It is perhaps useful to know that you can download a discount voucher from the aquarium's website. Alongside the sea creatures is a display of photographs showing films being shot in Lyme Regis, including *The French Lieutenant's Woman* and *Persuasion*. Mr Gallop proudly told me that the aquarium was used as a make-up room during the making of the latter.

"Along the seafront is a string of pastel-coloured wooden beach huts, well equipped and well used."

Along the seafront (Marine Parade) is a string of pastel-coloured wooden **beach huts**, well equipped and well used. The slightest bit of sun has holidaymakers throwing open their doors. Like magicians pulling rabbits from hats, they reach into their hut and produce with a flourish a never-ending supply of deckchairs, beach games, umbrellas and, of course, the all-important tea-making paraphernalia, and if this prospect tempts you, beach huts are available for daily, weekly or seasonal hire from the council (01297 445175 www.lymeregistowncouncil.gov.uk).

As well as the pebble beach, there is a manmade sandy one, complete with sand imported from Normandy, known as **Front Beach**. Lyme Regis is busy in summer and the area around Front Beach is where it shows. The sand is barely visible beneath the sun worshippers, the restaurants are buzzing and the shops are crowded with souvenir hunters.

The **Langmoor and Lister Gardens** provide a chance to step back from the crowds and admire the views of The Cobb and the coastline.

The Town Mill Complex

Mill Lane, DT7 3PU ✆ 01297 443579 🖰 www.townmill.org.uk ⊙ mill tours Easter–Oct Tue–Sun 11.00–16.00, Nov–Easter Sat–Sun 11.00–16.00, plus weekdays during school holidays

Around a cobbled courtyard at the Town Mill Complex, restored mill buildings house small shops showcasing local art, crafts and produce (including a potter, a cheesemonger and a brewer). The tour of the working watermill is worthwhile, with its volunteer millers overflowing with enthusiasm and knowledge about its workings and its history dating back to the 11th century. Powered by the River Lim, the mill continues to produce a small amount of stoneground flour, which is available in the mill shop. It also generates electricity, which powers the site.

Dinosaurland Fossil Museum

Coombe St, DT73PY ✆ 01297 443541 🖰 www.dinosaurland.co.uk ⊙ mid-Feb–Nov 10.00–17.00, opening hours Dec–Feb vary so it is best to check beforehand

The museum, which is in a former 18th-century chapel, has impressive displays of fossils from the local area and beyond, and interesting facts about their origins. There are dinosaur displays (good for children) and a rather odd exhibition of taxidermy of British animals. If you choose to search for fossils without doing a fossil-hunting tour, a visit to the museum will help you understand their formation.

Fossil hunting around Lyme Regis

Made from soft clay layered with a few hard bands of limestone that formed on the bottom of the sea during the early Jurassic period, some 190 million years ago, the grey cliffs of the Lyme Regis area regularly offer up some valuable clues about life on earth in geological ages past. The Jurassic fossils within the cliffs are derived from sea creatures that lived when dinosaurs roamed the land. Landslides and waves cause fossils to fall from the cliffs on to the beaches below, making them prime fossil-hunting territory.

Heading out with an expert will help you to get the most from your fossil-hunting expedition and give you a greater understanding of how they are formed. Contact details for guided fossil tours are provided on page 149.

I was lucky enough to go fossil hunting with enthusiastic expert Brandon Lennon. As the son of an international geologist, who also lives locally and fossil hunts, Brandon has a fine fossil-hunting pedigree. We were joined by Bradt founder, Hilary Bradt, who lives just over the border in Devon and is currently researching that county's side of the Jurassic Coast for her own Slow guide.

Brandon started by explaining the origins and significance of the Jurassic Coast; a large map erected by the local council on the seafront provided a handy prop and showed the relative ages of the coastline, with Lyme Regis and Charmouth being the oldest parts of the Dorset section at around 190 million years. As you head eastwards the cliffs are younger, and are a mere 65 million years old at Old Harry Rocks, the most easterly point of the Jurassic Coast. It was at this point that I got my first glimpse of Hilary's competitive streak, as she pointed out with delight that the Devon end of the Jurassic Coast is even older, approximately 250 million years old around Exmouth.

"We clambered across rocks and trudged through seaweed, keeping an eye out for spiral-shaped ammonites and other fossilised creatures."

Brandon then led us along Monmouth Beach, west of The Cobb, where we clambered across rocks and trudged through seaweed, keeping an eye out for spiral-shaped ammonites and other fossilised creatures. We were heading towards one of the area's best-known fossilised phenomena, the **ammonite graveyard**. About half way to the headland there was no mistaking that we had found what we were looking for: a ledge of limestone packed with the internal moulds of football-sized ammonites. Brandon explained that a catastrophic event or chemical reaction must have occurred to kill all these creatures at the same time. There were so many, and they were so clearly defined and uniform, that it looked as if an overly enthusiastic wallpaper designer had got carried away with an ammonite-shaped ink stamp. Hilary was initially convinced that the graveyard lies wholly within Devon but we eventually agreed that it straddles the Dorset/Devon border; at any rate, it is best accessed from Lyme Regis. The ammonites of the graveyard are intriguing to admire but you should not attempt to extract them; to do so would be dangerous and would damage this amazing site.

Brandon then handed each of us a sieve and we began sieving sand in rockpools to search for tiny fossils. Hilary hit the jackpot with several dainty, little ammonites. My find was less appealing – an ancient, fossilised gastropod. It was just as well that we had an expert on site because to the untrained eye it certainly didn't look like anything special, just a rather old and solid snail, and I would have discarded it if it hadn't been for Brandon's enthusiastic reaction.

TIPS FOR FOSSIL HUNTING

Brandon Lennon and the Lyme Regis Tourist Information Centre gave me the following tips for a productive and safe fossil-hunting trip.

- Fossil hunting is usually most productive after stormy weather or rough seas, as cliff falls are frequent and the shingle is rapidly turned over, exposing new fossils.
- Landslides are common, so it is important to stay away from the cliffs when searching the beaches.
- Sturdy footwear is essential to help you negotiate the rocks, which are slippery when covered in seaweed.
- Keep an eye on tide times – you don't want to get stranded. The best time to collect is 1½ hours either side of low tide.
- Only search the loose beach material and do not dig into the cliffs.
- You will see some fossil hunters carrying hammers. These are not essential fossil-hunting equipment but if you do decide to hammer at a rock, wear eye protection and heavy-duty gloves, and watch out for flying splinters.
- If you find something of possible scientific interest (a local expert can tell you), you will need to register it with the Charmouth Heritage Coast Centre (see page 154). While it will remain yours, scientists will have the right to ask to study it during the six months after registration.

Guided fossil tours are available from Lyme Regis Museum (☎ 01297 443370 🖱 www.lymeregismuseum.co.uk), Brandon Lennon (☎ 07944 664757 🖱 www.lymeregisfossilwalks.com) and Charmouth Heritage Coast Centre (☎ 01297 560772 🖱 www.charmouth.org/chcc).

Several yards back into Dorset, we seized upon a particularly interesting-looking rock, which Brandon skilfully tapped with a hammer to reveal the edge of an ammonite. He advised us to have it cut from the rock by local expert, Paddy Howe, who operates the **Fossil Workshop** (55 Broad St, DT7 3QF ☎ 01297 444720) in the basement of Alice's Teddy Bear Shop in the centre of Lyme Regis. It all felt rather illicit and exciting as Brandon led us into the teddy bear shop and quickly down the stairs to the workshop below. There was no sign indicating the presence of a fossil business, just shelves full of innocent-looking bears, and I began to wonder if the shop was a front for an underground fossil-polishing operation.

"It all felt rather illicit and exciting as Brandon led us into the teddy bear shop."

MARY ANNING – GROUNDBREAKING FOSSIL HUNTER

A female fossil hunter, dealer and palaeontologist who unearthed some of the most significant geological finds ever made, Mary Anning (1799–1847) was ahead of her time. Her discoveries were key to a fundamental shift in scientific thinking about the history of the earth, and challenged religious views.

Mary was born into a humble family of religious dissenters in Lyme Regis. She and her brother, Joseph, were the only survivors of ten children born to Richard Anning, a carpenter and cabinetmaker, and his wife Mary. At the age of 15 months, Mary survived a lightning strike, which killed three others; local legend had it the lightning turned her into a bright and observant child. Mary attended a Congregationalist Sunday School where she learnt to read and write. Congregationalist doctrine emphasised the importance of education for the poor, unlike the Church of England at the time. However, the family's position as dissenters against the Church of England caused them further discrimination than did poverty alone.

Richard Anning taught his children how to look for and clean fossils that had been hidden within the cliffs at Lyme Regis. They sold the 'curiosities' they collected on the seafront to the wealthy tourists who flocked to Lyme Regis in the summer.

Richard died in 1810, when Mary was 11 years old, and she supplemented the family's meagre income by continuing the fossil trade. Waves and landslides exposed new fossils, especially during winter, which needed to be collected quickly before they were washed out to sea. It was a dangerous living – landslides, treacherous tides and ferocious seas. In 1833, Mary narrowly avoided being killed by a landslide that buried her constant companion, a terrier named Tray. It has been suggested that Mary was the inspiration for the well-known tongue-twister 'she sells seashells on the seashore', written by Terry Sullivan in 1908.

Mary taught herself geology and anatomy and she, and her family, made some important discoveries. In 1811, Mary's brother Joseph found a skull protruding from a cliff. Over a period of months Mary painstakingly

As I waited for us to be swept up in a police raid, a more banal explanation came to light: Paddy's wife runs the teddy bear shop and the fossil workshop sign was away being repaired. Paddy demonstrated his skill and patience as he began to remove the rock around the fossil with special equipment. If you too are lucky enough to find a fossil, Paddy can identify and prepare it for you. Regardless, it is worth popping into the workshop to watch Paddy at work and see his fossil collection, some of which is for sale. Sadly, the rock around uncovered an almost complete 17-foot-long skeleton of a 'crocodile'. The specimen was bought by the local lord of the manor, who sold it to William Bullock for his Museum of Natural Curiosities in London. The find caused quite a stir and brought Mary to the attention of scientific circles. The specimen was later named *Ichthyosaurus*, the 'fish-lizard'.

In 1828, Mary made another important discovery – the first complete skeleton of a flying reptile recorded in England. It was named *Dimorphodon* after its two kinds of teeth and appears to have been a fish eater.

The Anning family had established themselves as fossil hunters but remained very poor. In 1820 one of their patrons, Lieutenant-Colonel Thomas James Birch, organised an auction of specimens he had purchased from them. The sale raised £400, which he donated to the Annings, and the publicity cemented Mary's fame.

Mary's gender and social class meant she could not fully participate in the scientific community of the day. As a woman, she was not eligible to join the Geological Society of London and rarely received due credit for her work. However, she was visited by, and corresponded with, eminent scientists of the time and her opinions were valued. In 1838, Mary was given an annuity raised by members of the British Association for the Advancement of Science and the Geological Society of London.

From humble beginnings she had gained the respect of the scientific community and captured the imagination of the public. She may not have been eligible to join during her lifetime but her death was recorded by the Geological Society. In 2010, the Royal Society included Anning in a list of the ten British women who have most influenced the history of science.

She died from breast cancer aged 47 and is buried in the churchyard of St Michael's in Lyme Regis, with her brother. A stained-glass window within the church, commissioned by the Geological Society of London, commemorates her life. On the wall of the Lyme Regis Museum is a blue plaque dedicated to her. The museum is believed to be on the site of Anning's home and her first fossil shop.

our fossil was not of a type that could be removed easily, so once the fossil was partly revealed (for the first time in hundreds of millions of years) Paddy was forced to stop to avoid damaging it. Nevertheless, it will go on display in my house as a reminder of our fossil-hunting day, and is all the more special because we found it.

Brandon explained to me that there is no reason why people should not take small fossils home from the beach, as it prevents them from being washed out to sea. The large ones, however, should be left alone.

Cruises, fishing trips & sailing lessons

At the shore end of The Cobb you can arrange fishing trips, self-drive hire boats, Jurassic Coast cruises or a water taxi to West Bay (page 160). Harry May's (✆ 07974 753287) mackerel-fishing and deep-sea fishing trips come highly recommended by locals. If you fancy getting in some sea time, a mackerel-fishing trip is a pleasant way to spend an hour pottering around the bay. On a deep-sea fishing trip your catch is likely to be cod, conger and skate.

RIVER COTTAGE & HUGH FEARNLEY-WHITTINGSTALL

For details of the busy schedule of events, see www.rivercottage.net

When I mentioned Dorset to an Australian friend recently she said, 'Oh, that's where God lives.' I was quite chuffed, thinking she was describing Dorset as God's own country, such is its beauty. She then clarified that she was talking about 'Hugh', that is to say television personality Hugh Fearnley-Whittingstall. I was surprised on a number of levels, firstly that the scruffy but likeable Hugh should attract such blasphemous praise and secondly that his back to basics food philosophy has such wide appeal, even on the other side of the globe.

Dorset and Hugh have been inextricably linked since 1998, when he moved into the original River Cottage to start growing and rearing his own food. River Cottage has in fact moved to a farm (Park Farm) just a smidgeon over the border in Devon but I believe Dorset still has a fair claim to Hugh. The River Cottage principles remain unchanged: less dependence on the outside world, food integrity, and the consumption of local, seasonal produce. The message is nothing new – it is the way my family and most of our Dorset farming friends have been living for years – but it is highly relevant in today's world of ready-made mush (I hesitate to use the word 'meals').

River Cottage HQ at Park Farm is the venue for courses inspired by the philosophy of the original River Cottage, including foraging, curing, gardening, bread-making and butchery. You can also enjoy an entertaining dinner at Park Farm, where you get to mingle with fellow guests over canapés, then potter around and draw inspiration from the flourishing fruit and vegetable garden and elaborate chicken enclosure, before sitting down to eat. Dinner is at two long tables and each course is accompanied by a talk from the chef, who explains the detail behind the dish. When I went I was struck by the convivial and collegiate atmosphere, although a little intimidated by the serious foodies who took notes throughout the evening. I began to worry that there was going to be an exam at the end of the meal – thankfully not.

River Cottage also has a canteen and deli in Axminster, where they sell local and organic food and drink.

Sailing lessons are available from Lyme Regis Sea School (✆ 01297 442644 🖱 www.lrss.org.uk), and the Lyme Regis Sailing Club (🖱 www.lymeregissailingclub.co.uk) offers temporary membership for visitors.

FOOD & DRINK

As you would expect of a bustling tourist town, Lyme Regis is packed with cafés and restaurants. They are concentrated along the main street and the seafront. Below is a selection.

Amid Giants and Idols 59 Silver St, DT7 3TZ ✆ 07928 790254 ⊙ Wed–Sun. Towards the top of town. This independent café serves speciality coffee, fine teas and fresh fruit smoothies, as well as homemade cakes.

Bell Cliff 6 Broad St, DT7 3QD ✆ 01297 442459 ⊙ daily. Centrally located restaurant and tea room with a small outdoor eating area with views over the bay. Does a good Dorset cream tea.

By the Bay Marine Parade, DT7 3JH ✆ 01297 442668 ⊙ daily 10.00–21.00. In a prime position overlooking the beach. Freshly cooked dishes with the emphasis on seafood.

Good Food Store 21 Broad St, DT7 3QE ✆ 01297 442076 ⊙ daily 08.30–17.00 in summer & closed Sun in winter. A deli, bakery and organic produce shop, which also has a café. Good, wholesome, local food and plenty of gluten-free options.

Hix Oyster & Fish House Cobb Rd, DT7 3JP ✆ 01297 446910 🖱 www.hixoysterandfishhouse.co.uk ⊙ daily 10.00–22.00, Nov-Mar closed Mon. Reservation recommended. Lyme's best-known and most exclusive restaurant, owned by celebrity chef Mark Hix. Great if you want to treat yourself or someone else, especially if you like fish. At the end of the gardens above the seafront, it has sweeping views over the bay and the service is very good. There is no parking here but you can drop people off and park nearby.

Pilot Boat Inn 1 Bridge St, DT7 3QA ✆ 01297 443157 ⊙ daily 11.00–23.00. Unassuming pub right in the centre of Lyme Regis. Traditional pub fare at reasonable prices. Plenty of vegetarian options.

River Cottage Park Farm, Trinity Hill Rd, Axminster, Devon EX13 8TB ✆ 01297 630313 🖱 www.rivercottage.net ⊙ see website for details of events. Hugh Fearnley-Whittingstall's River Cottage (Park Farm) near Lyme Regis organises fabulous events throughout the year, including hugely memorable dinners and fascinating courses focused on food and farming. You will need to book in advance as this is a working farm and not open to the public except during events (see opposite).

Tierra Kitchen 1a Coombe St, DT7 3PY ✆ 01297 445189 ⊙ Nov–Mar closed Mon–Wed. Vegetarian dishes lovingly prepared using carefully selected ingredients.

Town Mill Bakery 2 Riverside Studios, Coombe St, DT7 3PY ✆ 01297 444754. ⊙ daily. Bread, pastries and pizzas, made on site. Well known for their sourdough breads and use of local produce. Long, wooden tables reminiscent of school mealtimes and the open bakery provide a casual atmosphere.

2 CHARMOUTH

Fernhill Hotel (page 296) **Hensleigh House** (page 296)

Smaller than Lyme Regis, Charmouth is billed as the quieter of the two, although the beach can feel pretty crowded in the summer. The bulk of Charmouth is about half a mile back from the sea, spread along either side of the main street, which runs between the coast and the A35. You can drive down to the seafront, where there is ample paid parking close to the beach.

The seafront is decidedly low-key – there is no fancy esplanade lined with shops, amusement arcades and hotels; instead there is a pebble beach, fossil-rich cliffs, a fossil shop, a café and the **Charmouth Heritage Coast Centre** (Lower Sea Lane, DT6 6LL 01297 560772 www.charmouth.org/chcc; free admission). If you plan on collecting fossils or simply want to know more about the Jurassic Coast, the centre is worth a visit. The interactive displays and fossil touch table will appeal to most children, and there is a video microscope for you to examine your fossil finds. Displays on the coastal wildlife of the area, including two marine rock-pool aquariums, add another dimension. The centre provides a large and varied programme of events, including fossil hunting, ammonite-slice polishing and rock pooling.

Every Monday during the summer a large **flea market** is held in a field on the edge of Charmouth at Manor Farm Park.

At the western end of the village is a turning marked Stonebarrow Lane, which leads to **Stonebarrow Hill**. This National Trust land along the coast is a relatively uncrowded and peaceful vantage point from which to take in the sea views. Bridleways and the South West Coast Path pass through here and the small National Trust shop does a good trade selling teas, coffees and ice creams to walkers.

FOOD & DRINK

Fernhill Hotel DT6 6BX 01297 560492 www.fernhill-hotel.co.uk closed Sun evening & Mon. An elegant restaurant, good service and delicious food combine to make a meal here a very pleasant experience. The owners describe their food philosophy as 'we buy local first; free range, organic and fair-trade where possible; and ensure no GM or artificial additives are in our food'. The menu offers plenty of variety, including vegetarian, vegan, dairy-free and gluten-free options. A bar and grill are available for more casual dining, following the same food philosophy.

Hensleigh House Hotel Lower Sea Lane, DT6 6LW 01297 560830 daily. At the top of the hill on the way to the beach, the hotel has a simple conservatory restaurant serving cream teas.

3 MORCOMBELAKE

The small village of Morcombelake has long been associated with a Dorset icon, for it was here that **Moores Biscuits** (www.moores-biscuits.co.uk) opened their bakery in 1880. Today, this family business is in the hands of the fifth generation. Although Moores now has a factory in Bridport, the Morcombelake bakery is still active (01297 489821 Mon–Sat). Bread is baked on site from Tuesday to Friday. As well as baked goods, including some excellent doughnuts which I can personally recommend, the bakery has a deli, a display of historical Moores Bakery items and a collection of paintings of the West Country by Mrs Moores. The most famous of the biscuit selection is the Dorset Knob, a savoury biscuit baked three times.

"The most famous of the biscuit selection is the Dorset Knob."

FOOD & DRINK

Felicity's Farm Shop Morcombelake DT6 6DJ 01297 480930 http:// www.felicitysfarmshop.co.uk Mon–Sat 08.00–18.00, Sun 10.00–16.00. This large, family-run farm shop is conveniently located on the A35 and has plenty of parking (which is important around here). The shop is well stocked with local produce, deli items and gifts. Felicity's son, Tom, raises pigs nearby and his pork, bacon and sausages are deservedly popular. Local seafood is a particular feature with Portland crab often for sale, and there are tempting locally smoked meats and fish. This is the perfect place to stock up for a picnic or a self-catering stay, and if you can't wait to try the food there is a café on site selling take-away food, which you can enjoy on the outdoor picnic tables with a sea view. The Portland crab sandwiches are among my favourites.

4 CHIDEOCK

As you head eastwards from Morcombelake, the A35 passes through Chideock, a village of attractive golden stone and whitewashed cottages, many of them thatched, and with a couple of decent pubs.

In the centre of the village is the short and stocky **St Giles Church**. The oldest parts of the church date from the 13th century but what you see today is largely unchanged since the restoration of 1884–85. Its most intriguing feature is not usually visible but it makes an amusing anecdote: the belfry contains a peal of six bells, the oldest of which was cast in 1603 and is inscribed with the unfortunate spelling error 'Love dog'. It's a fine and worthy notion but not what they were going for, which was, of course, 'Love God'.

Behind St Giles Church is a Roman Catholic **memorial chapel**, built in 1852 by Charles Weld of Chideock Manor in memory of his parents. The walls and ceilings are beautifully painted; when it is open (times vary) it is worth a peek inside, or you can make an appointment (www.chideockmartyrschurch.org.uk).

"Seven Chideock men were put to death for their faith between 1587 and 1642."

Catholicism has a strong history in the village, which is displayed in the **museum** (daily 10.00–16.00; free admission) attached to the **Church of Our Lady Queen of Martyrs and St Ignatius** (North Rd, DT6 6LF www.chideockmartyrschurch.org.uk). When Catholicism was banned in England, local Catholics worshipped in secret in a barn which stood on the site of the present-day church. Seven Chideock men were put to death for their faith between 1587 and 1642; the church is a memorial to them and others who shared their fate.

The church is next to Chideock Manor (not open to the public) and was designed in Italian Romanesque style by Charles Weld in 1872, who was living in the manor house at the time. He painted much of the decoration himself. Nearby Ruins Lane leads to the site of Chideock Castle, which was destroyed in 1645 and where a cross now stands dedicated to the Chideock Martyrs.

5 SEATOWN, EYPE & GOLDEN CAP

Golden Cap Holiday Park (page 297), **Downhouse Farm** Higher Eype (page 297)
Highlands End Holiday Park Eype (page 297)

A turning in the centre of Chideock takes you to Seatown, a modest seaside hamlet nestled between cliffs. Seatown consists of a few houses, a pub and a good campsite, all huddled close to a golden shingle beach.

The land along the coast around Seatown is owned by the National Trust and offers some excellent walks. The hillside to the east of Seatown is steep and usually dotted with cows of assorted colours and sizes, who casually swagger to the cliff edge and gaze out to sea. From Seatown you can walk up and over the hill, and then another hill, to Eype Mouth. It is a hilly two miles and the Downhouse Farm Café at Eype provides an excellent stop for refreshments (page 158). The hamlet of **Eype** near Bridport has a shingle beach, which is reached down a steep path from a cliff top car park (payable), and a couple of sizeable campsites.

A walk to Golden Cap

OS Explorer map 116 or Landranger 193; start: Seatown, SY420917; 4 miles; difficult (steep climb along the cliff top). Refreshment at the pub in Seatown (page 158). For an easier walk, avoiding the steep climb, start the walk at Langdon Hill car park, SY412930.

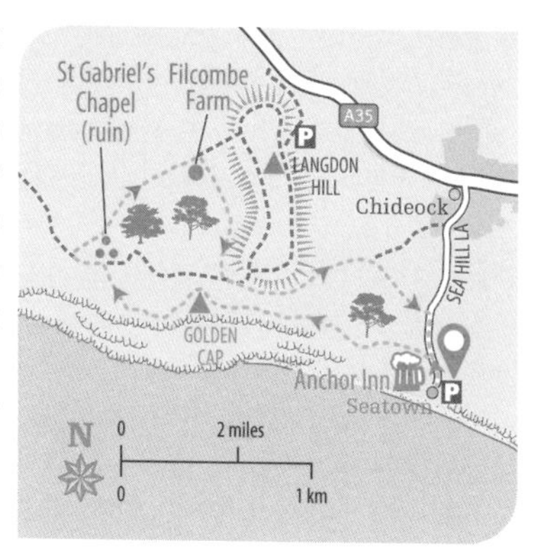

This walk takes you to the highest point on England's south coast and entails an appropriately steep section and far-reaching views. From the car park near the Anchor Inn in Seatown, walk up the hill into the village, climb the stile on the left and join the footpath, signed 'Coast Path Diversion'. Walk across the field, over a stile and through a small woodland. Cross another stile and bear right up the hill, signposted 'Golden Cap'.

Where the track forks, keep left. You will walk through open fields with Golden Cap directly ahead of you. It gets pretty steep in parts but the views give a great excuse for a pause. At the summit you will see a stone memorial to the Earl of Antrim KBE, chair of the National Trust 1966–77. The views of the coastline are spectacular, towards Lyme Regis in the west and West Bay in the east. Once you have had your fill of the view, follow the path down the steep hill to a gate and bear right over the fields towards the ruins of the 13th-century St Gabriel's Chapel. Keeping the chapel on your right, you will pass through two gates. Continue in the direction of Morcombelake. You will pass through Filcombe Farm and around the base of Langdon Hill Wood, which in spring is awash with bluebells and wild garlic. Head down the hill back to Seatown, where the Anchor Inn awaits.

To reach the National Trust car park at Langdon Hill, drive westwards through Chideock on the A35 and turn left at the top of the hill half a mile past the village centre, just before the dual carriageway ends. The turning you are looking for is a tiny, unmarked lane (known as Langdon Lane) just after the turning signposted 'Seatown'. A mostly level walk takes you around Langdon Hill Wood.

On the west side of Seatown is **Golden Cap**, which lives up to its name: the top of the cliff has a warm golden glow, which can be seen for miles around, and at 626 feet it is the highest point on the south coast of Britain. It can be reached on foot either from Seatown or from Langdon Hill Wood.

FOOD & DRINK

Anchor Inn Seatown DT6 6JU 01297 489215 daily for lunch & dinner, for breakfast at weekends. A Palmers Brewery pub in a super seaside location, and with a beer garden on the cliff top. Serves traditional pub food and plenty of fish dishes. Parking is paid but is refunded if you spend over £20 in the pub.

Garden Café Downhouse Farm, Downhouse Lane, Higher Eype DT6 6AH 01308 421232 www.downhousefarm.org Mar–Oct Tue–Sun 10.00–18.00. This outdoor café at the farm serves delicious homemade food. Dishes are prepared using the farm's own organic meats, vegetables and herbs, and there are plenty of vegetarian options. The bubble and squeak is delicious. It is found down a very narrow lane.

6 BRIDPORT & WEST BAY

Bridge House Hotel Bridport (page 296) **Washingpool Farm** North Allington (page 297)

Bridport

'A vibrant and quirky market town, whose population doubles in summer', is how Bob Smith of the Bridport District Tourism Association describes his home town. I met with Bob and Clive Edwards, a fellow member of the association, and their enthusiasm for the area in which they live and work was immediately apparent. They are rightly proud of Bridport's rope-making history, its market, its food culture and its arts scene. Yet, Bridport and the surrounding area have to work hard to compete with the likes of Lulworth Cove, Lyme Regis and the coastal towns over the border in Devon. To do that Bridport has had to be a little creative, which is probably one reason why it has a staggering number of events for such a small town. There is the food festival in June, the hat festival in September and the literary festival in November, to name but a few.

"There is the food festival in June, the hat festival in September and the literary festival in November, to name but a few."

The **Bridport Food Festival** (www.bridportfoodfestival.wordpress.com), launched in 2004 by celebrity chef and local food advocate Hugh Fearnley-Whittingstall (see box, page 152), is a fitting way to celebrate the area's local produce. The farms of the fertile Marshwood Vale and the seas off West Bay do their part to contribute, offering up delicious and natural food.

Bridport is still very much a market town, with street markets held on Wednesdays and Saturdays. The **Saturday market** is crammed with bric-a-brac stalls and attracts bargain hunters from miles around. Equally popular is the **farmers' market**, held on the second Saturday of each month in the Bridport Arts Centre.

Perhaps because it is surrounded by inspiring land and seascapes, Bridport has developed a flourishing artistic and literary community. There is a healthy population of art galleries where you can pick up a souvenir of your visit. The **Bridport Arts Centre** (✆ 01308 424204 ⊕ www.bridport-arts.com) runs a programme of free exhibitions and is the home of the literary festival and the coveted Bridport Prize International Creative Writing Competition. The Art Deco **Electric Palace** (✆ 01308 424901 ⊕ www.electricpalace.org.uk) is considered to be one of the best entertainment venues in the region, playing host to theatre, live music, cinema and art exhibitions.

Bridport has had a **rope-making industry** since the 13th century. The town was once well known for producing hangman's ropes, hence the mildly euphemistic saying 'to be stabbed with a Bridport dagger', meaning to be hanged. You may notice the long gardens around Bridport, which were once walks used for making lengths of rope. A **net-making industry** also survives in the town, with fishing and sporting nets being made in Bridport, including the nets for the Wimbledon Tennis Championships. Information about the rope- and net-making industries, and other local history, is on display at **Bridport Museum** (The Coach House, 25 South St, DT6 3NR ✆ 01308 458703 ⊕ www.bridportmuseum.co.uk).

Beer has been produced continuously since 1794 at **Palmers Brewery** (West Bay Rd, DT6 4JA ✆ 01308 422396 ⊕ www.palmersbrewery.com), which claims to be the only thatched brewery in the UK. It is run by the founder's great-grandsons, John and Cleeves Palmer. From Easter to the end of September you can take a **brewery tour**, but will usually need to book in advance. **Palmers Wine Store** is adjacent to the brewery.

As you are driving in the vicinity of Bridport, make sure you keep an eye out for **Colmer's Hill**, a remarkably round little hill topped with a few scraggly pine trees. It has been used for many years as a local landmark, including by smugglers when they were taking their contraband inland from the shore. You can walk to the top of the hill from the village of **Symondsbury**.

West Bay

A mile from the town is **West Bay**, Bridport's harbour, where the River Brit, a tidal river, flows into the sea through the sluice gates and harbour basin. A harbour was first recorded at West Bay in the 13th century and was known as Bridport Harbour until 1884. It was a centre of the boat-building industry until the late 19th century and many ships were built here during the Napoleonic Wars (1799–1815). West Bay has not been primped and preened to turn it into a glamorous, tourist honeypot; instead it continues as a working fishing harbour with a 'what you see is what you get' attitude and where unpretentious fish and chip kiosks are the lunch venue of choice. Above the pebble beach tower sandstone cliffs, and the pier looks out along the coastline from the Isle of Portland to Brixham in Devon. At **West Bay River Boat Hire** (☎ 07905 689994) you can hire a rowing boat to explore the River Brit.

If the scenery looks familiar here it may be because West Bay is one of a series of locations in the area used for the filming of the hugely popular television drama *Broadchurch*. You may recognise the rounded apartment block behind the harbour as the programme's police station.

Mangerton Mill

Mangerton Mill (page 297)

Mangerton DT6 3SG ☎ 01308 485224 ⏲ Easter–Oct Tue–Sun & Bank Holiday Mon

Tucked away down tiny lanes north of Bridport, this three-storey watermill on the River Manger dates from the 17th century, and has been the home of the Harris family for several generations. Last worked commercially in 1966, the family has restored it and it is now a workable grist mill. It is in a very peaceful location and even the rhythmic churning of the mill wheel is soothing. Visitors are free to explore the building at their own pace and wonder at the inner workings of the mill, which are surrounded by a collection of household and agricultural artefacts arranged in suitably higgledy-piggledy granddad's-shed fashion. The tea room serves homemade, locally sourced food; cream teas are a speciality. In the converted outbuildings are artist studios and gift shops.

Trout fishing is available in the lake and there is quiet, riverside camping area for just ten caravans. It is worth walking along the wooded edge of the River Manger to the sluice gates, from where water tumbles into a magical-looking pool shrouded by moss-gilded trees and ferns. It is the sort of scene meditation tapes invite you to imagine.

FOOD & DRINK

Bull Hotel 34 East St, Bridport DT6 3LF ✆ 01308 422878 www.thebullhotel.co.uk ⏲ for breakfast, lunch and dinner. The restaurant at this hotel has a reputation for upmarket, locally produced food. The stable yard has been converted into a relaxed cider, pizza and pie house.

Leakers Bakery 29 East St, Bridport DT6 3JX ✆ 01308 423296 www.leakersbakery.co.uk ⏲ Mon–Sat. Not a café, just a very special bakery selling their handmade bread and cakes, including the delicious Dorset cider and cheese cottage loaf. This is also where you will find the Jurassic foot loaf, in the shape of a dinosaur's footprint. G S Leaker bought this bakery in 1914 and it remained in the family until 2002: a granddaughter of the original Leakers is still responsible for baking the Dorset apple cakes.

Riverside Restaurant West Bay DT6 4EZ ✆ 01308 422011 ⏲ lunch Tue–Sun, dinner Tue, Wed, Fri & Sat. This seafood restaurant on the water at West Bay is reached by crossing a footbridge over the river. It's more pricey than some others in the area, although the lunchtime set menu is relatively good value.

Washingpool Farm Shop Dottery Rd, North Allington DT6 5HP ✆ 01308 459549 www.washingpool.co.uk ⏲ daily. On the B3162 to the northeast of Bridport is this well-stocked farm shop and licensed restaurant on a working farm. As well as vegetables and meat produced on the farm, the shop stocks a range of goodies from within a 50-mile radius. A tranquil spot for lunch close to town. Visitors are free to wander around the farm trail and there is a children's play area.

Watch House Café West Bay DT6 4EN ✆ 01308 459330 www.watchhousecafe.co.uk ⏲ hours vary, check the website. On East Beach is this sister to the well-known Hive Beach Café at Burton Bradstock (pages 163–4). It has a casual atmosphere and specialises in seafood and wood-fired pizza. Private hire available.

EAST OF BRIDPORT VIA THE BRIDE VALLEY TO ABBOTSBURY

As you travel east from Bridport you are heading towards some utterly captivating scenery – the Bride Valley, the start of **Chesil Beach** and the village of **Abbotsbury**. The River Bride, which in parts is more a stream than a river, rises in Littlebredy and runs along a 6½-mile course to the sea at **Burton Bradstock**. The surrounding valley is a bucolic blend of rolling hills, woodland and small stone and thatched villages that remain genuine Dorset, and not Dorset dressed up for the tourist trade, with scarcely a trinket shop in sight. Even the wildlife feels unthreatened – walking around the villages

"The Bride Valley area provides some good walking country."

of the Bride Valley I saw a stoat, a fox and numerous rabbits all happily going about their business. If you are looking for a quieter base within easy reach of the coast, Burton Bradstock and the Bride Valley are good options.

The **Bride Valley** area provides some good walking country, some of which incorporates Neolithic sites such as the **Kingston Russell Stone Circle** and its neighbour, the long barrow known as the **Grey Mare and her Colts**.

Abbotsbury does get busy during summer but it is a delightful village, best known for its swannery.

7 BURTON BRADSTOCK

Norburton Hall (page 297)

The village nestles at the base of the Bride Valley, at the point where the River Bride flows into the sea. Although there has been some modern development on the outskirts, photogenic thatched 17th- and 18th-century cottages remain around the church of St Mary the Virgin. The **post office** on Mill Street does everything a local post office should do and more; it doubles as a village shop, selling a range of local produce, including cheese, meat and bread.

A pleasant shingle **beach** lies on the edge of the village, shielded by golden cliffs that regularly yield up their fossils. Apart from a National Trust car park and the popular Hive Beach Café (see opposite), there are no other facilities of note at the beach. The South West Coastal Path leads from the beach up on to cliffs and towards West Bay, or eastwards towards West Bexington.

Just outside Burton Bradstock on the Bridport road is the **Bridport and West Dorset Golf Club** (Burton Rd, DT6 4PS 01308 421095 www.bridportgolfclub.org.uk), which is open to visitors on most days. The club, which was founded in 1891, is said to be the oldest in Dorset. If you play here and find you are off your game, you can always use the excuse that you were distracted by the spectacular views across Lyme Bay and Chesil Beach. Club member, Tony Edwards, and owner of Sea Fret House (page 296), told me it is pretty challenging to play a cliff top course with swirling winds. 'It is a real test of a golfer's skills, and the sixth is a keynote hole from an elevated tee over wilderness on to a green surrounded by five bunkers with the sea and the beach waiting to catch the wilder shots. The vistas rival anything on the Med, and I feel lucky we can play on such a course at an affordable price.'

Modbury Farm Shop

Modbury Farm, DT6 4NE ✆ 01308 897193 🖱 www.modburyfarm.co.uk

A visit to this farm shop is far more than a shopping experience. If you are in the area, I urge you to drop in. This is a true working farm. The shop is within the farmyard and, unusually for a farm shop, visitors are free to look at the animals. What better way to know where your food comes from than to see how it is produced?

Hard-working couple Julie and Tim Garry took me on a tour of their farmyard. Our first stop was the poultry house. Tim opened the door and out rushed a colourful assortment of chickens, turkeys, ducks and guineafowl. Among the excited feathered crowd was one who didn't quite seem to fit. Julie explained to me that the pigeon had appeared one day and begun to hang out with the farmyard birds. The tag on its leg gave it away as a racing pigeon who had gone off course (or was plain lazy). Bizarrely, the pigeon's identity crisis seemed to deepen when it developed a crush on a bantam cockerel. I witnessed this for myself – the apparently love-struck pigeon wandered around the farmyard clinging to the feathered ankles of the long-suffering bantam.

The mainstay of the farm is a milking herd of around a hundred pedigree Jersey cattle. Jerseys have always been among my favourite breeds. With kind eyes, long eyelashes, a quizzical expression and dainty figure, they almost look like cartoon cows.

Modbury Farm's unpasteurised (raw) Jersey milk is on sale in the shop and I can assure you it is nothing like its tasteless supermarket cousins. The shop also sells Modbury's own Angus-cross-Jersey beef, as well as organic vegetables and honey.

Modbury Farm Shop is two miles from Burton Bradstock on the Litton Cheney road. More information about raw milk is available on the US website 🖱 www.realmilk.com.

FOOD & DRINK

Anchor Inn High St, DT6 4QF ✆ 01308 897228 ⏲ daily for lunch & dinner. Behind the rather average pub exterior hides a clean, comfortable restaurant divided into several small rooms, which creates an intimate atmosphere. The menu is varied and creative, with a focus on seafood. The local scallops are excellent. Reservation recommended.

Hive Beach Café Beach Rd, DT6 4RF ✆ 01308 897070 🖱 www.hivebeachcafe.co.uk ⏲ during the day, & Fri & Sat evenings in summer. Times are dependent on the weather, so if in doubt, check. The name is misleading, for this is not your average beachside café. Trendy, well known and with a reputation for superb seafood, this restaurant draws quite a crowd. So trendy is it that they now sell more lobster for breakfast than they do for lunch. The manager told me that they're committed to sustainable fishing: you can even order a local fish with an identity tag which allows you to look up who caught the fish and when. Reservation recommended.

8 WEST BEXINGTON

Manor Hotel (page 296) **Sea Fret B&B** Puncknowle (page 296)

West Bexington is a small settlement tucked away off the B3157 between Burton Bradstock and Abbotsbury. A lane leads down to a car park that extends over the pebble beach, making it one of the most accessible beaches for those with limited mobility.

The beach is typically quieter than others in the area but is popular with beach fishermen, who can be seen casting their lines into the sea

CHILLIES FROM DORSET

Sea Spring Farm, West Bexington DT2 9DD 01308 897898 www.seaspringseeds.co.uk

Dorset is well known for its cream teas, its cheese and its apple cake. It is less well known for its chillies, yet one of the hottest chillies in the world, the **Dorset Naga**, was first grown in a polytunnel in a nursery behind a bungalow in West Bexington.

The Dorset Naga is the creation of Joy and Michael Michaud. The couple, who both have doctorates in agronomy, began growing chillies at West Bexington in the early 1990s and are widely acknowledged as the first commercial chilli-growers in the UK. Although the Dorset Naga is frequently referred to as the hottest chilli in the world, it is a title Joy shies away from, as there are a few other 'superhot' chillies and, depending on growing conditions, one could be hotter than the next in any given season. One thing is for certain, annual tests since 2005 have consistently shown that the Dorset Naga is exceptionally fierce; it is just one of the many varieties the Michauds have created, ranging from mild to extra hot.

Joy explained to me that growing chillies was an interest that became a way to make their 15-acre smallholding pay for itself. The gently sloping site, reflection of sunlight off the sea and mild coastal climate made their nursery one of the best places to grow chillies in Britain.

Joy and Michael sell the Dorset Naga online, and seeds for vegetable varieties (including their chillies), which they have tested themselves for quality. If you fancy growing your own Dorset Naga or any of the other special varieties, visit www.seaspringseeds.co.uk.

Joy and Michael have really helped to put Dorset on the chilli-growing map. The **Great Dorset Chilli Festival** (www.greatdorsetchillifestival.co.uk) is held annually at St Giles House in Wimborne St Giles.

whatever the weather. There is a small café but its opening hours are rather hit and miss. An alternative is the Manor Hotel, on the road down to the beach, which has a bar and restaurant (see below).

On the B3157, in the area known as Swyre, is **Vurlands Animal Park** (DT2 9DB ✆ 01308 897160). This 30-acre, family-run farm opened to the public in 2014. Visitors can wander between the paddocks and meet the farm animals and pets, and there are good views of the Bride Valley. There is a wildflower meadow, willow maze, children's play area and the Eggcup Tearooms (see below).

FOOD & DRINK

Eggcup Tearooms Coast Rd, Swyre DT2 9DB ✆ 01308 897160 ⊙ Oct–Mar closed Mon. Serves homemade lunches and cream teas, and roasts on Sunday in winter. The outdoor area has views of the Bride Valley.

Manor Hotel Beach Rd, West Bexington DT2 9DF ✆ 01308 897660 ⊙ daily. A pleasant restaurant with a flagstone floor plus an outdoor eating area. The bar is open all day, making it a good spot for post-beach refreshments. The menu features local produce and the portions are generous.

9 PUNCKNOWLE

Despite its spelling, Puncknowle is pronounced 'Punnel'. There is no agreed explanation for the 'Punck' part of the name but the second part is believed to refer to the knoll to the south of the village. On top of the knoll is a small, mysterious **stone house**. No-one is certain of its origins but its positioning high above the coast means it has long been used as a land and sea mark. In 1794 the knoll was the site of a signal station, one of a chain along the coast, and it has been suggested the house may have been associated with it. The house is built on a Bronze Age barrow and a cremation urn, now in the County Museum in Dorchester (page 102), was found under its foundations.

The **village** has a simple charm – narrow roads lined with thatched, stone cottages and farm buildings. Behind the high walls in the centre is the manor house, and next to it the church. Their positioning side by side is a reminder of how dominant the church and the big house were in England's rural villages. The manor is at the heart of a 2,000-acre farm, whose principal activity is dairy production.

On a visit to the Crown Inn, locals told me more about a quirky character with a broad Dorset accent whom I had met briefly earlier in the evening. Known as the Mayor of Swyre, Michael is something of a celebrity around these parts. He has never left the Bride Valley or married but he takes his mayoral duties seriously and wears a toilet chain and plug as his chain of office. Michael used to be employed helping move cattle safely around the village, but since the decline in farming he has redirected those skills and now helps escort children across the road.

FOOD & DRINK

Crown Inn Church St, DT2 9BN ✆ 01308 897711 ⏲ pub: closed Oct–Easter & Sun evening, village shop: Mon–Sat 09.00–21.00, Sun 09.00–18.00. A handsome, thatched 16th-century inn run by the local Palmers Brewery. Popular with locals and visitors, it serves tasty, traditional pub food. Dorset teas are served every afternoon, and it is dog-friendly. The pub also houses a small village shop selling local produce and household essentials.

10 LITTON CHENEY

The road from Puncknowle to Litton Cheney takes the most extraordinary route right through the centre of the farmyard of Looke Farm. Around the village several pretty stone bridges span the River Bride. Litton Cheney is another picturesque Bride Valley village with 17th- and 18th-century cottages reached by crossing the flagstones which lie over the stream running in front of them.

FOOD & DRINK

White Horse Inn DT2 9AT ✆ 01308 482539 ⏲ closed Mon lunch all year & Mon dinner in winter. Traditional country pub drawing a good local crowd. A resident dog sits on a bar stool, begging at the bar until it is rewarded with snacks.

11 LITTLEBREDY

At the head of the Bride Valley, Littlebredy is an idyllic hamlet in a magical setting. As I approached the village on my last visit the unmistakable Englishness of the scene struck me – the green rolling countryside, the neat hedgerows and the buzzards shrieking above.

Only cars belonging to Littlebredy's 85 residents are allowed into the community, so you will need to park and walk. The road above the church is a good place to leave the car. With its dainty spire, the **church of St Michael and All Angels** stands out against the deep green of the hill behind, making it look super-imposed on the scene. The church was largely rebuilt in 1850 and the spire was added to the 14th-century tower.

CHRISTINE MCFADDEN COOKERY COURSES AT LITTLEBREDY

For more information or to book a visit www.thedorsetfoodie.co.uk

Christine McFadden, Dorset-based cookery teacher and food writer, runs hands-on cookery classes in Littlebredy. Christine is the author of *The Farm Shop Cook Book, Pepper: The Spice that Changed the World* and *Cool Green Leaves and Red Hot Peppers*, all three nominated for international cookbook awards.

Christine's classes make the most of Dorset's abundance of top-notch produce, but also draw on flavours and cuisines from around the world. The emphasis is very much on seasonal, local and Slow, with time allocated to in-depth study of key ingredients – from their history, provenance and cultural importance to tutored tastings and how to cook them. Topics include Taste of North Africa, Glorious Greens and Fish Cookery.

Classes are limited to a maximum of seven people, and include a recipe folder to take away, delicious refreshments and a leisurely meal to finish.

There is a very pleasant circular walk from here, into the grounds of Bridehead House then along the River Bride and back up the hill to the church. Bridehead House was the manor house at the centre of the estate; it stands behind the village cricket ground and can be glimpsed from the road.

The lake in the grounds was formed by damming the springs that are the start of the River Bride. Water tumbles from the lake down a waterfall and into the river, which passes in front of Littlebredy's cottages. From the waterfall a footbridge takes you across the river, which is small at this stage, and on to a path that runs beside the water. You will pass thatched, stone cottages built in the 19th century but in the medieval style – essentially this is an early Victorian model village. Even the village hall (once a school), which is near the church, looks like a cottage. You come to a five-acre **Victorian walled garden** (01305 898055 Easter–Oct Wed, Sun & bank holidays 14.00–17.00), which belonged to the local estate. The gardens and walls are being restored by a not-for-profit community interest venture, and an experimental vineyard has been planted.

Fresh Face Furniture (The Old Forge, Estate Yard, DT2 9H 01308 482278 www.freshfacefurniture.co.uk), within the estate's old forge, is a small business which restores, hand-paints and sells furniture. They can also make and paint furniture according to your requirements.

The **Valley of Stones National Nature Reserve** lies on the southeastern edge of Littlebredy and its 24 acres are pleasant for walking and horseriding. It is named for the sarsen stones that have tumbled down the valley. The stones were formed at the end of the last ice age as the tightly cemented sandstone that capped the chalk hilltops gradually fragmented under freeze/thaw conditions. The chalk grassland is home to wildflowers and butterflies, and scarce lichens and mosses grow on the sarsens. It is managed by the grazing of cattle and sheep.

12 ABBOTSBURY

Abbey House (page 296) **Abbotsbury Tearooms and B&B** (page 296)

Approaching Abbotsbury by road from the west is an absolute delight, as you gaze down towards Chesil Beach, which is watched over by St Catherine's Chapel. There are a few lay-bys where you can pull over and admire the view but it can all get a bit frantic if there are streams of traffic in both directions. A more relaxing option is to head up to **Abbotsbury hillfort** to take in the views at your leisure. Before you begin the descent to Abbotsbury, take the small turning on your left signed 'Ashley Close only'. It is worth the short detour to the top of the hill, where you can park and walk along Abbotsbury hillfort for practically aerial views of **Chesil Beach** and the lagoon it shields, known as **The Fleet**. The hill forms the western end of the ridgeway, which protects Abbotsbury from the worst of the weather and gives it its own microclimate. The fort would have been of great strategic importance to the Iron Age population as news of any seaward invasion could be passed to the region's other hillforts, including Maiden Castle (page 106).

"Abbotsbury was the site of an abbey, built in 1044 around the Church of St Peter and populated with Benedictine monks from Cerne Abbas."

As the name indicates, Abbotsbury was the site of an abbey, built in 1044 around the church of St Peter and populated with Benedictine monks from Cerne Abbas. It was destroyed in 1539, during the Dissolution, and some of the stone was used to build the village you see today. Near the church and Abbey House you will see other scattered ruins of the abbey, but the most obvious reminder of the monastic days is the **Tithe Barn**, which now houses a **children's farm and play centre** (page 171). The barn was built in the 14th century to store the tithe payments (a tenth of the harvest) paid by local farmers to the abbot and at 272 feet is the longest tithe barn in England. Its thatched roof covers only half the building but even that takes around three years to re-thatch.

One of the best views of the Tithe Barn is from Abbey House, where you can have lunch or afternoon tea in the garden (page 171). In the corner of the garden is the Old Mill House, believed to be the only surviving Benedictine watermill in England. The **church of St Nicholas**, parts of which were built around the same time as the Tithe Barn, features some bullet holes in the pulpit. These are not the result of a violent reaction to a particularly dreary sermon, but rather they were caused when the Parliamentarians expelled a Royalist garrison from the church during the Civil War.

While Abbotsbury can get very busy during the day in summer, the crowds are largely made up of day trippers who perform a mass exodus shortly after 17.00, making it a more pleasant place to stay than you might expect.The village has model looks; it is crammed with golden stone cottages, many topped with thatched roofs and decorated with window boxes full of colourful flowers. Most of Abbotsbury is owned by Ilchester Estates (page 178) and only around 15 houses are freehold. Lyn from Abbotsbury Tearooms credits Ilchester Estates with keeping Abbotsbury beautiful because they take care of any repairs and alterations, ensuring all work is in harmony with the village.

"It is crammed with golden stone cottages, many topped with thatched roofs and decorated with window boxes full of colourful flowers."

Abbotsbury caters for the steady stream of tourists it receives with an abundance of tea rooms and art galleries. In the centre of the village, outside the 19th-century Strangways Village Hall, is a helpful sign listing the various businesses. An **Abbotsbury passport ticket** (available from the attractions or their websites) allows you reduced admission prices for the three main attractions: the swannery, the subtropical gardens and the children's farm.

St Catherine's Chapel

This lonely building dominates the village from its position high on a hill and beckons you to walk up to it for stunning views of the coastline. From Market Street in the centre of the village take Chapel Lane and follow the path up the hill, passing pretty stone walls and looking back for views over the village. From this angle it is easy to appreciate the vast size of the Tithe Barn.

The chapel was built in the 14th century and may have been used as a chantry by the monks. When they built St Catherine's Chapel they certainly meant it to last – it is constructed entirely of stone, including the roof, with walls four feet thick. It survived the Dissolution, probably because of its importance as a seamark for shipping.

St Catherine is the patron saint of spinsters and for centuries unmarried women have climbed up to the chapel to pray for a husband:

> **A husband, St Catherine; a handsome one, St Catherine; a rich one, St Catherine; a nice one, St Catherine; and soon, St Catherine!**

I know plenty of girlfriends who have tried everything to find one of those, so a girls' trip to St Catherine's Chapel may well be on the cards. When I last visited, there were several handwritten prayers in the wall of the building asking for husband-hunting help, and the resident white doves seemed to be a good omen. Non-denominational services are held monthly in summer and if your prayers to St Catherine bear fruit, it is good to know that you can get married here.

From the chapel there are far-reaching views of Chesil Beach and The Fleet, and you can walk half a mile down the hill to the swannery and the beach from here.

Abbotsbury Swannery

New Barn Rd, DT3 4JG ✆ 01305 871858 🖱 www.abbotsbury-tourism.co.uk 🕘 mid-Mar to end Oct daily 10.00–17.00

By far Abbotsbury's best-known attraction is the swannery on The Fleet lagoon, which is home to around 600 swans (and various other canny birds who have taken up residence and exploit the very pleasant living conditions). It was established by Benedictine monks during the 1040s, when they farmed the swans for food. Sir Giles Strangways bought the swannery from Henry VIII in 1543 and it is still owned by his descendants, the Ilchester Estates (page 178), making these the only swans in England not owned by the Queen.

Clearly the swans you see here today won't end up on anyone's plate – this is a sanctuary – and you won't see swans in pens, they are free to roam. The visit begins with a film and an exhibition about swans and the swannery. You can then wander along the paths among the nesting mute swans, and hides allow you to watch the birds out on the water. On display over the waterways are some rather dastardly looking old-fashioned duck traps.

Children have the opportunity to help with feeding at 12.00 and 16.00, and mid-May to late June is a particularly exciting time to visit as this is when the cygnets hatch. Also on site are a well-stocked gift shop and a café.

Abbotsbury Children's Farm

Church St, DT3 4JJ ✆ 01305 871817 www.abbotsbury-tourism.co.uk ⏲ Mar–Aug daily, Sep–Oct Sat–Sun & Oct half-term

The Tithe Barn is not nearly as peaceful these days as it was when the monks were running the show because it now contains a children's farm. As well as the usual farm animals and pets, there are indoor play areas and a bouncy castle.

Abbotsbury Subtropical Gardens

Bullers Way, DT3 4LA ✆ 01305 871387 www.abbotsbury-tourism.co.uk ⏲ daily 10.00–17.00

Established in 1765 by the first Countess of Ilchester as a kitchen garden, this has developed into a colourful 30-acre garden filled with rare and exotic plants from all over the world. Many of the plants were first introductions to Britain, discovered by the descendants of the countess. There are notable rhododendron, camellia and hydrangea collections. The plant centre sells some of the plants on show in the garden, and there's a colonial-style restaurant.

FOOD & DRINK

Abbey House Church St, DT3 4JJ ✆ 01305 871330 ⏲ Mar–Oct 10.00–17.00. Teas and lunches around the enormous fireplace or on the lawn, with views of the millpond and Tithe Barn.

Abbotsbury Tearooms and B&B 26 Rodden Row, DT3 4JL ✆ 01305 871143. Clean, comfortable tea rooms serving generous light lunches, cakes and high tea. On sunny days, the garden is a nice spot to eat.

Old Schoolhouse Tearooms 1 Back St, DT3 4JP ✆ 01305 871808 ⏲ Oct–Jul closed Mon. A traditional tea rooms, which almost has a French feel thanks to the red-and-white checked tablecloths. There is also a garden area. Good homemade light lunches and cakes, plus a range of preserves on sale.

FROM THE SOMERSET BORDER TO THE MARSHWOOD VALE

Once part of a wealthy monastic estate with Forde Abbey at its heart, the area between the Somerset border and the A35 coastal road remains remarkably unspoilt. The accurately named **Marshwood Vale** is marshy and wooded, which has protected it from the development of large settlements; instead the bowl-shaped valley has just a few scattered farms and hamlets. It is encircled by hills, including Dorset's two highest points: **Pilsdon Pen** and **Lewesdon Hill**, which make for superb walking country.

13 FORDE ABBEY

Forde Abbey, near Chard TA20 4LU ✆ 01460 220231 www.fordeabbey.co.uk ⊙ gardens: daily; house: Apr–Oct Tue–Fri, Sun & bank holidays 12.00–16.00

Founded by Cistercian monks over 800 years ago, Forde Abbey became one of the richest monasteries in the country. It was transformed into a private house in 1649 and lies at the heart of a family-run estate. The house is surrounded by 30 acres of beautiful gardens. If it inspires you to start your own garden makeover, there is a small garden nursery on site. Central to the garden are its lakes. At 12.00, 13.30 and 15.00 the centenary fountain is turned on in the Mermaid Pond in front of the house and throws water high into the air for 15 minutes, creating a good photo-opportunity.

"Once part of a wealthy monastic estate with Forde Abbey at its heart, the area between the Somerset border and the A35 coastal road remains remarkably unspoilt."

You enter the house via the Great Hall, one of the remaining monastic rooms, which doesn't really live up to its name and feels rather cold and bare. Upstairs is of greater interest, in particular the Saloon with its wall-hanging Mortlake Tapestries depicting scenes from St John's Gospel. The tapestries were made in London around 1620 as copies of those woven in Brussels a hundred years earlier for the Sistine Chapel at the instigation of Pope Julius II; elsewhere are a fair range of family heirlooms and some evocative 18th-century bedrooms. Aside from the Great Hall, some other remnants of the house's monastic days remain: the chapel, the monks' dormitory, the cloisters and the undercroft, which now houses a restaurant.

14 GUY MALLINSON WOODLAND WORKSHOP

Woodland Workshop, Yonder Hill, Holditch TA20 4NL ✆ 01460 221102 🖱 www.mallinson.co.uk

Spending a few days living in a wood and creating something from it has the potential to be supremely relaxing. Guy Mallinson, a cabinetmaker, runs two-hour to five-day woodwork courses in woodland not far from Forde Abbey. Two-hour courses are available for children. The courses, which cater for all levels, range from carving a bowl to making a chair from a tree. On site are luxury camping facilities with all mod cons.

15 CONEY'S CASTLE & LAMBERT'S CASTLE

Those Iron Age folk certainly kept themselves busy, for not far from Pilsdon Pen and Lewesdon Hill are two further Iron Age hillforts. Tucked away down narrow lanes near the village of Fishpond Bottom, they are preserved by the National Trust. They lie about a mile apart and are linked by a road and a footpath. As well as fine walking spots, they are ideal for a picnic overlooking the Marshwood Vale.

Both Coney's and Lambert's castles may have been built as border posts between the neighbouring tribes, the Durotriges (eastwards) and the Dumnonii (southwest), or as status symbols for local chiefs. More recently (from 1709 to 1947), Lambert's Castle was used as the venue for a fair, with the hilltop serving as a racecourse.

These hillforts are perhaps at their best when wearing their spring finery in the form of a layer of bluebells, particularly Coney's Castle with its magical woodland enveloping the ramparts. Lambert's is larger and less wooded than Coney's Castle and as a result the views of the surrounding countryside are clearer.

"These hillforts are perhaps at their best when wearing their spring finery in the form of a layer of bluebells, particularly Coney's Castle."

FOOD & DRINK

Bottle Inn Marshwood DT6 5QJ ✆ 01297 678484 🖱 www.bottle-inn.net. This traditional thatched pub dating from 1585 has made a name for itself as the home of the annual World Nettle Eating Championship, where brave (or should that be silly?) folk attempt to eat the most nettles in an hour. You won't be compelled to eat nettles here – regular pub food is also served.

16 WHITCHURCH CANONICORUM

A village of farms and cottages tucked back from the coast at the southern edge of the Marshwood Vale, Whitchurch Canonicorum has a **church** with an unusual dedication – to St Candida, also known as St Wite. Within the church is the 13th-century shrine containing St Wite's remains. The three oval openings were originally designed for the sick to insert their ailing limbs into, or if they couldn't make it to the church a handkerchief was inserted and taken to them. Today the openings are used for depositing prayers handwritten on small cards, and there were plenty of them when I was last there. The shrine is a rare survival as most were destroyed during the Reformation and this is the only church in England, other than Westminster Abbey, that still contains the original medieval shrine and relics of the saint to whom it was dedicated. St Wite has not conclusively been identified: one theory is that she was a Saxon woman killed by the Danes in one of their raids on Charmouth.

Near the altar is a rather splendid shrine to 'S John Ieffrey of Catherstone, Knight', who died in 1611. The recumbent stone figure dressed in a knight's armour is in excellent condition.

Buried in the churchyard is **Georgi Ivanov Markov**, the Bulgarian dissident writer who died in London in 1978 after being stabbed with an umbrella which was used to insert a ricin pellet into his calf. His assassination was allegedly organised by the Bulgarian Secret Police with the help of the Soviet KGB. It was their third attempt to dispose of him, and several prominent KGB defectors, including Oleg Gordievskiy, have asserted that the KGB was responsible for the killing. The inscription on Markov's gravestone, which is written in both English and Russian, states that he died 'in the cause of freedom'. He was buried here at the request of his English wife, whose family is from the area.

17 PILSDON PEN & LEWESDON HILL

Pilsdon Pen and Lewesdon Hill are the two highest points in Dorset. No-one ever seems quite sure which of the two is actually the higher, although I am reliably informed Lewesdon narrowly takes the title at 915 feet. These neighbouring hills have a lot in common: both were once Iron Age hillforts, both were once used as beacon sites to warn of impending invasion and both provide magnificent views of the Marshwood Vale. A round walk from Broadwindsor, incorporating both Pilsdon Pen and Lewesdon Hill, takes about four hours.

Pilsdon Pen is particularly easy to access and makes a brief but satisfying walk on its own. There is a car park opposite the start of the walk, on the B3164. From there it is a short, steep climb up the hillside until you reach the flat top, which was once the site of the Iron Age hillfort.

18 BROADWINDSOR CRAFT & DESIGN CENTRE

Broadwindsor DT8 3PX ✆ 01308 868362 broadwindsor-crafts.co.uk ◷ daily 10.00–17.00, closes at 16.00 in Jan & Feb

Former farm buildings house this craft centre and restaurant in the village of Broadwindsor, east of Beaminster. At the heart of the centre is a large gift shop selling country-style gifts, homewares, clothing and food; in the lead-up to Christmas there is a huge and colourful range of Christmas decorations. In the surrounding buildings, formerly pig pens, are studios showcasing the work of different local crafts people and artists. The **Earth Design** shop sells a range of semi-precious stones, jewellery and crystals reputed to heal all manner of ills and owner Clive was so convincing about the healing power of crystals that I was persuaded to buy two.

"The centre's farming links contribute to its charm."

The restaurant here serves homemade light lunches and cakes, and is a popular pit stop for walkers tackling nearby Pilsdon Pen and Lewesdon Hill. There is plenty of free parking and the centre is wheelchair accessible. It has been part of the local farming community since 1986 and its farming links contribute to its charm; the manager, Sarah, is a farmer's wife and the day I met her she had had to rush home earlier that morning to deal with escaped cows.

EASTWARDS FROM BEAMINSTER

19 BEAMINSTER & SURROUNDS

Bridge House Hotel (page 296)

Beaminster, a market town since 1284, positively glows on a sunny day thanks to the golden hamstone from which much of the town is built. In fact, if you look closely you may see ammonites and other fossils in the golden walls of the buildings, as stone from nearby Horn Park Quarry, from which much of the town is constructed, is rich in them. Narrow lanes of terraced cottages converge in the market square. It is surrounded by gently rolling hills, which provide easy walking country.

The Square is the focal point; at its centre is a covered market cross known as the Julia Memorial. This was erected in 1906 by Vincent Robinson of Parnham House, which lies south of the town, as a memorial to his sister, Julia.

"The small, independent shop seems to have survived better in Beaminster than elsewhere."

St Mary's Church faces a row of pretty terraced cottages of assorted shapes, sizes and colours. The community has come up with an ingenious solution to the problem of getting an ageing population into church. A small stone building at the end of the churchyard contains a lift allowing those with limited mobility or in wheelchairs to avoid the steps. Volunteers are usually on hand to guide visitors and the community has done an admirable job conserving and restoring the church and deservedly won an award for their efforts. The volunteer who showed me around told me proudly that they had installed under-floor heating, when each of the original flagstones was painstakingly lifted and replaced. Sadly the pews had to be removed due to wood rot, and have been replaced with chairs. The tower, which dates from the 1500s, is one of the most elaborate in the West Country: every three hours the church clock plays the hymn tune known as 'Hanover'. Within the church are large memorials to the Strobe family who once lived in nearby Parnham House, while the embroidery screen near the organ, which depicts nearby scenes, was made by local ladies as part of their millennium celebrations.

Beaminster has a small, local **museum** (Whitcombe Rd, DT8 3NB ✆ 01308 863623 🖱 www.beaminstermuseum.org ⏲ Easter–Oct Tue, Thu, Sat, Sun & bank holidays) telling the history of the town and surrounding villages.

BUCKHAM DOWN FAIR

An annual pony and dog show, Buckham Down Fair (🖱 www.buckhamfair.co.uk) takes place in August just outside Beaminster. The fair is the initiative of actor and television presenter, Martin Clunes, and his wife Philippa, on whose land it is held. Martin has made his Dorset retreat his permanent home and is very much a fixture of the local community. The Clunes family, like so many who live in Dorset, are horse and dog people. As well as a gymkhana and dog classes, the fair has stalls selling local produce, trade stands and fairground rides. This fun day out, which attracts several thousand visitors, is also an important fund-raising event: since it began in 2008, the fair has raised over £200,000 for local charities.

FOOD & DRINK

The small, independent shop seems to have survived better in Beaminster than elsewhere. Around The Square are several selling locally grown food, such as **Nick Tett Family Butchers** and **Fruit n' Two Veg**. Just around the corner, on Hogshill Street, is the **Village Bakery** – irrepressibly quaint and old-world.

Art Deco Café@Ann Day 3 Hogshill St, DT8 3AE 01308 861137 Tue–Sat 09.30–14.30. Operating for over 20 years, this café is run by a husband and wife team, a baker and an artist respectively. Homemade soda bread, soup and fish are on the menu, but no meat.

Beaminster Brasserie Bridge House Hotel, 3 Prout Bridge, DT8 3AY 01308 862200 www.beaminsterbrasserie.co.uk daily for breakfast, lunch & dinner. Head chef Steve gives local ingredients an international flavour at this elegant fine-dining restaurant. Local snails always appear on the menu – perhaps they are the ultimate Slow Food? – and dishes might include snail rarebit with Palmers beer. The meals are beautifully presented and the service is very professional. Surprisingly affordable.

Brassica 4 The Square, DT8 3AW 01308 538100 closed Mon. Upmarket restaurant in the market square, created by chef Cass Titcombe who co-founded Canteen Restaurant in London. The menu has a Mediterranean flavour but dishes are prepared using Dorset produce wherever possible.

Out of Town Farmshop Lane End Farm, Tunnel Rd, DT8 3HB 07518 982148 closed Sun & Mon. On the A3066, half a mile north of Beaminster, this small shop sells the farm's own meat and vegetables, plus homemade pies, cakes and preserves.

Mapperton Gardens

DT8 3NR 01308 862645 www.mapperton.com garden: Apr–Oct Sun–Fri

Mapperton, the home of the Earl and Countess of Sandwich, lies in a gloriously bucolic landscape two miles east of Beaminster. Its garden, hidden in a narrow, steep-sided valley below the house, is fascinating for its amalgamation of three styles at the hands of three different owners. The banks, terraces and long, rectangular fish ponds date from the Elizabethan period but in the 1920s a wealthy widow, Ethel Labouchère, created an Arts and Crafts garden in the Italianate style on the highest of the terraces, into the banks of which she built little rooms, complete with fireplaces for taking afternoon tea. It's possible she was influenced, or helped, by Harold Peto, creator of the (Arts and Crafts Italianate) garden at Iford in Wiltshire. The present owner's father (Victor Montagu) bought the property in the 1950s and made several important additions to the garden, including a classical-style orangery, overlooking Mrs Labouchère's fountains and topiary, and a pergola. He also converted one of the Elizabethan fish ponds into a swimming pool of near-Olympic proportions, while in the wild, stream-fed valley below the pool he planted an arboretum with some notable specimen trees. The current owners have done an admirable amount to improve the planting on all three levels of the garden over the past two decades. The Jacobean manor house is open for limited periods during the summer.

20 EVERSHOT

Acorn Inn (page 296) **Summer Lodge Country House Hotel Restaurant and Spa** (page 296)

Evershot is the second-highest village in Dorset, after Ashmore, although unlike Ashmore it doesn't feel particularly high. It is also where the River Frome rises, just behind St Osmund's Church in Back Lane.

Much of the village's undeniable charm derives from its mixture of architectural styles, from tiny 17th-century cottages to large Georgian houses. Although the main street is largely residential, Evershot has managed to keep its village shop, and the excellent bakery is thriving. The pavement is raised on one side of the village street; this protected pedestrians and residents of the more upmarket side of the street from the muck that collected in the road, presumably mostly donated by the local bovine population. The houses on the raised pavement side were therefore considered more desirable and expensive.

On the edge of Evershot is the heart of the vastly wealthy **Ilchester Estates**, which owns 15,000 acres of West Dorset, including Abbotsbury and Chesil Beach, and 40 acres of central London, including Holland Park. The estate is currently owned by Charlotte Townshend, a country sports enthusiast and active opponent of the ban on foxhunting. As the owner of the Abbotsbury Swannery (pages 170–1), she is the only person in the country, other than the Queen, who is allowed to own swans.

FOOD & DRINK

Acorn Inn 28 Fore St, DT2 0JW 01935 83228 www.acorn-inn.co.uk daily. A 16th-century coaching inn with excellent food and service, and an active skittles team.

Evershot Village Bakery 18 Fore St, DT2 0JW 01935 83379 Mon–Sat 08.00–15.00, Sat 08.00–12.30. Spelt and sourdough breads sell briskly, alongside a range of pizzas and sweet treats.

Summer Lodge Country House Hotel Restaurant and Spa Summer Lane, DT2 0JR ✆ 01935 482000 www.summerlodgehotel.co.uk daily. This elegant hotel has a fine-dining restaurant with excellent service, and an award-winning wine selection. Meals are taken in the conservatory, restaurant or cosy bar and afternoon tea is served daily in the drawing room.

21 THE KINGCOMBE CENTRE

Lower Kingcombe, DT2 0EQ ✆ 01300 320684 www.kingcombecentre.org daily; see advert on page 181

The marketing material gives Kingcombe the title of 'the jewel in Dorset's crown'. It certainly is very precious. The Dorset Wildlife Trust manages almost 1,000 acres of meadows and nature reserve at Kingcombe and Powerstock. The Kingcombe site was formerly a well-managed organic farm, owned by the Wallbridge family, and is now rich in wildflowers, butterflies and birdlife. Grazing is an important element of the conservation of this land so you can expect to see livestock as well as wildlife. You can simply wander and experience the English countryside as it used to be, have lunch in the café or take part in one of the many activities, events or craft and environmental studies courses on offer, such as beekeeping, hedgelaying and wildlife tracking.

I spent a wonderful and informative day on a **foraging course** with John Wright, known for his appearances on television's *River Cottage.* By the end of a day foraging with him, I was surprised I had survived my childhood. As an only child and a tomboy, I spent many hours building camps in the countryside surrounding our house and was often joined by my equally tomboyish friend, Gillian, who later put her countryside training to good use and married a Devon farmer. Gillian and I collected all manner of leaves, berries, even fir cones, and held 'tea parties' – by sheer fluke it seems, we managed to steer clear of the various toxic plants that John took care to point out on his course. As he said, 'it is just as important, if not more so, to know the plants you can't eat as it is to know the plants you can'. Particularly scary was the hemlock waterdropwort, Britain's most deadly plant, which seems cunningly disguised as some relation of parsley or celery.

"The Kingcombe site was formerly a well-managed organic farm."

John describes himself as one of those lucky people who has turned a hobby into a job. I had assumed he must have had some sort of botany studies background but he was actually a cabinetmaker, whose passion for mushrooms led him to become a self-taught forager. John runs a series of fascinating foraging courses, covering hedgerow, seashore, fungi and more. He maintains an interesting and helpful website (www.wild-food.net) and has written some lovely books on foraging, which are part of the River Cottage Handbook series, *Mushroom Handbook*, *Edible Seashore Handbook* and *Hedgerow Handbook*.

22 EGGARDON HILLFORT

This hugely atmospheric Iron Age hillfort, four miles east of Bridport, has superb panoramic views and is one of the most accessible hillforts in Dorset. On a clear day you can see right across Lyme Bay to south Devon, and across the Marshwood Vale to Pilsdon Pen.

The fort covers 20 acres of the hilltop. Its impressive ditches and banks seem to ripple as shadows cast by the clouds drift across them. The interior contains a large octagonal earthwork, thought to be the result of tree planting by a smuggler who owned the land and used the formation as a seamark for his ships. It is certainly worth a visit for the views, the history and the serenity.

UPDATES WEBSITE

You can post your comments and recommendations, and read the latest feedback and updates from other readers online at www.bradtupdates.com/dorset.

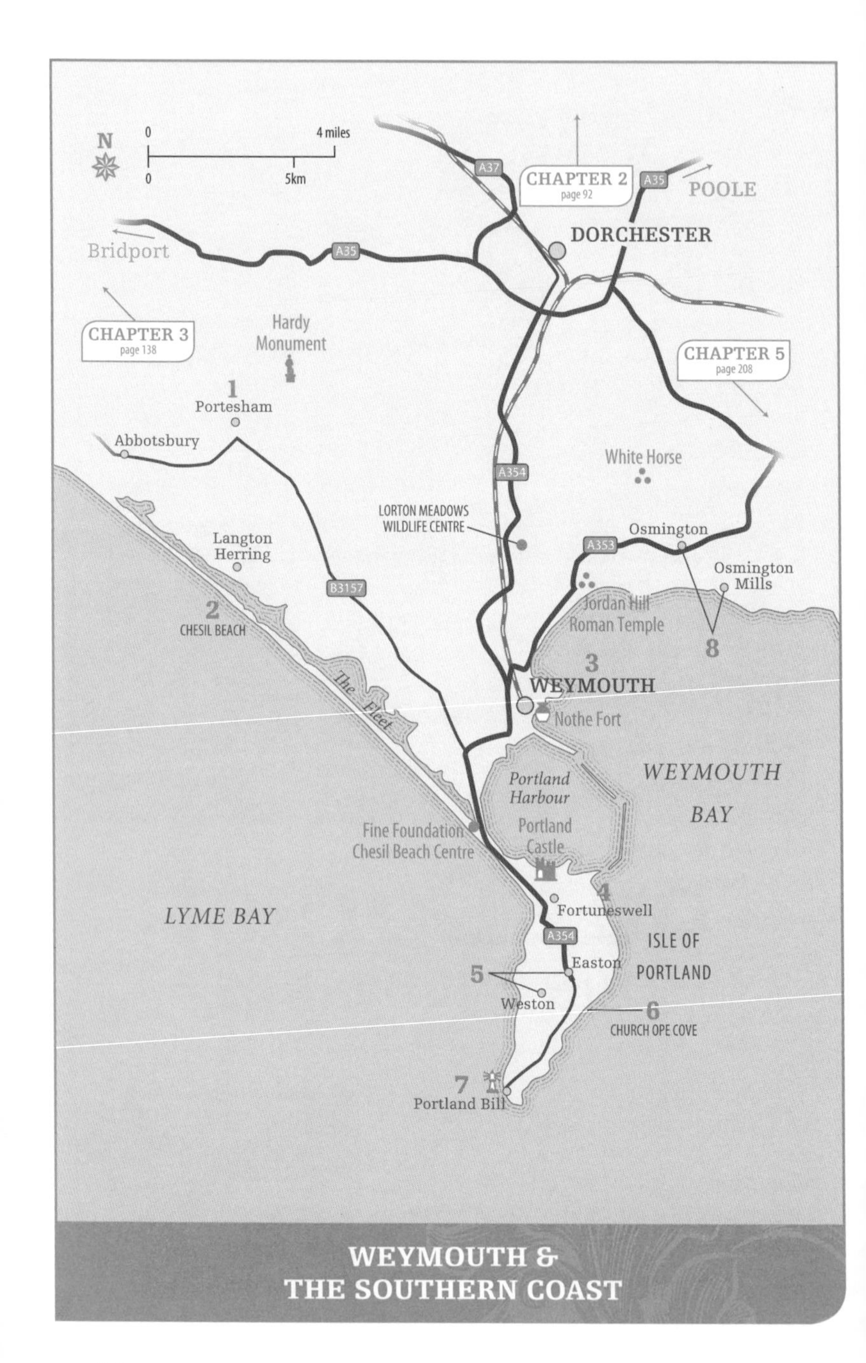

WEYMOUTH & THE SOUTHERN COAST

4
WEYMOUTH & THE SOUTHERN COAST

Along this portion of the Dorset coast the huge shingle bank of **Chesil Beach** stands separated from the mainland by a lagoon, creating a strange, but entirely natural, visual phenomenon. At the beach's southeastern end are the town of Weymouth and the peninsula known as the Isle of Portland. Depending on how you look at it, **Weymouth** is either confused about what it wants to be or multi-talented, having to juggle being a working town, a port and a seaside resort. Now it can add another achievement to its CV – Olympic venue. It was quite a coup for Weymouth, and for Dorset, when the Weymouth and Portland National Sailing Academy (WPNSA) was chosen to host the sailing events for the London 2012 Olympic and Paralympic Games. Thanks to the WPNSA, the area now has world-class facilities to complement its superb sailing waters.

Linked to Weymouth by a causeway is the **Isle of Portland**, famed for its Portland stone quarries and its lighthouse at Portland Bill, which warns shipping to steer clear of Dorset's southernmost point. A highlight of the island is Portland Castle, an extraordinarily well-preserved fort built by Henry VIII in the 1540s.

Smuggling became rife along the south coast after an act was passed in 1751 which dramatically increased the tax levied on spirits. Weymouth and the surrounding area was a smuggling hot spot, with a notorious gang operating around **Osmington Mills**. The quiet waters of **The Fleet** lagoon behind Chesil Beach were ideal for stowing contraband for collection at a more convenient time.

The **South Dorset Ridgeway** is a ridge of chalky downland running parallel to the coast from **Abbotsbury** in the west to the village of **Osmington** in the east. The ridgeway is extraordinarily rich in prehistoric sites such as long barrows, round barrows, stone circles and hillforts.

GETTING THERE & AROUND

Reaching Weymouth and Portland by road can be irksome, as the main route from Dorchester is very congested in the peak holiday months. For long-stay parking, try the Swannery car park.

Weymouth is the main entry point for the area as it has a mainline train station and connecting buses to get you to the more hidden places, including access points for the South Dorset Ridgeway such as Portesham.

PUBLIC TRANSPORT

Weymouth is three hours from London Waterloo by **train** and is also connected by train to other Dorset towns: Dorchester, Wareham, Poole and Bournemouth.

The **Jurassic Coast bus** (CoastLinX53) runs along the south coast, calling at Poole, Wareham, Wool, Weymouth, Abbotsbury, West Bay, Bridport, Chideock, Charmouth, Lyme Regis, Seaton, Beer and Exeter. Other parts of Dorset are relatively easy to reach by bus: **South West Coaches** operates an hourly service between Portland and Dorchester via Weymouth (210), and **Wilts & Dorset** operates buses to Blandford (⊗ www.morebus.co.uk). In summer, buses operate between Weymouth, Lulworth and Swanage, which is handy for the South West Coast Path; they stop at Norden Park and Ride station, the starting point for the Swanage Heritage Railway to Corfe Castle and Swanage.

In Weymouth, **First Buses** (⊗ www.firstgroup.com) are useful for getting around the town and the surrounding area, including Portland. From Easter to September open-top buses run from Weymouth Esplanade to Portland Bill. A Weymouth **Plus Bus** ticket gives you unlimited travel around Weymouth and Portland on participating operators' services (⊗ www.plusbus.info).

Information about local bus services and how to link up with the South Dorset Ridgeway is available at ⊗ www.travelinesw.com.

BY BOAT

White Motor Boats (☎ 01305 785000) operates a summer **ferry** from Weymouth (Brewers Quay) to Portland Castle, which takes around 40 minutes. The usual boat is *My Girl*, a veteran of World War II. The ferry leaves Brewers Quay at 10.30, 12.30 and 14.30 and returns from Portland Castle at 11.20, 13.20 and 15.20.

TOURIST INFORMATION CENTRE

There is no longer a tourist information centre in the area, but there is a tourist information point at the Pavillion Theatre in Weymouth (page 190) and a visitor information centre at the Heights Hotel in Portland (page 204), where you can pick up brochures and maps. For general information, see www.visitweymouth.co.uk.

During the summer, local boatmen operate **rowing-boat ferries** across the harbour from near the ferry terminal. This is a novel way of getting from the town to Nothe Fort and saves you the walk up to the Town Bridge.

Numerous **cruises** along the Jurassic Coast also depart from Weymouth.

CRUISE OPERATORS

MV Freedom 11 Redcliff View, DT4 8RW 07974 266867 www.mvfreedom.co.uk. Trips along the Jurassic Coast or around Portland Harbour in a boat specifically equipped for the disabled.

Weymouth Whitewater 07899 892317 www.weymouth-whitewater.co.uk. Rigid inflatable boat rides to Lulworth Cove, Portland or around Weymouth Bay lasting one to two hours.

CYCLING

Just as driving around Weymouth can be problematic due to traffic, so can cycling. The most cycle-friendly routes are outlined in *Active Travel Weymouth and Portland: A Guide to Walking and Cycling*, available from tourist information centres and online (www.dorsetforyou.com). The **Rodwell Trail** (www.rodwelltrail.org.uk) follows the track of the old Weymouth and Portland railway built in 1865, and is open to cyclists as well as walkers.

The **South Dorset Ridgeway** offers some good off-roading with fantastic views and a chance to stop off at the numerous prehistoric sites.

CYCLE HIRE

Jurassic Electric 07796 135256 www.jurassic-electric.co.uk. Offers guided electric bike tours of the area, and you can also hire an electric bike from them.

Jurassic Trails 10 Bowleaze Coveway, Preston, Weymouth DT3 6RY 01305 836428 www.jurassictrailscyclehire.co.uk. Based at the start of several family-friendly routes, known as the Jurassic Cycle Trails.

Weymouth and Portland Bike Hire 64 Weston, Portland DT5 2BZ 07783 456749 www.portlandbikehire.com. Free delivery and collection within the Weymouth and Portland area.

WALKING

The South West Coast Path runs along this stretch, diverting inland around Weymouth and passing above the **White Horse** near Osmington. A four-mile circuit from Osmington works well through fields to Sutton Poyntz, then up on to White Horse Hill for the high-level section on the coast path before dropping down near the White Horse into Osmington.

The **South Dorset Ridgeway** is part of the South West Coast Path and runs from West Bexington to Osmington Mills. Glorious views of the Jurassic Coast, chalk downland and river valleys are not its only draw card as this is an area packed with archaeological delights, reminders that the land has been inhabited for over 6,000 years. *Round-a-bout the Ridge* is a collection of four walks taking in the archaeology and scenery of the South Dorset Ridgeway. The nicely illustrated packs are available from tourist information centres and can also be downloaded from the publications section of the AONB website (www.dorsetaonb.org.uk).

The Visit Weymouth website (www.visitweymouth.co.uk) suggests walking routes using local buses. The **Rodwell Trail** (www.rodwelltrail.org.uk) follows the track of the old Weymouth and Portland railway, built in 1865, and links to the South West Coast Path.

Portland is easy to explore on foot and a nine-mile path runs around the peninsula. The fascinating southern tip around Portland Bill makes a perfect three-mile circuit past the three lighthouses. Southwell is a useful starting point, giving the pleasure of arriving at the Bill on foot, and taking in atmospherically decayed old quarries with rusting cranes and derricks, and a huge blow-hole on the east coast; follow the west coast until you're nearly level with the strikingly hideous factory on the skyline, then head inland back to Southwell.

HORSERIDING

Hacking is available in the countryside to the north and east of Weymouth and on the Isle of Portland.

RIDING STABLES

Chesil Equestrian Centre Weston Portland DT5 2JH 01305 823719 www.chesilequestriancentre.co.uk. Offers hacking for all levels of experience on the Isle of Portland. The coastal treks provide impressive sea views.

Ranch House East Farm Dairy, Osmington Mills DT3 6HB 01305 833578. Offers hacking near Weymouth for experienced riders.

WEST OF WEYMOUTH, INCLUDING CHESIL BEACH

1 PORTESHAM & SURROUNDS

The village of Portesham snuggles up against the base of the chalk hills of the South Dorset Ridgeway. **St Peter's Church**, which is largely 12th and 13th century, is reached over a flagstone across the flower-topped stream which flows gently alongside the main street. The handsome 18th-century **Portesham House** is where Vice-Admiral Sir Thomas Masterman Hardy once lived.

Standing high above Portesham on Black Down Hill is the **Hardy Monument**. It is not, as you may at first assume, a monument to the novelist Thomas Hardy but to the vice-admiral who served aboard Nelson's HMS *Victory* during the Battle of Trafalgar in 1805. During the battle the French and Spanish fleets were defeated but Nelson was fatally wounded. It was to Hardy that Nelson reputedly uttered his famous last words, 'Kiss me, Hardy'. Hardy spent his childhood in Portesham until joining the navy as a 13-year -old captain's servant. The monument is a 72-foot Portland stone tower built in 1844. It certainly isn't a thing of beauty, looking rather like a factory chimney protruding from the hilltop: its shape was intended to represent a telescope of the type Hardy may have used at sea. Once you know that, it doesn't seem so out of place. You used to be able to climb to the top of the monument for spectacular views but at the time of writing it was closed for an extended period for restoration; however, the views from the base are splendid, without the climb. The heathy surroundings make great strolling terrain, with the South Dorset Ridgeway passing the monument; bear in mind that, although the National Trust owns the monument and a small patch of land around it, the rest of the land is private.

From the Hardy Monument, you have several options for **walking**: one of the most pleasing (around seven miles) is to start from Portesham and walk up, then carry on eastwards on the well-marked track along the ridge of Bronkham Hill with its spectacularly profuse series of prehistoric tumuli, and down to Corton Farm, then back to Portesham by lanes and footpaths.

FOOD & DRINK

Kings Arms 2 Front St, DT3 4ET ✆ 01305 871342 ⏲ daily. Freshly cooked pub food. The large beer garden with wood-fired pizza oven is popular in the warmer months.

2 CHESIL BEACH

Stand on Portland Heights or outside St Catherine's Chapel high above Abbotsbury and look out to sea and you will be treated to the most extraordinary sight – a wide, golden, shingle bank rising out of the water and running along the coastline, with a lagoon sheltering sheepishly behind it. If you saw such a thing in Dubai you might assume it was the zany creation of a capricious sheikh, but this is Dorset and Chesil Beach is all natural.

Stretching for 18 miles between West Bay and Portland, Chesil Beach is the largest of three major shingle structures in Britain. The shingle bank, which reaches around 40 feet at its highest point, was formed by rising seas at the end of the last Ice Age. Its rounded pebbles have been graded in size by strong tidal currents; they are as small as peas at the western end and the size of oranges at the Portland end. For centuries the size of the pebbles has been helping locals, mostly smugglers and fishermen, pinpoint where they are landing on the beach.

The lagoon, known as **The Fleet**, extends from Abbotsbury to Portland and contains a mixture of salt and fresh water. Home to an abundance of birdlife, wading birds can be seen all year, while brent geese from Siberia and red-breasted merganser (fish-eating duck) visit in winter. The birds' ancestors must have had quite a shock back in 1942–43, when Barnes Wallis's famous bouncing bomb was tested on The Fleet in preparation for the Dambusters raids.

"If you saw such a thing in Dubai you might assume it was the zany creation of a capricious sheikh."

At the southern end of The Fleet, just before you head over the causeway from Weymouth to Portland, is the **Fine Foundation Chesil Beach Centre** (Portland Beach Rd, DT4 9XE ✆ 01305 206191 www.dorsetwildlifetrust.org.uk/chesil-beach-centre) and a pay-and-display car park with direct access to Chesil Beach. The centre is run by the Dorset Wildlife Trust and provides information on Chesil Beach, the Fleet and Portland. Binoculars allow you to watch seabirds feeding on the sand flats and there is live video from cameras on the bed of the lagoon. It is worth checking whether any sections of the beach are closed, as during nesting season (usually April to August) parts are off-limits to avoid disturbing the birds. The centre also runs a programme of events (see website for details), and there is a good café (page 196). From the centre is a boardwalk leading to Chesil Beach.

Since Chesil Beach is virtually physically impossible to walk along, the South West Coast Path follows the inland side of The Fleet, midway along which **Langton Herring** makes a handy access point for the water's edge.

Glass-bottom boat trips provide the opportunity to explore The Fleet and get a closer look at its bird and sealife (The Fleet Observer, Ferryman's Way, Wyke Regis, Weymouth DT4 9YU ✆ 01305 759692 🖱 www.thefleetobserver.co.uk ⏲ Easter–Oct).

3 WEYMOUTH

A bustling seaside town of around 52,000 people, Weymouth attracts thousands of holiday-makers in summer, earning it the rather dubious nickname of 'England's Bay of Naples', or more recently 'Weybiza'. It has an active harbour, constantly criss-crossed by fishing vessels and pleasure craft, and a ferry port which connects it to France and the Channel Islands. When it was announced as the venue for the sailing events of the London 2012 Olympic and Paralympic Games, work quickly began to spruce up the town, which had begun to look a little neglected.

Plague port & royal resort

Weymouth began as two medieval ports on either side of the mouth of the River Wey. The two towns, Weymouth and Melcombe Regis, were joined in 1571 by royal charter and a bridge was later built across the harbour between them. The portion now referred to as the town centre, which lies north of the River Wey, was actually Melcombe Regis, which has a grim claim to fame, for it was here that the bubonic plague, or Black Death, entered England in 1348.

During the 18th century Weymouth, like many coastal towns, was touted as a health retreat. King George III came to Weymouth in 1789 to try out one of the first bathing machines, a hut on wheels drawn into the water by horses where one could bathe supervised by an attendant. It is said that while he bathed 'God save the King' was dutifully sung from another hut. The king visited regularly until 1810, a fact which is commemorated by a chalk carving on a hillside at Osmington depicting the monarch on horseback (pages 205–6). The promise of healing properties and royal patronage made Weymouth highly fashionable and rows of elegant houses sprung up along the esplanade to cater for well-to-do visitors.

The **statue of George III** on the esplanade was erected in 1809 to mark the 50th anniversary of his succession. Nearby, at the end of King Street, is the colourful **Jubilee Clock**, which was built in 1887 to commemorate 50 years of the reign of Queen Victoria. A bronze **statue of Queen Victoria** sits in front of **St John's Church**, a fine Portland stone building completed in 1854.

During World War II, Weymouth suffered heavy damage. It also featured prominently in the D-Day landings in Normandy as a departure point for many British and American soldiers. A **memorial** on the esplanade, opposite the Royal Hotel, records that 517,816 troops and 144,093 vehicles embarked at Weymouth between 6 June 1944 and 7 May 1945.

The seafront & Lodmoor Country Park

Today, handsome Georgian terraced houses and some sizeable hotels line Weymouth's seafront. The earlier terraces have iron balconies, while the later ones (1820s) have bay windows. If you can manage to screen out the amusement arcades and tacky souvenir shops you can just about imagine how the seafront was back in the 18th and early 19th centuries. In summer the long sandy beach is given over to the usual seaside entertainment, including a funfair, traditional Punch and Judy show and the ever-popular donkey rides. There is also a shell-shaped pod where sand sculptors show off their skills.

"Handsome Georgian terraced houses and some sizeable hotels line Weymouth's seafront."

There is no longer a tourist information centre in Weymouth but there is an **information point** in the **Pavillion**, a theatre at the southern end of the seafront, where you can pick up information on local attractions and public transport. Near the Pavillion is the ferry terminal with services to the Channel Islands and France. A packet steamer service between Weymouth and the Channel Islands was launched in 1794. Although the purpose was originally trade, the link led to many Dorset families settling in the Channel Islands.

Near the Pavillion, **Sea Life Tower** takes people up to 174 feet on what looks like a rotating doughnut for views of the bay and the Jurassic Coast.

A colourful Gypsy kiosk can often be seen on the esplanade, where Romany Gypsy Zara Lee will tell your fortune. Zara's family has been telling fortunes on Weymouth Esplanade for 40 years and Zara, who told me she has had the gift since childhood, took over from her parents in 2008.

A land train operates between Easter and the end of September from the Pavillion along the seafront to **Lodmoor Country Park**. The 350-acre park contains a Royal Society for the Protection of Birds (RSPB) nature reserve and numerous more lively attractions, such as mini-golf, a miniature railway, Weymouth Sea Life Park and Sandworld. As parking is expensive at Lodmoor Country Park, catching the land train can help to keep costs down.

One of the town's best-known attractions is **Weymouth Sea Life Park** (Lodmoor Country Park, DT4 7SX ✆ 0871 4232110 www.sealifeweymouth.com ⊙ daily 10.00–18.00). As well as the displays of colourful fish you may expect, more unusual residents feature, such as baby crocodiles, seals, sharks, otters, rays and rescued green sea turtles. Many of the creatures have been rescued and cannot be released, or were born and bred at the park as part of its conservation work. You might like to plan your visit around particular feeding times or keeper talks (details on the website), and to take along swimwear and towels for the water rides. Admission is costly but various vouchers offer reduced rates.

"A land train operates between Easter and the end of September from the Pavillion along the seafront to Lodmoor Country Park."

For many years visitors to Weymouth have admired Mark Anderson's sand sculptures, and those of his grandfather, Fred Darrington, before him. Fred began creating them on Weymouth Beach in the 1920s, a skill he later passed on to his grandson. Mark's sand sculptures now have a more permanent home in the form of **Sandworld** (Lodmoor Country Park, DT4 7SX ✆ 07411 387529 www.sandworld.co.uk), which he co-founded in 2011. Incredibly, the intricately detailed works are created by Mark and his fellow sculptors using nothing but sand and water. His website (www.sculpturesinsand.com) shows many of his and Fred's creations.

Radipole Lake

Returning towards the town centre and heading away from the esplanade along King Street you will come to the Swannery car park, where a huge open-air **market** is held on Thursdays between Easter and autumn. This is also where you will find the visitor centre for the **Radipole Lake RSPB Reserve** (✆ 01305 778313 www.rspb.org.uk; see box, page 192),

RADIPOLE LAKE RSPB RESERVE

Sarah Cookson, RSPB Volunteer

The first time I visited the RSPB's Weymouth Wetlands Nature Reserve at Radipole Lake, I could hardly believe that I was still in the middle of a busy town with houses and shops on every side and the beach, amusement arcades and ice-cream sellers of the tourist resort just five minutes' walk away.

The noise and bustle fell away and so did the cares. I was in Weymouth's tranquil heart, a peaceful oasis for locals and holiday-makers alike. I had stumbled across a little piece of paradise with meandering paths overhung with arches of hawthorn and blackthorn, sweeping willows and buddleia adorned with butterflies and bees.

The paths led to surprising vistas over pools and lagoons, where kingfishers dived and ducks dabbled, and small nooks and stretches of the River Wey, where water vole plopped and otters played.

As well as breeding kingfishers, Weymouth Wetlands is home to bearded tits and a wide range of wildfowl and warblers, including the Cetti's. Bitterns, the UK's rarest bird species, regularly overwinter here. In 2009, a pair of marsh harriers nested on the reserve and successfully reared three young – the first breeding pair in Dorset for nearly half a century and the most urban in the country. These rare and magnificent birds of prey returned with six fledglings – what a coup!

Other creatures are thriving too –five species of bats as well as reptiles and amphibians, butterflies and moths and a whole host of other insects and plants.

So whether you're a dedicated wildlife watcher, want somewhere to take the family that's considerably less crowded than the esplanade or simply want a quiet walk in the 'countryside', Weymouth Wetlands is a great place to be. And I mean just be. It restores my soul on a regular basis and it's well on the way to becoming one of the country's finest urban wetlands, stuffed with breathtaking wildlife, right at the heart of the town.

a surprising chunk of tranquillity in the middle of town. The lake – which flows into Weymouth Harbour – and the surrounding wetland are home to an impressive line-up of bird species, including rare bitterns and Cetti's warblers. You don't need to be a knowledgeable ornithologist to enjoy the reserve – the visitor centre (⏲ daily 09.00–17.00 or 16.00 in winter) and handy display boards make it accessible to everyone. Simply getting away from the hustle and bustle and wandering through the wetland is a joy. Children can be entertained with specially created trails, bird events, and during the summer, family activities such as pond dipping and bug hunts, while paths make the reserve accessible to wheelchairs and pushchairs.

DORSET'S ANCIENT HABITATS

Dorset's geological diversity crammed into a small area has produced varied landscapes and habitats, from fertile vales to chalk downland, ancient woodland to unspoilt heaths. Dorset has the highest proportion of conservation areas of any English county.

1 Godlingston Heath on the Isle of Purbeck. 2 Duncliffe Hill: a pocket of well-preserved woodland in the Blackmore Vale. 3 The Wyndham Oak at Silton is one of England's oldest trees. 4 Dartford warblers can be found across Dorset's heaths and woodland.

ALEXANDRA RICHARDS

ERNI/S

DAVID CROSBIE/S

HISTORY & HERITAGE

Everywhere are reminders you are walking in the footsteps of much earlier Dorset inhabitants. The county is justifiably proud of its rich literary heritage; its landscapes inspired Thomas Hardy, William Barnes, Enid Blyton and more.

ALEXANDRA RICHARDS

NEAL SULLIVAN

ALEXANDRA RICHARDS

1 Medieval Knowlton Church lies on a Neolithic henge. 2 The Roman Town House in Dorchester. 3 The ruins of Old Sherborne Castle. 4 The bridge in Sturminster Newton is one of several in Dorset to carry this warning. 5 Exhibits at the agricultural museum at Mangerton Mill. 6 The sheep-washing pool at Winterborne St Martin. 7 Thomas Hardy set his famous works in his native Dorset – pictured here, his writing tools.

ALEXANDRA RICHARDS

HISTORIC HOUSES & GARDENS

Every corner of Dorset is endowed with carefully maintained historic houses and glorious gardens, many of which are open to the public. The survival of several large estates has helped to preserve Dorset's landscapes and character.

1 Kingston Lacy is one of Dorset's grandest houses. 2 The delightful garden at Cranborne Manor. 3 Athelhampton House dates from the 15th century. 4 Minterne Gardens is nestled in the Cerne Valley.

ALEXANDRA RICHARDS

ALEXANDRA RICHARDS

ALEXANDRA RICHARDS

Around Weymouth Harbour

More low-key than the seafront, **Weymouth Harbour** is a pleasant place to wander, divided into two distinct halves by the River Wey, as it was when it was two communities prior to 1571. On the old Melcombe Regis (north) side is **Custom House Quay**, where the buildings that were once at Weymouth's commercial shipping heart now stand at the centre of an area dominated by restaurants and shops. Being an old mariners' haunt, there is no shortage of historic pubs along this stretch. From here you can watch the fishing and pleasure boats on the harbour and explore the narrow streets that lead back into the town centre. **Custom House** is a fine brick building, as is the George Inn which towers over its neighbours. The **Royal Dorset Yacht Club** (11 Custom House Quay, DT4 8BG ✆ 01305 786258) occupies a chapel-like building, which was once an institute for seamen, known as the Sailor's Bethel.

The squat stone building at the end of Maiden Street is the original **Fish Market**, built in 1855, and appropriately still sells fish. It is worth taking a short walk along Maiden Street for a closer look at the stone building on the corner of St Edmund Street. I wouldn't ordinarily suggest people take a closer look at a **public convenience**; however. this one has a cannonball lodged in the wall above the first-floor window, believed to have been fired during the Civil War.

In summer, you can cross to Nothe Gardens on the other side of the harbour using a rowing-boat ferry from the ferry terminal. Alternatively, you can take the **Town Bridge**, a bridge which lifts every two hours during the day to allow tall ships to pass through. The bridge is reputed to be in the same place as the wooden one constructed in 1597 after Melcombe Regis and Weymouth were united.

Holy Trinity Church, erected in the 1830s, is one of the first buildings you are likely to see if you come across the bridge and it gives its name to Trinity Road, which runs alongside the harbour. Colourful buildings stand shoulder to shoulder facing the water, where the boats are busy bustling up and down. This side of the harbour has more residential buildings than the other, giving it a homely, village-like feel. Set back from the harbour is **Tudor House** (3 Trinity St, DT4 8TW ✆ 01305 779711 ⊘ www.weymouthcivicsociety.org), one of Weymouth's few remaining Tudor buildings. It is decorated and furnished in the style of a 17th-century middle-class home and guided tours provide an insight into domestic life at that time.

Nearby Hope Square is dominated by **Brewers Quay**, the converted buildings of the Devenish Brewery, which now house a series of bric-a-brac shops and the **Weymouth Museum** (01305 457982 www.weymouthmuseum.org.uk). Continuing along the peninsula, Nothe Gardens offer a peaceful retreat from the town, plenty of parking and views of the harbour. It is here that you will find **Nothe Fort**, part of Weymouth's 19th-century defences and now a fascinating museum (see below).

Continuing towards Portland, **Sandsfoot Castle** (www.sandsfootcastle.org.uk; free admission) sits across Portland Harbour from Portland Castle (page 199). The two were built by Henry VIII to protect against French and Spanish invasion after his divorce from Catherine of Aragon and his break with the Catholic Church. Unlike Portland Castle, Sandsfoot is a ruin, largely because the cliff on which it sits has been progressively eroded by the sea, although the construction of the Portland Breakwater in 1849 helped to slow the erosion. The ruin sits precariously on a cliff top and in recent years stabilisation work has been carried out and attractive gardens laid down on the approach to it. The castle and gardens are peaceful with views of the harbour, and the small café makes a good pit stop on the Rodwell Trail (page 186).

Nothe Fort

Barrack Rd, DT4 8UF 01305 766626 www.nothefort.org.uk Apr–Sep daily, & at specified times during the rest of the year – see website

At the end of a promontory on the south side of the entrance to Weymouth Harbour, Nothe Fort was built between 1860 and 1872 by the Royal Engineers with the help of inmates from Portland Prison. It was part of England's coastal defences and remained in active service until 1956. It is one of the best-preserved forts of its kind.

Today, it is an absorbing museum, displayed over three levels, charting its own history and Weymouth's, with particularly detailed information on the town's role in World War II. The Fort Artillery in their splendid Victorian artillery uniforms put on displays of musketry and cannon firing on alternate Sundays throughout the year and during special events.

The fort is great value for money and particularly good on a rainy day as much of it is under cover. In better weather, however, you can take in the views of the harbour from the picnic areas on the ramparts. The fort is wheelchair accessible and has a good café.

Lorton Meadows Wildlife Centre – Dorset Wildlife Trust

Lorton Lane, Upwey DT3 5QH ✆ 01305 816546 www.dorsetwildlifetrust.org.uk

On the northern edge of Weymouth, this is a Dorset Wildlife Trust reserve of unimproved grassland with views over Portland and Weymouth Harbour. The grassland attracts a variety of bird and butterfly species, including marbled white, common and holly blues and small and large skipper. Wildlife webcams enable you to watch resident barn owls, tawny owls, great tits and kestrels; there's also a small shop and a picnic area. Although the reserve is open all year and the wildlife centre is open between April and October, the wildlife centre opening times vary so it is best to call and check.

Boating, fishing & diving around Weymouth

For information on sailing, windsurfing, kitesurfing and angling, see www.visitweymouth.co.uk

From Weymouth you can take boat trips of varying durations, including along the Jurassic Coast (page 185).

With superb **sailing** waters, it is unsurprising that there are numerous sailing schools in the area. If you want to try your hand at **performance yachting**, Weymouth Sailing (✆ 07970 122718 www.weymouthsailing.co.uk) offers groups of up to eight people the opportunity to have a go on a state-of-the-art yacht. Sailing is either around Weymouth and Portland or along the Jurassic Coast to Swanage. The Andrew Simpson Sailing Centre (WPNSA, Osprey Quay, Portland DT5 1SA ✆ 01305 457400 www.andrewsimpsonsailing.co.uk) offers boat hire, as well as sailing and powerboat courses.

Weymouth and Portland are also popular for other watersports, including windsurfing, canoeing and diving. A permit is required for waterskiing in specially designated areas of Weymouth Harbour, available from the Harbour Master's Office (13 Customs House Quay, DT4 8BG ✆ 01305 838423). One of the largest **dive schools** in Weymouth is Underwater Explorers (Unit 1, Maritime Business Centre, Portland DT5 1FD ✆ 01305 824555 www.underwaterexplorers.co.uk).

The best source of information on **fishing** in the area is Weymouth Angling Centre (✆ 01305 777771 www.weymouthangling.com). Weymouth has one of the largest charter **angling** fleets in Britain, with turbot, brill, bass, plaice, pollack, cod and ray fishing available.

FESTIVALS

Weymouth and Portland's close relationship with the sea is celebrated in the annual **Spirit of the Sea Maritime Festival**, which takes place over a week in July. It incorporates cultural events, sporting activities and entertainment, including the Dorset Seafood Festival, a sailing regatta, live music and a carnival procession (www.spiritofthesea.org.uk). Another favourite on the Weymouth calendar is the colourful **Beach Kite Festival**, held in May (www.visitweymouth.co.uk).

FOOD & DRINK

Weymouth Harbour and the seafront are overflowing with eateries of varying kinds. Cheap and cheerful cafés and fish and chip shops dominate but there is the odd upmarket restaurant.

Chalbury Food & Wine 71 St Mary St, DT4 8PJ 01305 457244 daily. An inviting shop specialising in Dorset food, drink and gifts.

Crab House Café Ferry Man's Way, Portland Rd, Wyke Regis DT4 9YU 01305 788867 Wed–Sun for lunch & dinner. Located at the Weymouth end of Ferry Bridge (to Portland), this unassuming little shack has earned an enormous reputation for excellent seafood. It is also an oyster farm, so the oysters are as fresh as they get. The café has views of The Fleet and Chesil Beach. Reservation recommended.

Dining Room 67 St Mary St, DT4 8PP 01305 783008. Experienced chef Taher Jibet creates modern European dishes with a strong Mediterranean influence, using local produce.

Floods Seafood Restaurant 19 Custom House Quay, DT4 8BG 01305 772270 Mon–Sat for dinner. Family-run seafood restaurant serving catch straight from Weymouth's fishing fleet. Simple fish dishes, nicely presented. The restaurant is committed to using only sustainable fish stocks. Reservation recommended.

Mallams 5 Trinity Rd, DT4 8TJ 01305 776757 www.mallamsrestaurant.co.uk Mon–Sat for dinner. Locally sourced fish and meat in this popular harbourside restaurant.

Nothe Tavern Barrack Rd, DT4 8TZ 01305 839255 www.thenothetavern.co.uk daily for lunch & dinner. Pub at the entrance to Nothe Gardens, not far from the fort.

Taste Fine Foundation Chesil Beach Centre, Portland Beach Rd, DT4 9XE 01305 206196 daily. The café at the visitor centre uses as much locally sourced food as possible, with Portland crab sandwiches a speciality. You can watch the birdlife on The Fleet as you eat.

Tea Bush Tearooms 55a The Esplanade, DT4 8DG 07852 796298 daily 10.00–16.00. Built in 1783, this is one of the few buildings along this stretch of the esplanade that has changed little since its construction. The tea rooms still has its distinctive bay window and the range cooker downstairs is thought to be original to the building. On offer are unfussy, reasonably priced lunches, cream teas and ice creams, including old favourites such as Knickerbocker Glory.

THE ISLE OF PORTLAND

Despite its name, the Isle of Portland is a peninsula connected to the mainland by Chesil Beach and the A354, which runs alongside it. A place of maritime history and quarrying, Portland is a term familiar to many, either via the BBC's shipping forecast or linked to its most famous product, Portland stone.

As a Royal Manor, Portland has its own court leet and crown court. In recent times a popular car sticker has been seen around this part of Dorset, proclaiming 'Keep Portland Weird'. Evidently it has been that way for some time, which is perhaps why it feels like you are entering another country when you arrive here. Reverend John Hutchins (1698–1773), the Dorset historian, wrote:

> The people are a stout, hardy, industrious race and in general better informed than most labouring people; very healthy, but not long-lived, for, though at 60 many of the men appear strong and robust, they soon drop off and there are no instances of longevity, which may be accounted for from too great a use of spirits.

By all accounts they were not a friendly bunch: Portlanders used to throw stones at outsiders, whom they called 'kimberlins', to keep them from setting foot on their island. Hutchins commented:

> The natives are jealous of strangers coming to settle in the Island and ... in consequence they marry and intermarry so much among themselves that most of the Islanders are related.

They reportedly followed a bizarre marriage custom, whereby women did not marry until pregnant, at which point:

> She tells her mother, the mother tells her father; her father tells his father and he tells his son that it is then the proper time to be married.

The system only broke down when non-Portlanders got the local ladies pregnant and then reneged on the deal to get married.

Thankfully Portland has come a long way since Hutchins's days, the locals no longer throw stones at outsiders and its rugged curiosity value (rather than beauty) makes it worth a visit. Portland should perhaps be more attractive than it is – after all it is surrounded by the sea, overlooks Chesil Beach and there is no shortage of beautiful stone with which to build. While there are some attractive buildings of Portland stone, the island

STONE ISLAND

The Isle of Portland has been quarried since the 17th century. In his 1793 paper on Dorset, written for the Board of Agriculture and Internal Improvement, John Claridge wrote:

> As to quarries, the whole island of Portland seems to be one mass of the most beautiful stone, chiefly used in the metropolis and elsewhere for the most superb buildings, and universally admired for its close texture and durability, surpassing any other. The raising of it, is a laborious business, sometimes employing upwards of a hundred men, to break down a large jam of it, afterwards it is divided into blocks and then conveyed in cars by horses to the shore.

Indeed there is plenty of Portland stone to be admired in the 'metropolis' today, including St Paul's Cathedral, the Bank of England and the British Museum. The island still has working quarries; those which are disused have been colonised by plants and wildlife creating mini nature reserves.

also has many rows of boxy-looking houses and most of the villages turn their back on the sea.

The whole of Portland is a solid block of limestone, windswept and industrial in feel, owing to its many quarries, extant and defunct. Its long and fascinating history is neatly summarised in the island's museum (page 202); finds from the Culverwell Mesolithic site indicate that it is the oldest known settlement in Britain. The peninsula is easily explored on foot, along the nine-mile coast path. Several of its disused quarries, including Broadcroft, Kingbarrow and Tout (page 200), are now nature reserves, colonised by plants and wildlife.

4 FORTUNESWELL & SURROUNDS

Beach House (page 297)

The drive across the causeway, shielded on one side by the vast Chesil Beach, makes a memorably strange approach to Portland. Chesil Beach is so high at this point that it resembles an enormous desert dune and you might half expect to see a camel lolloping over the hill.

The modern complex on your left as you arrive on the Isle of Portland is **Osprey Quay**, home to the **Weymouth and Portland National Sailing Academy** (Osprey Quay, DT5 1SA ✆ 01305 866000 www.wpnsa.org.uk), the venue for the London 2012 Olympic and Paralympic sailing events.

It occupies the site of the former Royal Navy air station, and breathed new life into the area when it was founded in 1999 as a not-for-profit company to promote sailing at all levels and make the sport more accessible to a wider group of people. The academy has superb facilities and direct access to Weymouth Bay and Portland Harbour, reputed to be some of the best sailing waters in the world.

The road climbs to the top of a hill through Portland's largest residential settlement, known as Fortuneswell. From just in front of the Heights Hotel there are expansive views over Chesil Beach and Portland Harbour. It isn't exactly a beautiful view – the dense mass of housing and modern harbour buildings see to that – but it gives you your bearings. At one end of the Heights Hotel is a **visitor information centre**, where you can pick up brochures and maps. On Tuesdays in summer you may encounter the Portland **market**, near the hotel. Also nearby, on the island's highest point, **Verne Citadel** was built between 1848 and 1869 as a fort and became a prison in 1950, although at the time of writing the prison was empty. It is here that you will find the **Jailhouse Café** run by inmates on day release from the nearby prison at The Grove (page 202).

Portland Castle

Liberty Rd, Castletown DT5 1AZ ☎ 01305 820539 🌐 www.portlandcastle.co.uk ⏲ daily most of the year but parts are closed at times for private events; English Heritage

Overlooking the harbour, just beyond the National Sailing Academy and juxtaposed with a series of ultra-modern buildings is Portland Castle, is one of English Heritage's best-preserved Tudor monuments. It was built in the 1540s by Henry VIII to protect against French and Spanish invasion after his break from the Catholic Church.

A short, squat building, designed to make it less of a target, it has a rounded wall facing the sea to deflect incoming artillery. Its surroundings are unexceptional – the modern buildings tower over it – but once you are inside the castle walls it is a different story. The castle is built of Portland stone, which seems to be tough stuff as it remains in superb shape. I doubt the modern buildings around it will fare as well over the next 550 years.

The other reason Portland Castle is well preserved is that it saw less battle action than Henry VIII had perhaps anticipated. During the Civil War the Parliamentarians and Royalists alternately occupied the castle, and in the 19th century it became a private house. During World War I it was a sea plane station, and during World War II it was used as a base in preparation for the D-Day landings.

You are free to wander through the castle at your own pace (the audioguides are helpful) and browse a series of exhibits on its history. The rooms overflow with atmosphere, especially the Great Hall, and the enormous fireplaces the size of a modern apartment's kitchen transport you back to the time of Henry VIII. This is a great castle for firing up the imagination of children, who will enjoy the arrow slits, cannons and life-sized model of Henry Tudor.

5 EASTON, WESTON & SURROUNDS

Contemporary Cottages (page 297)

The unimaginatively named villages of Easton and Weston lie on the plateau in the centre of the island. They are not particularly appealing in their own right but there are a couple of interesting places to visit in the area.

As you travel southwards along Wide Street from Fortuneswell, towards Weston, you will see on your right the turning to **Tout Quarry** (Tradecroft Industrial Estate, DT5 2LN 01305 826736 www.learningstone.org daily; free admission). The road takes you into an industrial estate and an abandoned stone quarry that has been turned into a nature reserve and a sculpture park with a difference. You can wander through it on foot and look at the sculptures carved into the rock, and you may see local stonemasons at work. Stone-carving courses are available; details are on the website.

A little further south, off Weston Road, is the sizeable and commanding **St George's Church**, which appears almost as if it has been superimposed against the backdrop of a quarry and residential streets. It was consecrated in 1766 and replaced the church of St Andrew above Church Ope Cove, although St George's is now itself redundant. It is under the care of the Churches Conservation Trust and helpful volunteers are on hand to show you around. Built from Portland stone, the nave exudes residential rather than ecclesiastical style, but the belfry and steeple are more intricate and are reminiscent of St Paul's Cathedral. The interior is unusual, with the box pews arranged so everyone faces the twin pulpits

"Built from Portland stone, the nave exudes residential rather than ecclesiastical style."

DON'T MENTION THE 'R' WORD!

Whatever you do while on Portland, don't mention the 'R' word. The use of the word is taboo because rabbits have long been associated with bad luck, and instead locals refer to them as 'underground mutton', 'long-eared furry things' or 'bunnies'. The superstition is thought to derive from quarry workers, who would see rabbits rising from their burrows immediately before a rockfall and blamed them for increasing the likelihood of landslides.

in the centre of the chancel. The graveyard is packed tightly with over 2,000 sturdy headstones in assorted shapes, with many of the deaths related to seafaring or quarrying. Only one headstone is not made from Portland stone: the black granite headstone marks the grave of William Pearce who was killed by lightning in 1858 on Portland Beach. Some locals theorise that the dark-coloured stone was chosen to symbolise the fact that the lightning turned him black. A leaflet in the church provides details of some of the more interesting graves, including those of the victims of the **Easton Massacre**. When a press gang came to Portland in 1803 to take men to join the military, the locals resisted, believing that they were exempt because they had paid 'quit rent' as a substitute for military service, as was the right of people living in a Royal Manor. In the ensuing struggle with the press gang just near the church, three Portland men and one woman were shot and killed.

South of Easton are two Grade II-listed windmills, which date from at least 1608, although their exact date of construction is unknown. They were used to mill four until the late 1890s. Today they appear as cylinders, are rather overgrown, and sadly they are frequently vandalised.

6 CHURCH OPE COVE & SURROUNDS

Church Ope Cove is a small pebbly bay on the east side of the island, which can only be reached on foot. You can park opposite Pennsylvania Castle (a large private house) and follow the path down the steep hill, through the ruins of the medieval **church of St Andrew**. Dating from the 12th century, it was abandoned in 1756 and is Portland's earliest surviving building. The path takes you through woodland, then eerily through the middle of the plant-covered ruins and between the gravestones.

On the hillside above Church Ope Cove are the remains of **Rufus Castle**, also known as Bow and Arrow Castle. What little there is of the structure is almost entirely covered by a shroud of vegetation. The castle is believed to have been built by Richard, Duke of York between 1432 and 1460 as a coastal defence against the French during the final stages of the Hundred Years War.

Not far from Church Ope Cove on the way to Portland Bill is a viewpoint at **Cheyne Weares** with views as far as St Aldhelm's Head near Swanage, and a different perspective on the ruins of Rufus Castle.

HM Portland Prison in the village of The Grove was established in 1848 to provide labour to quarry the island's stone. Artefacts and photographs from the prison's early days make an interesting display at the Portland Museum and at the small **Grove Prison Museum** (The Governor's Community Garden, The Grove ✆ 01305 715726 ⏲ Thu–Sun 10.00–14.00). Inmates from here run the Jailhouse Café at Verne Citadel (page 204).

Portland Museum

217 Wakeham, DT5 1HS ✆ 01305 821804 www.portlandmuseum.co.uk ⏲ Easter–Oct Sun–Thu

The museum is built around two tiny 17th-century cottages and a small garden above Church Ope Cove. For a little island, Portland certainly has a big history and this museum covers it from Jurassic fossils, through prehistoric inhabitants to the more recent maritime links, prison and Portland stone. The displays on finds from archaeological digs on the island are fascinating and include information on the important Mesolithic site at Culverwell. There are also some interesting items from the days when the Romans inhabited the island, including a beautiful duck brooch inlaid with blue and cream enamel, and the sarcophagi in the garden of the museum. The museum's director drew my attention to the rare Iron Age ingots, which date from around 500BC, paraphernalia from the island's prison, and a fossilised freshwater turtle, unearthed on the island in 2010.

"HM Portland Prison in the village of The Grove was established in 1848 to provide labour to quarry the island's stone."

7 PORTLAND BILL & SURROUNDS

Old Higher Lighthouse (page 297) **Old Lower Lighthouse** (page 297)

Portland Bill is a narrow promontory, which forms the most southerly part of the Isle of Portland. Before you reach Portland Bill's lighthouses,

JURASSIC SAFARIS – 4X4 TOURS

01305 772324 www.jurassicsafari.co.uk; see advert in fourth colour section.

Husband and wife team Gary and Carol Fry offer 4x4 tours from Weymouth or Wareham along the Dorset coast. Tours start from two hours and cover different areas, such as the Isle of Portland, the Purbeck Hills, Thomas Hardy country near Dorchester or the area around Golden Cap. Both from farming families, Gary and Carol have lived in Dorset all their lives and have devised routes that take you off the beaten track, along country lanes and ancient byways. This means that not only will you see great views, you may see some good wildlife as well. The trusty Land Rover takes up to six people; it makes easy work of the off-roading and gives the whole experience a real 'safari' feel. Gary provides an enthusiastic commentary, using his local knowledge to full effect.

I ventured out with Gary and Carol around Golden Cap. I have driven and walked around the area extensively but the 4x4 tour provided views from a different perspective that made it seem like a whole new landscape. As with all their safaris, we were treated to one of Carol's homemade cakes when the time came for us to have our tea break.

Jurassic Safaris are ideal for those who lack the time, ability or inclination to walk to the best vantage points on the coast, but I expect that like me, even locals and regular visitors to the area who take one of these trips will see the area in a different way. The Land Rover is wheelchair accessible.

you will pass the **Culverwell Mesolithic site** (May–Aug first Sun of month, or by appointment by calling 01305 861576), which provides evidence that Portland has been inhabited for between 8,000 and 8,300 years, making it the oldest known site of permanent residence in Britain. One of the site's main features is a stone floor from the period, which represents the earliest known use of Portland stone for building purposes. You can learn more about the site and see some of the items uncovered here at the Portland Museum (see opposite).

Of the three lighthouses on the promontory, one is still operational. The red-and-white striped **Portland Bill Lighthouse** (DT5 2JT 01255 245156 www.trinityhouse.co.uk varied, check website) was built in 1906 and is 115 feet high. It guides vessels bound for Portland and Weymouth through the strong currents and acts as a marker for ships navigating the English Channel. Inside is a visitor centre with information on the Isle of Portland and the Jurassic Coast, as well as live footage of birds nesting on nearby cliffs. Tours of the lighthouse are available and include walking the 153 steps up to the light itself.

One of the disused lighthouses, built in 1788, has been transformed into the **Portland Bird Observatory and Field Centre** (The Old Lower Lighthouse, Portland Bill DT5 2JT ✆ 01305 820553 www.portlandbirdobs.org.uk), with basic hostel-style accommodation. The other, **Old Higher Lighthouse**, is a private residence but also offers guest accommodation (page 297).

FOOD & DRINK

There is a shortage of enticing eateries on Portland, although there are a couple with good views and decent food.

Blue Fish Café 16–17a Chiswell, DT5 1AN ✆ 01305 822991 ⊙ Wed–Sun 09.00–14.00 & Wed–Sat for dinner. Friendly, unpretentious restaurant that serves excellent seafood. Easily the best on Portland and probably one of the best in Weymouth.

The Heights DT5 2EN ✆ 01305 821361 ⊙ serves breakfast & afternoon tea, as well as lunch & dinner. It doesn't look like much from the outside, and the bistro has a bit of a chain restaurant feel, but it does have superb views over Chesil Beach and Weymouth Bay. The food is good and the service friendly.

Jailhouse Café The Verne, DT5 1EQ ✆ 01305 825186 www.jailhousecafe.co.uk ⊙ Mon–Fri 10.00–15.00. A café run by prisoners on day release from HM Portland Prison. The café provides training and work experience in preparation for release.

Lobster Pot Restaurant Portland Bill DT5 2JT ✆ 01305 820242 ⊙ daily 09.30–17.30. Unfussy café next to Portland Bill Lighthouse with sea views. Good, simple fare, including comforting Dorset cream teas.

The Pulpit Portland Bill DT5 2JT ✆ 01305 821237 ⊙ varied. A traditional pub overlooking Portland Bill.

EAST OF WEYMOUTH

Leaving Weymouth and heading east you are welcomed back into wild, untouched Dorset landscapes. Inland lies gentle chalk downland, river valleys, farms and scattered villages, while the coast features austere cliff faces.

8 OSMINGTON & OSMINGTON MILLS

Smugglers Inn (page 297) **Rosewall Camping** (page 297)

Although just four miles from Weymouth, Osmington seems a world away from the bustling town. Its narrow street is lined with thatched cottages and the backdrop of verdant hills leaves you in no doubt

SCREEN BITES FILM FESTIVAL

Gay Pirrie-Weir; screenbites.co.uk

Screen Bites, Dorset's food film festival, celebrated its tenth anniversary in 2014 with a gala evening at St Giles House, home of the Earl of Shaftesbury and his family pages 79–80).

An entirely local initiative, the festival brings films from all over the world to tiny communities in Dorset and highlights the county's vibrant culinary and cultural life. Screen Bites is unique, as it is the UK's only festival that balances food producers with food-themed films, responding to new products and new movies, and allowing audiences to meet the people who grow and produce the food they can buy, and eat, all within the small geographical area. Both the food and film communities in Dorset have seen an increase in interest in recent years, and Screen Bites has been at the forefront of this. Run by a small team of hard-working volunteers, for five weeks every year, the festival shows food-themed films and invites local food producers along to offer samples of their wares. Screen Bites has introduced almost 200 food producers to its audiences, in venues that range from intimate village halls to large arts and community centres. There have been screenings in National Trust houses, UK premieres and talks by those in the food and the film industries. Films from all over the world have been shown, such as *Vatel*, *Under the Tuscan Sun* and *Jadoo*. The festival has even been represented at the Chelsea and Hampton Court flower shows, with award-winning gardens based on edible playgrounds at local schools.

Events are unpredictable, and there have been spontaneous outbreaks of morris dancing, delicious after-film servings of Greek food (provided by a member of the audience) and an evening when the Fried Green Tomatoes on screen were complemented by the real thing, prepared in the village hall kitchen by a local farming co-operative. The award-winning website has full details of the festival from the beginning of September each year, and the growing band of Screen Bites groupies compete to be the first to book their tickets, sometimes travelling from the Devon border in the west to near Bournemouth to see their favourite films and eat their favourite local food. Visit the website to find out more about the festival's history and its current programme.

that you have re-entered rural Dorset. To the north of the village of Osmington is the **White Horse**, a depiction of George III on horseback, carved into the chalk hillside. It was created in 1808 in honour of the king, to commemorate the summers he had spent in the Weymouth area. Sadly, due to ill health, the king never returned to see it completed. At 279 feet long and 327 feet high, the carving is clearly visible from the

A353 to the east of Weymouth. A walk from Osmington or the nearby village of Sutton Poyntz allows a closer view.

On the coast is **Osmington Mills**, which has a rugged coastline and spectacular views towards Portland. The South West Coast Path runs along the top of the cliffs here, dipping down to the **Smugglers Inn**, a very popular pub with an inviting garden. It is easy to see why this building, parts of which date from the 13th century, has a long association with smugglers as its location is perfect for bringing contraband ashore – right on the coast at the bottom of a gulley. In the 18th and 19th centuries it was home to one of the area's most notorious smugglers, Emmanuel Charles; a file on the inn's history available at the bar makes interesting reading.

Jordan Hill Roman Temple

daily: free admission; English Heritage

On a hill at the back of a residential area between Weymouth and Osmington, off the A353, are the foundations of a 4th-century Romano-Celtic temple. All that remains of the building are the stone foundations in the form of a square. Built during the Roman occupation of the area, the temple would have served the local farming and fishing communities, and would have been visible from the sea.

Excavations of the site located a large cemetery to the north of the temple, where more than 80 skeletons were found, some originally in wooden coffins, others in stone cists. Various personal objects were buried with them, including pots, combs, jewellery, arrowheads and an iron sword; some are now on display in the County Museum in Dorchester (page 102).

FOOD & DRINK

Craig's Farm Dairy East Farm, Osmington DT3 6EX 01305 834591 www.craigsfarmdairy.co.uk daily. Tea rooms and farm shop on a working dairy farm, where the dairy's own ice cream is sold.

The Smugglers Inn Osmington Mills DT3 6HF 01305 833125 daily. A perfect stop-off for walkers on the South West Coast Path (with Burning Cliff above Ringstead Bay to the east and Black Head to the west) this large pub has lots of separate eating areas and a huge beer garden on either side of the stream, and its menu offers plenty of variety. There is a fee for the car park but you can redeem it at the bar for orders over £15. Dogs are welcome. Gets very busy in summer.

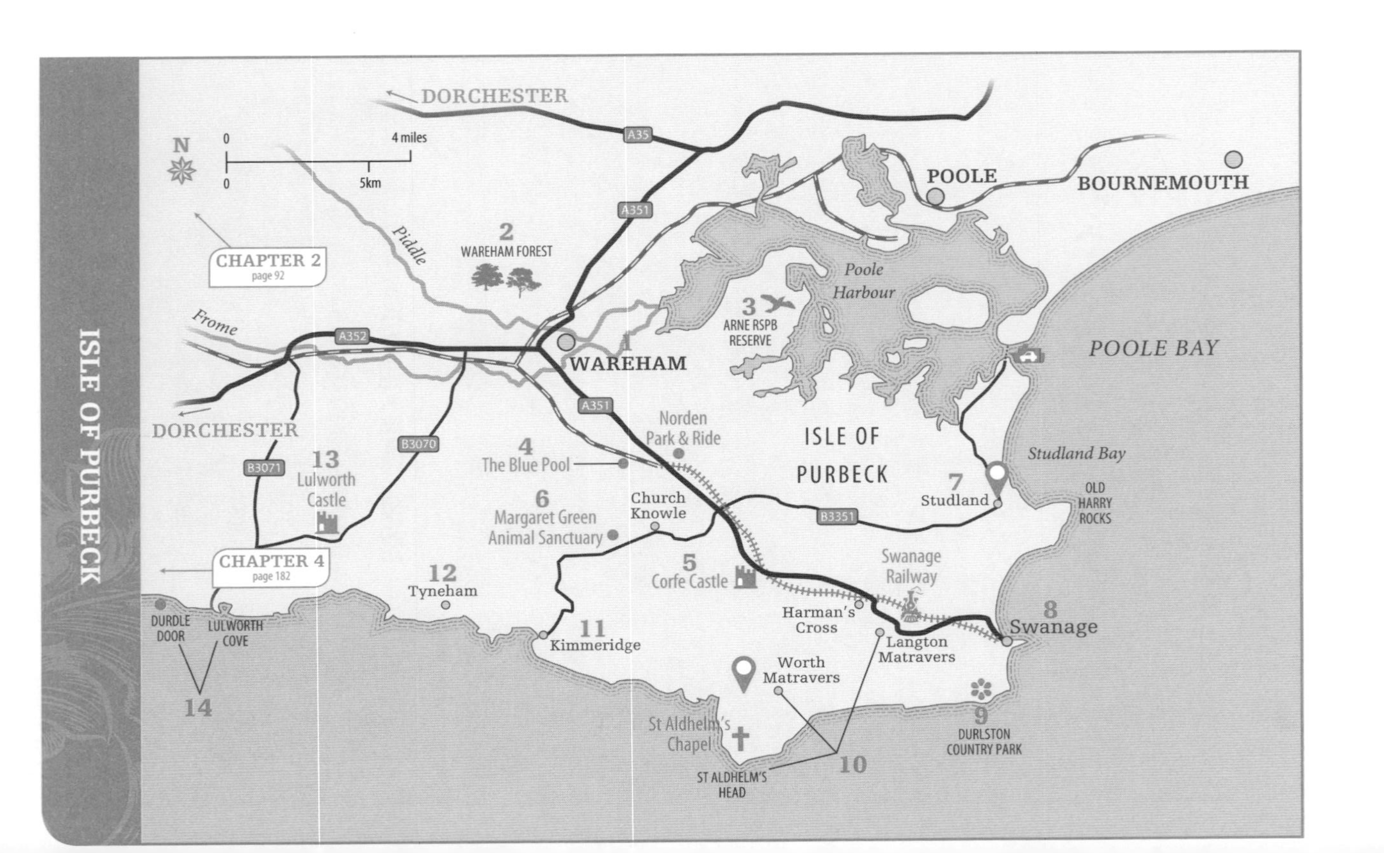

ISLE OF PURBECK
N
0
4 miles
0
5km
CHAPTER 2
page 92
CHAPTER 4
page 182
DORCHESTER
DORCHESTER
A35
A351
A351
A352
B3070
B3071
B3351
Piddle
Frome
2
WAREHAM FOREST
1
WAREHAM
3
ARNE RSPB
RESERVE
Poole
Harbour
POOLE
BOURNEMOUTH
POOLE BAY
Studland Bay
OLD
HARRY
ROCKS
ISLE OF
PURBECK
Norden
Park & Ride
4
The Blue Pool
6
Margaret Green
Animal Sanctuary
Church
Knowle
5
Corfe Castle
7
Studland
Swanage
Railway
8
Swanage
Harman's
Cross
Langton
Matravers
Worth
Matravers
9
DURLSTON
COUNTRY PARK
10
St Aldhelm's
Chapel
ST ALDHELM'S
HEAD
11
Kimmeridge
12
Tyneham
13
Lulworth
Castle
DURDLE
DOOR
LULWORTH
COVE
14

5
ISLE OF PURBECK

One glance at the map tells you that the Isle of Purbeck is not actually an island, but a peninsula of some 60 square miles bordered to the south and east by the English Channel and to the north by Poole Harbour and the River Frome. Nevertheless, I wouldn't be surprised to wake up one morning to the news that residents of the Isle of Purbeck are lobbying for independence from the rest of Britain. And I for one wouldn't blame them. The people who live here will proudly tell you how lucky they are to dwell in this enchanting corner of England. When extolling the virtues of the peninsula, locals may tell you that it inspired some of Enid Blyton's stories and that it has its own microclimate. Both claims are evidently true: Blyton was a regular visitor to the area from 1931 and the Isle of Purbeck does indeed have one of the highest sunshine records in England.

The peninsula is dissected by the **Purbeck Hills**, a chalk ridge which runs westward from the sea near Old Harry Rocks across the Isle of Purbeck to Lulworth Cove, and whose shape hints at the origin of the name 'Purbeck' – supposedly from the Saxon 'pur', meaning bittern or snipe, and beck meaning 'beak'. **Purbeck marble** has been quarried from the Isle of Purbeck's coastal plateau, especially the area between Swanage and **St Aldhelm's Head**, since Roman times and can be seen in many of England's grandest buildings.

Wareham, a pleasing ancient market town within Saxon earthen defences, marks the obvious gateway to the Isle of Purbeck and Poole Harbour. In the centre of the peninsula the towering ruins of **Corfe Castle** constitute one of Dorset's most-visited landmarks. **Swanage** is a seaside resort with all the associated entertainment, while **Studland Nature Reserve** provides sandy, unspoilt beaches and heathland. Off the coast from Studland the chalk stacks known as **Old Harry Rocks** mark the eastern end of the **Jurassic Coast**. The military training area around East Lulworth encompasses the fascinating deserted village of **Tyneham**, which can be visited when the firing ranges are not in use. Nearby are some of the Dorset coast's most photogenic landmarks, **Lulworth Cove** and **Durdle Door**.

You'll chance across plenty of opportunities here for Slow Travel, including a ride through the peninsula on the **Swanage Steam Railway**, and ideal country for cycling and **walking**. The South West Coast Path traces the outline of the peninsula and footpaths and bridleways criss-cross the hills. For me, the highlight has to be **horseriding** along Studland Beach as the sun is setting, illuminating the pale faces of Old Harry Rocks.

GETTING THERE & AROUND

The Isle of Purbeck is easily accessible by car: the A351 runs along the spine of the peninsula between Wareham and Swanage and minor roads branch off it. Crowds are drawn to Swanage and Studland in summer and the roads can become congested. Leaving the car at Norden to catch the Swanage Railway heritage service to Swanage is therefore a popular option.

Purbeck District Council publishes *Car Free Days in South Purbeck by Foot, Cycle, Bus, Train & Boat* and *Car Free Days in North Purbeck by Foot, Cycle, Bus, Train & Boat*, which can be downloaded from www.dorsetforyou.com. They suggest a series of car-free routes taking in some of the highlights of the area.

PUBLIC TRANSPORT

Three handy entry points to the Isle of Purbeck – **Wareham**, **Wool** and **Bournemouth** – have mainline **train stations** with connections to London. From Wareham you can access the main attractions by **bus**, including Corfe Castle, Swanage and Lulworth Cove. The Purbeck Breezer (route 50) links Bournemouth, Sandbanks, Studland and Swanage, crossing from Sandbanks to Studland on the **chain ferry** (see opposite); during the spring and summer months most buses on this route are open-topped, making for a very pleasant journey to the peninsula. For West Lulworth the closest mainline station is Wool.

The CoastLinX53 **Jurassic Coast bus** (page 14) stops at Wareham and link buses provide access to Corfe Castle and Swanage.

A memorably vintage way to travel is by the **Swanage Railway** (page 237), a heritage train service between Norden, Corfe Castle, Harman's Cross, Herston and Swanage. In the summer, many families heading to the beach opt to leave their car at the Norden Park and Ride and catch the train to Swanage. Another great use of this train is to walk from Swanage to Corfe Castle along the Purbeck Ridge and then catch the steam train back.

BY BOAT

A charming **chain ferry** (www.sandbanksferry.co.uk), which takes cars, buses and foot passengers, connects Studland and Sandbanks and has been operating since 1926. An area highlight in itself, it neatly avoids heavy traffic around Poole and Bournemouth. Crossings are every 20 minutes in the day, with the first leaving from the Sandbanks side at 07.00 and the last from the Studland side at 23.10. Cars can spend over an hour queuing to get on to the ferry at busy times but foot and bus passengers and cyclists can usually board straight away. From Sandbanks you can hop on another ferry to Brownsea Island (pages 265–7).

You can hardly miss the crowds of **sailing** enthusiasts who teem in the waters around the Isle of Purbeck. An idyllic way to arrive in the peninsula is to sail from Poole Harbour along the River Frome to Wareham Quay; Wareham has a public slipway and there is right of navigation on both the Frome and Piddle rivers. The Environment Agency controls over a hundred moorings on the River Frome; call the agency to check availability (01392 352223). If you don't have your own boat but want to get out on the river, you can **hire small craft** at Wareham Quay or take a cruise from Wareham or Poole Quay.

Short cruises operate from Swanage to Brownsea Island and Poole, providing magnificent views of the Jurassic Coast, including Old Harry Rocks. Specific **Jurassic Coast cruises** allow you to spend more time taking in the views of the cliffs and pinnacles, which are particularly impressive from sea level as their true size becomes apparent.

BOAT HIRE

Wareham Boat Hire Abbots Quay, Wareham BH20 4LW 01929 550688 www.warehamboathire.co.uk Mar–Oct daily. Hires canoes, kayaks, stand-up paddle boards, rowing boats and self-drive motorboats, as well as a wheelchair-friendly self-drive motorboat. Also offers kayak and canoe tours on the River Frome, and canoeing lessons.

CRUISE OPERATORS

Brownsea Island Ferries Poole Quay BH15 1HE ✆ 01929 462383 ⊕ www.brownseaislandferries.com. Operates cruises from Poole along the River Frome to Wareham Quay.

Dorset Cruises Parkstone Bay Marina, Turks Lane, Poole BH14 8EW ✆ 01202 724910 ⊕ www.dorsetcruises.co.uk. Offers a range of cruises, including between Poole and Swanage, or from Poole along the Jurassic Coast to Old Harry Rocks, and a river cruise from Poole Quay along the river to Wareham Quay on board a 1938 wooden ship. The Wareham cruise also operates in the evening.

Marsh's Boats The Stone Quay, Swanage BH19 2LN ✆ 01929 427309 ⊕ www.marshsboats.co.uk. From April to October offers cruises along the Jurassic Coast from Swanage, and fishing trips.

CYCLING

If you are arriving by train you can hop straight into the saddle at Wareham station, where bikes are available for hire. The Isle of Purbeck's roads get pretty busy in summer but there are some good **off-road** options, such as the Sika Cycle Trail (7 miles) at Wareham Forest (page 220) and the Rempstone Ride (12 miles) between Norden and Studland or Shell Bay. Local tourist information centres stock leaflets showing the Isle of Purbeck's cycle routes.

Bikes can be taken on the **chain ferry** between Studland and Sandbanks for a small fee, and also on the Swanage Railway.

A mountain bike ride on the Isle of Purbeck

Paul Connor

❋ OS Explorer map OL15; about 15 miles; moderate fitness required. Note that numbering on this route relates to the map opposite.

1 Jump the traffic queue at Sandbanks by taking your bike on the chain ferry (⊕ www.sandbanksferry.co.uk) to the Isle of Purbeck. Breathe in the sea air and take in the views during the quick crossing before hopping on your bike along a straight stretch of road for two miles. Half a mile after the road curves to the left take a sharp right turn. Don't go through the gate but take the gravel track towards Greenlands Farm. Turn left as you approach the farm (which is to your right) and the track soon bends to the right and fords a stream.

2 Stay on the bridleway through Newton Heath and Newton Copse, towards Game Copse and you will see views of Newton Bay. After Game Copse the track gradually curves to the left, joining another track

(leading you away from Ower Farm) before meeting a crossroads. Turn left and follow this track south for one mile and then take a short dog-leg turn to continue southeast to follow the track towards Kingswood Farm.

3 Turn left on to the B3351 for a few hundred yards of tarmac riding. Pause at the lay-by on your left for great views across the harbour before turning sharp right off the road up the bridleway. (If you wish to cut the ride short and avoid the steepest hills you can continue along the B3351 from here to Studland.)

4 The bridleway goes through a gate and up through woodland thick with the smell of wild garlic in spring. Gird your loins as the track steepens before emerging on the ridgeway.

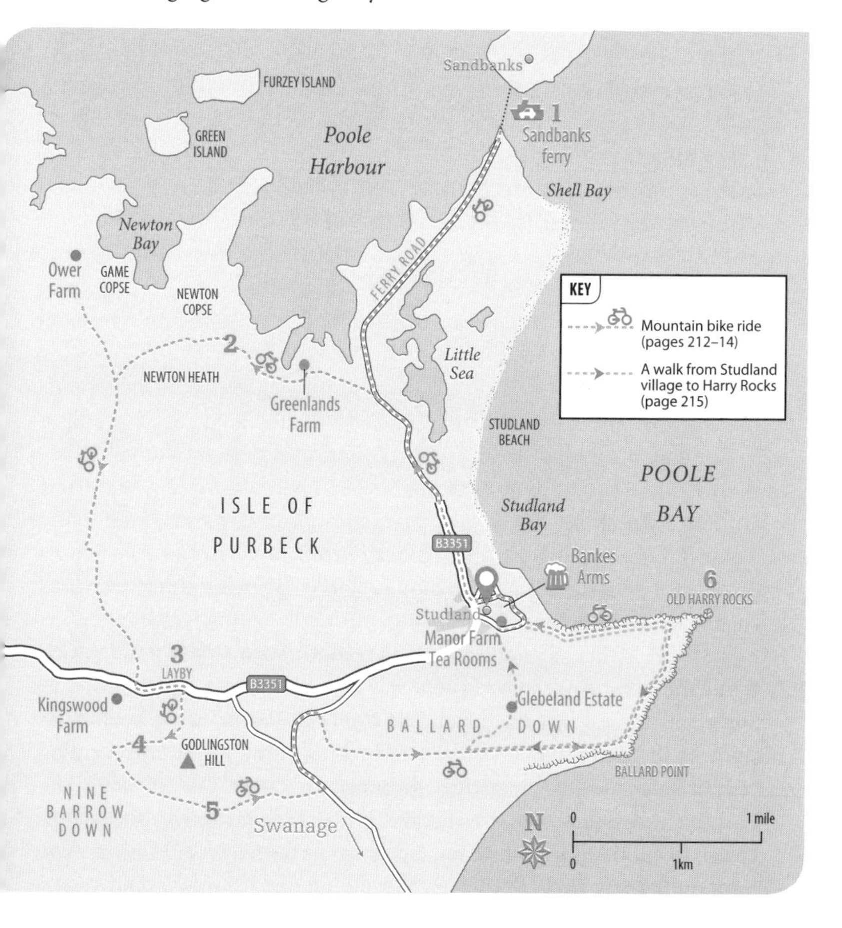

5 Turn left, heading east along the top of Nine Barrow Down and soak up the amazing views – small wonder this was chosen as a burial site in Neolithic times. The bridleway soon heads down Godlingston Hill. Be sure your brakes are in good order for this fast and at times bumpy descent. Turn left when you reach the road and after 500 yards on the tarmac turn right for the last steep climb, up a bridleway.

6 The ride from Ballard Down to Old Harry Rocks is a joy – a gentle sweeping ride downhill with panoramic views all around and The Needles just off the Isle of Wight in the distance. Pause a while at Old Harry Rocks before following the track to Studland. Where the track joins a lane, turn right. You pass the Bankes Arms, a tempting spot for a break, before continuing along the lane, turning left on to Rectory Lane, left on to Beach Road and then right (signposted Poole, Bournemouth) to join the road back to the ferry.

CYCLE HIRE

Cyclexperience Wareham station ✆ 01929 556601 🖱 www.purbeckcyclehire.co.uk. Bikes are available from Wareham station and, if booked 24 hours in advance, from Norden Park and Ride. Rucksacks, helmets and maps are provided free of charge.

Studland Cycle Hire Knoll Beach, Ferry Rd, Studland BH19 3AQ ✆ 07980 559143 🖱 www.studlandcyclehire.co.uk. Mountain bikes available for hire from the beach.

WALKING

The Isle of Purbeck offers the nearest really challenging coastal walking to London; a microcosm with extraordinary variety in a small area – within miles you can be walking through remote-feeling heathland around Agglestone Rock, past prehistoric burial mounds on Nine Barrows Down and up on to Ballard Down for views of Old Harry Rocks and Swanage. The landscape is startlingly diverse and seems to change in character at every turn.

Studland is the starting point of the **South West Coast Path**, which traces the outline of the peninsula and runs all the way to Minehead in Somerset (a total of 630 miles). The **Purbeck Ridge**, which forms the spine of the peninsula, provides far-reaching views of the surrounding countryside and the coastline. **Swanage to Corfe Castle** along the Purbeck Ridge is a classic walk, and if you run out of steam you can switch to another form of steam and catch the Swanage Railway heritage train on the way back. Even a short walk, such as the one to **Old Harry**

Rocks, will reward you with an exhilarating panorama of Studland Bay, Poole Harbour and the Jurassic Coast towards Swanage (see below). The walk from Worth Matravers to the cliff-top **St Aldhelm's Chapel** has a stunning coastline as well as an air of mystery (pages 242–3). For a short coastal walk you can't beat the stretch between **Lulworth Cove** and **Durdle Door**, with sweeping views of the undulating coastline. The **Range Walks** through the military firing ranges around Lulworth and **Tyneham** offer some very well-preserved countryside. They are open when the ranges are not in use, which is most weekends of the year; opening times are available at www.dorsetforyou.com and are well signed at the entrance.

A walk from Studland village to Old Harry Rocks

OS Explorer map OL15; start: Bankes Arms, SZ038824; 3 miles; easy. See map, page 213.

Although the beaches at Studland provide a view of Old Harry Rocks, the chalk stacks are much more impressive viewed up close. This can either be done by boat from the sea or by walking out along the chalk ridge towards the cliffs along a section of the South West Coast Path. There is a National Trust car park next to the Bankes Arms, where you can leave your car.

Early in the morning, in time to see the first rays of sunshine hitting the cliff faces, is a beautiful time of day for this walk. The waters are at their calmest then and the views towards the Isle of Wight are at their clearest. After a short descent and climb at the start, it is a mostly level walk along the chalk ridge. There are opportunities for bird and butterfly watching on the way, as well as views of Studland Bay and Poole.

You can return the same way or extend the walk by heading up the hill following the coastline to the summit of Ballard Down. As you approach Ballard Point, the South West Coast Path continues on towards Swanage. To walk back to Studland you need to head through the gate on the right. After the descent past the Glebeland Estate, you arrive at the edge of Studland. The **Manor Farm Tea Rooms** (01929 450311), within converted farm buildings, is a good spot to reward yourself with a Dorset cream tea. There are many other longer variants, such as walking through Studland Heath, past the prominent Agglestone Rock, then on a path southwest over the heath before climbing up on to the western end of Ballard Down and following the ridge to the cliff top, for a grand coast-path finale past Old Harry Rocks and back to Studland.

TOURIST INFORMATION CENTRES

General information www.visitswanageandpurbeck.co.uk
Swanage White House, Shore Rd, BH19 1LB 01929 422885
Wareham Wareham Library, South St, BH20 4LR 01929 552740

HORSERIDING

The Isle of Purbeck is blessed with a network of outstanding **bridleways**. Trails through **Wareham Forest** allow horse and rider to explore the heathland and mingle with wildlife (page 220). Sweetlands Riding School (Parkdean Holiday Park, Sandford BH16 6JZ 07725 530988 www.sweetlandsridingschool.co.uk) north of Wareham offers hacking in the forest. **Studland Beach and Nature Reserve** are criss-crossed with bridleways and provide a rare opportunity to ride along a sandy beach. A permit from the National Trust is required to ride your own horse on the beach, or you can head out on a ride with the team from Studland Stables (page 232).

For **hacking** in the Lulworth area, try Lulworth Equestrian Centre (Kennel Farm, Coombe Keynes BH20 5QR 01929 400396 www.lulworthequestriancentre.co.uk), which caters for all abilities.

WAREHAM TO SWANAGE & NORTH OF THE A351

The A351 cuts through the centre of the Isle of Purbeck peninsula, linking Wareham to the coastal town of **Swanage** and passing through **Corfe Castle** *en route*. The area north of the A351 is unspoilt, much of it being heathland, and is bordered to the north by the sheltered waters of Poole Harbour. It is here that you will find Arne RSPB Reserve, a wildlife-rich pocket of heathland and old oak woodland (pages 220–1). The Purbeck Ridge stretches to the sea at Handfast Point, near Studland, where the chalk stacks known as **Old Harry Rocks** stand proudly in the water.

An alternative to arriving on the peninsula via the A351 is to take the **chain ferry** from Sandbanks to Studland (page 211). As you cross from the hectic, glamorous side of the harbour, it seems as if you are venturing to another country as the wild heathland and Purbeck Ridge rise up before you.

1 WAREHAM

Although north of the River Frome and so not strictly in the Isle of Purbeck, Wareham dons the role of the gateway to the area. It is an ancient market town on the watershed of the Frome and Piddle rivers, surrounded on three sides by Saxon earthen defences; its fourth side is protected by the River Frome. Known as the **Town Walls**, these were a Saxon solution to the problem of Viking raids and were likely built in the 9th century as part of Alfred the Great's series of 'burh' (fortified) towns across Wessex. It seems Alfred was on to something, as the walls have lasted extraordinarily well, despite being tinkered with over the years. They were variously beefed up by the Normans, halved in size by Cromwell's troops during the Civil War and heightened on the west side during World War II to protect against tank attacks.

The Town Walls aside, Wareham may not strike you as particularly ancient. That is because much of the town centre was rebuilt in the Georgian style following a ferocious fire in 1762. However, the strict grid pattern of the streets following the points of the compass was laid out in Roman times, and some notable early buildings have survived, including medieval almshouses and one of Dorset's finest Saxon churches.

St Martin's on the Walls

if closed, you can borrow the key during shop hours from A F Joy Outfitters at 35 North Street

As you enter Wareham by road from the north, you cross the River Piddle then pass through a gap in the Town Walls and it is at this point that the history of the place resonates. Up on the walls to the left is the church of St Martin's on the Walls. If the church is open, there will be a steward on hand to guide you around. Most visitors to the church come to see the life-sized effigy of Lawrence of Arabia, but the church is enchanting in its own right. Dating from 1030 and the best-preserved Saxon church in Dorset, it contains fragments of **murals** of various ages. Painted above the chancel is the coat of arms of Queen Anne and the Ten Commandments, dated 1713.

"Dating from 1030 and the best-preserved Saxon church in Dorset, it contains fragments of murals of various ages."

To the left of the altar a remarkable 12th-century mural depicts the **story of St Martin**, who was born to pagan parents in AD316 and joined the Roman army at around 15 years of age. He is shown giving half of his cloak to a naked beggar; as the story goes, he later saw Christ wearing the cloak in a vision and converted to Christianity. One of the reasons for its survival is that the mural was made by fixing crushed stone into plaster, rather than painted. The Portland Stone **effigy of Lawrence of Arabia** is the work of Eric Kennington and was installed in the church in 1939. The effigy was homeless for some time after its completion. Kennington had designed it as a national memorial for Westminster Abbey but as there was already a Kennington bust of Lawrence in St Paul's crypt it was not accepted. Lawrence's brother bought the effigy, which eventually ended up at St Martin's, an appropriate choice because Lawrence, who lived locally at Clouds Hill (page 126), had contributed to the church's restoration. He had reportedly wanted to be buried here but is instead buried at nearby Moreton (page 125).

Around the Walls & quay

St Martin's Church is a logical point to begin the **Walls Walk**. This well-signed 1½-mile walk leads you around the town atop the grassy Saxon defences. A leaflet showing the points of interest along the route is available from the well-stocked **Wareham Information and Heritage Centre** on South Street. Highlights include passing along Wareham Quay and the views of the River Piddle, the water meadows and, in the distance, Wareham Forest. The walk also takes you through some rather unexciting modern housing estates, providing a rather disappointing backdrop to the romantic Saxon walls. Nowadays, one imagines the only Scandinavian invaders here are of the flat-packed furniture variety. As you walk around the town, don't get too excited about the signs to Wareham Castle in the southwest quarter of the town. All that remains of the Norman castle is a mound, on which stands a Victorian house.

"At the quay, you can hire a boat to potter along the River Frome."

Wareham was an important port until the 14th century, when Poole, with its much larger harbour, replaced Wareham in that role. The **quay** remains a focal point of the town but it is understated and has in no way suffered from overdevelopment. It is here that you can **hire a boat** to potter along the River Frome (page 211). You can either head inland along the river, where it is quiet and wildlife sightings are likely, or towards Poole Harbour, where you can admire the numerous yachts moored along the river. If you don't fancy taking to the water, there is a footpath along the river.

Wareham Town Museum

East St, in the Town Hall building ✆ 01929 553448 🖰 www.wtm.org.uk ⊙ Apr–Oct Mon–Sat 10.00–16.00; admission by donation

This small museum tells the story of the local area and its inhabitants through the ages. It has archaeology, geology and local history exhibits but the most detailed exhibit is that on Lawrence of Arabia. The **almshouses** opposite the museum date from 1741.

The venerable Rex

Rex Cinema 14 West St, BH20 4JX ✆ 01929 552778 🖰 www.therex.co.uk

Wareham's cinema is something of an institution. It began life in 1889 as the Oddfellows Hall, providing a venue for travelling theatre shows, concerts and banquets, and has operated as a cinema since 1920. In 2009, following a period of uncertainty about its future, the Rex was bought by the Purbeck Film Charitable Trust.

Full of character, the Rex still has its original gas lights and although they are no longer used, as you walk up the stairs you can see the black marks where they used to burn. The Rex holds a lot of memories for a lot of local people. Julie Sharman, one of the organisers of the Purbeck Film Festival (see box, page 223) told me, 'I remember the smell of gas from the lights as I walked into the cinema years ago, long before I worked for the festival.' Dougal Dixon, who has long been involved with the cinema, talks of an elderly lady working in the box office in the Rex's early days, who recalled that T E Lawrence (Lawrence of Arabia) used to come into Wareham from Bovington Camp on a Thursday afternoon and, if it was wet, he would go to the Rex to see a film. There can be no doubt that the Purbeck Film Charitable Trust is performing a valuable service by keeping this unusual little cinema open.

FOOD & DRINK

There is a small farmers' market in the Corn Exchange on North Street on the second and fourth Thursday of the month from 09.00 to 13.00. There is a small weekly produce market on East Street on Thursdays. A larger market operates on Saturdays at the quay.

Dorset Deli 10 South St, BH20 4LW ✆ 01929 553326 ⊙ May–Sep & Dec daily, Oct–Apr Mon–Sat. This deli aims to champion Dorset's artisan producers. It sells it own brand of ice cream, including unusual flavours like lavender, and superb bacon from their own farm. At times they can even tell you the name of the pig who provided the bacon, which is the ultimate in provenance but could be a little too much information for some.

Old Granary The Quay, BH20 4LP ✆ 01929 552010 ⏲ Mon–Sat from 09.00 & Sun from 10.00, until late. A Hall & Woodhouse pub-restaurant within an attractive former granary overlooking the River Frome. The deck is a great spot to sit and watch the river traffic. Local produce is used to create unfussy meals.

The Orchard at Holme West Holme Farm, BH20 6AQ ✆ 01929 554716 ⊕ www.holmeforgardens.co.uk ⏲ daily. On the B3070 Lulworth road is this garden centre with a farm shop stocking local produce and a café serving cream teas and light lunches. Nearby is Holme Fruit Farm, which offers pick-your-own fruit and vegetables from June to October.

Re-loved 7 North St, BH20 4AB ✆ 01929 552128 ⏲ Mon–Sat 09.00–17.00. Secondhand shop and traditional tea room where the vintage décor and cheerful bunting set the tone.

Salt Pig 6 North St, BH20 4AF ✆ 01929 550673 ⊕ www.thesaltpig.co.uk ⏲ daily 08.30–19.00. An urban farm shop selling a tempting selection of Dorset produce, including fresh local fish. The popular café serves good, simple food, such as pies and quiches. The owner, James, has a farming background (he previously worked as a shepherd) and a passion for local produce. He accurately describes the food as not frilly, not chefy. It can get busy at lunchtimes, so a good option is to get a take-away meal and eat it down at the quay.

2 WAREHAM FOREST

⛺ Wareham Forest Tourist Park (page 298)

A remote-feeling and surprisingly large heathy and pinewood expanse north of Wareham, Wareham Forest is dominated by commercial forestry but is varied enough for some pleasant walks and bike rides. Horseriders need a permit from the Forestry Commission (✆ 02380 286838), or if you don't have your own horse you can head out with a local stables, such as Sweetlands Riding School (Parkdean Holiday Park, Sandford BH16 6JZ ✆ 07725 530988 ⊕ www.sweetlandsridingschool.co.uk). The **Sika Trail** runs for seven miles (mostly level) around the forest, and takes its name from the sika deer, which you may well spot along the way. Roe deer are also present in the forest, as are Dartford warblers, nightjars and all six native species of reptile. The corrugated iron sheets which you may see lying around are refuges installed for the reptiles. You can camp within the forest (page 298).

3 ARNE RSPB RESERVE

RSPB Arne, Wareham BH20 5BJ ✆ 01929 553360 ⊕ www.rspb.org.uk/arne

Strikingly remote and peaceful, despite its proximity to Poole, Arne is a peninsula jutting out into Poole Harbour east of Wareham. The RSPB reserve, comprising heathland and old oak woodland, provides a habitat

ARNE'S GLORIES

Paul Morton, Warden, Arne RSPB Reserve

I am lucky enough to be a warden on the Arne RSPB Reserve. Being a local lad, I have been visiting the site since I was five years old. Yes, I am a keen birdwatcher and am fascinated with bird migration and behaviour, but the true spirit of Arne isn't just the birds, it's the sheer range of biodiversity.

Come to Arne at any time of the year, and you will be treated to some real wildlife spectacles. Visit in spring and all six native British reptiles can be seen emerging from their winter lairs, while our iconic Dartford warblers will be singing their scratchy song from the top of a gorse bush. When summer arrives the reserve explodes with life as hundreds of dragonflies emerge from our heathland ponds, many of them World War II bomb craters. The rare silver-studded blue butterflies carpet the illuminated purple bell heather, hobby can be seen dashing about in their aerial display and magical sunsets are elevated by the sound of the churring nightjars. Autumn is my favourite time of year, only because it hosts my favourite bird – the osprey. Poole Harbour is a magnet for these majestic 'fish eagles', which can be seen carrying large mullet to favourite eating posts. Migration is also in full swing and birds you wouldn't normally see, such as redstarts, pied flycatchers and wrynecks, can be found. Autumn is also the time when all manner of fungi appear on the reserve. If you think winter is a quiet time of year, then think again. Poole Harbour and Arne host some of the largest winter wader flocks in the UK. We are lucky enough to have the UK's largest winter avocet flock, thousands of brent geese and a multitude of wildfowl.

I hope you will agree there are plenty of reasons to visit this tranquil oasis nestled at the bottom of the Purbeck Hills.

for wildlife, including sika deer, and rare birds, such as the Dartford warbler and the nightjar. A very pleasant few hours can be spent wildlife spotting along the trails (guided or unguided) and then relaxing on the beach, which is usually delightfully uncrowded. The visitor centre shows footage from cameras, which have been installed in the nesting boxes around the reserve. Dogs are allowed but must be kept on a lead.

4 THE BLUE POOL

BH20 5AR 01929 551408 www.bluepooltearooms.co.uk Apr–Nov

Between Wareham and Corfe Castle, the Blue Pool and Tea House opened as a tourist attraction in the 1930s. What everyone got excited about was the extraordinary turquoise-blue hue of the pool, a former clay pit: it is the fine clay particles in suspension in the water that give it its characteristic colour. Walking through the 25 acres of heath and woodland which surround it, it is hard to imagine this was once an industrial site, as the plants have done such a good job of colonising the area. The original 1935 tea room remains, and has been joined by a gift shop, a plant centre and a museum showing the history of clay mining in the area. This is also where you will find the Wareham Bears, a collection of over 200 miniature teddy bears in various outfits and situations within their own houses.

Dogs are welcome but the water is not safe for swimming, either for dogs or for humans.

5 CORFE CASTLE

Mortons House Hotel (page 298) **Challow Farmhouse B&B** (page 298)

The hilltop ruins of Corfe Castle are magnificent from every angle (pages 224–5). Nestled at their base is the village of the same name, built in local grey limestone, some of which was salvaged from the ruins of the castle. The village thrived between the 12th and 14th centuries thanks to the Purbeck marble quarries. Stone was brought to the village to be worked and they made good use of it – many of the stone houses also have stone roofs.

Aside from the road running through it, the village has a tremendous sense of history commensurate with its position at the foot of the castle. Some curious traditions survive here. On Shrove Tuesday the **annual meeting of the Ancient Order of the Purbeck Marblers and Stonecutters** is held at Corfe Town Hall. Following the meeting, members kick a football three miles from the Town Hall to Ower Quay on Poole Harbour to preserve the right of way along which the quarried stone was transported. The tradition dates from 1695, when the company agreed to pay landowner, John Collins, a pound of pepper and a football in exchange for the right of way. Today the football is kicked into the sea and has pepper tipped over it, symbolising the peppercorn rent.

Small shops and pubs huddle around the village centre, with the castle looming above. The shops are suitably quaint: a traditional sweet shop, a baker and a fudge shop. There is even a **model village** (pages 225–6). The **Town Hall** is on West Street and is reputed to be the smallest in England. It houses a tiny, one-room **museum** (admission by donation). One of the strangest objects on display is the Poole punt and wildfowling gun, a contraption which allowed the hunter to lie flat on a narrow boat fitted with an enormous gun capable of killing 20 to 30 ducks with one shot.

THE PURBECK FILM FESTIVAL

Julie Sharman
Administrator, Purbeck Film Festival www.purbeckfilm.com

The Purbeck Film Festival is run by the Purbeck Film Charitable Trust Ltd and is the largest rural film festival in the UK.

In October each year the festival puts on around a hundred performances at venues throughout Purbeck and at the Lighthouse in Poole. The main cinema is the historic Rex in Wareham (page 219) but films are also shown at local village halls and other more unusual venues, such as Bovington Tank Museum. Wherever we can find a 13-amp plug and an enthusiastic local organiser, we can show a film.

The festival was originally set up as an initiative to increase tourism outside the main season and to celebrate a hundred years of cinema. The first event was so successful that the festival continued, and in due course the Purbeck Film Festival committee was formed. A Lottery grant gave the stability that was needed. We feel the Purbeck Film Festival serves an essential purpose – to bring the community together to celebrate film and to take film to rural venues.

Over the years, the Rex Cinema remained at the centre of the festival, so it was with great delight that after a lot of hard work by all the volunteers involved, the Purbeck Film Charitable Trust managed to raise the funds to purchase the Rex Cinema in April 2009, and turn it into a community, not-for-profit venue.

Also in the centre of the village is the **church of St Edward the Martyr**, dedicated to a Saxon king who is said to have been murdered at Corfe Castle in AD978 (see box, page 225). On the east gable of the church is a statue of the martyr. During the Civil War, Cromwell's men occupied, vandalised and stabled their horses in the church. They used the 14th-century Purbeck marble font with its carved octagonal bowl and stem as a horse trough. Thankfully it has now reverted to its original purpose.

There is little room for parking in the village. In 2013, the National Trust opened a visitor centre and car park opposite the castle on the way into the village. From there it is about a ten-minute walk to the village centre and castle. The other option is the Norden Park and Ride (page 211). It is here that you will find the volunteer-run Purbeck Mineral and Mining Museum (Norden Park and Ride, Norden BH20 5DW 01929 481461 www.pmmmg.org Sat, Sun, Tue, Wed 11.00–17.00), which allows visitors to explore part of the old Norden clay works, including a reconstructed narrow-gauge railway.

"Cromwell's men occupied, vandalised and stabled their horses in the church."

Corfe Castle: the castle itself

01929 481294 daily; National Trust

Corfe Castle is everything you want a ruined castle to be: built of moody grey stone, towering high on a conical mound and reached across a stone bridge. So it is unsurprising that its image adorns countless calendars, postcards and book covers. It was also reputed to be the inspiration for Kirrin Castle, which featured in Enid Blyton's The Famous Five series of children's books, although this claim has been challenged by numerous other castles. The building oozes history and drama and a wander around the ruins cannot help but stimulate the imagination. Just thinking of the characters who have lived and died here, and the momentous events that have taken place here, can induce the odd shiver.

The castle's location is no accident – it guards the only break in the Purbeck Ridge. The Domesday Book records a castle at this site and attributes its construction to William the Conqueror. Later kings, including Henry I, John and Henry III put their own stamp on the place, modifying and fortifying as they went. By the 13th century, the castle was being used as a treasure storehouse and prison. High-ranking, wealthy prisoners were held in the keep (the highest tower of the ruin), but the less privileged died a slow and miserable death in the dungeon under the Butavant Tower. In 1635, ownership of the castle passed to the Bankes family.

During the Civil War the castle was courageously held for the king by Lady Mary Bankes, who became known as 'Brave Dame Mary'. She, along with her daughters, servants and a garrison of five men, successfully defended it for three years. Corfe Castle eventually fell victim to betrayal in 1646 when one of her ladyship's own men smuggled in Parliamentarian troops. Later that year the castle was blown up by order of the House of Commons so that it could never again stand as a Royalist stronghold. A combination of undermining and explosives left the previously impregnable fortress in the ruined state in which it remains today. It is astounding that the gatehouse and outer towers have not tumbled down the hills during the intervening years, as their remains seem to be leaning out at impossible angles over the mound's steep slopes. While it may have been reduced to a skeletal impression of its former self, the castle, clinging tenaciously to the hilltop, maintains an air of majesty and enduring strength.

I could go on and on about Corfe Castle because I find it tremendously evocative. My mother tells me that my great-aunt, Elsie, was less

THE MURDER OF EDWARD THE MARTYR

Saxon King Edward, great-grandson of Alfred the Great, was murdered at Corfe Castle in AD978. Legend has it that his stepmother was responsible for his killing. Edward's father, King Edgar, died suddenly in AD975 leaving two sons, Edward by his first marriage and Ethelred by his third. England's ruling nobles chose 13-year-old Edward as king, much to the disgruntlement of his stepmother who would have much rather seen her own son, Ethelred, on the throne. She formed an alliance with anti-monastic noblemen who opposed Edward's close relationship with the Church. Since Ethelred was too young to replace Edward as ruler, she would rule as regent until he was ready to take over, so she devised a plan to get Edward out of the way for good.

Edward, who was hunting in the area, accepted an invitation from his stepmother to visit her at Corfe Castle, unaware of her plans for his demise. According to the 12th-century chronicler, William of Malmesbury,he was still on horseback when she:

> allured him to her with female blandishment and made him lean forward, and after saluting him, while he was eagerly drinking from the cup which had been presented, the dagger of an attendant pierced him through.

Edward fled on his horse but fell. His foot caught in the stirrup and he was dragged through the woods until he died.

He was initially buried at Wareham Priory but following a series of miracles and a growing number of pilgrims his body was moved to Shaftesbury Abbey. The first miracle is said to have occurred the night Edward died, when the blind woman in whose house the body was laid regained her sight. Circa 1008 Edward was canonised and became St Edward the Martyr.

impressed. Elsie was visiting from Australia, which, through no fault of its own, is devoid of splendid castles like Corfe. My parents decided to show Elsie the highlights of our beloved Dorset and took her to Corfe Castle, which at the time had some scaffolding on one side. My father explained that the structure had been reduced to a ruin some 400 years earlier, to which Elsie responded in disgust, 'I can't believe they took this long to get around to fixing it up!'

The Model Village

The Square, BH20 5EZ ✆ 01929 481234 🖱 www.corfecastlemodelvillage.co.uk ⏲ Apr–Oct Sat–Thu, Nov–Mar Fri–Sun, & daily in school holidays

If you find it hard to imagine what Corfe Castle would have looked like before Cromwell's troops got their hands on it, or if like Great-Aunt

Elsie you prefer your castles in one piece, then you may want to head to the Model Village. The model recreates the castle and the village as they would have been before the events of 1646. Being in the shadow of the real castle, it allows for an intriguing visual comparison of the two. The 1:20 scale model was built by Eddie Holland in 1966 in Purbeck stone and its detail is extraordinary, especially the 17th-century residents and the music playing in the miniature church. A delightful (normal-sized) garden on the site is complete with birdwatching hide, several original village stocks and a courtyard café.

The Olive Tree Cookery School

The Old Barn, Cat's Eye Cottage, Norden BH20 5DT ✆ 01929 477260
www.olivetreecookeryschool.com

Just north of Corfe Castle, on the A351, you will find the Old Barn, where Giuseppe and Sara offer a range of cookery courses, lasting from a few hours to three days. Class sizes are reassuringly small, around six, and their cosy converted barn is a great venue. Giuseppe's Sicilian background means that many of the courses have an Italian theme, but there are also plenty of courses on seafood, game, preserving and baking. I rather fancy the picnic course, where you spend the morning making a delicious picnic and then take it to your favourite spot for lunch. The course schedule varies, so check the website for details.

FOOD & DRINK

Castle Inn 63 East St, BH20 5EE ✆ 01929 480208 ⏲ daily for lunch & dinner. This pub on the road towards Swanage is highly recommended by locals. It has plenty of character and there is a pleasant outdoor area. Friday is fish day and the traditional Sunday lunches are very popular.

Clealls of Corfe 25 East St, BH20 5EE ✆ 01929 480170 ⏲ Mon–Sat 08.00–18.00, Sun 09.00–16.00. If the name of this village shop rings a bell, that may be because it was featured on the BBC's shop makeover programme, *Mary Queen of Shops*. It seems Mary Portas's advice has paid off – the shop is thriving. A good range of local beer and wine is sold here.

Corfe Castle Tearooms The Square, BH20 5EZ ✆ 01929 481294 ⏲ daily. National Trust tea rooms in an 18th-century building. A good choice on a sunny day because you can take your tea in the garden, right at the base of the castle.

Greyhound The Square, BH20 5EZ ✆ 01929 480205 ⏲ daily. This pub sits beneath the castle, and its beer garden looks up to the ruins. Local produce is used and there are good vegetarian and gluten-free options.

6 MARGARET GREEN ANIMAL SANCTUARY

Church Knowle BH20 5NQ ✆ 01929 480474 🖱 www.margaretgreenanimalrescue.org.uk
⏲ daily 10.00–16.00; admission by donation

Margaret Green Animal Rescue is a charity with three sanctuaries in Devon and Dorset. They do exemplary work caring for domestic and farm animals in need – cats, rabbits, goats, chickens and ponies among them – finding new homes for them where possible. They rescue and re-home over 1,000 animals each year. The sanctuary at Church Knowle is open to the public and visitors can walk around between the animal enclosures. When I visited, children seemed to be enjoying this almost as much as a zoo, and parents have the satisfaction of knowing their donation goes to a very worthy cause.

FOOD & DRINK

New Inn Church Knowle BH20 5NQ ✆ 01929 480357 🖱 www.newinn-churchknowle.co.uk ⏲ for lunch & dinner, Nov–Easter closed Mon. Maurice Estop and his family have run the New Inn since 1985. Licensee records for the pub date back to 1881 and, amazingly, Estop is only the fourth name on the licence in over 160 years. Maurice prides himself on serving reasonably priced traditional pub food and seafood, such as the delicious cottage pie made to his grandmother's recipe. Maurice's Blue Vinny (Dorset blue cheese) and crab soups are so popular that they are now available in take-away containers. You can choose a bottle of wine to go with your meal at the well-stocked walk-in wine store. A small number of camping spots are available in the field behind the New Inn.

7 STUDLAND

Pig on the Beach Studland Bay (page 298)

Much of the area around Studland is owned by the National Trust, bequeathed by Ralph Bankes in 1981 and one of the largest gifts the trust has ever received. Each year Studland attracts great numbers of visitors who come to enjoy its splendid beach.

My Australian friends are always teasing me that British beaches are ugly, covered in lumpy puddles and utterly devoid of sand. Studland is one beach to prove them wrong. A four-mile, sheltered stretch of sand with views of Old Harry Rocks and the Isle of Wight, Studland Beach really is beautiful. The water here is shallow a long way out, so is ideal for families, and there are plenty of watersports available. The beach is divided into four areas: South Beach, Middle Beach, Knoll Beach and Shell Bay. At Shell Bay a chain ferry covers the short distance to Sandbanks (page 211).

Studland Beach and Nature Reserve is run by the National Trust, and beach hut hire can be arranged through the National Trust office (✆ 01929 450259). A large area of protected heathland, woodland and sand dunes behind the beach adds greatly to its appeal and provides for walking, cycling and horseriding. In summer, when the heather is flowering, **Godlingston Heath** is glorious. The mass of yellow gorse flowers in spring is equally spectacular. From a mound in the midst of the heathland **Agglestone Rock** proudly surveys its surroundings. Also known as 'Devil's Nightcap', this 400-ton sandstone rock gets geologists excited. Local legend has it that the devil was sitting on The Needles off the coast of the Isle of Wight and, in a characteristically demonic temper tantrum, threw his cap at the mainland. Its intended target was Corfe Castle but it fell short and landed in its current position. The geologists' explanation for its presence is less colourful – it is a natural rock outcrop made of Agglestone grit, which was left behind when softer layers of rock around it eroded. The reserve around it is a haven for rare wildlife, including Dartford warblers, nightjars and all six British reptile species (adders, grass snakes, smooth snakes, slow worms, common lizards and sand lizards).

"In summer, when the heather is flowering, Godlingston Heath is glorious. The mass of yellow gorse flowers in spring is equally spectacular."

Little Sea Lagoon behind Knoll Beach was closed to the sea by the dunes around 1880 and now contains fresh water, being stream fed. Over 3,000 waterfowl spend the winter in this 79-acre body of water, including tufted ducks, pintails and pochards. Little egrets and teal are present all year round. Three bird hides are strategically positioned around the lagoon. It is hard to believe that just a short distance away is Wytch Farm, western Europe's largest onshore oilfield; thankfully, the refinery is well hidden in a pine forest on Wytch Heath.

The beaches at Studland have been popular with **naturists** since the 1920s. Those pioneering naturists were taking a risk greater than sand in places where sand shouldn't be because in those days exposure was illegal. Naturists can now relax on the right side of the law in a designated zone on **Knoll Beach**. Signs clearly mark the naturist area, including the instruction 'naturists please dress before passing this point'. I've always found this request strangely immaterial because it is not as if there is a giant curtain across the beach shielding the naturists from the view of the 'textiles' (the term naturists use to refer to the clothed masses).

Most people bypass Studland village in favour of the beach. The houses are spread over a wide area, although the centre of the village is tiny and consists mostly of Edwardian buildings. Studland village was apparently the inspiration for Toy Town in Enid Blyton's Noddy books. The **church of St Nicholas** dates from the 11th century; it blends Saxon and Norman architecture and is featured in Simon Jenkins's excellent book *England's Thousand Best Churches*. The original building was almost entirely destroyed by the Vikings but was later rebuilt by the Normans. The short, squat tower is the most striking architectural feature; it is thought the foundations could not support a full-sized one.

During World War II Studland was used as a training ground for the D-Day landings. A relic from this time is **Fort Henry**, a bunker on top of Redend Point, near the Pig on the Beach Hotel. It was from here in April 1944 that King George VI, Winston Churchill, General Montgomery and General Eisenhower watched troops training for the landings. Sadly, during the exercise the sea became rough and six tanks sank, killing six crew members.

To the west of Studland is the **Isle of Purbeck Golf Club** (BH19 3AB ✆ 01929 450354 🖰 www.purbeckgolf.co.uk), which was once owned by Enid Blyton and her husband. There is a nine-hole course for golfers of all abilities and an 18-hole course for more accomplished players. The courses wind through the heathland and have expansive views over both the nature reserve and the sea.

Studland is the starting point for walks to **Old Harry Rocks**, the stark white chalk stacks which stand in the water just off the cliffs at Handfast Point. Carved by millions of years of erosion by the sea, Old Harry Rocks mark the most easterly point of the Jurassic Coast, which is also the youngest. They are said to take their name from a 15th-century pirate, Harry Paye, who regularly attacked ships leaving Poole Harbour. Standing at Handfast Point on a clear day you can see a similar chalk formation off the coast of the Isle of Wight, called **The Needles**. They serve as a physical reminder that the Isle of Wight was once joined to the mainland at this point by a chalk seam, of which both Old Harry Rocks and The Needles were part. A further reminder is visible at **Redend Point**, at the northern end of Studland's South Beach. This small headland of brown, reddish and yellow sandstone bears a striking resemblance to the multi-coloured sand cliffs at Alum Bay on the Isle of Wight.

Horseriding at Studland

A National Trust permit is required to ride your own horse on the beach at Studland and the relevant forms can be downloaded from the National Trust website (www.nationaltrust.org.uk). It is advisable to contact the National Trust's Purbeck office (01929 450259) before applying to discuss availability. Only five permits are issued per day and you will need to allow a few days for processing.

If you don't have access to your own horse, never fear because **Studland Stables** has a yard full of horses and ponies to suit all abilities.

"The smell was irresistible for Tom, who carefully peeled back his lips in expert fashion to pluck a few gorse flowers from the prickly bushes."

It was a warm afternoon in May when my Australian travelling companion, Neal Sullivan, and I set off to Studland Stables, eager to view the surrounding countryside on horseback. Neal and I have very different levels of riding experience. Although he fancies himself as a stockman and dreams of droving 2,000 head of cattle across the Australian Outback, Neal is a beginner. Studland Stables went out of their way to accommodate our different levels of ability. They organised two rides for us, the first suitable for beginners, like Neal, and the second allowing me to fulfil my dream of a good canter along the beach.

We were welcomed by Helen and Stuart Spreadborough, the owners of Studland Stables, who are extremely friendly and professional. They took care to discuss our requirements and select suitable horses for us. Neal, like most men, always wants to have the biggest horse, so he was delighted with his mount – a handsome 18hh shire cross named Tom.

Helen, Neal and I rode out of the yard and were soon on **Godlingston Heath**, which was flushed with a springtime show of yellow gorse flowers. Their strong coconut scent prompted us to nickname it the 'piña colada ride'. The smell was irresistible for Tom, who carefully peeled back his lips in expert fashion to pluck a few gorse flowers from the prickly bushes.

Having climbed to the top of a rise, we were rewarded with views over Studland Beach and Nature Reserve, Old Harry Rocks, Sandbanks and Poole Harbour. As we admired the scenery, we spotted something that looked quite out of place – a large boulder protruding from the heath – it was the unmistakable **Agglestone Rock**.

We headed back to the stables without even setting hoof on a road, making this ride ideal for beginners. The ride boosted Neal's already healthy confidence and as we were unsaddling our steeds he began to talk of joining the mounted police. The following day, when the soreness kicked in, he fell remarkably silent on his mounted police plans.

My list of things to do in my lifetime includes 'ride along a deserted beach'. I never expected to fulfil that wish in Dorset, so I was delighted when Helen and I saddled up fresh horses and set off for the sand. I had half expected to have to dodge naturists as we cantered along the beach, but a cool evening must have caused them to retire early. We rode along the deserted sand as the setting sun cast a golden glow on Old Harry Rocks, pausing to allow the horses to splash in the water, much to their delight and mine. We reached **Shell Bay** and the chain ferry, then turned and cut back through the dunes towards the stables.

"We rode along the deserted sand as the setting sun cast a golden glow on Old Harry Rocks, pausing to allow the horses to splash in the water."

As we rode, Helen explained to me how she, Stuart and their two daughters had ended up at Studland Stables. Helen and Stuart had busy careers in London and often discussed their dream of one day moving to their favourite area, the Dorset coast. Horse-lover Helen had heard that there was a place in Studland where you could ride on the beach. For years she had planned to experience it for herself but never got around to it. In 2007, Helen learnt that the stables were on the market and, out of curiosity, sent off for details. She showed Stuart the brochure and was surprised by his lukewarm reaction. It turned out Stuart had bought Helen a voucher for a beach ride at Studland Stables as a birthday present and when he saw the brochure he feared his surprise had been discovered. They headed down to Dorset for the birthday ride. Helen had never ridden anywhere so beautiful or with such a variety of scenery. Both fell in love with the area and made the bold decision to give up their busy city lives and take on the stables. Their courage in making the lifestyle change so many of us talk about is inspirational. Earlier that day, as we rode to the top of the hill above Agglestone Rock and the spectacular views opened up in front of us, Helen proclaimed with a broad smile 'This is my office!' And what a beautiful office it is.

RIDING STABLES

Studland Stables Ferry Rd, BH19 3AQ 01929 450273 www.studlandstables.com. For riders of all abilities: 60-minute heathland rides. For able riders: Two-hour beach, forest or Old Harry Ride. Full-day Corfe Castle rides.

Watersports around Studland

The waters off Studland offer some great opportunities for the watersports enthusiast, from boat cruises along the coast to windsurfing and waterskiing.

WATERSPORTS PROVIDERS

Shell Bay Sailing Ferry Rd, BH19 3BA 01258 880512, 07853 986345 www.shellbaysailing.co.uk Apr–Sep daily. A small family-run sailing school with boat hire and courses for adults and children.

Studland Sea School Middle Beach, Studland BH19 3AP 01929 450430 www.studlandseaschool.co.uk. Situated on the beach at Studland. Offers canoeing courses and hire of kayaks, wetsuits, snorkelling equipment, fishing tackle and body boards. They also run kayaking tours, including a half-day tour to Old Harry Rocks and a full-day tour to Poole Harbour and Brownsea Island.

Studland Watersports Knoll Beach, Ferry Rd, BH19 3AQ 07980 559143 www.studlandwatersports.co.uk. Offer a wide range of watersports, including waterskiing, sailing, windsurfing and kayaking.

FOOD & DRINK

Bankes Arms Manor Rd, BH19 3AU 01929 450225 daily. Traditional pub atmosphere and food. This is also the home of the Isle of Purbeck micro-brewery. Well placed for the start or finish of a walk out to Old Harry Rocks.

Manor Farm Tea Rooms Church Rd, BH19 3AJ 01929 450311 times vary, so call ahead to check. Delightful tea rooms in converted farm buildings. Light lunches, cakes and cream teas are on offer at reasonable prices.

Pig on the Beach Manor Rd, BH19 3AU 0845 0779494 www.thepighotel.com daily. Uncomplicated, seasonal food prepared using ingredients from the kitchen garden, or from within a 25-mile radius, and served in trendy, shabby chic surroundings.

Shell Bay Seafood Restaurant Ferry Rd, BH19 3BA 01929 450363 www.shellbay.net the bistro is open from 09.30, & Apr–Aug the restaurant serves lunch & dinner daily, Sep Tue–Sun. Closed Nov–Mar. This restaurant is in a fantastic location, right on the water overlooking Brownsea Island and Poole Harbour, and just 250 yards from the Sandbanks ferry. Diners from the Sandbanks side of the harbour can catch the last ferry back at around

23.00. The menu features some creative seafood dishes and a few options for non-seafood eaters. The menu is very reasonably priced, given the location and the quality of the food.

8 SWANAGE

Swanage Haven B&B (page 298)

If you have spent some time enjoying the slow pace of rural Dorset you may need to be prepared for a change of gear as Swanage's atmosphere of seaside-holiday jollity can come as a bit of a shock. Swanage is a typical British seaside town, complete with amusement arcades and beach crowds. Take some time to get to know Swanage, however, and the deeper aspects of its personality emerge.

With this in mind, I took time to wander the town's out-of-the-way places, as well as the seafront, and found that there is much to like about Swanage. For a start, there is a lovely sandy **beach**, which is where the British seaside town bit comes in. It has everything you would expect – deckchairs, beach huts, a Punch and Judy show and tacky souvenir shops. It is a wide sweeping bay, with chalk cliffs at the northern end leading out to Old Harry Rocks, and on a clear day you can see the Isle of Wight from the beach.

At the southern end of the beach is the typically ornate **Victorian pier**, which was constructed in 1896 for shipping stone from local quarries. Horses were used to pull carts of stone along the narrow-gauge tramway which ran along the seafront and on to the pier. In 1994, the Swanage Pier Trust took control of the structure, which was by then in a sorry state, organised extensive repairs and has since managed to keep it open. Today, you can walk out along the pier for a small charge, which goes towards its upkeep. Above the pier, **Prince Albert Gardens**, a hillside park, makes a very pleasant spot for a picnic overlooking the bay.

SWANAGE CARNIVAL & REGATTA

Swanage comes into its own at the end of July/early August each year, when it holds the annual Swanage Carnival and Regatta (www.swanagecarnival.com). The week's events include various sporting competitions (including a half marathon, swimming and sailing), a carnival procession, sand sculpture competition and spectacular fireworks on the main beach. Swanage is even busier than usual during carnival week, so be prepared.

Beyond the pier, at Peverill Point, is the **Swanage Lifeboat Station** (✆ 01929 423237 🖱 www.swanagelifeboat.org.uk), opened in 1875 at the request of local residents. Consisting of a boathouse and slipway, it is open to visitors from April to October (see website for timings).

As you head northwards along the seafront from the pier, you pass the **Mowlem Theatre** (✆ 01929 422239 🖱 www.mowlemtheatre.co.uk), a venue for theatre and film since 1967. It is by no means a handsome building but has become one of the town's landmarks, and the upstairs bar has views of the bay.

Before it was a seaside resort, Swanage was a quarrying and fishing town. Stone and building contractor John Mowlem (1788–1868) and his nephew George Burt (1816–94) were highly influential in the town's development – so much so that George Burt is referred to as 'the king of Swanage', a nickname supposedly bestowed by Thomas Hardy. The town owes its most interesting architectural features to Mowlem and Burt, who scavenged them from London when they delivered their stone there. The elaborate façade of **Swanage Town Hall** once adorned the Mercers' Hall in London and looks rather out of place in Swanage High Street. It dates from 1670 and was brought to Swanage in 1883. The **Wellington Clock Tower** at **Peverill Point** came from the old London Bridge. The clock tower was erected at one end of London Bridge in 1854, but apparently caused traffic chaos so was removed and brought to Swanage in 1863. **Purbeck House** (now a hotel) in the High Street, which has obvious castle aspirations, was the house George Burt built for himself using marble chippings from the Albert Memorial. The house also includes a bollard from Millbank Prison, an archway from Hyde Park Corner and floor tiles from the Palace of Westminster.

"The Wellington Clock Tower was erected at one end of London Bridge in 1854, but apparently caused traffic chaos so was removed and brought to Swanage in 1863."

Behind Swanage Town Hall is a small, stone **lock-up** inscribed 'Erected for the Prevention of Vice and Immorality by Friends of Religion and Good Order – 1803'. It used to stand in the St Mary's churchyard and was considered a necessary measure for dealing with the town's rowdy revellers. It looks to me as if it would have served as a powerful deterrent. **St Mary's Church** is near to the pretty, spring-fed millpond. Apart from the 14th-century tower, the church is largely 19th and 20th century.

CHOCOCO

Commercial Rd, BH19 1DF ☎ 01929 421777 🖱 www.chococo.co.uk

Husband and wife team, Claire and Andy Burnet, have been making delicious, fresh chocolates in the Isle of Purbeck since 2002.

I met up with Claire at the Chococo café in Swanage to learn more about this creative company (where, appropriately, I had one of the finest hot chocolates I have ever tasted). Chococo's philosophy and techniques are groundbreaking. Claire explained that they are one of the first, if not the first UK chocolate maker, to produce a truly fresh product, using cream from a local farm blended with chocolate direct from the country where it was grown, and seasonal, natural flavours. What they do not use are artificial additives and preservatives.

I was staggered by the range of flavours, such as 'Bob's Bees' (made with honey from Swanage beekeeper, Robert Field), 'Mellow Mint' (made with fresh mint from a Swanage garden) and 'Piddle Beer' (made with beer from the Piddle Brewery). They even create edible chocolate boxes – a brilliant way to reduce packaging waste.

So how do a husband and wife come to set up a chocolate-making company in Swanage? Claire and Andy were both working in high-pressure jobs for large companies in London, when they decided they wanted a 'slower' lifestyle. Connections to Swanage drew them to this part of the world: Andy's family was from Swanage, Claire and Andy were regular visitors to the area and they were married in the town. Claire told me that she had always known that if she was going to survive as Andy's wife, she needed to like both Swanage and sailing; thankfully she likes both.

When discussing how they would make a living in Swanage, Claire suggested, almost flippantly, that they make chocolates. Her parents had lived in Brussels for a time and Claire and her family relished the fine chocolates available there and lamented that they couldn't find anything comparable in England. Andy laughed at Claire's suggestion, pointing out their total lack of expertise, but he agreed to go on a chocolate-making course with her and see what it was all about. Making chocolate is a highly scientific process and Andy, who has a science background, was in his element. He was won over by the course and their business began.

As I talked to Claire I was baffled at how she could stay so slim while working with temptation on a daily basis. She explained that good-quality dark chocolate is low in sugar and low GI (glycemic index), and in fact many of the Chococo staff have lost weight since joining.

Claire and Andy are proud of their ethical approach. They care about the provenance of their ingredients and about the people who produce them, and make every effort to minimise their carbon footprint.

If you fancy having a go at making chocolate yourself, Chococo offers workshops at their Swanage premises. Their delicious goodies can be bought in their Swanage shop, in premium retailers and online.

The High Street is lined with tempting shops and eateries, such as the **Mulberry Tree Gallery** (57 High St), selling local and locally themed art and ceramics. The **Tilly Mead** area on Commercial Road is a complex of small, independent shops, including local handmade chocolate company **Chococo** (see box, page 235). It is a pleasant area to wander and, if you need to buy a gift for the cat-sitter, dog-sitter or house-sitter, you are likely to find one here.

Swanage Museum & Heritage Centre

The Square, BH19 2LJ ✆ 01929 423850 www.swanagemuseum.co.uk ⊙ Mar–Nov daily, Dec–Feb weekends; free admission

Well worth a look, this free museum shows an informative film on the Isle of Purbeck and displays depict the local shops as they may have looked in the early 1900s. A good way to get to know Swanage is to take one of the **guided walks** offered by two local historians. There is no charge but voluntary contributions are gratefully received. The walks run from Easter to the end of September, and it is advisable to book. Groups usually meet outside the heritage centre at 14.30 on Tuesdays and Thursdays.

Water-based activities around Swanage

For those who tire of lying on the beach and wandering the shops, there are plenty of water-based activities. If you fancy a spot of fishing, the **Swanage Angling Centre** (✆ 01929 424989) at the pier end of the High Street can arrange bait, tackle and a skipper. The waters around Swanage, in particular beneath the pier and the local shipwrecks, are popular with divers.

WATERSPORTS PROVIDERS

Ocean Bay Waterports North Beach, Ulwell Rd, BH19 1LH ✆ 07721 938949 www.oceanbaywatersports.co.uk. Offers jet-ski, pedalo and kayak hire, as well as deckchair and beach hut hire. You can launch your own vessel using their concrete slipway.

DIVE OPERATORS

Divers Down The Pier, BH19 2AR ✆ 01929 423565 (Apr–Oct) www.diversdownswanage.co.uk. Established in 1958, this is reputed to be the oldest dive school in England.

Swanage Boat Charters Larks Rise, 279b High St, BH19 2NH ✆ 01929 427064 www.kyarra.com

Swanage Diving 64 Ulwell Rd, BH19 3DG ✆ 07917 794075 www.swanagediving.co.uk

The Swanage Railway

Station House, BH19 1HB ✆ 01929 425800 ⊛ www.swanagerailway.co.uk

You don't need to be a train buff to be charmed by the lovingly restored steam and diesel trains of the Swanage Railway. The railway operates over almost six miles between Swanage and Norden, which is just northwest of Corfe Castle and four miles from Wareham. Trains first ran to Swanage in 1885 and continued until 1972, when the line closed. The painstaking restoration, re-opening and maintenance of the railway is the work of the Swanage Railway Trust.

Every summer thousands of families use the railway to travel to and from the beach at Swanage. You can leave your car at the Norden Park and Ride (off the A351) and take the train to Swanage via Corfe Castle, Harman's Cross and Herston. The train travels at no more than 25mph and provides expansive views of Corfe Castle and the surrounding countryside (keep your eyes peeled – on some days deer, pheasants and other wildlife can be seen in the fields). The railway stations and the uniforms of the staff are those of a bygone age and add to the romanticism of the journey. Once you arrive in Swanage, the beach is just 100 yards from the station.

Martin Payne of the Swanage Railway Company, which is responsible for the day-to-day running of the railway, explained to me that around 450 volunteers work to keep the railway functioning, and it has to be said they do a fantastic job. The railway holds a series of special events throughout the year. One of Martin's favourites is the December Santa Special, when families clamber aboard and eagerly await Father Christmas, who passes through the train handing out presents to the children.

FOOD & DRINK

Swanage has a good selection of eateries, from casual fish bars to smart restaurants. Swanage market, including a farmers' market, is held every Friday in the main beach car park on Victoria Avenue (BH19 1AP). The Isle of Purbeck produces some wonderful food, such as St Aldhelm Blue cheese from the Windswept Cow Cheese Company at Worth Matravers, Robert Field honey and Purbeck Ice Cream. These and other local delicacies are available from the **Purbeck Deli** (26 Institute Rd, BH19 1BX ✆ 01929 422344 ⊛ www.thepurbeckdeli.co.uk) where you can pick up a selection and head to Prince Albert Gardens or Durlston Park for a picnic.

Bull & Boat 2 Ulwell Rd, BH19 1LH ✆ 01929 422222 ◷ bar & restaurant daily 09.00 until late. This bistro overlooking the water at the Studland end of the seafront enjoys the best restaurant views in Swanage; you can even moor your boat here. The décor is contemporary, as is the food.

Cauldron Bistro 5 High St, BH19 2LN ☎ 01929 422671 ⊙ hours vary. What a find! Terry and Margaret Flenley have been here for 22 years and could have retired by now, but instead they chose to open their restaurant 'just for fun'. They only serve five tables per night and it is almost like eating in someone's home. The menu is created daily, with specials handwritten on individual cards, and all the food is homemade to order using local ingredients. I tried coquilles St Jacques, one of my favourite dishes, and it was splendid; I washed it down with delicious homemade lemonade. Other dishes on the menu sounded tasty too, such as the pan-roasted quail and the wild boar sausages. Space is limited so it is best to book in advance.

Chococo Central Commercial Rd, BH19 1DF ☎ 01929 421777 🖱 www.chococo.co.uk ⊙ daily. The Chococo chocolate shop has a café attached, which serves homemade cakes and, of course, superb hot chocolate.

The Corner 1 Institute Rd, BH19 1BT ☎ 01929 424969 ⊙ Tue–Sat. It may not have sea views, but this restaurant scores on the merits of its cuisine. The menu is contemporary and creative, using local ingredients where possible.

Crows Nest Inn 11 Ulwell Rd, BH19 1LE ☎ 01929 422651 ⊙ daily; carvery Sun lunch, no Sun dinner. Locals rate this as one of the best pubs in Swanage, with dishes like locally sourced wild boar and apple faggots and slow-roasted rack of Dorset lamb.

Gee Whites 1 High St, BH19 2LN ☎ 01929 425720 ⊙ daily. Popular open-air fish bar and ice-cream parlour near Swanage pier. The place for lunch on a sunny day.

9 DURLSTON COUNTRY PARK

Lighthouse Rd, Swanage BH19 2JL ☎ 01929 424443 🖱 www.durlston.co.uk

Within a few hundred yards of the hilly, southern fringes of Swanage, Durlston Country Park has 280 acres of countryside overlooking Purbeck's Marine Research Area, with meadows and coastline ideal for walking, wildlife watching and picnics. The logical starting point is the **visitor centre** within Durlston Castle, another of George Burt's legacies and more of a seaside villa than a castle. The centre has displays on the area's natural history; you can watch Durlston's nationally important guillemot colony via a live video feed and listen to sounds from the seabed picked up by an underwater microphone. There are monthly exhibitions and a good café. The website lists ranger-led guided walks and events run throughout the summer.

I was lucky enough to meet ranger Ben Wallbridge, a descendant of the Wallbridges who farmed at Kingcombe before it became a nature reserve (pages 179–80). Ben and I chatted about Durlston as he sat with a snoozy black Labrador lying across his lap. Ben's enthusiasm for the place was obvious as he told me that Durlston was one of the newest of England's 224 national nature reserves: 'It is rare because of the diverse habitats and geology it contains: sea cliffs, coastal limestone downland, haymeadows, hedgerows and woodland.' The dog had clearly heard it all before as it began to snore but, undeterred, Ben went on to tell me that Durlston has been owned by Dorset County Council since the 1970s and at one point narrowly escaped being turned into a housing estate.

Parking at Durlston is paid but the money goes towards maintaining the park and, as Ben explained, that is quite a job for the team of rangers, estate workers and volunteers.

The walks along Durlston's cliffs take you past **Anvil Point Lighthouse** and disused **quarries**, which once supplied John Mowlem and George Burt's stone company. Walking along the cliffs between Swanage and the park you will pass the **Great Globe**, a handcrafted Portland limestone representation of the world decorated with astronomical facts and quotations. Burt had it created to attract people to the area; at ten feet in diameter it is one of the largest stone spheres in the world. As you walk, look out to sea for **bottle-nosed dolphins**; according to Ben Wallbridge, Durlston is one of the best places in Britain for spotting them.

BEYOND SWANAGE TO LULWORTH COVE

Some of the most exciting **walking** in southern England can be found on this stretch of coast, with its demanding hilly cliff paths and intriguing military ranges inland.

The area between Swanage and St Aldhelm's Head is known for its Purbeck stone quarries and the coast here has an irrepressible bleakness.

Lulworth Cove and **Durdle Door** are, justifiably, both tourist magnets and very busy in the summer months. Large tranches of the countryside around East Lulworth are within the army ranges, including the atmospherically deserted village of **Tyneham**, empty since its compulsory evacuation in 1943. Although the warning signs look forbidding, military occupation has preserved the landscape in time, making for some hugely rewarding walks within the ranges (the Range Walks), obviously only open when the firing ranges are not in use (most weekends and at certain times during school holidays).

10 LANGTON MATRAVERS, WORTH MATRAVERS & ST ALDHELM'S HEAD

▲ **Tom's Field Camping** (page 298)

The area around Langton Matravers and Worth Matravers has long been the heart of Purbeck's quarrying industry. These two appealing villages are a living illustration of the uses of Purbeck stone, being constructed largely of that material.

There are around a dozen different types of Purbeck stone but by far the best known is **Purbeck marble**. Just as the Isle of Purbeck isn't really an island, Purbeck marble isn't really a marble, but a hard limestone made up of river mud and packed with the shells of millions of freshwater snails which lived in the great river that once flowed through the south of the peninsula. It takes its name from the fact that it can be polished. Purbeck marble is usually blue-grey but can have a green or reddish tint. It has been quarried from this area since Roman times, when it was the material of choice for tombstones. Widely used in the Middle Ages, Purbeck marble can still be seen in churches, abbeys and cathedrals throughout England, as fonts, altar tables, flooring and columns. Some of its most notable appearances are in Durham Cathedral, Westminster Abbey, Lincoln Cathedral and Salisbury Cathedral.

"Just as the Isle of Purbeck isn't really an island, Purbeck marble isn't really a marble, but a hard limestone made up of river mud and packed with the shells of millions of freshwater snails."

In a former coach house behind the church in Langton Matravers, the **Purbeck Stone Museum** (St George Close, BH19 3HZ ✆ 01929 423168 🖱 www.langtonia.org.uk ⏲ Apr–Sep Mon–Sat) tells the story of the local geology, stone and quarries. Following World War II, three local men (Jim Bradford, John Dean and Reg Saville) began separate collections of items relating to the history and geology of the area. Their combined collections now form the bulk of the exhibits in the museum, which also has a reconstruction of a section of an underground quarry. Reg Saville, now in his nineties, explained to me that the museum was created in response to local demand when, in 1960, the tradition of underground quarry-mines (begun in the late 17th century) was stopped by order of the Privy Council for reasons of safety. The local community was eager to ensure that the hardships of the past should not be forgotten.

If you are inspired to unleash your creativity on a slab of Purbeck stone, **Burngate Stone Carving Centre** (Kingston Rd, Langton Matravers BH19 3BE 01929 439405 www.burngatestonecentre.co.uk) offers stone-carving courses from beginner to advanced. A have-a-go course takes just two hours. Details of the courses are on the website; book in advance.

Also in Langton Matravers is **Putlake Adventure Farm** (01929 422917 www.putlakeadventurefarm.com), where as well as farm animals and the usual opportunities to feed and groom the patient creatures, there is an indoor play area for Purbeck's inclement days.

From Langton Matravers fields lined with grey stone walls lead you to **Worth Matravers**, the last settlement before the coast. The village is more beautiful than Langton Matravers, with stone cottages huddled around a duck pond that was formerly part of Worth Manor Farm. Not far from the duck pond is the well-known and highly idiosyncratic **Square and Compass pub** (page 244). The Newman family has held the licence here since 1907 and current licensee, Charlie Newman III, represents the fourth generation. Charlie is passionate about palaeontology and attached to the pub is a small museum showing off fossils found in the area. Charlie told me that his mother's family has lived in the village since 1660. Sadly, long-term residents like Charlie's family have become a rare breed in this village, where over 60% of the houses are now holiday homes.

> *"St Aldhelm's Chapel has a mystical quality, perched on the cliff and often shrouded in sea mist."*

In the graveyard of the **church of St Nicholas** is the tombstone of Benjamin Jesty, who in 1774 became the first person to inoculate against smallpox when he administered a low dose of the milder cowpox to his family. Jesty's groundbreaking move is yet another in Dorset's long list of bizarre claims to fame.

St Aldhelm's Head & Chapel

Worth Matravers is the starting point for walks to St Aldhelm's Head, for sweeping views of the coast and a visit to the cliff-top **St Aldhelm's Chapel**, dedicated to the first bishop of Sherborne, St Aldhelm. The chapel has a mystical quality, perched on the cliff and often shrouded in sea mist. The square, squat shape is very unusual for an ecclesiastical building, which is one of the reasons why many people, including Reg Saville of the Purbeck Stone Museum, believe its original purpose was not as a place of worship. As

A walk to St Aldhelm's Head & Chapel

OS Explorer OL15 or Landranger 195; start: Renscombe Farm, SY964774; approximately 3.5 miles; difficult (some steep hills).

From the car park at Renscombe Farm, west of Worth Matravers, it is around one mile to St Aldhelm's Head. Next to the map displayed in the car park is a pedestrian gate. Head through the gate and diagonally across the field in the direction of **Chapman's Pool**. When you reach the coast (after about a quarter of a mile) you will be looking down (from around 400 feet) over Chapman's Pool, a brilliantly clear bay with a jumble of fishing huts on one side. Low rumblings from the Lulworth army range can often be heard echoing around the hills.

Turn left and head along the **cliff-top path**, bordered by a drystone wall. The farmland here runs almost to the edge of the cliffs, and it seems not an inch of land is wasted. You may well encounter some very contented cows along the way, as I did. You will come to a memorial to members of the Royal Marines killed between 1945 and 1990, and which includes stone benches and a table, where you are invited to sit and take in the scene.

The cliffs are steep and dramatic here and care needs to be taken. You will come to a long set of steps that run down and up a deep 'v' between hills. The part heading up the hill is extremely steep and has no handrail – if you don't like heights you probably won't enjoy this section.

At the top of the hill you will see white coastguards' cottages built in 1834 and the tiny St Aldhelm's Chapel.

Reg points out, there is no tradition of ecclesiastical buildings being square in England and the corners point to the cardinal points of the compass, which is unheard of in a medieval sacred building. Although little is known about the chapel's origins, it is possible that it was built as a lookout for Corfe Castle. The first known mention of it was during the reign of King Henry III (1216–72), when it was referred to as a chapel served by a chaplain. The mounds around the chapel suggest it is on the site of a pre-Conquest Christian enclosure and that it probably rests on an earlier timber building. The vaulting is 12th century and there are medieval graves outside. By the 17th-century the chapel was falling into disrepair and appears to have gone out of use; however, the initials and dates from that period carved into the stonework indicate that it was still visited. The central column was

"The vaulting is 12th century and there are medieval graves outside."

To head back to the car park without retracing your steps take the track that runs between the chapel and the line of coastguards' cottages. When the track divides, bear left. You will pass a small working quarry *en route* to the car park.

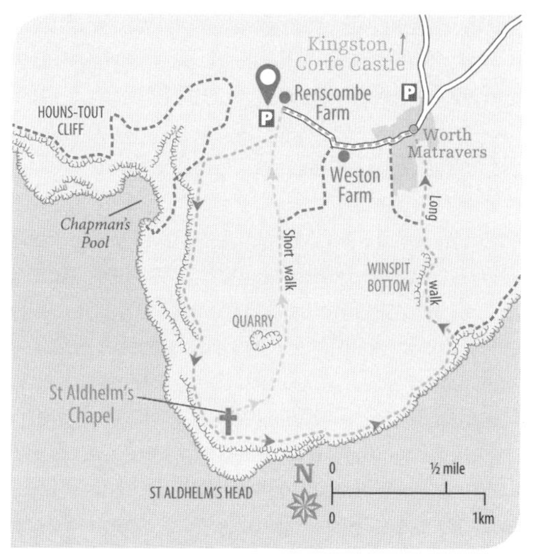

You can extend the walk to five miles by carrying on along the coast from the chapel for another mile and then turning inland up **Winspit Bottom**, a steep-sided dry valley with its slopes etched in outstanding medieval terracing known as lynchets. At the road at Worth Matravers turn left to Renscombe Farm.

evidently used as a wishing pillar, mostly by young ladies who would drop a pin into it through a hole and typically wish for a suitable husband. The building was restored in the 19th century and church services were held again from 1874. In 2005, a new altar made of stone from St Aldhelm's Quarry was installed. Today services are held on special occasions, such as Easter Day (for details see www.thedubber.co.uk).

A local legend has evolved to explain the chapel's presence: when in 1140 a bride and groom were sailing around the headland watched by the bride's father, their boat capsized and they were drowned; the father is said to have built the chapel in their memory.

Near the chapel are a modern coastguard station and a **memorial to the radar research station** at Worth Matravers. The station's work in developing radar was crucial to turning the tide of World War II and was critical to the development of modern telecommunications.

FOOD & DRINK

Ship Inn Langton Matravers BH19 3EU ✆ 01929 426910 ⊙ closed Mon. Traditional, unfussy pub food in the centre of the village.

Square and Compass Worth Matravers BH19 3LF ✆ 01929 439229 ⊙ daily, Oct–Mar closed 15.00–18.00. A supremely idiosyncratic pub run by Charlie, the fourth generation of the Newman family to hold the licence here. Charlie is keen on palaeontology and there is a collection of fossils on display. Food is limited to homemade pasties and pies, which you can wash down with the pub's homemade cider. The pub is popular with locals and has regular live music.

11 KIMMERIDGE

Clavell Tower (page 298)

The small village of Kimmeridge lies about a mile from the bay of the same name and consists of a clutch of stone and thatched cottages in the midst of some fine farmland. The bay is part of a privately owned estate and you pay a toll to drive on the road from the village to the bay, where there is plenty of parking. The bay lies within the **Purbeck Marine Wildlife Reserve**, one of the first underwater reserves in the country. It is wide and sheltered, backed by dark shale cliffs and with calm waters for swimming: the shallow waters mean this is fine rock-pooling country. The **Fine Foundation Marine Centre** (✆ 01929 481004 ⊙ Apr–Oct Tue–Sun 10.30–17.00) is run by the Dorset Wildlife Trust; it has displays on the marine life and organises events for children.

Archaeological evidence indicates that Iron Age residents of the area manufactured and exported jewellery, such as rings and bangles, made from Kimmeridge shale on rudimentary lathes.

The oil field at Kimmeridge is part of BP's Wytch Farm operation; its 'nodding donkey' has been pumping continuously since 1961, making it the UK's oldest working oil pump.

"The bay lies within the Purbeck Marine Wildlife Reserve, one of the first underwater reserves in the country."

On top of the cliff to the east of Kimmeridge is **Clavell Tower**, its soft pink-and-cream colouring and its Tuscan colonnade combining to give it a certain wedding-cake quality. It was built as a folly in 1830–31 by Reverend John Richards, who took the name Clavell when he inherited the Smedmore Estate. The three-storey tower fell into disrepair and due to coastal erosion ended up perilously close to falling into the sea. Between 2006 and 2008 the

Landmark Trust dismantled the tower, repositioned it 82 feet further back from the cliff and restored it. Since completion it has been available to rent as luxury holiday accommodation (page 298).

Seen from the road to the east of the village is **Smedmore House** (BH20 5PG ✆ 01929 480719 www.smedmorehouse.co.uk), an impressive country home constructed of Portland stone and set in the midst of an 18,000-acre estate. It is available for short-term rental.

FOOD & DRINK

Clavell's Village Café and Farm Shop BH20 5PE ✆ 01929 480701 ⏲ Apr–Oct daily 09.00–17.00 & evenings Jul–Sep, plus some evenings at weekends in spring & autumn, Nov–Mar closed Mon. Part of the 2,000 acres of farmland owned by the Hole family, in a quiet location on the lane to Kimmeridge Bay. Much of the produce is grown on the farm and the food served in the café is excellent. The portions are farmer's portions – large.

12 TYNEHAM

Ministry of Defence Ranges, East Lulworth BH20 5QF ✆ 01929 404819 www.visit-dorset.com ⏲ Tyneham village & the footpaths through the surrounding firing ranges (the Range Walks) are open to the public on certain weekends, when not being used by the army

In November 1943, 106 households in this area, including all the houses in Tyneham, received notice from Winston Churchill's war cabinet that they had one month to leave their homes as the area was to be used as an army training facility. It was meant to be a temporary arrangement but in 1948 the village was compulsorily purchased by the British Army and the villagers were never to return. Most of its buildings are now ruined, although the schoolhouse and church are preserved as museums showing what life was like in the village prior to the evacuation. The Tyneham Valley has escaped any form of development and is essentially frozen in time. It has become a haven for wildlife living among the ruined buildings.

"The Tyneham Valley is essentially frozen in time and has become a haven for wildlife living among the ruined buildings."

A visit to Tyneham is a fascinating and moving experience, showing how the villagers lived and how their lives were thrown into disarray by World War II. Each of the ruined dwellings contains a board with a description and photographs of the family who lived there. The **schoolhouse**, built in 1856, is as it would have been when the villagers left, right down to the children's names on the coat hooks.

Being such a small community, the school catered for children aged four to 14 in the same classroom: a school photo from 1928 and children's school work bring the history to life.

When the villagers left they pinned a note to the door of the church:

> Please treat the church and houses with care; we have given up our homes where many of us have lived for generations to help win the war to keep men free. We will return one day and thank you for treating the village kindly.

The **church** contains the names and photographs of local inhabitants at the time of the evacuation. In the gallery is the restored Bible that was last used in the church and a list of the parishioners. There is also a touching memorial to an Elizabeth Tennant, who died in 1769 and was a servant to the lady of the manor house: 'servant to Mrs Bond of Tyneham in which station she continued 34 years. To the memory of her prudence, honesty and industry this monument is erected'.

On the other side of the car park from the main part of the village is an abandoned farm, in which is displayed vintage agricultural machinery and used ordnance. From there it is a three-quarter mile walk to the stunning **Worbarrow Bay**. On a sunny day the water here can be so clear and blue, offset against the crisp white of the cliffs, that it could almost be the Mediterranean. As the bay can only be accessed on foot, it tends to be quieter than other beaches in the area. It is a hilly four-mile walk along the coast from the bay to Lulworth Cove.

There is no café at Tyneham or Worbarrow but both make excellent picnic spots if you come prepared.

Above Tyneham, **Whiteways Viewpoint** provides far-reaching views towards Poole and Studland. From here it is a short drive to East Lulworth; the 'tank crossing' signs you pass *en route* are a reminder of this area's primary use.

13 LULWORTH CASTLE

East Lulworth BH20 5QS ✆ 01929 400352 ⌂ www.lulworthcastle.com ◷ Sun–Fri 10.30–17.00 (check website as it closes for weddings)

Square with round towers in each corner, this large house was built in 1608 as a hunting lodge in the form of a stylised castle. The property was bought by Humphrey Weld in 1641 and has remained in the family, at the centre of a 12,000-acre estate, ever since. The castle was gutted by fire in 1929 and what you see today is the result of extensive restoration work completed in 1998. Nevertheless, the castle is really just a shell and the only rooms inside are a cellar and kitchen.

Visitors can climb the **tower** to take in spectacular views of the surrounding estate, walk around the park and woodland and enjoy a picnic in the grounds. In the grounds of the castle, the **chapel of St Mary** (1786) was the first free-standing Roman Catholic church to be built in England after the Reformation. George III approved the building on condition that it did not look like a chapel. He is reputed to have said, 'build a mausoleum and you may furnish it inside as you wish'. It looks more like a Georgian house than a chapel from the outside but the inside is more ecclesiastical with a large, painted dome.

Lulworth Castle House, the modern (1977) home of the Weld family, occasionally opens to the public (see website). It contains paintings and furnishings from the old castle.

14 LULWORTH COVE & DURDLE DOOR

Limestone Hotel & Restaurant West Lulworth (page 298) **Bindon Bottom** West Lulworth (page 298) **Durdle Door Holiday Park** Lulworth Cove (page 298)

The Lulworth Estate covers some 20 square miles and includes Lulworth Cove and Durdle Door, two of the most spectacular and best-known features of the Jurassic Coast World Heritage Site. Lulworth Cove is scallop-shell shape (almost a full circle) sculpted by the sea, which broke through a fault in the limestone beds at the mouth of the cove and ate away at the soft clay inland. Durdle Door, an impressive limestone arch eroded by waves, lies half a mile to the west.

The hilly coastline and looping bays backed by pale-coloured cliffs are topped with grassland and colourful flowers; if you walk only one small section of the South West Coast Path, let it be this one. The stretch west from Lulworth Cove over Hambury Tout to **Man o' War Bay** and Durdle Door is only 1¼ miles. It is steep in parts but at the top of those climbs you are rewarded with almost aerial views of the coastline. You can park either in the car park above Durdle Door or at Lulworth Cove but bear in mind that the refreshments are at the Lulworth Cove end. Another popular walk from Lulworth Cove is the one eastwards to the **Fossil Forest**, which can be done only when the Lulworth Range Walks are open (page 215). The 'forest' is a ledge in the Purbeck limestone cliff made up of doughnut-shaped layers of mud and algae, in the centre of which trees once grew.

The approach to West Lulworth and Lulworth Cove is via a narrow lane; there is a car park at Lulworth Cove but like all car parks on the estate it is payable. The **Lulworth Heritage Centre** near the car park makes a handy starting point. The free exhibition contains information on the geology, geography and social history of the area, including its long farming tradition. You won't be surprised to learn, given the shape of the cove, that it was a popular haunt for smugglers, who exploited its seclusion. The heritage centre stocks local maps, walking guides and wildlife identification guides, which can come in handy when exploring the area.

"You won't be surprised to learn, given the shape of the cove, that it was a popular haunt for smugglers, who exploited its seclusion."

From there it is a short stroll to **Lulworth Cove** along a narrow street lined with the usual trappings of a seaside touristy spot – guesthouses, tea rooms, and shops selling brightly coloured buckets, spades and rock-pooling nets. Thankfully, however, it lacks that slick, smarmy, touristy feel and instead retains the scruffy charm of a fishing village enhanced by the presence of rickety rowing boats lying at odd angles beside the street. Running down one side of the street is a stone wall and on the other side a stream, one of the many springs which feed the cove and make its waters some of the coldest in Dorset. The water pools in a pond part way down the hill, where families of ducks go about their daily business apparently oblivious to the steady stream of visitors pounding up and down the street.

As you walk down the hill you will see a mint-coloured cottage, the **Dolls House** (✆ 01929 400587), which is said to have been brought from Canada and re-built here in 1860. Within is a delightfully old-fashioned fudge shop. In the 1920s and 1930s, the cottage was reportedly home to one Jimmy Carter, not the former US president but a fisherman renowned for smearing his boat with dripping to keep tourists from sitting on it. Tourists are given a much warmer welcome today and can take tea in the courtyard here.

At the cove, boats lie scattered around the slipway and moored in the calm water, reinforcing that fishing village feel. The cove is ringed by a well-sheltered shingle beach and the waters are popular with snorkellers. Lulworth Marine (The Coach House, Main Rd, West Lulworth BH20 5RQ ✆ 01929 400560) offers **boat trips** from the cove.

The bulk of the village of **West Lulworth** lies a mile back from the sea and contains a mixture of architectural styles, including thatched cottages and grand Victorian stone villas. It has some good bed and breakfast accommodation, as well as a village shop.

The car park above **Durdle Door** is reached by driving through the large Durdle Door Holiday Park (page 298). On a clear day the views along the coast stretch as far as Portland. It is a steep walk down (and back up!) to Durdle Door, where there is a pebbly beach. The sea washes back and forth through the arch, making a washboard of the rocks below. Adventurous visitors can be seen swimming or kayaking through the arch, but it is a risky pastime. On the way down to the beach is a lookout point with views of Durdle Door in one direction and **Man o' War Bay** in the other. The beach at Man o' War Bay is accessible only at low tide.

Before you head to Lulworth Cove and Durdle Door it is useful to be aware that when the army ranges are in use, firing may be heard.

FOOD & DRINK

Many of the shops in this area sell **Purbeck Ice Cream** (www.purbeckicecream.co.uk). Like many dairy farmers, Peter and Hazel were driven to diversify when milk quotas were introduced; Purbeck Ice Cream was the result. It is made down the road at Kingston.

Castle Inn Main Rd, West Lulworth BH20 5RN 01929 400311 daily. A traditional thatched pub near Lulworth Castle, known for its food and variety of local beers and ciders. Extremely dog-friendly – there are even dog treats at the bar.

Lulworth Cove Inn Main Rd, West Lulworth BH20 5RQ 01929 400333 daily 11.00–23.00. A popular Hall & Woodhouse pub in a prime location, just a few hundred yards from Lulworth Cove.

Weld Arms East Lulworth BH20 5QQ 01929 400211 daily. A 17th-century thatched pub near Lulworth Castle believed to have been popular with the local smugglers. Serves traditional pub meals and some more upmarket dishes. There is a garden with a children's play area.

DORSET ONLINE

For additional online content, photos, accommodation reviews and more on Dorset, why not visit www.bradtguides.com/dorset.

POOLE, BOURNEMOUTH & THE EAST

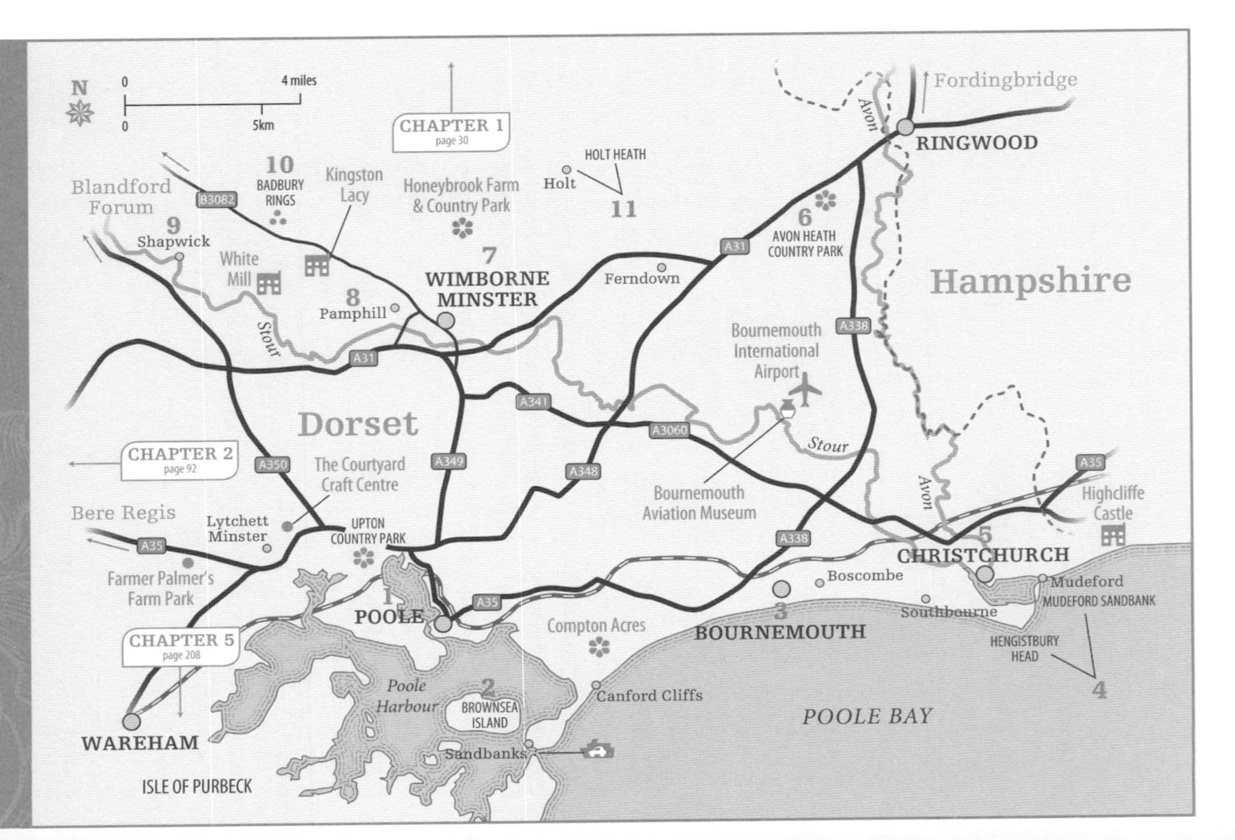

6
POOLE, BOURNEMOUTH & THE EAST

Poole and Bournemouth, Dorset's two largest towns, virtually combine into one large conurbation, with Christchurch as an appendage to make this by far the most densely populated part of Dorset. Although heavily urbanised, it has Slow corners to be discovered and I hope to help you find them.

The historic town of **Poole** sits on the second-largest natural harbour in the world, after Sydney, and its sheltered waters offer ideal conditions for all manner of watersports. Eight islands are dotted around the harbour, most of them privately owned, but the National Trust's **Brownsea Island** is open to the public and provides an unblemished, car-free sanctuary and a vantage point to watch the harbour's abundant birdlife. Many visitors, however, are drawn to the island by the possibility of catching a glimpse of the red squirrel as this is one of the few places in Britain where it remains.

Seven miles of sandy beaches stretch around Poole Bay from Sandbanks to Hengistbury Head near Bournemouth. **Sandbanks** is a small spit jutting out across the mouth of Poole Harbour, mirroring Studland on the Isle of Purbeck; a useful chain ferry links the two and replaces a long drive around the harbour. Sandbanks is the pick of the Poole Bay beaches: glamorous and well known for its exclusive real estate.

Bournemouth and Christchurch are relative newcomers to Dorset – until 1974, when the county boundary was moved, they were part of Hampshire. It is said that in Dorset terms it takes around 40 years to be accepted as a local, so they should be feeling just about settled by now. **Bournemouth** was created as recently as the 19th century and quickly developed all the accoutrements of a British seaside town: the pier, beach huts and souvenir shops. **Christchurch** has a very different feel as it dates from Saxon times, lies on the sedate rivers Stour and Avon and has as its focal point the magnificent Priory Church.

Rural East Dorset offers a pleasing mix of open rolling countryside, cherished heathland and forest, while just over the border into Hampshire is the gorgeous New Forest National Park. **Wimborne Minster** is a pleasing historic town with a minster church dating from the 8th century. A short distance from Wimborne Minster is the National Trust's **Kingston Lacy Estate** with one of Dorset's most imposing houses at its centre. **Badbury Rings**, an Iron Age hillfort, lies on the estate and offers some pleasant walking; a popular point-to-point course is nearby.

GETTING THERE & AROUND

Bournemouth International Airport lies north of Christchurch and links Dorset to other UK and European cities; an airport shuttle operates to Bournemouth town centre. Bournemouth Flying Club (✆ 01202 578558 ⊕ www.bournemouthflyingclub.co.uk) is based at the airport and offers trial lessons flying over the Dorset coast, Solent and the Isle of Wight.

The A35 links Poole, Bournemouth and Christchurch but traffic can be frustratingly heavy in the area, particularly during summer, so you may wish to consider some car-free options to get around the coastal area.

PUBLIC TRANSPORT

South West Trains connect London Waterloo to Christchurch, Bournemouth, Poole and Weymouth. If you arrive in Poole by **train**, a **Plus Bus** ticket gives you unlimited bus travel on most local bus services around the urban area of Poole, Bournemouth and Christchurch (⊕ www.plusbus.info).

Information on buses in the area is available at ⊕ www.morebus.co.uk. Poole's distinctive sky-blue **town centre bus** (route 1; Mon–Sat) loops around the major attractions. Parking in Sandbanks in summer can be troublesome but there are buses from Bournemouth and Poole. Regular buses link Poole and Bournemouth to Wimborne Minster, and to Swanage on the Isle of Purbeck.

BY BOAT

If you are arriving in your **own boat**, Poole Quay Boat Haven (✆ 01202 649488 ⊕ www.poolequayboathaven.co.uk) has serviced pontoon berths for visitor use and is within walking distance of the town centre.

Permanent berths are also available. The harbour master can answer any queries about navigation and regulations (☎ 01202 440210 🖱 www.phc.co.uk). Further east, mooring is available at the Christchurch Sailing Club (☎ 01202 483150 🖱 www.christchurchsailingclub.co.uk).

Sailing is part of the area's identity and regattas are held throughout the summer. At the heart of it all are Poole Yacht Club (🖱 www.pooleyc.co.uk), Parkstone Yacht Club (🖱 www.parkstoneyachtclub.com), Royal Motor Yacht Club (🖱 www.rmyc.co.uk) and Christchurch Sailing Club (details above).

Small ferries provide a time-saving and enjoyable way to get around the Poole and Christchurch harbours; bikes and dogs are usually welcome on board. From Sandbanks you can hop on a chain ferry to the quieter side of the harbour, Studland, in the Isle of Purbeck (page 211). Poole Quay is the departure point for ferry cruises around the harbour and along the Jurassic Coast. You can reach Brownsea Island via ferry from Sandbanks or Poole Quay. A short ferry ride from Christchurch Quay or Mudeford Quay to Mudeford Sandbank allows you to avoid the drive around the harbour, and from the sandbank you can walk up on to Hengistbury Head.

BOAT OPERATORS

The following offer ferries to Brownsea Island and/or boat cruises.

Blue Line Cruises Poole Quay BH15 1HJ ☎ 01202 467882 🖱 www.citycruisespoole.com. Jurassic Coast cruises and Swanage day cruises.

Brownsea Island Ferries Poole Quay and Sandbanks ☎ 01929 462383 🖱 www.brownseaislandferries.com. Provides ferries half-hourly from Poole Quay and Sandbanks to Brownsea Island. Also harbour cruises, Jurassic Coast cruises and trips to Swanage. A Wareham River cruise from Poole Quay takes around 75 minutes. In winter there are RSPB-guided birding trips.

Dorset Cruises Poole Quay BH15 1HJ ☎ 0845 4684640 🖱 www.dorsetcruises.co.uk. Brownsea Island, harbour and Jurassic Coast cruises. River cruises to Wareham.

Greenslade Pleasure Boats Poole Quay BH15 1HJ ☎ 01202 669955 🖱 www.greensladepleasureboats.co.uk. Brownsea Island ferries. Harbour cruises, river cruises to Wareham. Private hire.

Poole Sea Safari Poole Quay BH15 1HJ ☎ 07792 820245 🖱 www.pooleseasafari.com. A 12-seater rib zooms up and down the Jurassic Coast, giving you striking (albeit fleeting) views of the geology and wildlife. Departing from Poole Quay, you can expect to see Brownsea Island, Sandbanks, Old Harry Rocks, Swanage Bay and Durlston Country Park.

BOAT HIRE & WATERSPORTS PROVIDERS

Watersports are big business in Poole Harbour and there are plenty of companies offering everything from windsurfing to waterskiing. Hiring a boat or kayak is a relaxing way to explore Poole Harbour and get up close to the birdlife.

Castaway Boat Charters Poole Quay BH15 4EL 07860 793450 www.castawaycharters.co.uk. Full-day, half-day and evening charters exploring the harbour.

Poole Boat Hire Cobbs Quay Marina, Poole BH15 4EL 01202 687778 www.pooleboathire.co.uk. Powerboat hire; no experience necessary.

Poole Harbour Watersports School 284 Sandbanks Rd, Poole BH14 8HU 01202 700503 www.pooleharbour.co.uk. Kayak and stand-up paddle harbour tours, windsurfing and kitesurfing.

Rockley Watersports Rockley Point, Poole BH15 4LZ 01202 677272 www.rockleywatersports.com. Based at Poole Park, and offers sailing, windsurfing and powerboating courses.

Superhawk Marine Charters Cobbs Quay Marina, Poole BH15 4EL 01202 694427 www.superhawkmarine.com. Sunseeker Superhawk 48-foot luxury powerboat charters. Experienced skipper provided for up to 12 passengers.

Watersports Academy Banks Rd, Sandbanks BH13 7PS 01202 708283 www.thewatersportsacademy.com. Dinghy lessons and hire, kayak hire, windsurfing, kitesurfing, wakeboarding and waterskiing.

CYCLING

You may think that the built-up area along the coast would be unsuitable for riding but there are off-road cycle routes and cycling does present the opportunity to avoid the traffic. Poole has around 48 miles of cycle network and the town is well equipped with bike stands. A 7½-mile **Heritage Cycle Route**, part of National Cycle Route 25, takes you around places of historical interest in Poole and alongside the harbour to Upton Country Park. The **Castleman Trailway** runs almost 17 miles along the route of the defunct Southampton to Dorchester railway, linking three country parks: Avon Heath, Moors Valley and Upton. It also allows you to ride from Upton Country Park to Wimborne Minster. The trailway is open to walkers and cyclists and part of it to horseriders. The **Bourne Valley Greenway** for walkers and cyclists runs 4½ miles from Canford Heath in Poole to Bournemouth seafront, taking you through heathland and past the Alder Hills Nature Reserve, run by the Dorset Wildlife Trust.

Bournemouth has a good **promenade** for cycling, although you can't ride on it between 10.00 and 18.00 in July and August due to the high volume of pedestrians. You can cycle from Bournemouth Gardens to Hengistbury Head along the seafront, and extend it by continuing down Harbour Road and through Wick to Tuckton Gardens on the River Stour. Alternatively, you and your bike can catch the **ferry** from Mudeford Sandbank to Christchurch.

For a full day out, you can take bikes on the train from Bournemouth to Brockenhurst for riding the hundred miles of cycle paths around the **New Forest National Park**.

CYCLE HIRE

Front Bike Hire The seafront, Bournemouth ✆ 01202 557007 www.front-bike-hire.co.uk. A few hundred yards from the pier.
On yer bike 88–90 Charminster Rd, Bournemouth BH8 8US ✆ 01202 315855 www.onyerbike.co.uk
Watersports Academy Sandbanks Hotel, 15 Banks Rd, Poole BH13 7PS ✆ 0800 4840048 www.fjbhotels.co.uk

WALKING

This bit of Dorset is by no means as rich in great walks as the county is further west, with most of the coast built up – but the waterside provides plenty of interest, notably around Poole Harbour, which can be explored by a series of scenic trails (www.pooleharbourtrails.org.uk). A leaflet detailing the routes is available from Poole Tourist Information Centre. One of these, the **Cockle Trail**, helps you uncover the town's heritage with points of interest marked and explained.

A stroll around **Brownsea Island**, perhaps followed by a picnic, is a memorable way to spend a day and provides the opportunity for wildlife watching and views of Poole Harbour from a different perspective.

The **Stour Valley Way** follows the river for 64 miles from its source in Stourhead to the sea at Christchurch, with some rewarding sections at the Christchurch end of the walk. The path ends at **Hengistbury Head**, which provides pleasant walking and excellent views of Christchurch Harbour and along the Bournemouth coastline. If you park at the base of the head you can walk over the headland to **Mudeford Sandbank** and catch the land train along the harbour on the way back. From Mudeford Sandbank you can catch a ferry either to Christchurch Quay or to Mudeford Quay, where local fishermen sell their daily catch (page 273).

TOURIST INFORMATION CENTRES

Bournemouth Westover Rd, BH1 2BU ✆ 0845 0511700 🖱 www.bournemouth.co.uk
Christchurch 49 High St, BH23 1AS ✆ 01202 471780 🖱 www.visitchristchurch.info
Poole 19 The Quay, BH15 1HJ ✆ 01202 262534 🖱 www.pooletourism.com
Wimborne Minster 29 High St, BH21 1HR ✆ 01202 886116

The Stour Valley Way runs through the village of Shapwick, from where a short detour leads to the Iron Age hillfort of **Badbury Rings**; the site is imprinted with history and atmosphere and provides good views of the surrounding countryside. The nearby **Kingston Lacy Estate** is criss-crossed with footpaths and bridleways and offers some very pleasant walking country.

HORSERIDING

Rural East Dorset offers some decent riding, including the opportunity for beach rides; horseriding is allowed on **Highcliffe and Mudeford beaches** but horses are not permitted on the seashore between Easter and October from 10.00 to 21.00.

Ringwood, which lies near the Dorset/Hampshire border, is the gateway to the **New Forest**'s superb riding (itself not in Dorset and therefore outside the scope of this book), and there are no restrictions for riding across New Forest District-covered beaches (Barton on Sea, Calshot, Milford on Sea or Hordle Cliffs). Between April and July, New Forest stallions are let out into the forest to breed with the mares and it is best to keep your distance from them. Another thing to be aware of is that the New Forest Hounds drag hunt on Tuesday and Saturday from November until the end of February, so unless you are content to join the chase involuntarily, those days may be best avoided. The Forestry Commission has produced a code of conduct for riding in the forest, available online (🖱 www.thenewforest.co.uk).

The **Kingston Lacy Estate** near Wimborne Minster has 22 miles of pleasant public bridleways with shared access for cyclists.

RIDING STABLES

Arniss Farm Godshill, Fordingbridge SP6 2JX ✆ 01425 654114 🖱 www.arnissequestrian.co.uk. Set in 50 acres, with 2 all-weather arenas and hacking in the New Forest without having to venture on to roads. Runs summer camps for children.

Bagnum Riding Stables Charles Lane, Ringwood BH24 3BZ ✆ 01425 203902 ⌖ www.bagnumridingstables.co.uk. Well positioned for rides in the New Forest.
Fir Tree Farm Equestrian Centre Ogdens, Fordingbridge SP6 2PY ✆ 01425 654744 ⌖ www.fir-tree-farm.org.uk. Has direct New Forest access for hacking; also offers Equine Assisted Learning and reiki for humans and horses.
Stocks Farm Equestrian Centre Christchurch Rd, West Parley BH22 8SQ ✆ 01202 570288 ⌖ www.stocksfarmequestrian.co.uk. In countryside near Bournemouth International Airport and Ferndown. You will need to do a 30-minute assessment before going out on a hack.
Sweetlands Riding School Flowers Drove, Lytchett Matravers, Poole BH16 6BX ✆ 01202 630180 ⌖ www.sweetlandsridingschool.co.uk. Offers hacking, including three-hour pub rides incorporating a pub lunch.

POOLE & SURROUNDS

Poole Quay and **Poole Old Town** offer some good pottering territory – historic buildings, numerous eateries, independent shops and the chance to gaze with envy at the fabulous Sunseeker motorboats under construction there.

Poole Harbour's 110 miles of coastline, shallow waters and eight islands are a haven for wildlife, in particular birds. The best place to appreciate the area's flora and fauna is **Brownsea Island**, where the Dorset Wildlife Trust manages a conservation area with hides overlooking the lagoon. The harbour draws almost as many watersports enthusiasts as it does wildfowl and plays host to events throughout the year, including windsurfing and kitesurfing championships.

The **beaches**, in particular Sandbanks, attract people to the area but if they get too busy there are some waterside parks where you can relax and admire the harbour. Perhaps the best of these is **Upton Country Park**, a great spot for a picnic in front of the 18th-century manor house.

1 POOLE

Haven Hotel (page 299) **Hotel du Vin** (page 299) **Round Island Cottages** (page 299) **Weston Cottage** Broadstone (page 299)

Although modern development dominates Poole, a historic core remains around the quay and Poole Old Town, testament to the town's long seafaring history. The earliest evidence of that history was discovered in 1964: a 33-foot boat hollowed from an oak tree found preserved in mud off Brownsea Island and dated to around 295BC; it is now on display in Poole Museum. While being on the sea has its advantages, it has also meant the town had its fair share of seaborne invasions – both the Romans and the Vikings landed here. The Romans took over an Iron Age settlement at Hamworthy on the western side of the harbour and built a road between it and their settlement at Badbury Rings, near Wimborne Minster. In 1015 Canute used Poole Harbour as a convenient base from which to attack Wessex. Poole began to emerge as an important port in the 12th century and, gradually taking over from Wareham, was the biggest port in Dorset by 1433. In the 18th century it was the main British port trading with North America, bringing great wealth to its merchants. It was central to the Newfoundland trade, whereby Poole's ships sailed to Newfoundland laden with salt and provisions, collected salted cod caught off Newfoundland and delivered it to the West Indies and southern Europe, and then returned with wine, salt and olive oil. More recently, Poole played an important role as one of the principal departure points for the World War II D-Day landings.

Today, an easy and sedate way to get around is the **Poole Land Train**, which runs every 15 minutes past the hour from Poole Quay and travels for 45 minutes around the town; stops include the High Street and Poole Park. Look out for Poole's **town crier**, David Squire – he took on the role in 1958 and is reputed to be the longest-serving town crier in the world. The **tourist information centre** on Poole Quay is helpful and has leaflets on various trails around the town, including the **Cockle Trail**, which leads you around the older parts of Poole – shells inlaid in the pavement mark significant points with background provided in the leaflet, which you can also download (🖱 www.pooletourism.com). Cyclists can pick up a leaflet on a 7½-mile heritage cycle route around the town.

Poole suffered some bombing during World War II, and in the 1950s and 1960s over half the buildings dating from before 1850 were demolished. In 1975, a conservation area was established around the southwest end of High Street and across to West Street, in order to preserve the remaining old buildings. Within this zone, known as **Poole Old Town**, some medieval buildings survive but the predominant style is Georgian. Church, Market and Thames streets in particular have some fine Georgian buildings, many of which were houses built in the 18th century to accommodate the town's prosperous middle class, made wealthy by sea trading. **Poole House** in Thames Street has a typically flamboyant façade, while another highly decorative example sporting

HARRY PAYE

One particularly lively event on Poole's calendar takes place in June when the Harry Paye Charity Fun Day brings assorted crowds of sightseers and 'pirates' to the quay, with various forms of re-enactments and children's entertainment. It gives a nod to local boy Harry Paye, a colourful privateer and pirate who led naval raids along the coasts of France and Spain in the late 14th and early 15th centuries. He caused a fair amount of mayhem along the way, capturing ships, razing cities and holding prisoners to ransom. In 1406 he captured 120 French and Spanish vessels in an expedition, brought them back to Poole and distributed the booty to the residents. It is said that the wine from one of the ships kept the people of Poole happy for a whole month.

Baroque decoration is **West End House** in St James Close; built in the early 18th century for Newfoundland merchant, John Slade, it was in the late 19th-century home to the Carter family, founders of Poole Pottery.

At the end of Market Street, the **guildhall** dates from 1761, with twin exterior flights of steps curving up to the first floor, which once housed the courtroom; the ground floor was originally open and occupied by market stalls. Behind the guildhall in 1886, Alderman Horatio Hamilton, once mayor of Poole, was shot repeatedly by John King, a disgruntled harbour pilot following a dispute over a boat; you may be able to spot the bullet holes.

The large **St James's Church** (⏲ May–Sep Tue–Fri 11.00–16.00) was built in 1820 from Purbeck stone, although there has been a church here since the 13th century. The interior has a nautical feel: its grainy wooden pillars, which arrived on ships from Newfoundland, are reminiscent of the masts of sailing ships, and galleried seating extends all around. **St George's Almshouses** in Church Street have been restored but a plaque erected in 1904 reveals that they were built in the time of Henry V (reigned 1413–22) and 'have been devoted to the use of the poor for 500 years'. A niche in the wall was used for Poole's first street lamp.

The quay

A colourful variety of fishing boats are moored in this lively, industrious part of town, and early risers will see the daily catch of crabs and flat fish. Mussels are also regularly farmed and clams are racked within the harbour. Poole still has a thriving fishing industry with a strong fleet of some 80 to 90 professional fishermen.

The quay is also the departure point for **boat trips** around the harbour, to Brownsea Island and along the coast. A statue of Baden-Powell gazes out from the quay towards Brownsea Island, where he held the first scout camp, and the distant Purbeck Hills.

At the western end of the quay is the **Town Bridge**, a lifting bridge built in 1927 and sporting green copper cladding, which gives access to Hamworthy, where Sunseeker builds its luxury powerboats and the ferry port operates services to France and the Channel Islands. **Hamworthy Park** (Lulworth Av, BH15 4DH) is on the waterfront and has views of the harbour, a small sandy beach, promenade, tennis courts, paddling pool (◷ during summer), playground facilities and a café. It is lesser known than Poole Park (page 262) and tends to be quieter in busy periods.

On the oldest part of the quay, at the edge of Poole Old Town, stands the **Custom House**, which now houses a restaurant. It was rebuilt in 1813 in the style of the original building of 1747 that was later destroyed by fire. In front of it is the beam that was once used to weigh goods for customs duty. In 1747, following the seizure of one of their shipments, the notorious Hawkhurst Gang of smugglers raided the Custom House to retrieve their contraband. The shipment from Guernsey contained about 30 hundredweight of tea, 39 casks of brandy and rum, and a bag of coffee; it had been destined to land at Christchurch Bay when it was intercepted off the coast. About 30 members of the gang broke into the Custom House and escaped on horseback with the tea; several of them were later captured and hanged.

"On the oldest part of the quay, at the edge of Poole Old Town, stands the Custom House."

Nearby, in one of the 19th-century warehouses that once served the busy port, **Poole Museum** (4 High St, BH15 1BW ✆ 01202 262600 ◷ Oct–Apr Tue–Sat; free admission) displays over four floors of exhibits on the area's history and prehistory, plus a colourful collection of Poole Pottery. Poole's seafaring history features prominently, including its murkier side – smuggling and piracy. The museum's star attraction is the log boat dating from around 295BC found off Brownsea Island in 1964 (see pages 265–7). From the museum's terrace café there are views of the quay and Poole Old Town; the museum is accessible to those with limited mobility and is child-friendly. Attached to it, in a medieval warehouse building, is a local history centre where people researching the area or their family tree can draw on local archives.

Behind Poole Museum is **Scaplens Court and Garden** (free admission), used during school term time as a learning centre for local children but open to the public during August. The building dates from around 1500 and contains exhibits of Poole's domestic life; around the stone fireplace are initials believed to have been scratched by troops during the Civil War when it was known as the George Inn. There is also a carefully restored walled herb garden. Scaplens Court is the starting point for **ghost walks** around the town with Granny Cousins (✆ 07977 969080).

"Along the quay you pass a series of historic pubs that have served Poole's thirsty seafarers for centuries."

Heading eastwards along the quay you pass a series of historic pubs that have served Poole's thirsty seafarers for centuries, and the old seaman's mission, now the Oriel Restaurant. The front of the Poole Arms is covered with tiles made a little further along the quay by the forerunners of Poole Pottery, 'Carter's Industrial Tile Manufactory'. **Poole Pottery's factory shop** (The Quay, BH15 1HJ ✆ 01202 668681 www.poolepottery.co.uk) stands on the site of Carter's original factory, which opened in 1873 and where many of the tiles used in London underground stations were made. Production ceased when the company went into administration in 2006 but it was subsequently taken over and the pottery is now produced in Stoke-on-Trent. Live demonstrations at the shop allow you to watch distinctive pieces being created and for a few pounds you can even paint your own pottery. The café here specialises in local produce.

At the eastern end of the quay, **Poole Old Lifeboat Museum and Shop** (Fisherman's Dock, BH15 1RA ✆ 01202 666046 www.poole-lifeboats.org.uk ⊙ Apr–Dec 10.00–16.00; free admission), in a lifeboat station established in 1882, tells the story of the Royal National Lifeboat Institution (RNLI) and has a shop selling RNLI memorabilia. The centrepiece of the museum is the *Thomas Kirk Wright*, one of the first lifeboats to reach Dunkirk on 30 May 1940. She was one of the flotilla referred to as 'Dunkirk's Little Ships', sent to rescue members of the British Expeditionary Force from the beaches. On her third and final rescue voyage she was hit by German gunfire but managed to limp back to Poole on one engine; she returned to service at Poole until 1962. The RNLI has its headquarters in Poole at West Quay Road (BH15 1HZ ✆ 01202 662228) and maintains a library and archive on its work, which you can visit by appointment.

Poole Park, to the east of the town centre off Parkstone Road, is a green open space which snakes around a large saltwater lake separated from the sea by a thin strip of land where the railway runs. The lake has plenty of wildfowl, including some very friendly Canada geese, and is also suitable for watersports. Rockley Watersports (☎ 01202 677272) has a boathouse here offering all manner of water-based activities, including sailing, windsurfing, pedalo hire and kayaking. For landlubbers there are tennis courts, a bowling green, indoor and outdoor children's play areas and an ice-skating rink. A miniature railway runs from one end of the lake to the other, and you'll also find a restaurant and café.

Poole's beaches

Poole is blessed with some fine, golden sand beaches that wouldn't look out of place on a tropical island.

Heading east from the town the first beach you come to, **Shore Road**, lies within the harbour and has a dedicated launch zone for kitesurfers and windsurfers. The next beach along is Poole's best known, **Sandbanks**, a sandy peninsula stretching across the harbour mouth and connected to Studland on the Purbeck side of the harbour by a chain ferry (page 211). Sandbanks is well known for its luxurious homes and is reputed to have the fourth-highest land value in the world by area. While it may exude an air of exclusivity, it is packed in summer. The beach ranks among the finest on the south coast; the water is clean and shallow for around 200 yards offshore. In July the beach plays host to the **British Beach Polo Championships**, which draws top national and international teams, and is coupled with music events in the evening. When the inaugural tournament was held in 2008, it was the first of its kind in the UK – the sport was more usually seen on the beaches of Dubai and Miami. The polo is played in an arena with an oversized orange ball, designed not to get lost in the sand; spectators are pretty close to the action and get a real appreciation of the speed, agility and skill involved.

"Poole is blessed with some fine, golden sand beaches that wouldn't look out of place on a tropical island."

The stretch of sand continues from Sandbanks in the direction of Bournemouth and includes the beaches of **Canford Cliffs**, **Branksome Chine** and **Branksome Dene Chine**. They have views towards the Isle of Purbeck and Old Harry Rocks, and Canford Cliffs has the area's oldest beach huts, dating from 1927. Although officially belonging to Poole, the Branksome beaches seem more part of Bournemouth because of their location; the surrounding area is largely residential, with wooded hills running down to the beaches.

If you are looking for a **dog-friendly beach**, note that the main beaches are closed to dogs between May and September but you can always take your dog to Rockley Point at Hamworthy, the beach at Hamworthy Park, Branksome Dene Chine or the western end of Sandbanks.

Upton Country Park

BH17 7BJ ✆ 01202 261306 www.uptoncountrypark.com ⏲ park: daily 09.00–dusk (free), house: certain Sun, see website for details

A tranquil escape, just four miles from Poole town centre: walk or cycle through the hundred acres or so of lush gardens, parkland, woodland and coastline, or simply have a picnic and enjoy the views. You can download a nature trail map of the park from the website, and there's a hide for watching birds on the harbour. Segway and pétanque pitches are available and above the tea rooms the **Gallery Upstairs** (www.thegalleryupstairs.org.uk) shows works by professional and non-professional artists. In the restored **walled garden**, a water feature operates from May to September (⏲ daily 11.00–13.00 & 14.00–16.00). A plant centre sells plants that grow in the park (⏲ daily 12.00–16.00).

Upton House, which was built in 1816 and is now a venue for corporate events and private functions, is usually closed to the public but guided tours are available on certain Sundays. The house was built for Christopher Spurrier, one of the many Poole merchants made wealthy by the Newfoundland trade. He was declared bankrupt in 1830 after trade plummeted and things didn't get better – he reputedly managed to gamble away the family silver by losing a bet on a maggot race.

Compton Acres

164 Canford Cliffs Rd, BH13 7ES ✆ 01292 700778 www.comptonacres.co.uk ⏲ Mar–Oct daily 10.00–18.00, Nov–Feb daily 10.00–16.00

Between Poole and Bournemouth and covering ten acres, this garden displays over 3,000 species and is enhanced by views of Poole Harbour, Brownsea Island and the distant Purbeck Hills. A margarine entrepreneur bought the property as a seaside residence in 1920 and four years later created a garden to reflect his worldwide travels and interest in horticulture.

It is divided into distinctly themed areas, including Italian, Japanese and heather gardens; the wooded valley area is at its best in spring, when the bluebells and other bulbs are in flower. Plants and gifts are on sale and there are two cafés, a deli and a children's play area.

Farmer Palmer's Farm Park

Wareham Rd, Organford BH16 6EU 01202 622022 www.farmerpalmers.co.uk
Feb–Dec daily from 10.00

Off the A35 between Poole and Bere Regis, this farm park evolved from a working farm and is aimed at children under eight. The barn has farm animals and pets and there is the opportunity for interactive experiences. Each day at 13.45 a milking demonstration shows the children where milk comes from; trailer rides, woodland walks, play areas and a bouncy castle are also on offer.

The Courtyard Craft Centre

Huntick Rd, Lytchett Minster BH16 6BA www.thecourtyardcraftcentre.co.uk

Just west of Poole, this complex of converted farm buildings houses a variety of small, independent shops. Many are craft-related and include a pottery, where you can often see the potter at work. The tea rooms offer hot meals, as well as cream teas (daily 10.00–17.00). The centre runs a programme of classes and events, and is pet-friendly.

FOOD & DRINK

Poole general market takes place on the High Street on Thursday and Saturday, while a farmers' market is held in Falkland Square (outside the Dolphin Shopping Centre) on Thursday (09.00–14.00). Unsurprisingly, Poole does seafood very well; **Frank Greenslades** (New Quay Rd, BH15 4AF 01202 672199) has been selling freshly caught seafood since 1884, including local crab, lobster and scallops. A string of eateries along Poole Quay features casual cafés, pubs and restaurants.

Branksome Beach Restaurant & Terrace Bar Branksome Chine BH13 6LP 01202 767235 daily for breakfast, lunch & afternoon tea; & evenings in summer. On the beach, the restaurant has impressive sea views, which are magnified in the upstairs terrace bar. Serves modern British cuisine made using locally sourced, seasonal produce. One of the area's more upmarket dining options.

Courtyard Tearooms 48a High St, BH15 1BT 01202 670358 Mon–Fri 11.00–16.00, Sat 10.00–16.30. Tea rooms in a 16th-century building with plenty of character, tucked away in the Old Orchard Plaza. Serves a huge range of teas, homemade cakes and light lunches. Free Wi-Fi.

Cruel Sea 5 Bank Chambers, Penn Hill Av, BH14 9NB ✆ 01202 736362 ⏲ for lunch Tue–Sun, dinner Mon–Sun, breakfast Sun. A trendy bar serving fish, meat and vegetarian tapas-style dishes. Created by Pete Miles of Storm restaurant (see below), it follows the same seafood philiosphy of fresh, locally caught and sustainable. Fresh fish is also on sale.
Custom House The Quay, BH15 1HP ✆ 01202 676767 ⏲ daily for breakfast, lunch & dinner. An à la carte restaurant upstairs and a more casual café/bar downstairs. Serves modern English and French cuisine and seafood specialities. Good views of the quay, and the Georgian building has an elegant atmosphere.
Deli on the Quay D17 Dolphin Quays, The Quay, BH15 1HU ✆ 01202 660022 ⏲ daily. A deli and café overlooking the quay. Wholesome food and welcoming atmosphere.
Parkstone Bay Café Parkstone Bay Marina, Turks Lane, BH14 8EW ✆ 01202 733155 ⏲ daily. An informal, licensed café tucked away in a quiet spot at the marina, overlooking the water.
Sandbanks Beach Café Banks Rd, BH13 7QQ ✆ 01202 708621 ⏲ daily. Large, casual café on the beach. Has a bit of a school canteen feel but is well positioned and the homemade cakes are good.
Storm 16 High St, BH15 1BP ✆ 01202 674970 ⏲ summer daily for dinner, Mon–Sat for lunch & winter Tue–Sat for dinner; best to ring to confirm lunch opening. A fish restaurant owned by a fisherman – which indeed sounds like a recipe for success. Pete Miles still goes out fishing and ensures the fish that ends up on your plate is as fresh as it can be, and he adheres to sustainable fishing principles. Everything is made from scratch, using as much local produce as possible. Cookery courses are also available.

2 BROWNSEA ISLAND

Quay Cottage (page 299)
✆ 01202 707744 ⏲ Mar–Oct landing fee payable on arrival; foot-passenger ferry from either Poole Quay or Sandbanks (page 253); limited dedicated car parking at Sandbanks; National Trust

A car-free haven for wildlife as well as the starting point of the Boy Scout movement, Brownsea is the largest of the islands in Poole Harbour and one of Dorset's treasures. The journey to the island gives the impression that you are travelling to a magical, faraway land; arriving by boat, the first thing you see is the island's few stone houses and the castle, with a backdrop of woodland. The first castle on Brownsea was built in the time of Henry VIII as one of a string of defences; in the 18th century it was rebuilt as a residence. In the late 19th century it burnt down and was again rebuilt; today the John Lewis Partnership rents it as a hotel for its employees and it is not open to the public.

The **visitor centre** is a good starting point and provides information on the island's history, flora and fauna. Exploring the island independently is straightforward and rewarding, or you can take a **guided walk** or **tractor-trailer tour**. There really is great pleasure in walking around an island where there are no roads and no traffic, and absorbing sea views. Around the quay and visitor centre are traces of the communities that have lived here, including **St Mary's Church**, built in 1853 by the island's then owner, Colonel Waugh. The church has remained virtually unchanged since its construction and there is no electricity and no water supply, but its services are often well attended.

The island was the site of Major-General Robert Baden-Powell's original experimental scout camp in 1907, which gave rise to the international scouting movement. A **memorial** commemorates the first camp and a permanent scout campsite now exists on the island.

The island has plenty of space for picnics, or there is a National Trust tea room near the ferry. In summer, the **Brownsea Island Theatre Company** (✆ 01202 251987 ⌖ www.brownsea-theatre.co.uk) puts on open-air productions in this atmospheric location. You can prolong your stay at Brownsea by renting the National Trust cottage (see page 299).

Wildlife on the island

Indications are that the island was inhabited as early as the 5th century BC. Until the 16th century it was mostly heathland but successive owners farmed the island, planted deciduous and coniferous woodlands, reclaimed marshland from the harbour, created meadows and excavated peat bogs to form two large lakes. The National Trust acquired Brownsea Island in 1963, after the last owner, Mrs Bonham-Christie died in 1961. She had owned the island since 1921 and virtually lived as a recluse; she ordered almost everyone off the island, reducing its population from 70 to six. She let the island run wild, free from farming and forestry, and in part that is what preserved it.

The whole island, with its combination of woodland, heathland, wetland, seashore and lagoon, is rich in wildlife. Over 100 native and introduced species of trees grow on Brownsea, providing a shady canopy for walks. Pheasants roam the woodland, the descendants of those introduced for shooting parties, while the pine forest is the domain of goldcrests, woodpeckers, nuthatches and treecreepers. The open heath supports diverse butterfly species, common lizards and nightjars.

The northern half of the island, including the lagoon, is managed by the Dorset Wildlife Trust (DWT) and you can enter this area for a small fee, which goes towards the trust's conservation work. Chris Thain, DWT reserve manager, who lives on the island and is devoted to conservation work here, told me a large part of their work has been the removal of the rhododendrons that have spread invasively throughout the island. A trail leads around the DWT part of the island, where you can watch wildlife and admire the views of the harbour. This area is where you are most likely to catch a glimpse of **red squirrels**, a key attraction for many visitors. Food is put out for them at The Villa, which serves as the DWT's visitor centre providing detailed information on the wildlife.

Poole Harbour islands, including Brownsea Island, and the Isle of Wight are the only natural locations in southern Britain where red squirrels live. At the time of writing the population of red squirrels here was 200. They flourish on the island because the mature pine trees provide an ideal habitat and their competitor, the grey squirrel, has never been introduced here. The squirrels are most active at sunrise and sunset for about three hours, they sleep during the day and shelter when the weather is inclement or very hot.

You may also see **sika deer** – they were introduced to the island from Japan in 1896 and were one of the first populations in the country.

A series of hides allows you to watch the lagoon's abundant and diverse **bird population**. The lagoon was reclaimed from the harbour in the 1850s to create 70 acres of farmland; from the 1930s it was rarely drained, creating a rich non-tidal wetland. In spring and autumn waders stop off during their migration, including little stint, curlew sandpiper, ringed plover, spotted redshank and ruff. Also in spring, common and sandwich terns return from overwintering off the western coast of Africa and nest on gravel islands in the lagoon. Each pair usually rears two chicks and from May to September you can see them diligently feeding their young. From autumn to early spring large flocks of waders, including avocets and black-tailed godwits, make their home here, as do spoonbills. Colourful shelducks are present all year.

A freshwater marsh is home to an entirely different array of bird species, including water rail, reed bunting and reed warbler, an African migrant which spends the summer here. The marsh also supports many insects, including 24 species of dragonfly.

BOURNEMOUTH & CHRISTCHURCH

Colourful, vivacious, even shameless, **Bournemouth** is what you may have come to expect from a British seaside resort; what you may not expect is the high quality of the beaches, which draw crowds of eager sun worshippers in summer. **Christchurch** is more refined, imprinted with history spanning generations and with the elegant **Christchurch Priory** at its heart. The River Stour meets the sea here and you can spend a very sedate afternoon pottering along the river in a boat hired from the quay. Small ferries cross the harbour, providing plenty of opportunity for relaxing, car-free travel.

The area is within easy reach of the peaceful and beautiful New Forest National Park, with its excellent walking and horseriding, although as it is in Hampshire I don't discuss it in detail here.

3 BOURNEMOUTH

Langtry Manor (page 299)

There is little truly 'Slow' about Bournemouth, a large and relatively new settlement that has exploded around the coastal resort, but I have endeavoured to uncover the elements that give Bournemouth its distinctive character.

Prior to 1810, the area where Bournemouth now stands was little more than rugged heathland leading down to a deserted coastline. Smugglers landed their contraband here and took advantage of the chines (small ravines running down to the sea, carved into the cliffs by streams) to hide their illicit goods. The smuggling activity and threat of invasion by Napoleon's forces prompted the government to authorise the protection of the coast by Dorset Volunteer Rangers. The commander of the local Cranborne troop was Captain Lewis Tregonwell, who is credited with founding Bournemouth. Tregonwell took a liking to the area he was charged with protecting, built a summer residence here and planted the valleys with pine trees. The Victorians considered the sea air scented with pine to be therapeutic, in particular for those suffering with tuberculosis, and a series of villas sprung up in the area to cater for wealthy, ailing, visitors. The villas are still visible at the southern end of Tregonwell Road and Tregonwell's house has been incorporated into the Royal Exeter Hotel.

Hotels specialising in seawater treatments followed, such as the Mont Dore, built in the 1880s and now part of the town hall. One of those who came for rehabilitation was **Robert Louis Stevenson**, who wrote *Kidnapped* while living in Alum Chine Road. As well as creating grand villas, the prosperous Victorians added expansive parks and **gardens**, which, along with the pine trees, are characteristic of Bournemouth. The Lower, Central and Upper gardens break up the urban sprawl and maintain a Victorian feel, while Alum Chine has tropical gardens by the sea.

For many years, Bournemouth was considered a retirement town but the council has taken steps to attract other demographics. The university and a large number of schools teaching English as a foreign language have brought young people but it lacks that seat of learning atmosphere, perhaps because the institutions are relatively new and have not yet become an integral part of the town's identity. With students and youngsters comes a lively **nightlife** and in summer stag and hen parties invade the town. It also has a strong **gay** scene, similar to Brighton but on a smaller scale. Bournemouth is subject to incessant entertainment, with events running throughout the year; one of the best known is **Bournemouth Air Festival** (⊕ www.bournemouthair.co.uk), held over four days in August when aircraft display teams provide an exciting spectacle, and there is live music, fireworks and outdoor films.

The seafront

Bournemouth's main draw card is its sandy **beaches**, with views across the bay towards the Isle of Wight. The beaches referred to as Bournemouth's (as opposed to Poole's) lie at the centre of the seven-mile stretch of sand that runs from Sandbanks to Hengistbury Head. As a general rule, the further you head east (towards Hengistbury Head) from Bournemouth, the quieter the beach. For the full English-seaside experience, you can hire **beach huts** by the day, week or month, or even buy one (☎ 0845 0550968 ⊕ www.bournemouthbeachhuts.co.uk). Over 250 beach huts stretch across the seafront from Alum Chine to Southbourne and come equipped with four chairs, a gas ring and curtains. Boscombe Beach has a modern take on the beach hut: beach pods designed by fashion guru, Wayne Hemingway, come complete with kitchenette, French doors and private balcony. Between May and September, **dog-friendly beaches** are at Alum Chine, Middle Chine, Fisherman's Walk and Hengistbury Head, near Christchurch.

A **land train** runs along the seafront – westwards from Bournemouth Pier to Alum Chine and eastwards to Boscombe Pier, via Boscombe Precinct and Gardens. Bournemouth's **pier** has a cheap-and-cheerful, British-seaside flavour, and looked in need of some attention when I last visited. You need to pay a small fee (which gives you a ticket valid from April to November) to walk to the end of the pier, where entertainment includes a restaurant, a climbing wall and a zipline back to the beach.

The town centre

The busy commercial centre of the town is slightly inland, around **The Square**, where varied architecture adds interest. An attractive Victorian arcade leads through to a pedestrian shopping mall, where you will find the usual high street shops and the odd stoic independent.

If you enjoy Victorian churches, have a look in **St Stephen's**, north of The Square and widely recognised as Bournemouth's most interesting. It was designed by renowned architect John Loughborough Pearson and built in 1881–98. According to John Betjeman in 1952, 'it was worth travelling 200 miles and being sick in the coach' to view the interior. Light and airy, it features towering columns, dramatic stone vaulting and a decorative wrought-iron screen, which separates the chancel from the main body of the church. The floors of the choir, sanctuary and lady chapel contain around 60 different types of coloured marble. The stained glass is reputed to be the best in Bournemouth; the life and death of St Stephen are depicted in the west window and a rose window in the north transept commemorates the first vicar here.

To see the town from a different perspective, you can head into the air in the **Bournemouth Balloon** (BH1 2AQ ✆ 01202 313649 🖱 www.bournemouthballoon.com). The hot air balloon is tethered by a steel cable and hovers at 500 feet; day and night flights operate when weather conditions allow. It takes off from the **Lower Gardens**, between The Square and the seafront. The large gardens maintain a Victorian feel: a stream runs through them and wide paths and bridges are ideal for promenading. There are kiosks, where you can hire a deckchair and buy refreshments, and entertainment such as minigolf. When I last visited, extroverted grey squirrels were hassling visitors for food.

Just above the Lower Gardens and just below The Square is the **tourist information centre** (page 256), which is packed with brochures on the area, including handy maps of the town.

Boscombe & Southbourne

To the east of Bournemouth, **Boscombe** developed from the middle of the 19th century and has a neat seafront and some pleasant gardens, including the Italianate Gardens, Boscombe Cliff and Boscombe Chine. The A35, Christchurch Road, is dotted with antique shops. It is trying to shake off its long-held reputation as the seedy end of Bournemouth through a series of initiatives, such as Boscombe Spa Village, the redevelopment of the once run-down seafront to create a modern, surfy vibe. Key to this is **Boscombe Surf Reef** (🖱 www.thesurfreef.co.uk), an artificial reef designed to create waves for surfing fans. When it was built in 2009, it was a European first, made up of 55 giant sandbags placed 240 yards offshore on the seabed over an area the size of a football pitch. The reef has attracted a good deal of controversy; it cost three million pounds to install but has been plagued with technical problems.

East of Boscombe towards Hengistbury Head is **Southbourne**, where a funicular railway built in 1935, **Fisherman's Walk Cliff Railway**, runs the 128 feet between the coastal road and the promenade. Similar railways can be found at West Cliff and East Cliff, and opened in 1908. All three railways operate between April and October, labouring up their respective hills and looking as if they are about to run out of energy before they reach the top.

The Oceanarium

Pier Approach, West Beach BH2 5AA ☎ 01202 311993 🖱 www.oceanarium.co.uk 🕒 daily 10.00–17.00

This oceanarium on the seafront displays aquatic creatures from around the world. A walk-through tunnel passes underwater allowing you to see sharks, turtles and other fish. In 2014, the oceanarium acquired two loggerhead turtles, which were bred in captivity in a partner aquarium in France in 2011. You may wish to time your visit around daily feeding presentations, details of which are on the website. There is a café overlooking the beach.

Russell-Cotes Art Gallery & Museum

East Cliff Promenade, BH1 3AA ☎ 01202 451858 🖱 www.russellcotes.com 🕒 Tue–Sun & Bank Holiday Mon 10.00–17.00

Sir Merton Russell-Cotes was a mayor of Bournemouth (1894–95) and a local philanthropist. Built in 1901, this extravagant Victorian house contains artwork and souvenirs collected by the Russell-Cotes family during their worldwide travels in the late Victorian era. The abundance of statues, paintings and gold paint gives an effect somewhere between grand and gaudy. Regular exhibitions provide the opportunity to purchase artwork by local and other artists. On a hillside above the beach, the shaded gardens and views of the coastline are a highlight and there is a good café.

FOOD & DRINK

Bournemouth is packed with bars, restaurants and nightclubs, concentrated around the town centre and along the seafront.

All Fired Up 35–37 Bourne Av, BH2 6DT ✆ 01202 558030 ⏲ Mon–Wed & Fri–Sat 09.30–18.00, Thu 09.30–22.00, Sun 11.00–17.00. Just off The Square, a café where you can paint your own ceramics.

Beau Monde Lower Gardens, Exeter Park Rd, BH2 5AY ✆ 01202 311181 ⏲ Feb–Nov for breakfast, lunch & dinner. Serves light bites and coffee and cake all day. This bistro is worth considering for its relatively quiet location overlooking the Lower Gardens.

Chez Fred 10 Seamoor Rd, Westbourne BH4 98N ✆ 01202 761023 ⏲ Mon–Sat for lunch & dinner, Sun for dinner. Serves ethically sourced fish and chips; eat-in or take-away.

Larder House 4 Southbourne Grove, BH6 3QZ ✆ 01202 424687 ⏲ Mon–Sat 11.00–late, Sun for lunch. A wood-fired oven is at the heart of things here, producing artisan breads and pizzas.

L'Assiette 141 Belle Vue Rd, Southbourne BH6 3EN ✆ 01202 420537 ⏲ Tue–Sat for lunch & dinner, Sun for lunch. French and British cuisine made using locally sourced ingredients.

West Beach Pier Approach, BH2 5AA ✆ 01202 587785 ⏲ daily 09.00–22.00. A modern, relatively upmarket seafood restaurant and bar near the pier, with sea views.

4 HENGISTBURY HEAD & MUDEFORD SANDBANK

One of the few uninhabited parts of this built-up coastline, the sandstone promontory known as **Hengistbury Head**, a nature reserve, offers a quiet retreat for walking, cycling and wildlife watching. It has hidden depths too – as a place of great archaeological significance.

In February 2014, a sleek new **visitor centre** opened here (BH6 4EN ✆ 01202 420909 🖱 www.visithengistburyhead.co.uk; free admission). It provides information on the area's intriguing archaeology and natural history, and there is a pleasant garden, planted with wild flowers.

Archaeological investigations of the headland have revealed a wealth of activity from at least 10500BC. Its visible lumps and bumps include Bronze Age barrows and Iron Age earthworks dating from its time as a busy cross-Channel trading centre. Italian amphorae, Breton pots and raw purple glass are among the imports that have been unearthed here, some of which are on display in the visitor centre.

Heath, grassland, woodland, reed beds and water meadow are all present on the headland, which supports 500 plant species and over 300 bird species, including Dartford warbler and skylark. In 1989 the endangered natterjack toad was reintroduced to Hengistbury Head, where temporary pools near sand dunes and heathland are ideal for breeding. At dusk you may hear the call of the male natterjack, so loud it can be heard from over a mile away. Human activity in the 19th century left acidic ponds on the head, now a significant element of the nature reserve and home to 16 species of dragonfly.

"Heath, grassland, woodland, reed beds and water meadow are all present on the headland."

The headland and the long sand spit trailing from the end of it (Mudeford Sandbank) provide natural protection for Christchurch Harbour. The unspoilt sandbank has a spine of colourful beach huts running along it and is a good vantage point for watching the harbour's birdlife. Facilities are limited but there is a good restaurant, **Beach House** (page 280), with a small shop adjoining it.

The headland and sandbank are easily reached from both the Christchurch and Bournemouth sides. A ferry shuttles visitors the short distance to the sandbank from Mudeford Quay on the northeastern side of Christchurch Harbour (Mudeford Ferry ✆ 07968 334441 ⌖ www.mudefordferry.co.uk ⏲ Easter–Oct 10.00–17.00, weekends in winter weather permitting; bikes and dogs allowed). Bournemouth Boating Services (✆ 01202 429119 ⌖ www.bournemouthboating.co.uk) operates a vintage ferry between Tuckton Tea Gardens, Christchurch Quay and Mudeford Sandbank.

From the large car park at the base of Hengistbury Head, near the visitor centre, you can walk or catch the land train to **Mudeford Sandbank**. The car park has a helpfully positioned café and is the departure point for the **land train** (✆ 01202 425517 ⏲ daily 10.00–17.00, which runs 1½ miles around the harbour to the sandbank. The train has been running since 1968 and provides a scenic, atmospheric and fun way to get to the beach at Mudeford (dogs also carried).

It is a pleasant walk from the headland to the sandbank and the views from the top over Christchurch, Bournemouth and the Isle of Wight make it worth the climb.

5 CHRISTCHURCH & SURROUNDS

Grove Farm Meadow Holiday Park (page 299)

Although a close neighbour, the delightful, historic town of Christchurch, on the rivers Stour and Avon, is a world away from the bustle and modernity of Bournemouth. It is certainly worth visiting for its attractive riparian scenery and historic buildings, the most notable of which is its medieval church, Christchurch Priory.

Christchurch Priory (pages 276–8) lies in a park-like area on the River Avon and the town's key historic features are conveniently clustered around it. Christchurch's bowling green must surely have the best outlook of any of its kind, for it stands next to the ruins of **Christchurch Castle**, probably built by the Normans around 1100 to protect the town's river access. The castle was taken by Cromwell's troops during the Civil War and when hostilities ended Cromwell had it torn down, leaving it in the ruined state in which it remains. Steps lead to the top of the motte on which the castle was built and it is worth the short climb to see the remaining stonework and for the views over the town. Within the castle precinct beside the river are the roofless remains of **Constable's House**, a 12th-century chamber block with a rare surviving Norman chimney. From here you can walk along the mill stream (Convent Walk) past the priory and onwards to the point where the stream meets the River Stour, near Place Mill. In the **Priory Gardens** is a handsome mausoleum for a Mrs Perkins, who died in 1783. She reportedly had a horror of being buried alive and so asked that she be laid to rest in the mausoleum at the entrance to the school so she could be heard if she revived. She left instructions that the coffin should not be sealed and she should be able to unlock the door of the mausoleum from the inside. Her wishes were carried out but when her husband died in 1803, her body was removed, the mausoleum sold and re-erected here.

A sculpture by Jonathan Sells in the gardens has a humorous take on the history of the priory; the images include one monk climbing on the shoulders of another to feed birds. It was erected in 1994 to commemorate the priory's 900th anniversary.

Place Mill (BH23 1BY ✆ 01202 487626 ⏲ Apr–Oct Tue–Sun & bank holidays 11.00–17.30) was used to grind corn until 1908 and, although no longer in working order, it has been restored and opens in spring and summer as an art gallery.

Near Place Mill is the quay, where you can **hire small boats** and potter upstream along the River Stour. I spent a very relaxing hour taking a boat up the river, which flows gently at this point, passing carefree swans, ducks and moorhens drifting in and out of the reeds and golden water lilies. The river gives you a totally different perspective on the town and you can't help but covet the houses with gardens running down to the water and private moorings. You can also hire a boat further upstream from **Tuckton Tea Gardens** (✆ 01202 429119 ⏲ Feb–Dec), a riverside café. The **Wick Ferry** (✆ 01202 429119 ⏲ Easter–Oct 10.00–17.00) runs across the River Stour between Wick Village (on the Hengistbury Head side of the harbour) and Christchurch. Simply beckon to Tony, the lively Italian skipper, and he will gladly pick you up. A **vintage ferry service** (✆ 01202 429119 ⏲ Easter–Oct 10.00–17.00) operates boats built in 1934–35 between Tuckton Tea Gardens, Wick Ferry, Christchurch Quay and Mudeford Sandbank.

From the quay you can often see ponies or cattle grazing on the meadows almost surrounded by water, creating the illusion of an island inhabited by marooned livestock. Behind the meadows, **Stanpit Marsh Nature Reserve** juts out into the harbour on the northern side, giving the waterway its narrow appearance. A visitor centre fleshes out detail on the resident wildlife of this habitat, made up of salt marsh with creeks and salt pans, reed beds, freshwater marsh, gravel estuarine banks and sandy scrub. Although it is boggy in parts, you can walk through the reserve. In the 18th century Stanpit Marsh was a favourite haunt of smugglers, who landed their contraband at Mudeford Quay and brought it across the harbour and up the narrow channels that cut across the marsh.

Christchurch town centre is a pleasing blend of Georgian and older buildings, such as that containing the **New Forest Perfumery Gift Shop and Tearooms** (11 Church St), which dates from the 13th century. Full of character inside and out, it is distinguishable by its medieval timber frame and thatched roof. On the other side of the road is Ducking Stool Walk, which leads along the river to a replica **ducking stool**, installed in 1986. Records show that the ducking stool was used in Christchurch from at least the mid 14th century. It was a humiliating punishment largely reserved for scolds (women accused of verbal abuse or other anti-social behaviour). The last recorded use of a ducking stool in England is 1809.

It is worth popping into the **Red House Museum and Gardens** (Quay Rd, BH23 1BU ✆ 01202 482860 ⏲ Tue–Fri 10.00–17.00, Sat 10.00–16.00; free admission) for an insight into the archaeology and social history of the area. The building was constructed in 1764 as a workhouse; upstairs is a collection of finds excavated during the building of Bournemouth, while the ground floor has an array of more recent items and changing art and photography exhibitions. In a barn at the back of the house is a Royal Horse Artillery fire engine of 1795; the pretty garden is brimming with heritage plants and there is a small café.

"A characterful cobbled street lined with shops and restaurants leads to the longest parish church in England."

A pleasant coastal walk leads from **Mudeford Quay**, a working quay piled high with lobster pots, to **Highcliffe Beach**. The beach stretches for four miles and is divided into areas known as Avon, Friars Cliff, Steamer Point and Highcliffe Castle. You will pass colourful beach huts and have views across to the Isle of Wight and The Needles; a couple of cafés along the way provide handy stopping-off points. Avon Beach offers excellent windsurfing and plays host to the national championships.

St Catherine's Hill Nature Reserve lies north of the town and provides commanding views of the town and surrounding area. It has probably served as a lookout point since prehistoric times and there is evidence of Bronze Age and Iron Age settlement here. The heathland and coniferous forest provide a habitat for smooth snakes, sand lizards, Dartford warblers, nightjars and abundant butterflies. You can leave your car in the small car park at the bottom of St Catherine's Hill Lane, or on surrounding residential roads, and walk up from there. A suggested walk is available online at www.dorsetforyou.com.

Christchurch Priory

✆ 01202 485804 ⏲ Mon–Sat 09.30–17.00, Sun 14.15–17.30; free recitals Thu 12.30–13.15

A characterful cobbled street lined with shops and restaurants leads to the longest parish church in England – it is so long it looks almost as if it has been stretched lengthways. There is so much to see within that it is just as well there are hugely knowledgeable volunteer guides on hand to point you in the right direction. The church has been considerably added to since it was first built in the 11th century and therefore displays a catalogue of architectural styles from Norman to

Renaissance. Thankfully, during the Dissolution Henry VIII abandoned his plans to pull down the church in a merciful response to a plea from the townspeople, instead giving permission for it to be used as the parish church.

At the end of the 11th century Ranulf Flambard (later Bishop of Durham) decided to build a church to replace the 7th-century Saxon one that existed on the site of the current priory but he elected to build it on St Catherine's Hill, about two miles away, so the new Norman church would be visible for miles around. The townspeople objected – they wanted the church built in the town on the same spot as the Saxon one. Flambard ignored their wishes and in 1094 preparations began to build the church on St Catherine's Hill. After the stones that were laid out on the hill were repeatedly moved overnight to the site of the Saxon church, Flambard conceded to build the church there, citing divine intervention.

Talk of miraculous happenings continued throughout the construction. It is said that a mysterious carpenter helped with the building and was never present for meals or to collect wages. Then there is the **miraculous beam**, still visible at the rear of the lady chapel – a large beam was cut from the New Forest for the roof but when it was brought to the church it was found to be too short. The workers returned the following morning to find it was the perfect length and already installed in its intended position. The mysterious carpenter was not seen again and was assumed to be Jesus. Until that point the intended name was church of the Holy Trinity but because of the miracles it became known as Christchurch.

"A mysterious carpenter helped with the building and was never present for meals or to collect wages."

The **lady chapel** was completed and vaulted early in the 15th century, and features what is thought to have been the first pendant vault (a decorative pendant hanging from the vaulted ceiling) in England. Above the lady chapel, reached by climbing 75 steps, is St Michael's Loft, originally a school for novice monks and later for local boys; it now contains a **museum** on the history of the priory (⏲ May–Oct).

The absorbing **reredos** behind the high altar is essentially Jesus's family tree caricatured – it illustrates the prophecy in the book of Isaiah: 'And there shall come forth a shoot out of the stem of Jesse, and a branch shall grow out of his roots.' It dates from around 1350 and is remarkably well preserved.

The oak **misericords** are mostly from the 1520s, although four date from the early 13th century and are thought to be the oldest in England. Misericords are seats designed to prevent monks falling asleep during services – if they did so, the seats fell forward with a loud crash. Each seat has a carving, either human or animal or a blend of the two. Look out for the depiction of a fox in the pulpit and geese underneath, a cheeky ecclesiastical metaphor.

The large **memorial** of 1500 to Margaret, Countess of Salisbury, is ornately carved and exquisite but tells a chilling tale. The countess was punished for the sins of her son, when Henry VIII had her beheaded at the age of 74 because her son had published criticisms of the king. Henry VIII refused to allow her to be buried in her chantry in Christchurch and she was interred in the Tower of London's cemetery for traitors.

For a small fee, you can climb the 176 steps to the top of the 15th-century **tower** accompanied by a steward; you are rewarded with memorable views over the town, harbour and surrounding countryside.

Boating around Christchurch

The boating companies at the quay provide boat hire for pottering along the River Stour and some also offer cruises in the area. Alternatively, you can opt for a high-speed rigid inflatable boat (RIB) trip around the bay or across to the Isle of Wight. Most boat-hire companies only operate between Easter and October.

BOAT HIRE & CRUISES

Adventure Voyages Mudeford Quay, BH23 4AB ☎ 01202 488662 www.adventurevoyages.co.uk. Offers 20-minute blasts around the bay in an RIB, or longer trips across the Solent to the Isle of Wight.

Bournemouth Boating Services 323 Belle Vue Rd, Bournemouth BH6 3BA ☎ 01202 429119 www.bournemouthboating.co.uk. Operates the Wick Ferry across the River Stour between Wick village and Christchurch. Hires out self-drive motorboats for exploring the river from Christchurch Quay, Tuckton Tea Gardens and near the Wick Ferry. Rowing boats are also available for hire at Tuckton Tea Gardens, near the café (Feb–Dec). On Saturday evenings in summer they offer hour-long boat cruises followed by a barbecue in the gardens.

Mudeford Ferry Mudeford Quay ☎ 07968 334441 www.mudefordferry.co.uk. As well as the ferry to Mudeford Sandbank, offers daytime and evening harbour cruises.

Quay Leisure Hire Christchurch Quay, BH23 1BY ☎ 07813 278698. Hires out self-drive boats and operates the wheelyboat (wheelchair accessible).

Fishing around Christchurch

Anglers are well catered for, with opportunities for excellent sea, coarse and fly fishing in the waters in and around Christchurch. The harbour is good for bass and mullet during spring and summer, while Mudeford and Hengistbury Head yield mackerel, sea bream, wrasse and the occasional cod. Some of the best river fishing in England is available at the acclaimed Royalty Fishery on the River Avon and the Throop Fishery on the Stour, where you can expect to hook barbel, chub, roach, carp and pike. Permits are available from Davis Tackle (75 Bargates, BH23 1QE ✆ 01202 485169 ⊛ www.davistackle.co.uk) and you can pick up a leaflet on fishing from the tourist information centre.

Highcliffe Castle

Rothesay Dr, Highcliffe BH23 4LE ✆ 01425 278807 ⊛ www.highcliffecastle.co.uk ⊙ Feb–Dec 11.00–17.00

There can be few stately homes with a better location than Highcliffe, which stands looking out to sea from its cliff top. The house was built in the 1830s by Lord Stuart de Rothesay, an eminent diplomat, using materials salvaged from medieval French buildings, including gargoyles and coloured glass windows. It is this Norman and Renaissance carved stone, along with the castle's Gothic revival features, that makes it appear older than it is. It remained a family home until the 1950s but was severely damaged by fire in the following decade, and only the shell of the building remains. Nevertheless, it is widely recognised as one of the best surviving houses in the Romantic and Picturesque styles of architecture. Highcliffe was bought and renovated by Christchurch Borough Council and now hosts a range of events throughout the year, from concerts to murder mystery suppers. The interior has not been restored but each room has information and a photograph showing what it would have looked like in its prime; visiting the inside doesn't take long (low admission fees reflect this) but every Sunday, Tuesday and Thursday at 14.00 you can take a volunteer-led hour-long tour of the unrestored parts of the building not normally open to visitors, including the wine cellars, kitchens and servants' areas. You can linger in the 14-acre cliff-top grounds (a good spot for a picnic), and wander down to the beach below.

The tea rooms serve Dorset cream teas, cakes and light lunches and there is a gift shop.

Bournemouth Aviation Museum

Merritown Lane, Hurn BH23 6BA ☎ 01202 473141 www.aviation-museum.co.uk daily

On the B3073 Bournemouth International Airport perimeter road, this is emphatically a hands-on museum, run as a charity and staffed by enthusiastic and knowledgeable volunteers. You are encouraged to climb into aircraft and twiddle the knobs; a flight simulator allows you to play pilot. I saw plenty of excited children clambering into the helicopter, fighter planes and double-decker bus and wrestling with the controls. The aircraft are scattered in a field, rather than in a hangar, and the planes taking off and landing at the airport add to the atmosphere.

"You are encouraged to climb into aircraft and twiddle the knobs."

FOOD & DRINK

A farmers' market takes place on the first Friday of the month in Saxon Square (09.00–13.00), while the regular weekly market is on Mondays. An annual food festival in May (www.christchurchfoodfest.co.uk) features demonstrations and special offers in the town's eateries.

Beach House Mudeford Sandbank, Hengistbury Head BH6 4EN ☎ 01202 423474 dependent on the weather but usually 09.00–17.00 & evenings at the weekend, plus additional evenings in summer. An excellent casual restaurant among the beach huts on Mudeford Sandbank, with views across Christchurch Harbour to the Priory. Not surprisingly, the restaurant specialises in fresh seafood. Adjacent, a small shop sells essentials. If you arrive in your own boat, you can moor outside the restaurant. Pet-friendly.

Boat House 9 Quay Rd, BH23 1BU ☎ 01202 480033 daily 09.00–late. A very trendy restaurant and bar in an enviable position on the quay. The menu is creative but unfussy and features wood-fired pizzas and breads. Local ingredients are used and the food is freshly prepared. The live music in the bar on Friday and Saturday evenings and Sunday afternoon attracts a crowd. There is outdoor seating and a crazy golf course.

Cheese & Alfies 10 Church St, BH23 1BW ☎ 01202 487000 Mon–Sat 08.00–17.00, Sun 09.00–16.00 & Tue–Sat for dinner. A popular restaurant close to the Priory. Its name honours the owners' two sons, Charlie (aka Cheese) and Alfie. There is a good supply of books tucked into the backs of the chairs if you fancy a read while eating, and it is very child friendly. Serves a decent breakfast, a delicious hot chocolate and plenty of vegetarian dishes. Cookery classes are also held here.

Coast 74 High St, BH23 1BN ☎ 01202 496800 daily. Owner Sally prides herself on her coffee, including exotic single estate coffees, and her locally sourced light lunches and cakes.

New Forest Perfumery Giftshop & Tearooms 11 Church St, BH23 1DP ✆ 01202 482893 ⏲ daily. In a 14th-century thatched building with oodles of character; there is also a pleasant courtyard. Homemade lunches, cakes (including gluten free) and, of course, perfumes.
Old Mill Tearooms The Quay BH23 1BY ✆ 01202 474942 ⏲ daily 10.00–16.30. Small, unpretentious tearooms on Christchurch Quay. A good spot to stop off after taking a boat up the River Stour.
The Paddle 397 Waterford Rd, Highcliffe BH23 5JA ✆ 01425 275148 ⏲ Wed 08.00–17.00, Thu–Sat 08.00–22.00, Sun 09.00–16.00. A relaxed and popular café, where homemade cakes and wood-fired pizzas take centre stage.
Tuckton Tea Gardens 323 Belle Vue Rd, Tuckton BH6 3BA ✆ 01202 429119 ⏲ Feb–Dec. A riverside café in a peaceful setting, offering minigolf and boat hire. During the summer they run Saturday night barbecue cruises, when a one-hour river cruise is followed by a barbecue in the gardens.

6 AVON HEATH COUNTRY PARK

BH24 2DA ✆ 01425 478470 ⏲ 08.00–dusk; admission is free but parking is charged

Two miles west of Ringwood off the A31, Avon Heath is an important area of lowland and wet heath, acid grassland and heather. It is managed in conjunction with the RSPB and is home to various rare species, including Dartford warblers, nightjars and woodlarks; grazing by livestock is part of its conservation strategy.

"Avon Heath is an important area of lowland and wet heath, acid grassland and heather."

You can walk or cycle along marked trails, and for families there are activity trails and play equipment. A visitor centre provides information on the park and there's a hide for watching the wildlife visiting the feeders. It's dog-friendly, and you can picnic or use the café.

WIMBORNE MINSTER & SURROUNDS

Wimborne Minster is an appealing riverside town with an impressive minster church. Nearby is the National Trust **Kingston Lacy Estate** with its manor house, parkland and **Badbury Rings**, an Iron Age hillfort in an appealing countryside setting. Kingston Lacy has the distinction of being the National Trust's largest lowland property, with a working estate encompassing three villages, a dozen farms, a farm shop and an extensive network of footpaths and bridleways.

7 WIMBORNE MINSTER

Number 9 (page 299) **Deans Court Cottages** (page 299) **Wilksworth Farm Caravan Park** (page 299)

If you're arriving from the north, Wimborne Minster, often shortened to Wimborne, is the last pleasantly sized Dorset town before you hit the heavily populated area around Poole and Bournemouth. Although it is just five miles north of Poole, it retains a rural flavour and streets full of character, which make for pleasant wandering. Bright floral displays heighten the overall impression of a well cared for town. For its size, Wimborne has a very well-stocked and equipped **tourist information centre**; it sells a booklet containing a town trail, which leads you around some of the less obvious places of historical interest, marked with green plaques.

The town stands on the confluence of the rivers Stour and Allen and dates back to the early 8th century. It became an important market town although trade had slowed by the 18th century when John Hutchins noted in his *History of Dorset*, 'the town of Wimborne is much more remarkable for what it was formerly than for what it is now'.

Whatever the changing fortunes of the town, its principal feature has remained constant through the ages, the **minster of St Cuthburga** (pages 284–5), the two towers of which dominate the town's skyline.

Narrow streets following medieval lines lead away from the minster to the well-preserved town centre with its abundance of historic buildings. One of them, a town house dating from the 16th century, contains the delightful **Priest's House Museum and Garden** (23–27 High St, BH21 1HR 01202 882533 www.priest-house.co.uk Apr–Oct Mon–Sat 10.00–16.30). A series of rooms shows the area through various eras, including finds from the excavation of a nearby Roman site, a representation of a Victorian kitchen and an elegant Georgian room. A childhood gallery has a colourful array of toys and games, which might hold a few surprises for today's children, and a long, narrow garden running down to a stream behind the house is dotted with historical agricultural and horticultural implements and is also where you will find the tea room. This is a child-friendly museum with interactive displays, quizzes and trails to follow; children can even dress up in Victorian or Roman dress.

To the northwest of the minster, the **Cornmarket** with its market house of 1738 is the original marketplace. The **markets** have now moved to Mill Lane, where they take place every Friday (07.30–13.30), Saturday

(⏲ 07.30–13.00) and Sunday (⏲ 08.00–15.00) and a farmers' market is held on the second Saturday of the month (⏲ 09.00–13.00). Friday features a renowned antique bazaar, which draws bargain hunters from quite a distance. Erected as a corn mill in 1771, the **Town Mill** at the end of Mill Lane now houses a café overlooking the River Allen. Nearby is **Dreamboats** (Station Rd, Riverside Point ☎ 07794 507001 🖱 www.dream-boats.org.uk; ⏲ Apr–Sep weekends, public holidays & school holidays), where you can hire a rowing boat and mess about on the River Stour. It is a registered charity staffed by volunteers and was created in 2000 to promote enjoyment of the river, in particular for children.

The town is blessed with some good **independent shops**, such as Gullivers Bookshop (47 High St, BH21 1HS ☎ 01202 882667 ⏲ Mon–Sat 09.00–17.30), which has been selling books on Dorset, maps, jigsaw puzzles and stationery since 1969. As you wander the town centre, you may hear the bellowing tones of the local **town crier**, Chris Brown, also known as DJ Dapper Dan (🖱 www.rocknrolltowncrier.com). He is always happy to stop for a chat and is a great source of knowledge on the area. When not performing his town crier role, he has a reggae show on a local radio station.

Wimborne always seems to have plenty going on. The **Tivoli Theatre** (West Borough, BH21 1LT ☎ 01202 885566) is a very active Art Deco cinema and theatre built in 1936 in a Georgian town house. It fell into disrepair and was closed in 1980 but thanks to a committed band of volunteers, known as the Friends of the Tivoli, was restored and re-opened in 1993. A highlight on the local calendar is the annual **Wimborne Folk Festival** (🖱 www.wimbornefolk.co.uk) in June, one of the largest folk-dancing and music events in the country. Wimborne also hosts the longest fireworks display in Dorset, as part of its 5 November Guy Fawkes celebrations. Held in the grounds of St Michael's Church of England Middle School, it draws a good crowd from the surrounding area.

Wimborne has a rather grim skeleton in its closet: it was the birthplace of one of the chief suspects in the Jack the Ripper murders. **Montague John Druitt** was born in Wimborne in 1857 into a medical family – his father William was the town's leading surgeon. They lived at the substantial Westfield House, which has now been converted into flats; he was educated at Winchester College and New College, Oxford and went on to become a schoolmaster and a barrister. Druitt was found drowned in the River Thames on 31 December 1888, believed to have committed suicide; his death coincided with the cessation of the Jack the Ripper murders. Druitt is buried in Wimborne Cemetery, now something of a macabre tourist attraction.

Just north of Wimborne on the River Allen, **Walford Mill Craft Centre** (Stone Lane, BH21 1NL ✆ 01202 841400 www.walfordmillcrafts.co.uk ⏲ Mon–Sat 10.00–17.00, Sun 11.00–16.00) has exhibitions of crafts, plus a craft shop and restaurant. Some of the artisans have studios on site and you can see them at work. The centre also runs craft classes.

The minster

⏲ Mon–Sat 09.30–17.30, Sun 14.30–17.30, guides available in summer

As you approach the minster church in summer, pink flowering chestnuts provide a decorative surround. Its foundations date back to around AD705, when Cuthburga, sister of Ine, king of the West Saxons, founded a nunnery here. In its heyday it housed around 500 nuns (there was also a monastery) but it was destroyed by the Danes in 1013 and never rebuilt. The Saxons obviously considered the church significant as King Alfred buried his brother Ethelred here in AD871 after he was mortally wounded in a battle near Cranborne.

The largely Norman building dates from around 1120 to 1180, although the transepts are 14th century and the western end is from 1500. On the northern exterior of the west tower a **quarter jack** strikes his bells every quarter of an hour. He was created in 1612 and reportedly began life as a monk but during the Napoleonic Wars was given a makeover to create the appearance of a grenadier. Attached to the quarter jack on the inside of the tower is a colourful **astronomical clock** built in the 14th century by a monk at Glastonbury in Somerset. Its rudimentary depiction of the solar system is rather beautiful and resembles a drawing from a children's storybook in its simplicity, but its operation is remarkably clever. The sun points to the time of day and the gold-and-black sphere represents the moon; both move around the face of the clock. The sphere shows the moon's phases with appropriate portions showing black and gold: when there is a full moon it is completely golden and when there is an eclipse it is completely black.

Opposite the clock is the simple memorial to **Isaac Gulliver**, better known as 'the King of the Smugglers'. In 1782, the government offered a pardon to smugglers who joined the navy, or who could find substitutes to undertake military service on their behalf. For a man of Gulliver's means, buying a substitute was no problem and thus he cleared his name and became a respected member of Wimborne society. It is also said that he uncovered a French plot to kill King George III and this contributed to his receiving a pardon.

The minster contains other fascinating tombs, such as that of **Anthony Ettricke**, known as 'the man in the wall', whose plans to be interred in Wimborne Minster on his death were scuppered when he fell out with church authorities and announced he would not be buried either in the church or outside it. He subsequently relented but to save face was buried in the wall. All in all his demise was rather farcical: he had predicted he would die in 1693 and had that date engraved on his memorial but ended up living until 1703 and so the date had to be altered. In the north chapel is an ornate and colourful monument of 1606 to **Sir Edmund Uvedale**, whose effigy is lying on his side in full armour and appears to have two left feet. While it would nice to think this was a hint that he was an appalling dancer, it is believed to have been the result of a restoration by a sculptor who was having a bad day.

Above the choir vestry and reached via a spiral staircase is the **chained library** (⏲ times vary), established in 1686. With over 400 leather-bound books it is the second largest of its kind in England and was one of the earliest public libraries. It holds some literary treasures, including the Regimen Animarum written in 1343 on vellum (lambskin) with a quill pen and ink made from oak apples. Only two other copies survive and this one is believed to be the finest of the three. Also in the library are the collected works of St Anselm of 1495, some of the earliest printings of the Gospels, Bibles in Hebrew, Greek and Latin, and a book bound for the court of Henry VIII.

Wimborne Model Town

16 King St, BH21 1DY ✆ 01202 881924 ⊕ www.wimborne-modeltown.com ⏲ Apr–Oct daily 10.00–17.00

This intricately detailed 1:10 scale model of Wimborne Minster was begun in the 1940s and finished in 1951 yet it still bears a striking resemblance to the town today, aside perhaps from the goods on sale in the shops. Seeing what was on offer in a rural town centre in the post-war years will be quite a revelation for many. Children may enjoy the model railway based on Thomas the Tank Engine and there is also a putting green and giant outdoor games. The model is surrounded by beautiful gardens and the tea rooms are good value. In the mid-1980s the model town had fallen into disrepair and a group of townsfolk managed to save it from developers; they found a new site for it and it re-opened here in 1991.

FOOD & DRINK

Kings Head The Square, BH21 1JG ✆ 01202 880101 ⏲ daily for lunch & dinner. A large 18th-century inn in the town centre, serving traditional pub food.

Number 9 9 West Borough, BH21 1LT ✆ 01202 887557 ⏲ Mon 10.00–15.00, Tue–Sat 10.00–15.00 & 18.00–late. A 2AA rosette restaurant offering good-quality food and service. Indoor and outdoor seating and a relaxed atmosphere.

Number 9 on The Green 7 Cook Row, BH21 1LB ✆ 01202 887765 ⏲ Mon–Sat 09.00–16.30. This sophisticated café in a characterful building opposite the minster offers breakfast, light lunches and cream teas, and theme nights on Friday and Saturday evenings. Uses local produce, including goodies from the Long Crichel Bakery.

Riverside Café 10a The Old Mill, Mill Lane, BH21 1JQ ✆ 07816 462184⏲ Mon–Sat 09.30–16.30. An informal café on the River Allen, with indoor and outdoor seating. It serves unpretentious, traditional dishes and is a good option for the budget-conscious. The building is reputedly haunted by a 15-year-old girl who worked at the mill and drowned in the mill race while trying to escape the unwanted advances of the miller.

Squash Court Deans Court Lane, BH21 1EE ✆ 01202 639249 ⏲ Tue–Sat. This 1932 squash court has a new purpose – as a vintage shop. There is a pleasant courtyard and quirky, shabby chic café and it's in a quiet spot centred around the Deans Court historic house (🖱 www.deanscourt.org). The café sources food locally, including from the Deans Court kitchen garden.

Tickled Pig 26 West Borough, BH21 1NF ✆ 01202 886778 ⏲ Mon–Sat for lunch & dinner. Showcases local, seasonal produce with flair. Many of the vegetables and salads come from their own organic kitchen garden. Cookery courses also available.

8 PAMPHILL

524 Pamphill Green Cottage Little Pamphill Green (page 299)

Around a rambling green in this delightful village of the Kingston Lacy Estate huddles a group of 17th- and 18th-century cottages, many of them thatched. **St Stephen's Church** at the northern end of the green was built in 1907 in Arts and Crafts Gothic style as a memorial to Walter Ralph Bankes, who left £5,000 in his will for the purpose of 'building and endowing a church at Kingston Lacy'. The interior is simple with fine carved oak from the Kingston Lacy Estate. The nearby Pamphill First School and Nursery began life as an almshouse and school in 1698, and the 17th-century manor house was built by a steward to the Bankes family. **Abbott Street Forge** served the estate from the 19th century until 1945, when it closed. It swung into operation again in 1997, when Giles Stuart fired up the old brick forges to produce fine, handcrafted ironwork (✆ 01202 888573 🖱 www.abbottstreetforge.co.uk). He receives a steady flow of commissions for interior and exterior restoration work, particularly from the National Trust. In December he and his wife hold an exhibition and open up the forge to visitors, who can see Giles in action. In spring, Pamphill's **Abbott Street Copse** is awash with bluebells, offering up an unmistakably English scene.

"I was surprised and delighted to see a tractor and trailer heavily laden with hay crossing the river."

It is a short stroll along quiet lanes from the village to the **River Stour** (or you can drive and leave your car in the parking area just off Cowgrove Road), where there is an inviting picnic spot at Eyebridge. A bridge leads over the river to Eye Mead, a wetland habitat with abundant birdlife. National Trust signs suggest walks along the river, including towards Cowgrove, another small village on the Kingston Lacy Estate. When I visited one evening in late summer I was surprised and delighted to see a tractor and trailer heavily laden with hay crossing the river just above the weir.

FOOD & DRINK

Barford Ice Cream Barford Farm, BH21 4BY ✆ 01258 857969 🖱 www.barford-icecream.co.uk ⏲ times vary so check website but are usually Easter–Sep Tue or Wed–Sun 11.30–17.30, weather permitting. West of Pamphill towards Sturminster Marshall, this is is the home of Barford Ice Cream, made on the Kingston Lacy Estate using milk from a small Jersey herd. The flavours are intriguing – whisky and orange marmalade, for example. The sorbets are 50% fruit, most of the ice creams are gluten free, and diabetic-friendly options are also available. During the warmer months, you can drop in, sample their wares and buy a tub of your favourite to take home. You buy your ice cream from a little wooden shed and can enjoy it in the attractive garden. There is no indoor seating so it is really a fair-weather activity.

Pamphill Dairy Farm Shop and Restaurant Pamphill BH21 4ED ✆ 01202 880618 🖱 www.pamphilldairy.co.uk ⏲ daily. Close to the church in a converted dairy and milking parlour, this complex comprises a well-stocked farm shop, butcher, café and various small outlets, including a gift shop and an antique shop. Products on sale at the butcher include Kingston Lacy's Red Devon beef. The popular café serves wholesome, farmhouse cooking.

Vine Inn Pamphill BH21 4EE ✆ 01202 882259 ⏲ daily. A classic country pub offering local cider, simple food and two tiny, characterful bars.

Kingston Lacy House & Estate

Wimborne Minster BH21 4EA ☎ 01202 883402 ⏲ house: Mar–Oct Wed–Sun 11.00–17.00; garden: daily; National Trust

One of Dorset's grandest houses, Kingston Lacy was the home of the Bankes family from 1665 until 1981, when Ralph Bankes bequeathed the magnificent 8,500-acre estate to the National Trust. Today it draws a steady flow of visitors for its sumptuous interior, outstanding collections of art and Egyptian artefacts, and serene grounds.

The house was built in 1665 for Sir Ralph Bankes after the family's original home, Corfe Castle, was destroyed by Cromwell's troops during the Civil War. It was significantly altered in 1835 at the behest of William Bankes, who employed the noted architect Sir Charles Barry (whose other projects included work on the Houses of Parliament and Westminster Bridge) to refurbish it in flamboyant Italian Renaissance style. The house's lavish interior is in large part the legacy of William Bankes, who was an avid traveller, collector and Egyptologist and who enjoyed displaying his trinkets at the family home. From 1841 he lived in Italy, where he had fled to avoid prosecution for homosexual acts, but he continued to collect and send back furniture and fittings for the house, and may have made the occasional clandestine visit to his beloved Kingston Lacy.

"One of Dorset's grandest houses, Kingston Lacy was the home of the Bankes family from 1665 until 1981."

A grand marble staircase leads from the entrance hall; William Bankes bought it in Italy and it was part of Barry's brief in the refurbishment that he alter the house to accommodate it. Perched in niches in the walls on the first floor loggia are bronze statues of King Charles I, Sir John Bankes and Dame Mary Bankes. Dame Mary is depicted holding the keys to Corfe Castle, which she successfully defended during the Civil War until Cromwell's men gained access via subterfuge and destroyed the building (page 224). The real keys to Corfe Castle hang over the fireplace in the library, which is adorned with family portraits and Guido Reni's ceiling fresco, *The Separation of Night and Day*. Still sporting their 18th-century design are the library and saloon, created when Henry Bankes (William's father) renovated the house in the 1780s. The saloon contains some of the house's exceptional art collection, including paintings by Rubens and Titian. William Bankes built the oppressively flamboyant Spanish room to display his Spanish art collection; the room is a monument to opulence, with gilded leather wall hangings and a gilded ceiling taken from a Venetian palace. The Egyptian room contains objects Bankes collected while on expeditions in Egypt and represents the largest private collection of Egyptian artefacts in the UK. The Egyptian theme extends to the grounds of the house, where an obelisk from the 2nd century BC has stood since 1827. Its journey from Egypt to Kingston Lacy reportedly took 20 years and a team of 19 horses was needed to haul it into place.

The house is surrounded by formal gardens and 250 acres of landscaped parkland, grazed by Red Devon cattle. The garden features an Edwardian Japanese area and a Victorian fernery, which contains over 20 varieties of ferns. Paths lead from the formal gardens through the park and woodland, awash with daffodils and bluebells in spring. Longer walks, bridleways and cycleways lead around the estate, and are mapped in a leaflet available at Kingston Lacy. The red-brick stables of 1880 house a restaurant which serves a wealth of local food, including the estate's Red Devon beef.

White Mill

Sturminster Marshall BH21 4BX ✆ 01258 858051 ◷ Apr–Oct Sat–Sun & bank holidays; National Trust

Even if it isn't open, it is worth driving along the narrow road past White Mill and over the charming bridge nearby to enjoy the incredibly picturesque riverside scene they create. Made of red brick, this former corn mill on the River Stour has a doll's house quality. Just over half a mile west of Pamphill, White Mill was last rebuilt in 1776 and was worked by tenants of the Kingston Lacy Estate until the late 19th century. The National Trust took over the mill when it was given the estate but it was not until the early 1990s that efforts were made to conserve it, using a photograph from 1900 to assist in the accurate restoration of the exterior of the mill; even the dovecotes on the wall are copies of those seen in the photograph. Although some restoration work has been done on the interior, the wooden drive gear, which dates from the 1776 rebuilding, is too fragile to work. The wheels are thought to be elm, which is resistant to water and to vibration, while the teeth are likely made of apple wood. Apple was traditionally used to make the teeth as it is more fragile than elm and should anything go wrong the teeth would shear off before more substantial parts were damaged. Local legend tells that the bells from the ruined church at Knowlton were stolen and dropped into the millpond by the thieves, and that they can still be heard ringing.

The statuesque eight-arch **stone bridge** near the mill is thought to date from the 16th century, but its predecessor is referenced in documents from 1175 as 'a bridge on the River Stour adjacent to the White Mill'. Carbon dating of the wooden pilings on which it stands indicate they are 12th century, making this the oldest bridge site in Dorset. A plaque warns: 'Any person wilfully damaging any part of this county bridge will be guilty of felony and upon conviction liable to be transported for life by the court.' The bridge is the ideal vantage point for views along the river, which flows freely here and on the mill side divides around an island draped with silvery willows.

9 SHAPWICK

Across the B3082 from Badbury Rings is the turning to the small village of Shapwick, which lies just over a mile down the lane. On the River Stour, it is an ideal spot to stop off during a walk along the **Stour Valley Way**. At its centre, opposite the Anchor pub is the village cross, believed to be of Saxon origin. In 1880 it was destroyed in a brawl and in 1920 the remains were converted into a war memorial. **St Bartholomew's Church** was originally built in the 11th and 12th centuries near an old Roman ford, where the Dorchester to Old Sarum road crossed the river. It is remarkably close to the river and has been known to flood, including during a funeral in 1870 when a torrent of water carried the coffin off down the river, never to be seen again. Little did the unsuspecting occupant know that they were going to receive an impromptu burial at sea. The tower, with its heathstone and flint banding, is thought to have been added in the 14th century, when the height of the roof was raised: coffin lids from that period can be seen supporting the north wall of the nave. Much restored in the late 19th century, the church was until the Reformation connected with a priory. Henry VIII expelled the prior and gave the land and houses to 'my belovit cousin Hussey, the little man but a great General'. The Commissioners of Henry VIII left 'ye one silver cuppe'; this is probably the chalice still used in the church today, which dates from 1527, and is one of the finest of its type in England. In the floor of the church, near the altar, is a gravestone bearing the inscription, 'Anne Butler here beneath is laid, a pious prudent modest maid – 1659': an epitaph of which any girl could be proud.

FOOD & DRINK

The Anchor at Shapwick West St, DT11 9LB ☎ 01258 857269 ⏲ Mon–Sat for lunch & dinner, Sun 12.00–15.00. A refurbished pub with a sophisticated modern British menu, which incorporates local produce. An ideal stop-off for those walking the Stour Valley Way.

10 BADBURY RINGS

The road to Badbury Rings announces that you are in for something special, with the stately avenue of beech trees along the B3082 providing a fitting approach. It stretches for over two miles and is made up of 731 trees planted in 1835. Sadly, the trees are nearing the end of their natural lives and gaps in the avenue are starting to appear.

Badbury Rings is a memorable spot for a stroll, with far-reaching views from the ramparts of the surrounding countryside, and an abundance of wildflowers, including 14 species of orchid. The Iron Age hillfort was built on a site that was occupied much earlier, as evidenced by the four Bronze Age (2200–800BC) round barrows, the most notable of which are the three that lie just to your right as you travel up the track to the car park. The hillfort itself consists of three concentric, circular ditches with high walls that protect a large central area where the settlement would have been. From the bottom of the ditch to the top of the rampart would have reached a height of some 40 feet and, even accounting for 2,000 years of erosion, the ditches are still formidable today. Above the rampart a timber palisade would have been constructed to further protect the settlement on top of the hill, now covered by a small wood. The circular depressions visible in the ground, roughly ten feet in diameter, are evidence of the wattle-and-daub roundhouses.

"The circular depressions visible in the ground, roughly ten feet in diameter, are evidence of the wattle-and-daub roundhouses."

Badbury Rings is believed to have been one of several settlements in the area belonging to an ancient Dorset tribe known as the Durotriges. It would almost certainly have fallen to the invading Romans, and was probably taken by the Second Legion Augusta, led by Vespasian under Emperor Claudius. Evidence of the important Roman road from Old Sarum to Dorchester can be seen running to the west of the hillfort; the 22-mile portion of the road from Old Sarum to Badbury Rings is known as Ackling Dyke and is visible as an embankment. To the north this crosses a north–south road, which probably ran from Bath to Poole. The Romans are thought to have built a town just outside the rings, which they called Vindocladia – the place of white walls. It has been suggested that Badbury Rings could be the Mons Badonicus, where King Arthur and his army defeated the invading pagan hordes of the early 5th century, the Jutes, Angles and Saxons. Ravens, which have always been associated with Arthur, bred here until the late 19th century.

Just below the rings is the **point-to-point** racecourse, the scene of much drama and excitement during the season. I have fond memories of going point-to-pointing there as a child – it was usually freezing cold, wet and muddy but nothing could detract from the enjoyment of the day.

11 HOLT & HOLT HEATH

Holt was originally the centre of the Royal Forest of Wimborne, mentioned in the Domesday Book, and the area is still well wooded. The **church of St James** is unusual for Dorset, being of red brick. It was completely rebuilt in 1836 but records show a church was repaired here in 1493 so that inhabitants would not have to walk to Wimborne Minster for services, which was particularly troublesome during the winter months.

"The heath is home to large populations of Dartford warbler, stonechat and nightjar and it is Dorset's only site for breeding curlew."

At 1,200 acres, **Holt National Nature Reserve** is one of Dorset's largest areas of lowland heathland and has to its northwest two areas of ancient woodland (Holt Forest and Holt Wood); the National Trust owns the area and manages it in association with Natural England. The reserve offers a quiet retreat from the busy East Dorset coast, and the chance of a leisurely walk or ride. It is best to keep to the paths as the heathland can be very boggy in parts.

The reserve is particularly fine in July and August when wildflowers are prolific. The heath is home to large populations of Dartford warbler, stonechat and nightjar and it is Dorset's only site for breeding curlew. All six British species of reptile (adder, grass snake, smooth snake, slow worm, sand lizard and common lizard) are present. The heath had traditionally been maintained by grazing but this ceased following World War II. In 2010, grazing was reintroduced in the form of a small number of cattle and New Forest ponies, which it is hoped will help to reverse the deterioration by reducing the invasive scrub.

Honeybrook Farm & Country Park

Stanbridge BH21 4JD ✆ 01202 881120 ⌂ www.honeybrook.org ⏲ Tue–Sun 09.30–17.00; entry fee per car payable

Honeybrook Farm lies 1½ miles north of Wimborne Minster on the B3078 and is part of the Gaunts Estate. The working farm offers fun and learning for children, who can interact with farm animals, and it has three play areas as well as a programme of nature-based outdoor activities. You can buy produce from the farm in the shop, sample it in the café, or tuck into it at the picnic area.

ACCOMMODATION

The accommodation listed in this book is by no means exhaustive; rather, it is my selection of places to stay, with no fee having been paid by the businesses concerned. I have selected a variety of accommodation options covering a range of budgets and styles, including campsites, B&Bs, self-catering and luxury boutique hotels. Each has been selected because I feel it is special in some way, perhaps for its location or historical connections, and because it aligns with the Slow Tourism ethos.

For further reviews and additional listings, go to www.bradtguides.com/dorsetsleeps.

The hotels, B&Bs and self-catering options are indicated by 🏠 under the heading for the area in which they are located. Campsites are indicated by ⛺.

Further information on accommodation is available online at www.dorsetforyou.com and www.visit-dorset.com.

1 NORTH DORSET – THE BLACKMORE VALE, CRANBORNE CHASE & SHERBORNE

Many of North Dorset's farms offer true countryside breaks, with good B&B and self-catering accommodation. Staying on a working farm can be a great way to get a feel for the area, which was built on the agricultural industry. There are also some enticing upmarket country house hotels and plenty of pubs. North Dorset receives fewer visitors than the coast and so tends to be less expensive, although Sherborne can be pricey. **The Blackmore Vale** is relatively central for exploring the rest of Dorset, so makes a good base.

Hotels

Crown Inn Crown Rd, Marnhull DT10 1LN 01258 820224 www.thecrownatmarnhull.co.uk
Eastbury Hotel Long St, Sherborne DT9 3BY 01935 813131 www.theesastburyhotel.co.uk
Grosvenor Arms The Commons, Shaftesbury SP7 8JA 01747 850580 www.thegrosvenorarms.co.uk
Museum Inn Farnham DT11 8DE 01725 516261 www.museuminn.co.uk
Plumber Manor Sturminster Newton DT10 2AF 01258 472507 www.plumbermanor.co.uk
Stock Hill House Gillingham SP8 5NR 01747 823626 www.stockhillhouse.co.uk

B&Bs

Glebe Farm Ashmore SP5 5AE ✆ 01747 811974 🖱 www.glebefarmbandb.co.uk
Golden Hill Cottage Stourton Caundle DT10 2JW ✆ 01963 362109
🖱 www.goldenhillcottage.co.uk 🖱

Self-catering

Ellwood Cottages Woolland, Blandford Forum DT11 0ES ✆ 01258 818196
🖱 www.ellwoodcottages.co.uk
Todber Manor Manor Farm, Todber DT10 1JB ✆ 01258 820384 🖱 www.todbermanor.co.uk
Whistley Farm Milton-on-Stour, near Gillingham SP8 5PT ✆ 01747 840962
🖱 www.whistleyfarm.com. See advert in fourth colour section.

Camping

The Ark Naish Farm, DT9 5LJ ✆ 01963 23597 🖱 www.honeybuns.co.uk
Inside Park Fairmile Rd, Blandford Forum DT11 9AD ✆ 01258 453719
🖱 www.theinsidepark.co.uk
Stock Gaylard Yurt Holidays Stock Gaylard Estate, Sturminster Newton DT10 2BG ✆ 01963 23511 🖱 www.stockgaylard.com

2 DORCHESTER & THE PIDDLE & FROME VALLEYS

Dorchester is a handy base if you are travelling by public transport, but there are also some lovely out-of-the-way villages with good accommodation which will really allow you to experience what this unspoilt area has to offer. **Cerne Abbas** is one such place and well positioned for exploring Dorchester, Sherborne, the Blackmore Vale and even the coast. For those with an interest in Hardy, **Higher** and **Lower Bockhampton** will appeal. The Landmark Trust lets out two beautifully restored properties in this area, Wolfeton Gatehouse and Woodsford Castle (see below).

Hotels

Fox Inn Ansty, near Dorchester DT2 7PN ✆ 01258 880328 🖱 www.foxinnansty.co.uk
New Inn 14 Long St, Cerne Abbas DT2 7JF ✆ 01300 341274
🖱 www.thenewinncerneabbas.co.uk. See advert in fourth colour section.

B&Bs

Abbots B&B 7 Long St, Cerne Abbas DT2 7JF ✆ 01300 341349
🖱 www.abbotsbedandbreakfast.co.uk
The Old Mill West St, Bere Regis BH20 7HS ✆ 01929 472641
🖱 www.theoldmillbereregis.com. See advert in fourth colour section.

Self-catering

Dorset Resort Bere Regis BH20 7NT ✆ 01929 472244 🖰 www.dorsetgolfresort.com
River Cottage at Athelhampton Dorchester DT2 7LG ✆ 01305 848363 🖰 www.athelhampton.co.uk
Wolfeton Gatehouse Dorchester DT2 9QN ✆ 01628 825925 🖰 www.landmarktrust.co.uk
Woodsford Castle Near Dorchester DT2 8AS ✆ 01628 825925 🖰 www.landmarktrust.org.uk

Camping

Green Valley Yurts Longmeadow, Godmanstone DT2 7AE ✆ 07970 298427 🖰 www.greenvalleyyurts.com

3 THE MARSHWOOD VALE & WEST DORSET

The West Dorset coast has an abundance and variety of accommodation. If you are after peace and tranquillity during the summer months, consider looking beyond Lyme Regis for a place to lay your head. The area between Burton Bradstock and Abbotsbury has some good, quieter options. There are also some nice places to stay inland, including some good B&Bs.

Hotels

Acorn Inn 28 Fore St, Evershot DT2 0JW ✆ 01935 83228 🖰 www.acorn-inn.co.uk
Bridge House Hotel 3 Prout Bridge, Beaminster DT8 3AY ✆ 01308 862200 🖰 www.bridge-house.co.uk
Bridge House Hotel 115 East St, Bridport DT6 3LB ✆ 01308 423371 🖰 www.bridgehousebridport.co.uk
Fernhill Hotel Charmouth DT6 6BX ✆ 01297 560492 🖰 www.fernhill-hotel.co.uk
Hensleigh House Hotel Lower Sea Lane, Charmouth DT6 6LW ✆ 01297 560830 🖰 www.hensleighhouse.co.uk
Manor Hotel Beach Rd, West Bexington DT2 9DF ✆ 01308 897660 🖰 www.manorhoteldorset.com
Summer Lodge Country House Hotel Restaurant and Spa Summer Lane, Evershot DT2 0JR ✆ 01935 482000 🖰 www.summerlodgehotel.co.uk

B&Bs

Abbey House Church St, Abbotsbury DT3 4JJ ✆ 01305 871330 🖰 www.theabbeyhouse.co.uk
Abbotsbury Tearooms and B&B 26 Rodden Row, Abbotsbury DT3 4JL ✆ 01305 871143 🖰 www.abbotsbury-tearooms.co.uk
Dorset House Pound Rd, Lyme Regis DT7 3HX ✆ 01297 442055 🖰 www.dorsethouselyme.com
Sea Fret B&B Coast Rd, Puncknowle DT2 9DQ ✆ 01308 897435 🖰 www.seafret.co.uk

Self-catering

Norburton Hall Shipton Lane, Burton Bradstock DT6 4NQ ✆ 01308 897007 🖱 www.norburtonhall.com

Washingpool Farm North Allington, Bridport DT6 5HP ✆ 01308 459549 🖱 www.washingpool.co.uk

Camping

Downhouse Farm Downhouse Lane, Higher Eype DT6 6AH ✆ 01308 421232 🖱 www.downhousefarm.org

Golden Cap Holiday Park Seatown DT6 6JX ✆ 01308 422139 🖱 www.wdlh.co.uk

Highlands End Holiday Park Eype DT6 6AR ✆ 01308 422139 🖱 www.wdlh.co.uk

Mangerton Mill Mangerton, Bridport DT6 3SG ✆ 01308 485224

4 WEYMOUTH & THE SOUTHERN COAST

Accommodation in Weymouth is typically of the cheap and cheerful variety; there are innumberable B&Bs and guesthouses along the seafront.

Hotels

Smugglers Inn Osmington Mills DT3 6HF ✆ 01305 833125 🖱 www.smugglersinnosmingtonmills.co.uk

B&Bs

Beach House 51 Chiswell, Portland DT5 1AW ✆ 01305 821155 🖱 www.beach-house-bandb.co.uk

Self-catering

Contemporary Cottages 4 Weare Close, Portland DT5 1JP ✆ 07976 152723 🖱 www.contemporarycottage.co.uk

Old Higher Lighthouse Portland Bill DT5 2JT ✆ 01305 822300 🖱 www.oldhigherlighthouse.com

Old Lower Lighthouse Portland Bill DT5 2JT ✆ 01305 820553 🖱 www.portlandbirdobs.org.uk

Camping

Rosewall Camping Osmington Mills DT3 6HA ✆ 01305 832248 🖱 www.weymouthcamping.com

5 ISLE OF PURBECK

For many visitors to the Isle of Purbeck, Wareham will be their first stop but not necessarily their base, because it doesn't feel as if it's in the Isle of Purbeck proper. **Corfe Castle** is a peaceful and picturesque place to stay, right in the centre of the peninsula and allowing easy access to all the local attractions. **Swanage**, like many British seaside towns, is crammed with guesthouses and hotels of varying quality, but is a handy place to stay if you are travelling by public transport. **Studland** is a quieter option and within easy reach of the Sandbanks ferry, although accommodation is limited. The whole of the Dorset coast is busy in summer, but in **Lulworth Cove** the overcrowding is exacerbated by the single road in and out. As well as the enormous campsite at **Durdle Door**, the Lulworth Estate has cottages for rent (01929 400100 www.lulworth.com). Lists of accommodation in the area are available at www.isleofpurbeck.com.

Hotels

Limestone Hotel & Restaurant West Lulworth BH20 5RL 01929 400252 www.limestonehotel.co.uk
Mortons House Hotel 45 East St, Corfe Castle BH20 5EE 01929 480988 www.mortonshouse.co.uk
Pig on the Beach Manor Rd, Studland Bay BH19 3AU 0845 0779494 www.thepighotel.com
Purbeck House Hotel 91 High St, Swanage BH19 2LZ 01929 422872 www.purbeckhouselouisalodge.com

B&Bs

Bindon Bottom Main Rd, West Lulworth BH20 5RL 01929 400256 www.bindonbottom.com
Challow Farmhouse B&B Sandy Hill Lane, Corfe Castle BH20 5JF 01929 480052 www.challowfarmhouse.co.uk
Swanage Haven B&B 3 Victoria Rd, Swanage BH19 1LY 01929 423088 www.swanagehaven.com

Self-catering

Clavell Tower Kimmeridge 01628 825925 www.landmarktrust.org.uk

Camping

Durdle Door Holiday Park Lulworth Cove BH20 5PU 01929 400200 www.lulworth.com
Tom's Field Camping Langton Matravers BH19 3HN 01929 427110 www.tomsfieldcamping.co.uk
Wareham Forest Tourist Park North Trigon, Wareham BH20 7NZ 01929 551393 www.warehamforest.co.uk

6 POOLE, BOURNEMOUTH & THE EAST

Poole, **Bournemouth** and **Christchurch** have an extensive range of accommodation from self-catering apartments and cottages to upmarket hotels. The coastal region is very busy in summer, although Christchurch is slightly quieter than the Poole and Bournemouth conurbation. **Brownsea Island** is a very special place and a National Trust cottage is available for rent there. Staying in rural East Dorset allows you to be within easy reach of the coast without being in the thick of it.

Hotels

Haven Hotel Sandbanks BH13 7QL ✆ 0800 4840048 www.havenhotel.co.uk
Hotel du Vin Thames St, Poole BH15 1JN ✆ 0844 7489265 www.hotelduvin.com
Langtry Manor 26 Derby Rd, East Cliff, Bournemouth BH1 3QB ✆ 01202 553887 www.langtrymanor.co.uk
Number 9 9 West Borough, Wimborne Minster BH21 1LT ✆ 01202 887557 www.number9wimborne.co.uk

B&Bs

Weston Cottage 6 Macaulay Rd, Broadstone BH18 8AR ✆ 01202 699638 www.westoncottage.org.uk

Self-catering

524 Pamphill Green Cottage Little Pamphill Green, Kingston Lacy Estate, BH21 4EE ✆ 0344 3351287 www.nationaltrustcottages.co.uk
Deans Court Cottages Wimborne Minster BH21 1EE ✆ 01202 849314 www.deanscourtcottages.co.uk
Quay Cottage Brownsea Island, Poole Harbour ✆ 0344 3351287 www.nationaltrustcottages.co.uk
Round Island Cottages Poole Harbour ✆ 01202 882885 www.roundisland.co.uk

Camping

Grove Farm Meadow Holiday Park Stour Way, Christchurch BH23 2PQ ✆ 01202 483597 www.meadowbank-holidays.co.uk
Wilksworth Farm Caravan Park Cranborne Rd, Wimborne Minster BH21 4HW ✆ 01202 885467 www.wilksworthfarmcaravanpark.co.uk

INDEX

Entries in **bold** refer to major entries; those in *italic* indicate maps.

INDEX OF ADVERTISERS

NOTES

ALEXANDRA RICHARDS

CHURCHES

From tiny village churches to grand minsters and abbeys, Dorset's religious buildings encapsulate the history of local families and showcase local building materials and the work of generations of skilled craftsmen.

1 St Catherine's Chapel at Abbotsbury overlooks The Fleet and Chesil Beach. 2 The church at Littlebredy in the beautiful Bride Valley 3 The relics of the patron saint of Dorset, St Wite, are enshrined in the church at Whitchurch Canonicorum. 4 The ornate ceiling of Sherborne Abbey.

PHOTOSEEKER/S

ALEXANDRA RICHARDS

ALEXANDRA RICHARDS